Next Generation Content Delivery Infrastructures:

Emerging Paradigms and Technologies

Giancarlo Fortino
University of Calabria, Italy

Carlos E. Palau
Universitat Politecnica de Valencia, Spain

Managing Director:	Lindsay Johnston
Senior Editorial Director:	Heather A. Probst
Book Production Manager:	Sean Woznicki
Development Manager:	Joel Gamon
Development Editor:	Myla Merkel
Acquisitions Editor:	Erika Gallagher
Cover Design:	Nick Newcomer

Published in the United States of America by
Information Science Reference (an imprint of IGI Global)
701 E. Chocolate Avenue
Hershey PA 17033
Tel: 717-533-8845
Fax: 717-533-8661
E-mail: cust@igi-global.com
Web site: http://www.igi-global.com

Library of Congress Cataloging-in-Publication Data

Next generation content delivery infrastructures : emerging paradigms and technologies / Giancarlo Fortino and Carlos E. Palau, editors.
     p. cm.
  Includes bibliographical references and index.
  Summary: "This book delivers state-of-the-art research on current and future Internet-based content delivery networking topics, bringing to the forefront novel problems that demand investigation"-- Provided by publisher.
  ISBN 978-1-4666-1794-0 (hardcover) -- ISBN 978-1-4666-1795-7 (ebook) -- ISBN 978-1-4666-1796-4 (print & perpetual access) 1. Web site development. 2. Information storage and retrieval systems. I. Fortino, Giancarlo, 1971- II. Palau, Carlos E., 1970-
  TK5105.888.N4825 2012
  004.67'8--dc23
                                    2012002872

British Cataloguing in Publication Data
A Cataloguing in Publication record for this book is available from the British Library.

All work contributed to this book is new, previously-unpublished material. The views expressed in this book are those of the authors, but not necessarily of the publisher.

Editorial Advisory Board

Table of Contents

Detailed Table of Contents

Chapter 1

Benjamin Molina, Universitat Politecnica de Valencia, Spain

Carlos E. Palau, Universitat Politecnica de Valencia, Spain

Manuel Esteve, Universitat Politecnica de Valencia, Spain

Content Distribution Networks (CDN) appeared a decade ago as a method for reducing latencies, improving performance experienced by Internet users, and limiting the effect of flash-crowds, so as balance load in servers. Content Distribution has evolved in different ways (e.g. cloud computing structures and video streaming distribution infrastructures). The solution proposed in early CDN was the location of several controlled caching servers close to clients, organized and managed by a central control system. Many companies deployed their own CDN infrastructure– and so demonstrating the resulting effectiveness. However, the business model of these networks has evolved from the distribution of static web objects to video streaming. Many aspects of deployment and implementation remain proprietary, evidencing the lack of a general CDN model, although the main design concepts are widely known. In this work, the authors represent the structure of a CDN and the performance of some of its parameters, using queuing theory, simplifying the redirection schema and studying the elements that could determine the improvement in performance. The main contribution of the work is a general expression for a CDN environment and the relationship between different variables like caching hit ratios, network latency, number of surrogates, and server capacity; this proves that the use of CDN outperform the typical client/server architecture.

Chapter 2

Mukaddim Pathan, Commonwealth Scientific and Industrial Research Organization (CSIRO), Australia

James Broberg, University of Melbourne, Australia

Rajkumar Buyya, University of Melbourne, Australia

Extending the traditional Content Delivery Network (CDN) model to use Cloud Computing is highly appealing. It allows developing a truly on-demand CDN architecture based upon standards designed to ease interoperability, scalability, performance, and flexibility. To better understand the system model, necessity, and perceived advantages of Cloud-based CDNs, this chapter provides an extensive coverage and comparative analysis of the state of the art. It also provides a case study on the MetaCDN Content Delivery Cloud, along with highlights of empirical performance observations from its world-wide distributed platform.

Chapter 3

Tieying Zhang, Institute of Computing Technology, Chinese Academy of Sciences, China
Xueqi Cheng, Institute of Computing Technology, Chinese Academy of Sciences, China
Weisong Shi, Tongji University, China & Wayne State University, USA

In recent years, Peer-to-Peer (P2P) streaming systems have attracted enormous attention from both industries and academia. P2P streaming technology not only improves system scalability but also enables resource aggregation. This chapter reviews the field of P2P streaming by summarizing the key concepts and giving an overview of the most important systems. Design and implementation issues of P2P streaming systems are analyzed in general, and then six case studies for P2P live streaming, P2P on-demand streaming, and P2P download-based streaming separately are discussed. This chapter will help people in the research community and industry understand the potential properties of P2P streaming. For people unfamiliar with the field, it provides a general overview. Comparison of P2P steaming designs with different architectures is intended for developers and researchers.

Chapter 4

Israel Pérez-Llopis, Universitat Politecnica de Valencia, Spain
Carlos E. Palau, Universitat Politecnica de Valencia, Spain
Manuel Esteve, Universitat Politecnica de Valencia, Spain

Wireless video streaming, and specifically IPTV, has been a key challenge during the last decade, including the provision of access to users on an always best connected basis using different wireless access networks, including continuous seamless mobility. There are different proposals including IP based video streaming, DVB-H, or MediaFLO to carry out IPTV and video streaming on demand to users in a wireless environment, but one of the most relevant elements is the architecture of the service, with all the components of the delivery process. In this work the authors propose an alternative architecture based on a wireless Content Delivery Network, optimized to distribute video to mobile terminals in order to create a triple screen platform; considering that the main available wireless access networks are WiFi, WiMAX, and 3G, this work focuses on the last two. Surrogates within the CDN architecture act as video streaming servers, while the origin servers in the content providers carry out the transcoding process in order to be compliant with individual client requirements.

Chapter 5

Giancarlo Fortino, DEIS – University of Calabria, Italy
Carlos Calafate, DISCA – Universitat Politècnica de València, Spain
Pietro Manzoni, DISCA – Universitat Politècnica de València, Spain

In this work the authors apply raptor codes to obtain a reliable broadcast system of non-time critical contents, such as multimedia advertisement and entertainment files, in urban environments. Vehicles in urban environments are characterized by a variable speed and by the fact that the propagation of the radio signal is constrained by the configuration of the city structure. Through real experiments the authors demonstrate that raptor codes are the best option among the available Forward Error Correction techniques to achieve our purpose. Moreover, the system proposed uses traffic control techniques for classification and filtering of information. These techniques allow assigning different priorities to contents in order to receive firstly the most important ones from broadcasting antennas. In particular, as vehicle speed and/or distance from the broadcasting antenna increase, performance results highlight that these techniques are the only choice for a reliable data content delivery.

Chapter 6

Zhiming Zhao, University of Amsterdam, The Netherlands
Paola Grosso, University of Amsterdam, The Netherlands
Jeroen van der Ham, University of Amsterdam, The Netherlands
Cees de Laat, University of Amsterdam, The Netherlands

Moving large quantities of data between distributed parties is a frequently invoked process in data intensive applications, such as collaborative digital media development. These transfers often have high quality requirements on the network services, especially when they involve user interactions or require real time processing on large volumes of data. The best effort services provided by IP-routed networks give limited guarantee on the delivery performance. Advanced networks such as hybrid networks make it feasible for high level applications, such as workflows, to request network paths and service provisioning. However, the quality of network services has so far rarely been considered in composing and executing workflow processes; applications tune the execution quality selecting only optimal software services and computing resources, and neglecting the network components. In this chapter, the authors provide an overview on this research domain, and introduce a system called NEtWork QoS Planner (NEWQoSPlanner) to provide support for including network services in high level workflow applications.

Chapter 7

Nadia Ranaldo, University of Sannio, Italy
Eugenio Zimeo, University of Sannio, Italy

Broadband network technologies have improved the bandwidth of the edge of the Internet, but its core is still a bottleneck for large file transfers. Content Delivery Networks (CDNs), built at the edge of the Internet, are able to reduce the workload of network backbones, but their scalability and network reach is often limited, especially in case of QoS-bound delivery services. By using the emerging CDN internetworking, a CDN can dynamically exploit resources of other cooperating CDNs to face peak loads and temporary malfunctions without violating QoS levels negotiated with content providers. In this chapter, after a wide discussion of the problem, the authors propose an architectural schema and an algorithm, based on the divisible load theory, which optimizes delivery of large data files by satisfying an SLA, agreed with a content provider, while respecting the maximum budget that the delivering CDN can pay to peer CDNs to ensure its revenue.

    Jewel Okyere-Benya, Eindhoven University of Technology, The Netherlands
        & Politecnico di Torino, Italy
    Georgios Exarchakos, Eindhoven University of Technology, The Netherlands
    Vlado Menkovski, Eindhoven University of Technology, The Netherlands
    Antonio Liotta, Eindhoven University of Technology, The Netherlands
    Paolo Giaccone, Politecnico di Torino, Italy

Evolving paradigms of parallel transport mechanisms are necessary to satisfy the ever increasing need of high performing communication systems. Parallel transport mechanisms can be described as a technique to send several data simultaneously using several parallel channels. The authors' survey captures the entire building blocks in designing next generation parallel transport mechanisms by firstly analyzing the basic structure of a transport mechanism using a point to point scenario. They then proceed to segment parallel transport into four categories and describe some of the most sophisticated technologies such as Multipath under Point to Point, Multicast under Point to Multipoint, Parallel downloading under Multipoint to Point, and Peer to Peer streaming under Multipoint to Multipoint. The Survey enables the authors to stipulate that high performing parallel transport mechanisms can be achieved by integrating the most efficient technologies under these categories, while using the most efficient underlying Point to Point transport protocols.

    Giancarlo Fortino, DEIS – University of Calabria, Italy
    Wilma Russo, DEIS – University of Calabria, Italy

Technologies and applications that enable multi-party, multimedia communications are becoming more and more pervasive in every facet of daily life: from distance learning to remote job training, from peer-to-peer conferencing to distributed virtual meetings. To effectively use the evolving Internet infrastructure as ubiquitously accessible platform for the delivery of multi-faceted multimedia services, not only advances in multimedia communications are required but also novel software infrastructures are to be designed to cope with network and end-system heterogeneity, improve management and control of multimedia distributed services, and deliver sustainable QoS levels to end users. In this chapter, the authors propose a holistic approach based on agent-oriented middleware integrating active services, mobile event-driven agents, and multimedia internetworking technology for the component-based prototyping, dynamic deployment, and management of Internet-based real-time multimedia services. The proposed approach is enabled by a distributed software infrastructure (named Mobile Agent Multimedia Space – MAMS) based on event-driven mobile agents and multimedia coordination spaces. In particular, a multimedia coordination space is a component-based architecture consisting of components (players, streamers, transcoders, dumper, forwarders, archivers, GUI adapters, multimedia timers) that provide basic real-time multimedia services. The event-driven mobile agents act as orchestrators of the multimedia space and are capable of migrating across the network to dynamically create and deploy complex media services. The effectiveness and potential of the proposed approach are described through a case study involving the on-demand deployment and management of an adaptive cooperative playback service.

Chapter 10

Jesús M. Barbero, OEI/EUI, Technical University of Madrid, Spain

The spreading of new systems of broadcasting and distribution of multimedia content has had as a consequence a larger need for aggregation of data and metadata to traditionally based contents of video and audio supply. Broadcasting chains of this type of channels have become overwhelmed by the quantity of resources, infrastructures, and development needed for these channels to provide information. In order to avoid this kind of shortcoming, several recommendations and standards have been created to exchange metadata between production and distribution of taped programs. The problem lies in live programs; producers sometimes offer data to channels, but most often, channels are not able to face required developments. The key to this problem is cost reduction. In this work, a study is conducted on added services which producers may provide to the media about content; a system is found by which additional communication expenses are not made, and a model of information transfer is offered which allows low cost developments to supply new media platforms.

Chapter 11

Alfredo Cuzzocrea, ICAR-CNR, Italy & University of Calabria, Italy
Marcel Karnstedt, DERI, NUI Galway, Ireland
Manfred Hauswirth, DERI, NUI Galway, Ireland
Kai-Uwe Sattler, Ilmenau University of Technology, Germany
Roman Schmidt, Ecole Polytechnique Federale de Lausanne, Switzerland

Range queries are a very powerful tool in a wide range of data management systems and are vital to a multitude of applications. The hierarchy of structured overlay systems can be utilized in order to provide efficient techniques for processing them, resulting in the support of applications and techniques based on range queries in large-scale distributed information systems. On the other hand, due to the rapid development of the Web, applications based on the P2P paradigm gain more and more interest, having such systems started to evolve towards adopting standard database functionalities in terms of complex query processing support. This goes far beyond simple key lookups, as provided by standard distributed hashtables (DHTs) systems, which makes estimating the completeness of query answers a crucial challenge. Unfortunately, due to the limited knowledge and the usually best-effort characteristics, deciding about the completeness of query results, e.g., getting an idea when a query is finished or what amount of results is still missing, is very challenging. There is not only an urgent need to provide this information to the user issuing queries, but also for implementing sophisticated and efficient processing techniques based on them. In this chapter, the authors propose a method for solving this task. They discuss the applicability and quality of the estimations, present an implementation and evaluation for the P-Grid system, and show how to adapt the technique to other overlays. The authors also discuss the semantics of completeness for complex queries in P2P database systems and propose methods based on the notion of routing graphs for estimating the number of expected query answers. Finally, they discuss probabilistic guarantees for the estimated values and evaluate the proposed methods through an implemented system.

Foreword

As more aspects of our work and life move online and the Web expands beyond a communication medium to become a platform for business and society, Content Delivery Networks (CDNs) have recently gained momentum in the Internet computing landscape. The integration of existing emerging as well as stable technologies, such as Peer-to-Peer, Grid, and the latest IT trend—Cloud computing opens new perspectives in Internet technologies, raising new issues in the architecture, design, and implementation of existing CDNs. The rapid proliferation of next-generation content delivery infrastructures has the potential to change radically the way computer applications and services are constructed, managed, and delivered.

In the last few years there have been an increasing number of initiatives to develop next-generation content delivery infrastructures. The key driving forces behind this trend includes the ubiquity of broadband and wireless networking, the failing cost of storage, the overcapacity of today's large corporate data centers and progressive improvements in networking technologies. In this context, adaptive Content Networks for media streaming, mobile dynamic CDNs, Content Clouds, QoS-based resource management, and SLA-based allocation policies have been developed. There is also considerable investment in this field from commercial CDN providers such as Akamai, Limelight Networks, Mirror-Image, Savvis, and Edgestream as well as academic bodies such as CoDeeN (Princeton University, USA), Coral CDN (New York University, USA), MetaCDN (University of Melbourne, Australia) and Globule (Vrije University, The Netherlands).

The current volume is a major contribution in the field of content delivery networking, opening new perspectives with profound implications. It presents many of the most relevant current development and research results in a coherent and self contained manner. Each chapter is accompanied by examples or case studies to show the applicability of the described techniques or methodologies. What I really like in this book is that each chapter balances the theoretical and practical aspects very well. The content flow is natural and easy to read by a wide range of audiences including undergraduate university students, postgraduate students, and research engineers.

Regarding its content, the book provides exhaustive coverage of the most important fundamental issues related to the next-generation content delivery infrastructures such as CDN modeling and performance, peer-to-peer streaming, broadcasting media content in urban environments, parallel transport mechanisms, structured peer-to-peer database systems, SLA policies for CDNs, and wireless multimedia communications. It also provides interesting insights on the most relevant applications such as video production and distribution, media delivery services, content delivery clouds and mobile agent-based services. Overall, the broad range of topics of the present book makes it an important reference on the area of content delivery networking.

George Pallis
University of Cyprus, Cyprus

George Pallis *received his BSc (2001) and Ph.D. (2006) degree in Department of Informatics of Aristotle University of Thessaloniki (Greece). Currently, he is Lecturer at the Computer Science Department, University of Cyprus. Previously, he was visiting Lecturer and Marie Curie Fellow at the same department. His research interests include content distribution networks, cloud computing, Web data caching, information retrieval, online social networking, vehicular networking, and Web data clustering. He has published in top journals and conference proceedings in his area of study and he has co-edited abook on Web data management. He is member of the editorial board in the IEEE Internet Computing magazine and the International Journal on Internet and Distributed Computing Systems. He is member of IEEE and ACM.*

Preface

We are in the midst of an Internet computing revolution. One vision of 21st century computing is that users will access Internet services and "resource-hungry" applications (e.g. gaming, streaming media, video on demand, and voice-over-IP) over lightweight portable devices rather than through some descendant of the traditional desktop PCs (e.g. smartphones and tablets). In this context, distributing and processing Internet-based data in an efficient and cost-effective manner is a challenging issue in Internet technology, and of course, in the Future Internet architecture and services.

Content Delivery Networks (CDNs) have emerged to overcome the inherent limitations of the Internet in terms of user perceived Quality of Service (QoS) when accessing Web data. They offer infrastructure and mechanisms to deliver content and services in a scalable manner, and enhance users' Web and media experience. Specifically, a CDN is an overlay network across Internet, which consists of a set of servers (distributed around the world), routers, and network elements. Edge servers are the key elements in a CDN, acting as proxy caches that serve directly cached content to users. With CDNs, content is distributed to edge cache servers located close to users, resulting in fast, reliable applications, Web services, and media for the users. Once a user requests for content on a Web provider (managed by a CDN), user's request is directed to the appropriate CDN server. The perceived high end-user performance and cost savings of using CDNs have already urged many Web entrepreneurs to make contracts with CDNs. For instance, Akamai – one of the largest CDN providers in the world – claims to be delivering 20% of the world's Web traffic (n.d.). While the real numbers are debatable, it is clear that CDNs play a crucial role in the modern Internet infrastructure and will play it more and more in the Future Internet Architecture more focused in services and content.

The main value proposition for traditional CDN services has shifted over time. Initially, the focus was on improving end-user perceived experience by decreasing response time, especially when the customer Web site experiences unexpected traffic surges. Nowadays, CDN services are treated by content providers as a way to use a shared infrastructure to handle their peak capacity requirements, thus allowing reduced investment cost in their own Web site infrastructure. Moreover, recent trends in CDNs indicate a large paradigm shift towards a utility computing model, which allows customers to exploit advanced content delivery services without having to build a dedicated infrastructure. These trends foster the necessity and success of a well-designed content-utility system to provide highly scalable Web content delivery over the Internet. One approach to address these issues is to exploit the recent emergence of "Cloud Computing." Cloud Computing is a recent trend in Information Technology (IT) that moves computing and data away from desktop and portable PCs into computational resources such as large Data Centers ("Computing") and make them accessible as scalable, on-demand services over a network (the "Cloud"). The main technical underpinnings of Cloud Computing infrastructures and services include virtualization, service-orientation, elasticity, multi-tenancy, power efficiency, availability, and economics of scale. The perceived advantages for Cloud-service clients include the ability to add more capacity at peak demand, reduce cost, experiment with new services, and to remove unneeded capacity. The use of Clouds for content delivery is highly appealing as Cloud providers (e.g. Amazon S3, Amazon CloudFront, Mosso Cloud Files, and Nirvanix Storage Delivery Networks) charge customers for their utilization of storage and transfer of content (*pay-as-you-go*), typically in order of cents per gigabyte. They also offer SLA-backed performance and uptime guarantees for their services.

The integration of Cloud Computing in content delivery opens new perspectives in Internet technologies, raising new issues in the architecture, design, and implementation of existing CDNs. Moreover, the evolution of next-generation Internet-based Content Networks (CNs) in a large-scale heterogeneous environment demands for adaptation within the research community in terms of the technologies used. Therefore, the integrated uses of existing content delivery technologies and emerging technologies (i.e. Cloud Computing, Peer-to-Peer (P2P), utility computing, mobile computing, and agent technology) are anticipated to augment the effectiveness and boost the efficiency of future CN infrastructures.

Given the continued, intense activity in this area, the editors of this book invited researchers and practitioners to submit papers to this book describing research efforts and experiences in the domain of content delivery and management, and related applications.

This book has a three-fold integrated contribution: (i) to deliver the state-of-the art in the current research about Internet-based content management and delivery; (ii) to promote the content networking discipline by integrating different perspectives and by innovating through sound propositions; (iii) to challenge the future research by indicating open research issues and addressing key problems that will enhance the evolution of next-generation Internet-based content (delivery) networks.

After a rigorous review phase, the editors selected the following 11 papers as representative of ongoing research and development activities.

The first chapter, "CDN Modeling and Performance," written by Benjamin Molina, Carlos E. Palau, and Manuel Esteve, focuses on the modeling the structure of a CDN and evaluation of the performance of some of its parameters, using queuing theory, simplifying the redirection schema, and studying the elements that could determine the improvement in performance. The main contribution of such work is a general expression for a CDN environment and the relationship between different variables like caching hit ratios, network latency, number of surrogates, and server capacity; this proves that the use of CDN outperform the typical client/server architecture.

In the second chapter, "On the Performance of Content Delivery Clouds," the authors (Mukaddim Pathan, James Broberg, and Rajkumar Buyya) extend the traditional CDN model to use Cloud Computing. Such an extension will allow for the development of a truly on-demand CDN architecture based on standards designed to ease interoperability, scalability, performance, and flexibility. This chapter provides an extensive coverage and comparative analysis of the state of the art in order to better understand the system model, necessity, and perceived advantages of Cloud-based CDNs. It also provides a case study on the MetaCDN Content Delivery Cloud, along with highlights of empirical performance observations from its world-wide distributed platform.

The third chapter, written by Tieying Zhang, Xueqi Cheng, and Weisong Shi, entitled "P2P Streaming Content Delivery Systems," reviews the research area of P2P (Peer-to-Peer) streaming by summarizing the key concepts and giving an overview of the most important systems. In recent years, P2P streaming systems have attracted enormous attention from both industries and academia. Design and implementation issues of P2P streaming systems are analyzed in general, and then revisited six case studies for P2P live streaming, P2P on-demand streaming and P2P download-based streaming separately. The authors believe that this chapter will help people in the research community and industry understand the potential properties of P2P streaming. For people unfamiliar with the field, it provides a general overview. Comparison of P2P steaming designs with different architectures is intended for developers and researchers.

Israel Pérez-Llopis, Carlos E. Palau, and Manuel Esteve wrote the forth chapter, entitled "Wireless Multimedia Content Distribution Architecture," in which they focus on wireless video streaming, an important technology enabling ad-hoc video streaming on mobile devices. In particular, this chapter proposes an architecture based on a wireless CDN, optimized to distribute video to mobile terminals to create a triple screen platform, considering that the main available wireless access networks are WiFi, WiMAX, and 3G. Surrogates within the CDN architecture act as video streaming servers, while the origin servers in the content providers carry out the transcoding process in order to be compliant with individual client requirements.

The fifth chapter is entitled "Robust Broadcasting of Media Content in Urban Environments," written by Giancarlo Fortino, Carlos Calafate, and Pietro Manzoni. In this work, raptor codes technology is applied to obtain a reliable broadcast system of non-time critical contents, such as multimedia advertisement and entertainment files, in urban environments. Vehicles in urban environments are characterized by a variable speed and by the fact that the propagation of the radio signal is constrained by the configuration of the city structure. Through real experiments it is shown that raptor codes are the best option among the available Forward Error Correction techniques to achieve its purpose. Moreover, the system proposed uses traffic control techniques for classification and filtering of information. These techniques allow assigning different priorities to contents in order to receive firstly the most important ones from broadcasting antennas. In particular, as vehicle speed and/or distance from the broadcasting antenna increase, performance results highlight that such techniques are the only choice for a reliable data content delivery.

The sixth chapter, "Quality Guaranteed Media Delivery over Advanced Network," written by Zhiming Zhao, Paola Grosso, Jeroen van der Ham, and Cees de Laat, focuses on quality of service in advanced networks in which multimedia flows can transit and workflows need to be defined not only according to their functional tasks but also to the network performances. In this chapter, authors provide an overview on this interesting research domain, and introduce a system called NEtWork QoS Planner (NEWQoSPlanner) to provide support for including network services in high-level workflow applications.

Nadia Ranaldo and Eugenio Zimeo, in the seventh chapter, "Optimizing Content Delivery in QoS-aware Multi-CDNs," focus on the emerging CDN internetworking in which a CDN can dynamically exploit resources of other cooperating CDNs to face peak loads and temporary malfunctions without violating QoS levels negotiated with content providers. Specifically, they propose an architectural schema and an algorithm, based on the divisible load theory, which optimizes delivery of large data files by satisfying an SLA (Service-Level-Agreement), agreed with a content provider, while respecting the maximum budget that the delivering CDN can pay peer CDNs to ensure its revenue.

In the eighth chapter, entitled "Mechanisms for Parallel Data Transport," Jewel Okyere-Benya, Georgios Exarchacos, Vlado Menkovski, Antonio Liotta, and Paolo Giaccone present a survey on parallel transport mechanisms, a technique to send several data simultaneously using several parallel channels, necessary to satisfy the ever increasing need of high performing communication systems. Their survey captures the entire building blocks in designing next generation parallel transport mechanisms by firstly analyzing the basic structure of a transport mechanism using a point-to-point scenario. They then proceed to segment parallel transport into four categories and describe some of the most sophisticated technologies, such as Multipath under Point to Point, Multicast under Point to Multipoint, Parallel downloading under Multipoint to Point, and Peer to Peer streaming under Multipoint to Multipoint.

The ninth chapter is dedicated to mobile agent technology and paradigm used in the context of multimedia content delivery. In particular, the authors (Giancarlo Fortino and Wilma Russo) present a paper entitled "Mobile Agent-Based Services for Real-Time Multimedia Content Delivery." They propose a holistic approach based on agent-oriented middleware integrating active services, mobile event-driven agents, and multimedia internetworking technology for the component-based prototyping, dynamic deployment and management of Internet-based real-time multimedia services. The proposed approach is enabled by a distributed software infrastructure (named Mobile Agent Multimedia Space – MAMS) based on event-driven mobile agents and multimedia coordination spaces. In particular, a multimedia coordination space is a component-based architecture consisting of components (players, streamers, transcoders, dumper, forwarders, archivers, GUI adapters, multimedia timers) that provide basic real-time multimedia services. The event-driven mobile agents act as orchestrators of the multimedia space and are capable of migrating across the network to dynamically create and deploy complex media services. A case study involving the on-demand deployment and management of an adaptive cooperative playback service allows showing the effectiveness and potential of the proposed approach.

In the tenth chapter, "Remote Delivery of Video Services over Video Links," Jesús M. Barbero focuses on new systems of broadcasting and distribution of multimedia content. Specifically the author first proposes a study on added services which media broadcasting producers may provide to the media delivery about content; then, a system is defined by which additional communication expenses are not made and a model of information transfer is offered, which allows low cost developments to supply new media platforms.

The eleventh chapter was written by Alfredo Cuzzocrea, Marcel Karnstedt, Manfred Hauswirth, Kai-Uwe Sattler, and Roman Schmidt, and it is entitled "Estimating the Completeness of Range Queries over Structured P2P Databases: Fundamentals, Theory and Effective Applications to Distributed Information Systems." This chapter is focused on a base technique for implementing range queries that are a very powerful tool in a wide range of data management systems and are vital to a multitude of applications and systems included P2P CDNs. In particular, authors propose a method for estimating the completeness of query answers and discuss the applicability and quality of such estimation. Moreover, they present an implementation and evaluation for the P-Grid system and show how to adapt the technique to other overlays.

This book was conceived due to the direct and indirect involvement of many researchers, academicians, developers, designers, and industry practitioners.

The editors hope that through this book we are delivering the state-of-the-art research on current and future Internet-based content delivery networking topics, bringing to the attention of the community novel problems that must be investigated. They hope that this book will serve as a valuable text for students especially at graduate level and reference for researchers and practitioners working in the CDN domain and its emerging consumer applications. The contributors envision this book to establish a pathway for the integrated use of existing technologies for the development of future-generation Content Networks.

REFERENCE

Akamai. (n.d.). *Perspectives*. Retrieved from http://www.akamai.com/html/perspectives/index.html

Acknowledgment

We would like to express our gratitude to the authors of accepted papers and the reviewers for their contributions to this book, as well as to IGI Global to have fully and enthusiastically supported such an initiative.

We'd like to thank authors for their precious contributions that allow us to edit such an interesting book, the Editorial Advisory Board Members (Manuel Esteve, Universidad Politecnica de Valencia - Spain, Juan G. Lalinde, EAFIT University - Colombia, Carlo Mastroianni, ICAR/CNR - Italy, George Pallis, University of Cyprus - Cyprus, Mukaddim Pathan, University of Melbourne - Australia, Weisong Shi, Wayne State University - USA) for advertising the book call for chapter and supporting the review process, and George Pallis for writing the foreword of this book.

The Editors,

Giancarlo Fortino
University of Calabria, Italy

Carlos E. Palau
Universidat Politecnica de Valencia, Spain

Chapter 1
CDN Modeling and Performance

Benjamin Molina
Universitat Politecnica de Valencia, Spain

Carlos E. Palau
Universitat Politecnica de Valencia, Spain

Manuel Esteve
Universitat Politecnica de Valencia, Spain

ABSTRACT

Content Distribution Networks (CDN) appeared a decade ago as a method for reducing latencies, improving performance experienced by Internet users, and limiting the effect of flash-crowds, so as balance load in servers. Content Distribution has evolved in different ways (e.g. cloud computing structures and video streaming distribution infrastructures). The solution proposed in early CDN was the location of several controlled caching servers close to clients, organized and managed by a central control system. Many companies deployed their own CDN infrastructure– and so demonstrating the resulting effectiveness. However, the business model of these networks has evolved from the distribution of static web objects to video streaming. Many aspects of deployment and implementation remain proprietary, evidencing the lack of a general CDN model, although the main design concepts are widely known. In this work, the authors represent the structure of a CDN and the performance of some of its parameters, using queuing theory, simplifying the redirection schema and studying the elements that could determine the improvement in performance. The main contribution of the work is a general expression for a CDN environment and the relationship between different variables like caching hit ratios, network latency, number of surrogates, and server capacity; this proves that the use of CDN outperform the typical client/server architecture.

DOI: 10.4018/978-1-4666-1794-0.ch001

INTRODUCTION

Few things compare with the growth of the Internet over recent years. A key challenge for Internet infrastructure has been delivering increasingly complex data of different types and origin to a growing user population. The need to scale led to the development of clusters (Mendonça et al, 2008), global content delivery networks (Verma, 2002) and, more recently, P2P structures (Androutsellis-Theotokis et al, 2004). However, the architecture of these systems differs significantly, and the differences affect their performance, workloads, and the role that caching can play (Gadde et al, 2000; Sariou et al, 2002).

Content Delivery Networks (CDNs) are overlay networks across the wide-area Internet which consist of dedicated collections of servers, called surrogates, distributed strategically throughout the Internet. The main aim of the surrogates is to be close to users and provide them with content in a low-latency mode. The surrogates are normally proxy caches that serve cached content directly with a certain hit ratio; the uncached content is previously obtained (if possible) from the origin server before responding. When a client makes a request for content inside a CDN, it is directed to an optimal surrogate, which serves this content within low response time boundaries – at least compared to contacting the origin site (Cardellini et al, 2003). CDNs such as Akamai (Akamai, 2011) or Limelight Networks (Limelight Networks, 2011) are nowadays used by many websites as they effectively reduce the client-perceived latency and balance load (Johnson et al, 2000). They accomplish this by serving content from a dedicated, distributed infrastructure located around the world and close to clients. The content is replicated either on-demand, when users request it, or replicated beforehand, by pushing the content on the content servers (Dilley et al, 2002; Verma et al, 2002). CDN services can improve client access to specialized content by assisting in four basic areas:

- *Speed*, reducing the response and download times of site objects (e.g. streaming media), by delivering content close to end users.
- *Reliability*, by delivering content from multiple locations; a fault-tolerant network with load balancing mechanisms can be implemented.
- *Scalability*, both in bandwidth, network equipment and personnel.
- *Special events*, by incrementing capacity and peak loads for special situations by distributing content as it is needed (Yoshida, 2008).

CDNs improve performance and availability of web and some media content by pushing the content towards the network edges and providing replication and replica location services. Intelligent replica placement improves response time by serving content from a topological location near the client (in terms of network hops), avoiding the congested backbone networks and network access (Mao et al, 2002). Replica location services direct requests for objects to nearby replicas by means of redirections through DNS, based on extensive measurements and monitoring of network performance (Shaikh et al, 2001). The overall performance of a CDN is largely determined by its ability to direct client requests to the most appropriate server (Johnson et al, 2000; Doyle et al, 2002; Khan et al, 2008). Content providers, such as websites or streaming video sources, contract with commercial CDNs to host and distribute content (Cranor et al, 2001). They are attractive for content providers because in some cases the responsibility is offloaded to the CDN infrastructure. Most CDNs have servers in ISP points of presence, so clients can access topologically nearby clients with very low latencies. They are capable of sustaining large workloads and flash-crowds due to a large number of servers, or few but powerful servers (Dilley et al, 2002). The main features of a CDN are:

- Decentralizes content storage by moving content closer to clients.
- Preserves WAN bandwidth by delivering content locally, and maximizes user performance.
- Content management tools help optimize network performance and prioritize mission critical data (Fei, 2001).

CDNs are perfectly integrated in web architecture and the minimum unit managed by them is an object, which are named by URLs. Unlike the web, content providers do not need to manage web servers, since client requests are redirected to replicas hosted by the CDN (Verma et al, 2002). CDNs typically host static content (images, advertisements, media clips, etc.) although dynamic content could contain embedded objects served by the CDN (Pallis et al, 2006).

PREVIOUS WORK

Content Delivery Networks have become a popular method for providing scalable access to web content, currently static and streaming media content. This type of service can be offered by private companies (Akamai, Limelight, Inktomi, etc.) or it can be individually implemented by means of specific vendor products (Cisco, Nortel, etc.) and solutions. With regard to CDN developments, there are different proposals. The Globule approach introduces object-oriented replication between peers in order to create an overlay network the authors have called user-centric CDN (Pierre et al, 2006). In (Karbhari et al, 2002) we find the development of Application CDN (ACDN), based on the RaDaR system developed in AT&T, a similar approach has been used by NETLI, acquired by Akamai in 2007 (NETLI, 2011). SPREAD (Rodriguez et al, 2000) is another replication system for content delivery but not exactly a CDN, which replicates content through interception of network traffic. CoDeeN is another development of a CDN

by Princeton University, but it only works over PlanetLab platform (PlanetLab, 2011).

CDNs are overlay networks on top of the Internet that deliver content to users from the network edges, thus reducing response time compared to obtaining content directly from the origin server, as depicted on Figure 1. If client 1 downloads content from a certain site, it traditionally contacts a centralized server, located in the origin site. The communication may traverse several ISPs and WANs, thus being unable to predict content latency and jitter. If the desired content requires some temporal constraints, a decentralized solution is mandatory in order to avoid, or at least reduce, network unpredictability. Following the example of Figure 1, if client 1 contacts surrogate S_C to retrieve content (path S_2), it will perceive a reduction in the response time compared with contacting the origin server (path S_1). Furthermore, network usage is reduced and optimized on an S_2-path, as backbone traffic is reduced.

As can be seen, reducing response time implies reducing network latency and decreasing server processing time. Due to a lack of a global management of the Internet, companies have traditionally scaled-up with a more powerful server or scaled-out locally in cluster-based architectures. A CDN is a global scale-out approach that tries to reduce network latency by avoiding congestion paths, thus resulting in a reduction of perceived response time. Leading CDN companies have placed from hundreds up to thousands of servers throughout the world, being able to serve content to any client from a nearby surrogate. Correctly managing such huge content networks is extremely important.

Previous research has investigated the use and effectiveness of CDNs, although the proprietary and closed nature of these systems tends to impede investigation (Dilley et al, 2002). Recent studies confirm that CDNs reduce average download response time, but that DNS redirection techniques add noticeable overhead because of DNS latencies. Most of these studies have been empirical

Figure 1. General CDN scenario on the Internet

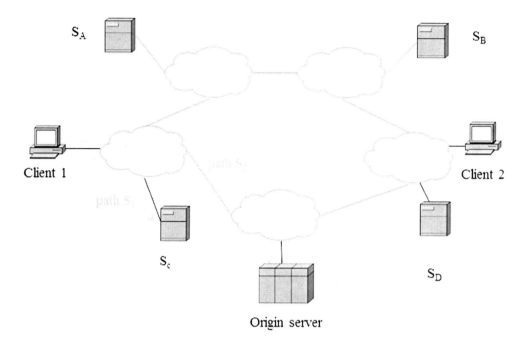

Origin server

ones, studying and evaluating response times on real CDNs (Mao et al, 2002; Khan et al, 2008), effectiveness of DNS redirection (Mao et al, 2002; Krishnamurthy et al, 2001), server selection (Doyle et al, 2002; Khan et al, 2008), or server location (Mendonça et al, 2008). Previous works on the literature have tried to model the behavior of CDNs using different techniques, but usually simplifying the nature of such systems and losing generality. These studies have focused mainly in two topics: server placement (Wu et al, 2011) or evaluation of response time. Different techniques have been used for the evaluation of the second parameter: linear time response of web servers (Agrawal et al, 2001), water filling schema (Masa et al, 2003) or queuing theory (Calo et al, 2002). This chapter starts from basic assumptions in (Agrawal et al, 2001) and introduces new features that resemble a more realistic and general model. This way we can study the impact on performance of important parameters such as the caching hit ratio, network latency, number of surrogates and server capacity. Moreover, it is worthwhile es-

tablishing some dependencies and relationships among these parameters, as simulation results are always finite and cover only a limited variability range of the CDN parameters.

CDN are complex systems, with many distributed components collaborating to distribute content. CDN facilitate and optimize the management and delivery of static and streaming content over heterogeneous all-IP networks. (Wee et al, 2003) The common problems CDN researchers and operators have to solve are:

• Content placement, which involves how many servers to use, where to position them and how to distribute content across them. It has been treated as the Facility Location Problem.(Turaga et al, 2005) The goal of the algorithms is to specify the surrogate server locations that improve performance with low infrastructure costs, and determine the best distribution strategy for the contents stored in the CDN. Adequate replica placement benefits clients, ISP and servers. (Vakali et al, 2003)

- Surrogate server placement is a significant problem and there have been different approaches proposed to the problem. In (Khan et al, 2008) the authors minimize the number of autonomous systems traversed by when clients issue a request for a specific content. Other authors propose the use of an unrealistic tree topology network (Li et al, 1999); a greedy solution (Qiu et al, 1999) or try to profit P2P content placement solutions to the CDN environment. (Clarke et al, 2001) However, commercial CDNs use different techniques based mainly on popularity, state of the network and available resources at the servers. (Androutsellis-Theotokis et al, 2004; Vakali et al, 2003; Wang et al, 2002). Each CDN operator use a different approach, e.g.: Akamai has more than 12.000 surrogates deployed in PoPs all around the world (1000 networks in 162 countries), while other CDN have deployed a reduced number of surrogates. (Vakali et al, 2003)

- Content discovery is the process of identifying surrogates that store the desired content or a relevant part of it. P2P networks use mechanisms based on flooding and forward routing algorithms (Androutsellis-Theotokis et al, 2004), but CDNs are more static and centrically managed. Different approaches exist: a user-centric alternative more related with P2P systems (Pierre et al, 2006); support by a central content manager with knowledge of every object stored in the surrogates of the network (Mao et al, 2002; Peng, 2003)

- Content Management is close related with request redirection. There are different techniques to redirect client requests to the objects stored in a CDN (Wang et al, 2002). Although most CDN use DNS-based redirection schemes (Mao et al, 2002; Park

et al, 2004), others use URL rewriting, in which the origin server redirects clients to different surrogate servers by rewriting the dynamically generated pages. CDN provide special scripts that transparently parse web page content and replace embedded URL (Krishnamurty et al, 2001), e.g.: Akamai with the use of the Akamaizer tool and Akamai Resource Locator (ARL). (Akamai, 2011) An example of DNS CDN content management in an open development is CoDeeN with CoDNS (Park et al, 2004). PRISM introduces the usage of an XML identification of the contents to locate the streaming sources within a CDN (Cranor et al, 2001)

Current uses of CDN are mainly focused on video streaming, although static web content is still a business. CDN operators are currently entering in the cloud systems, but the basic operations and redirection of a client to the most adequate surrogate is still modeled in the same way. With regard to video streaming and CDN there are different contributions in the literature. PRISM provides content naming, management, discovery and redirection mechanisms to support high quality media streaming over an IP-based CDN (Cranor et al, 2001). TVCDN is another work related with streaming and CDN, but it still is a preliminary work in which the authors provide description of a content management system for TV distribution; again the authors rely on an existing CDN infrastructure.(Caviglione et al, 2011) Another work related with streaming distribution is MARCONINet (Dutta et al, 2002), that provides an infrastructure for audio delivery to mobile and fixed users, using multimedia proxies and content management but not exactly using a CDN. And finally in (Roy et al, 2003) the authors present different techniques and procedures to develop a CDN focused on streaming distribution for mobile users. Akamai (Akamai, 2011), SinoCDN (SinoCDN, 2011), Limelight Networks

Figure 2. General CDN architecture

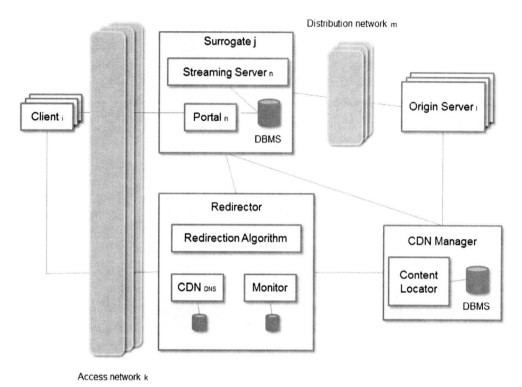

(Limelight Networks, 2011) or Voddler (Voddler, 2011) are the main CDN companies devoted to streaming media.

CDN REFERENCE ARCHITECTURE

CDN systems are focused on delivering both web and streaming media content. A CDN general architecture description can be found in different papers in related literature (Peng, 2003). The architecture used in this paper is straight-forward and depicted in Figure 2. It relies on the HTTP protocol and also in IETF streaming protocols. The architecture includes also control protocols and mechanisms in order to deliver content adequately. The main components of the architecture are: Origin Server, Surrogates, Clients, Access Network, Distribution Network, Content Manager and Redirector, and it has been developed and

specified in (Molina et al, 2006). All these components will be used in the CDN model specified and analyzed in the following section.

Origin Servers

Origin servers are located at the content providers, containing the information to be distributed or accessed by clients. This information can be classified using different criteria, but the most used is the one who separates between static and dynamic contents. Currently, the main kind of media objects managed by CDN providers are static, although different efforts are carried out to deal with dynamic information, services and applications, what has lead to the establishing the relationship between CDN providers and cloud computing operators. If the CDN service is contracted by a content provider, it delegates its URI name space for objects to be distributed and delivered by the CDN system. The Origin server distributes the delegated content to the surrogates of the CDN by means of the Distribution Network. The origin servers provide the contents directly to the surrogates which cache it and wait for client requests. In the model we will consider an origin server and all the surrogates containing the same information, other configurations are possible but we have used it to keep the model as simple as possible for better understanding.

Surrogates

Surrogate servers are replica servers of the origin servers, acting as proxy/cache servers with the ability to store and deliver content. A CDN is usually classified according to its structure, number of surrogate servers, location of these servers and the algorithm executed to determine the server who serves each issued request. Surrogates share content among themselves, i.e. the most popular content is replicated among the surrogates, or a complete origin server is replicated in the surrogates, different policies are policies are possible. Typically, surrogates are composed of three components (Peng, 2003; Molina et al., 2006):

- Portal, a HTTP-based web server which provides access to the contents stored in the CDN.
- Streaming Server, a media streaming server in charge of distributing the multimedia content, if the CDN allows the distribution of this kind of content, as in the model we will study the redirection mechanism it is not relevant for the outcome of the model.
- DB, contains information about stored content, on-going sessions and statistics accessible by the monitor and content manager.

Clients

Clients are individuals with different devices (e.g. PC, special set-top boxes or smart-phones) which request and download a particular piece of content served by the CDN through the most convenient surrogate. Interaction of clients with the CDN is better modeled if clients are considered as clusters, rather than individual clients. Clusters of clients experience similar latency and bandwidth constraints, and can be modeled as a unique request generator for simplicity, usually clients in the same LAN use to have common interests, and web caching uses this premise in order to analyze and improve performance. In the specified model, clients will be located at a certain distance from surrogates, and depending on the measured rtt will access one or another surrogate.

Access Network

Clients access the service provided by the CDN through different Access Network, if the client is multihomed, it can even use more than one network at the same time (Lazaro et al., 2007). These networks can be fixed or mobile, narrow or broadband, currently the common point among all these networks is the IP protocol. All-IP networks and seamless mobility between networks are key paradigms to analyze access networks. Surrogates are usually located in the ISP points of presence (POP) in order to serve the cluster of clients accessing the Internet by each ISP, although to provide better service for load balancing and fault tolerance, they can be attached to more than one network. Multicast can improve the process delivery within an access network served by one or more surrogates, if the core IP network of the ISP supports it; if several networks from different ISP are involved BGP operation will be needed.

Distribution Network

The distribution network supplies content from the Origin Servers to the CDN in order to store the conten in the Surrogates. There are different approaches, but the two mostly considered are satellite networks and overlay trees over the

Internet. In most cases the distribution from the Origin Servers to the Surrogates takes the form of a bulk transfer, in order to optimize the bandwidth consumption, and avoid as much as possible the unpredictability and problematic performance of the Internet, using multicast where available in order to reduce bandwidth consumption.

The use of the Distribution Network for object transfer between origin servers and the Surrogates is done when any content is not available in any of the Surrogates. Techniques like Digital Fountain or data compression can be used to perform this bulk transfer. The most simple business model is the full copying of the origin servers in the surrogates, although different authors propose the selection of objects to be stored, in order to reduce usage cost of the CDN (Qiu et al., 2001).

Content Manager

The core intelligence of the CDN resides in two components: the content manager and the redirector. Both working together, would provide the best server to each request issued by a client. The main task of the Content Manager is to control the objects stored in each Surrogate, providing this information to the Redirector in order to get each client served by the most suitable Surrogate.

The main component of the Content Manager is the Content Locator, it is in charge of determining:

- Number of replicas of a media object.
- Surrogate or surrogates designated to store a new object.
- Elimination of non-popular objects from the surrogates.
- Interaction of the CDN with the origin servers.
- Update objects in the surrogates when a new version is available in the origin servers.
- Move media objects among surrogates, depending on the demand pattern.

There are two types of messages involved in the process of content management: update messages and report messages. The former are sent by the Content Manager to the Surrogates in order to inform them about changes in the policies or update control information. The latter are sent back by the surrogates in order to inform the content manager about exceptional situations, e.g. a flash-crowd is detected.

The information managed by the Content Locator is stored in a database named $DB_{Content}$ and it is used by the redirector, together with the information collected by the monitor in order to decide the response to provide to each client request. The model will simplify this issue, considering that all surrogates store the full origin server content.

Redirector

This module provides intelligence to the system, because it estimates the most adequate surrogate server for each different request and client. It has three differentiated modules:

- CDN_{DNS}, accepts requests from the client local DNS and sends the corresponding response routing the client to the most adequate surrogate. Several approaches exist to perform the redirection task, i.e. Akamai uses many DNS servers distributed around the globe organized in two hierarchies. The addresses and names of the surrogates, and some additional information, is stored in the DB_{DNS}, which keeps all the registers and information needed to reply to client requests for a certain content. (Akamai, 2011)
- Monitor Module, periodically gets statistical information from different key elements of the CDN architecture and conducts a variety of measurements to obtain information about the network (e.g. routers and link usage) and the components of the CDN. The Monitor uses SNMP and other

Figure 3. Simple CDN scenario

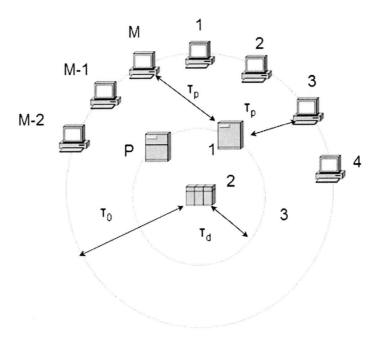

monitoring protocols to gather data. All such information is stored in a database (DB$_{Monitor}$). The archived data are used to feed the redirection algorithm and determine the best Surrogate for each client request in terms of QoS.

- Redirection Algorithm, which selects the optimal surrogate on the basis of the information gathered by the Monitor, using different heuristics, but always with the aim of providing the best surrogate, to each request in a certain time.

THE CONTENT DISTRIBUTION MODEL

The CDN model is composed of three main elements, as shown in Figure 3.

- One *origin server*, placed at a central location

- P *surrogates*, placed somewhere between clients and the origin server, and
- M *client clusters*, dispersed throughout the world. A client cluster is a way of joining multiple single users located within a certain zone. We will analyze this scenario, obtaining therefore results for the whole group and not for single users. However, our general approach enables the easy extraction of a model based on single clients.

As a first approach, we can assume that all client clusters (in the following also clients) are uniformly distributed in a circle with roundtrip-time (RTT) τ_0 around the origin site. The surrogates between origin and clients are τ_d and τ_p away respectively (in terms of RTT). A client generates requests, that are served either by the origin server or surrogates. The mechanism telling the client which is the suitable server to contact is not considered; instead we assume that requests will be routed to the surrogates with a certain

Figure 4. Model of a M/M/1 queue

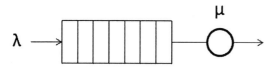

probability p. Otherwise, the client contacts the origin server with the opposite probability (1-p).

The normal performance metric considered in all CDN analysis is the mean response time experienced by the users. To start with an initial formula we can consider the following expression for the mean response time:

$$R = p \cdot R_{srrgt} + (1 - p) \cdot R_{origin} \qquad (1)$$

where R_{srrgt} is the mean response time associated with contacting a surrogate (and be served by it) and R_{origin} is the average response time associated with contacting the origin server (and be served by it). Further on, the mean response time can be represented using a linear model as:

$$R = N \cdot \tau + S \qquad (2)$$

where N is a scaling factor that incorporates the effect of network loss rates, retransmission and, in general, the volume of exchanged data required for the request; τ is the network latency factor (round-trip-time) associated and S is the request processing time, which will be modelled as a M/M/1 queue system. An M/M/1 queue (Kleinrock et al, 1996) consists of a FIFO buffer with packets arriving randomly according to a Poisson process and a processor, called a server, that retrieves packets from the buffer at a specified service rate, as depicted in Figure 4.

So it follows for the average response time that:

$$R = p \cdot \left[N\tau_p + \frac{1}{\mu_p - \lambda_p} \right] + (1 - p) \cdot \left[N \cdot \tau_s + \frac{1}{\mu_s - \lambda_s} \right]$$

$$(3)$$

The appearing variables in the above expression will be described separately for a better comprehension.

The variable p is the probability a request will be satisfied by a surrogate. However, a client will not always be routed to the same surrogate. Although theoretically it would be desirable for a client to be redirected to its closest surrogate, it is a fact that the common routing mechanism (DNS redirection) does not always correctly guess client location, thus redirecting it to another surrogate. Even supposing a correct estimation, it could be useful to balance between near surrogates due to overloading conditions. So we can represent the value of p for the i-th cluster as the sum of the probabilities of contacting the P surrogates:

$$p_i = \sum_{j=1}^{P} p_i^j \qquad (4)$$

The variable τ_p is the latency associated with contacting the surrogates. Note that this value is highly variable and different for each client cluster. Thus, the latency value for the i-th cluster to the j-th surrogate will be expressed as $\tau_p^{i,j}$.

The variables μ_p and λ_p are the mean service rates and the perceived incoming mean arrival rate at each surrogate. Once again, these values may be different per surrogate. Supposing that the i-th cluster generates packets at rate λ_i, then the arrival rate perceived by the j-th surrogate from cluster i will be:

$$\lambda_i^j = p_i^j \lambda_i \qquad (5)$$

Due to the stability condition ($\mu_p > \lambda_p$) we could just get a factor k (k>1) so that $\mu_p = k \lambda_p$. The value of k is important: a low value can limit capacity conditions where processing time is slow; a high value can suppose a practically instantaneous processing time, where only latency values

Table 1. Parameters and expressions for an M/M/1 queue system

Parameter	Expression
mean arrival rate λ mean arrival time T	$\lambda = \dfrac{1}{T}\left(\dfrac{packets}{second}\right)$
mean packet size	$\bar{p}$ (bits/packet)
service capacity	C (bits/ second)
mean service rate	$\mu = \dfrac{C}{\bar{p}}\left(\dfrac{pakets}{second}\right)$
mean delay	$\overline{W} = \dfrac{1}{\mu - \lambda}\left(\dfrac{seconds}{packet}\right)$ with $\mu > \lambda$

significantly affect the global response time. The same considerations can be applied to the origin site for the variables p, τ_s, μ_s and λ_s. However, this time the origin site is absorbing M exponential distributions from each client cluster, which can be modelled as another exponential distribution with a new arrival rate as the sum of each individual arrival rate.

Before coming to the general expression, it is important to note that the previous formula (formula 3) enables the response time to be obtained for both for a client cluster and for the overall system. The latter case, which will be here considered, is the average of the mean response time obtained for all M clusters:

$$\overline{R} = \frac{1}{M}\sum_{i=1}^{M} R_i \qquad (6)$$

So we can present our general expression as:

$$\overline{R} = \overline{R_s} + \overline{R_0} \qquad (7)$$

with the following expressions for $\overline{R_s}$ and $\overline{R_0}$:

$$\overline{R_s} = \frac{1}{M}\cdot\sum_{i=1}^{M}\sum_{j=1}^{P}\left[p_i^j\left(N\cdot\tau_p^{i,j} + \frac{1}{\mu_p^j - \sum_{l=1}^{M}\lambda_l^j}\right)\right] \qquad (8)$$

$$\overline{R_0} = \frac{1}{M}\sum_{i=1}^{M}\left(1 - \sum_{j=1}^{P}p_i^j\right)\left(N\tau_0^i + \frac{1}{\mu_s - \sum_{l=1}^{M}(1 - p_l)\lambda_l}\right) \qquad (9)$$

where M is the number of client clusters, P is the number of surrogates, p_i^j stands for the probability of the i-th client cluster contacting the j-th surrogate, N represents the number of required packets for a client-server transaction, $\tau_p^{i,j}$ is the mean roundtrip time between the i-th cluster and the j-th surrogate, μ_p^j stands for the mean service rate of the j-th surrogate, λ_l^j represents the mean arrival rate that the l-th cluster sends to the j-th surrogate, τ_0^i is the mean RTT between the i-th cluster and the origin site, μ_s stands for the mean service rate of the origin site, and $(1-p_l)\lambda_l$ represents the mean arrival rate that the l-th cluster sends to the origin site

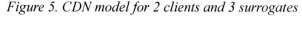

Figure 5. CDN model for 2 clients and 3 surrogates

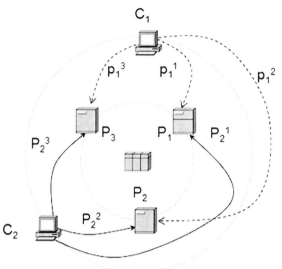

MODEL EXPLANATION

Before translating our expression into simulation scenarios, it could be of interest to better understand it by using some graphical and mathematical techniques. As there are M client clusters and P surrogates to serve them, one may ask whether P=M, just to associate one optimum surrogate close to each client cluster. However, it is not necessarily true as at the design phase it is extremely difficult to define client clusters. Even so, one may assign various surrogates for the same client cluster (P>M), if there is a need to serve content by client profile, which could be the business situation of premium and normal users. If a CDN provider is deploying its network, it is cost-safe to begin with few surrogates (P<M) and later grow by aggregating more servers. Independently of the business strategy, technical reasons such as congested servers due to flash crowds suggest serving content from different surrogates.

Let's start from the situation depicted in Figure 5, composed of 2 client clusters and 3 surrogates.

Client 1 generates requests with a mean rate of λ_1. As it is served by various surrogates, the general approach is to suppose that a certain percentage of requests will be served by surrogate P_1 and another by surrogate P_2 and P_3. A certain number of requests with probability $1-p_1$ ($p_1 = p_1^1 + p_1^2 + p_1^3$) will be directed to the origin server. As can be logically deducted from the previous picture (Figure 5), the probabilities of contacting the surrogates vary. Each client will usually contact its closest surrogate, and a hierarchy in the assigned weights by distance is established. So, if client 1 is next to surrogate P_1, then the nearest surrogate is P_2 and then P_3, it follows that $p_1^1 > p_1^2 > p_1^3$. We can therefore construct a matrix that contains all the probabilities of the surrogates, where the row indicates the client cluster and the column is associated with the correspondent probability of contacting the j-th surrogate. In the case of our system, an example could be:

$$P_p = \begin{bmatrix} 0.4 & 0.1 & 0.2 \\ 0.0 & 0.3 & 0.2 \end{bmatrix} \qquad (10)$$

Note that the sum of each row is $\neq 1$. This is because a certain number of requests are directed to the origin server (those that have not been

Figure 6. Latency threshold for a client cluster

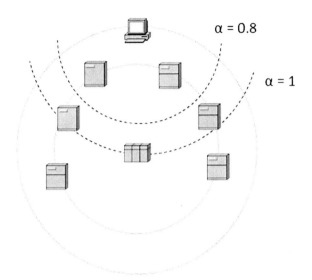

previously cached). So we can construct a vector from the mean caching hit ratios that specify the probability of contacting the origin server by each client. Following the example, we have:

$$\vec{p}_s = \begin{bmatrix} 1 - (0.4 + 0.1 + 0.2) \\ 1 - (0.0 + 0.3 + 0.2) \end{bmatrix} = \begin{bmatrix} 0.3 \\ 0.5 \end{bmatrix} \quad (11)$$

Generalizing the expression for M clients and P surrogates, we obtain a matrix with M rows and P columns and a vector with M rows.

$$P_p = \begin{bmatrix} p_1^1 & p_1^2 & p_1^3 & \cdots & p_1^P \\ p_2^1 & p_2^2 & p_2^3 & \cdots & p_2^P \\ \cdots & \cdots & \cdots & \cdots & \cdots \\ p_M^1 & p_M^2 & p_M^3 & \cdots & p_M^P \end{bmatrix}_{M \times P} \quad (12)$$

$$\vec{p}_s = \begin{bmatrix} 1 - \sum_{j=1}^{P} p_1^j & 1 - \sum_{j=1}^{P} p_2^j & \cdots & 1 - \sum_{j=1}^{P} p_M^j \end{bmatrix}^T \quad (13)$$

Another aspect to consider is that a client may never contact a specific surrogate ($p_i^j = 0$ for a

certain i,j). For example, client 2 will not retrieve any content from surrogate P_1. This is due to the fact that (in terms of latency) the origin server is nearer than surrogate P_1, that is $\tau_p^{2,1} > \tau_0^2$. This relationship can be used as a criterion to assign the probability weights, so that

$$\begin{bmatrix} if \ \tau_p^{i,j} < \tau_p^{k,l} \rightarrow p_i^j > p_k^l \ , \forall \ i,k \in [1..M], \forall \ j,l \in [1..P] \\ if \ \tau_p^{i,j} > \tau_0^i \rightarrow p_i^j = 0 \ , \forall \ i \in [1..M], \forall \ j \in [1..P] \end{bmatrix} \quad (14)$$

The behaviour can be illustrated on Figure 6. Normally, a client contacts few surrogates – and mainly those that are nearby. A threshold can be assigned introducing a factor α (α <1) so that $\tau_p^{i,j} < \alpha \cdot \tau_0 i$. If the number of surrogates is high, then reducing the value of α also reduces the assigned surrogates. In the example of Figure 6, a reduction from α =1 to α = 0.8 supposes contacting only 3 servers instead of 5. On the contrary, if the number of surrogates is small it should be possible to obtain content from distant surrogates (α >1). This situation is only under conditions of severe congestion in the origin server and nearby surrogates.

SIMULATION RESULTS

As can be appreciated, the expression for the main response time corresponds to an n-dimensional function represented with a non-fixed value of n. For example, the probability of a client contacting a surrogate, represented by p_i^j, is really a set of variables whose size depends on the number of clients (M) and surrogates (P). Similar behaviour occurs with latencies (τ_p^{ij}, τ_0^i), capacities (μ_p^j, μ_s) and mean traffic rates (λ_i). So we will simulate a CDN for various values of M clients and P surrogates and we will try to extract some general conclusions. The simulation procedure has to consider the following variables as input parameters:

- The number of clients (M). The clients will be uniformly distributed around the origin server and mutually separated by ($2\pi/M$) radians. To introduce some randomness, the first client is shifted by a random angle (uniformly distributed) between 0 and ($2\pi/M$) radians, and the rest are just placed equidistantly. So it follows:

$$\text{client 0: } \alpha_{c0} = rand\left[0, \frac{2\pi}{M}\right] \quad (15)$$

$$\text{client i: } \alpha_{ci} = \frac{2\pi}{M} \cdot i + \alpha_{c0}, \text{ i} = 0..M \quad (16)$$

Note that the first client begins with index 0, while in previous pictures it had index 1. This is only done to enable a simpler mathematical description. Analogous treatment will happen with the surrogates.

- The number of surrogates (P). The same randomizing procedure as with clients happens with the surrogates:

$$\text{surrogate 0: } \alpha_{s0} = rand\left[0, \frac{2\pi}{P}\right] \quad (17)$$

$$\text{surrogate j: } \alpha_{sj} = \frac{2\pi}{P} \cdot j + \alpha_{s0}, \text{ j} = 0..P$$
$$(18)$$

- The number of necessary retransmissions (N).
- A certain hit ratio per each client cluster (p_i, i=1..M).
- A minimum and a maximum value of the latency between each client and the origin server (τ_0^{min}, τ_0^{max}). As each client must not be the same latency away from the server, a random value between this interval will be taken for each client (τ_0^i).
- A minimum and a maximum value of the latency between each surrogate and the origin (τ_d^{min}, τ_d^{max}). All surrogates are not the same value τ_d^j (j=1..P) away from the origin server, so a random value will be taken between these two boundaries.
- A minimum and a maximum value of the mean traffic rate sent by each client (λ_{min}, λ_{max}), as they can have different traffic characterizations. Once again, a random value between minimum and maximum will be taken.
- A threshold factor (α) indicating the area or zone for each client to contact surrogates, as described previously in Figure 5. Surrogates placed outside this area will not serve any content to the associated client.
- A capacity factor (k) representing the necessary increase with respect to the mean arrival rate, so that the stability condition for an M/M/1 queue is satisfied ($\mu > \lambda$). Though it could be set differently for each surrogate, we will take the same value of the parameter k for all of them.

Figure 7 shows an example for 8 clients and 4 surrogates. Note that both clients and surrogates do not have the same distance (in terms of latency) from the origin server. Each are inside a ring whose thickness is determined by [τ_0^{min}, τ_0^{max}] and [τ_d^{min}, τ_d^{max}] respectively. However, the distance in radians between them is deterministic, as both are uniformly distributed around the ring depending on the values of the parameters M and P.

Figure 7. CDN structure for M=8 and P=4

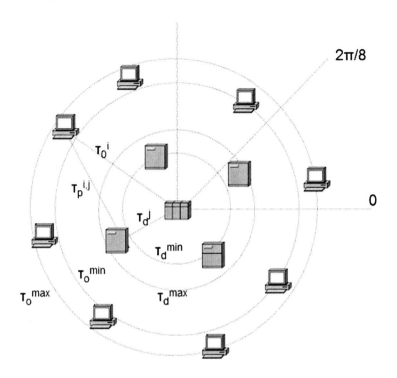

With the above geometric distribution the distance between a client i and a surrogate, j can be automatically calculated applying the cosinus theorem, without introducing it as an input parameter. So it follows that:

$$\tau_p^{i,j} = \left(\tau_o^i\right)^2 + \left(\tau_d^j\right)^2 - 2 \cdot \tau_o^i \cdot \tau_d^j \cdot \cos \beta^{i,j} \quad (19)$$

$$\beta^{i,j} = \left|\alpha_{ci} - \alpha_{sj}\right| = \left|\left(\frac{2\pi}{M} \cdot i + \alpha_{c0}\right) - \left(\frac{2\pi}{P} \cdot j + \alpha_{s0}\right)\right| \quad (20)$$

The even property of the cosinus function makes it unnecessary to use the absolute module.

In this way, we can create the following matrix and vector:

$$T_p = \begin{bmatrix} \tau_1^1 & \tau_1^2 & \tau_1^3 & \dots & \tau_1^P \\ \tau_2^1 & \tau_2^2 & \tau_2^3 & \dots & \tau_2^P \\ \dots & \dots & \dots & \dots & \dots \\ \tau_M^1 & \tau_M^2 & \tau_M^3 & \dots & \tau_M^P \end{bmatrix}_{M \times P} \quad (21)$$

$$\vec{\tau}_s = \begin{bmatrix} \tau_0^1 & \tau_0^2 & \dots & \dots & \tau_0^M \end{bmatrix}^T \quad (22)$$

The latency matrix T_p is related with the probability matrix mentioned in the previous chapter P_p, that is, P_p can be automatically obtained from T_p, $\vec{\tau}_s$, α and the caching hit ratio. The method to obtain P_p is very simple. For each row i of the matrix T_p a threshold given by $\alpha \cdot \vec{\tau}_s(i)$, described graphically in Figure 6, discriminates between the surrogates being contacted by the i-th client. Thus we can construct a mask matrix M_p (dimension MxP) whose elements $m_p^{i,j}$ comply with the following condition:

$$m_p^{i,j} \begin{cases} 1 & , if \ T_p(i,j) \leq \alpha \cdot \vec{\tau}_s(i) \\ 0 & , if \ T_p(i,j) > \alpha \cdot \vec{\tau}_s(i) \end{cases} \quad (23)$$

The mask matrix M_p serves as a starting point (together with T_p) for constructing another intermediate matrix P_w that assigns probability weights

Figure 8. Response times for M =8, P =4, N=5, α=1, k=1.2, hit_ratio=0..1, $\tau_0^{min} = \tau_0^{max} = 2$ sec, τ_d^{min} $= \tau_d^{max} = 1$ sec, $\lambda_{min} = \lambda_{max} = 100$

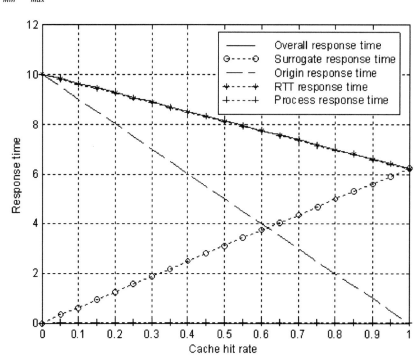

for a client i to contact a surrogate j. Therefore, the sum of each row in P_w must be 1. The steps for constructing P_w are the following:

Create an auxiliary matrix by multiplying the latency matrix T_p with the mask matrix by components. This means, it is not a matrix multiplication (note that the matrix dimensions do not allow it), but a component by component multiplication, resulting in a new MxP matrix similar to T_p, but discriminating between those latencies that are greater than our imposed threshold. So it follows for this auxiliary matrix:

$$aux^{i,j} = \tau_p^{\,i,j} \cdot m_p^{i,j} \qquad (24)$$

As each row sum of M_p must be 1, it may seem sensible to divide each element of a row i by the sum of all the elements of the row. However, this process would result in a greater weight for a greater distance, which is not our intention; on

the contrary, the link between a client and a nearby surrogate must suppose a greater weight than a more distant surrogate (distant surrogates have been previously avoided). A method to achieve this is by weighting the difference between latency and the sum of latencies in a row:

$$\tilde{p}_w^{\;i,j} = 1 - \frac{aux^{i,j}}{\displaystyle\sum_{j=1}^{P} aux^{i,j}} \qquad p_w^{i,j} = N(\tilde{p}_w^{\;i,j})$$

$$(25)$$

where the N operator implies normalization, that is, the sum of elements within a row must be 1.

Once the simulation function has been described, it is now time to obtain some graphs and interpret their behaviour. Figure 8 depicts response times for a possible CDN scenario for various values of caching hit ratios and a reduced number of clients and surrogates. Easy parameter relationships have been established to analytically validate the results. For example, the caching hit ratio is the same for all clients sending traffic with the same mean rate. The parameter α has been set to 1 to be sure that each client would contact at least one surrogate. For simplicity, there is no latency ring for clients nor surrogates.

Note that the mean response time can be seen in two ways: (i) as the response times of the surrogates and the origin, or (ii) as the response time associated with latency and process.

The first approach enables an analysis of working conditions and when to send, or not, content to the surrogates; the second approach indicates where response time is mainly affected by network congestion, or server overload.

As can be seen in Figure 8, all response times follow a linear behaviour. Once identified, further conclusions can be made. The lowest value of mean response time is obtained for the highest caching hit ratio, that is, when all content is served by the surrogates and none of it by the origin server. The reduction of response time is perhaps insignificant in absolute terms, but significant in relative terms (representing a 40% reduction).

Besides, the overall process time is very reduced (nearly imperceptible), so only the roundtrip affects the mean response time. Maybe the set value of factor k leads to underload conditions in all servers. Anyway, the latency value of this scenario is considerable for a real CDN.

After the first observations, it would be interesting to support them with a mathematical viewpoint. Let's consider only the response time associated with the roundtrip time $(\overline{R}_t)$.

$$\overline{R}_t = \frac{1}{M} \sum_{i=1}^{M} \left\{ \sum_{j=1}^{P} p_i^j \cdot N \cdot \tau_p^{i,j} + \left(1 - \sum_{j=1}^{P} p_i^j\right) \cdot N \cdot \tau_0^i \right\}$$
(26)

As all clients have the same hit rate p and are the same roundtrip time away from the origin server, it follows that:

$$\left(1 - \sum_{j=1}^{P} p_i^j\right) = (1-p), \tau_0^i = \tau_0, p_i^j = p \cdot p_w^{i,j} \ , \forall i$$
(27)

So $\overline{R}_t$ is simplified to the following expression:

$$\overline{R}_t = (1-p) \cdot N \cdot \tau_0 + \frac{p \cdot N}{M} \cdot \sum_{i=1}^{M} \sum_{j=1}^{P} p_w^{i,j} \cdot \tau_p^{i,j}$$
(28)

Note that the model only considers nearby surrogates for the clients, where we can assume a similar latency for the surrogates a client will contact $(\tau_p^{i,j} \cong \tau_p^*)$, so it follows that:

$$\overline{R}_t = (1-p) \cdot N \cdot \tau_0 + p \cdot N \cdot \tau_p^*$$
(29)

corresponds to the equation of a linear function with variable p. As $\overline{R}_t(p=0) = N \cdot \tau_0 > N \cdot \tau_p^* = \overline{R}_t(p=1)$ we can conclude that for the roundtrip time it is desirable to offload all the content to the surrogates.

Considering now the response time associated with the required process time $(\overline{R}_p)$, we start from the following expression:

$$\overline{R}_p = \frac{1}{M} \sum_{i=1}^{M} \left\{ \sum_{j=1}^{P} \left(\frac{p_i^j}{\mu_p^j - \sum_{l=1}^{M} \lambda_l^j} \right) + \frac{\left(1 - \sum_{j=1}^{P} p_i^j\right)}{\mu_s - \sum_{l=1}^{M} (1-p_l)\lambda_l} \right\}$$
(30)

Figure 9. Response times for M =8, P =4, N=5, α=1.01, k=1.01, hit_ratio=0..1, $\tau_0^{min} = \tau_0^{max} = 2$ sec, $\tau_d^{min} = \tau_d^{max} = 1$ sec, $\lambda_{min} = \lambda_{max} = 100$

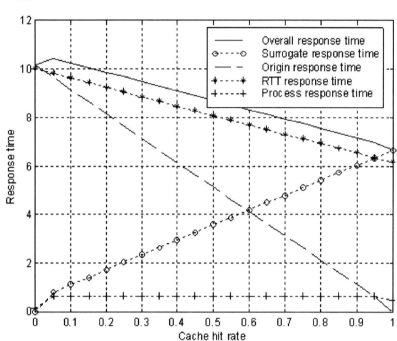

As the same capacity factor k is set to all clients, the previous expression can be simplified to:

$$\overline{R}_p = \frac{P+1}{(k-1) \cdot \lambda \cdot M}$$

$$as \quad \sum_{i=1}^{M} \sum_{j=1}^{P} \frac{p_w^{i,j}}{\sum_{l=1}^{M} p_w^{l,j}} = P \tag{31}$$

The first property of $\overline{R}_p$ that attracts attention is the fact that it is independent of the caching hit rate, that is, it remains constant. This can be observed in Figure 8 and Figure 9.

The previous expression is valid for values of caching hit rates in the interval $]0..1[$. If p=0, then the mean process time is the one required by the origin server:

$$\overline{R}_p = \frac{1}{M} \sum_{i=1}^{M} \left\{ \frac{1}{(k-1) \cdot \sum_{l=1}^{M} \lambda_l} \right\} \tag{32}$$

$$= \frac{1}{(k-1) \cdot M \cdot \lambda}$$

As $\overline{R}_p (p=0) = \frac{1}{P+1} \overline{R}_p (p \neq 0)$, it justifies the notorious jump or discontinuity for the graph of process response time in Figure 8. Similar behaviour occurs in the CDN scenario depicted in Figure 8; however, the effect remains unnoticeable as the process time is very reduced.

If p=1, then the mean process time is required by the surrogates:

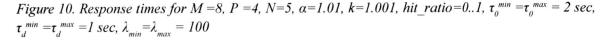
Figure 10. Response times for M =8, P =4, N=5, α=1.01, k=1.001, hit_ratio=0..1, $\tau_0^{min} = \tau_0^{max} = 2$ sec, $\tau_d^{min} = \tau_d^{max} = 1$ sec, $\lambda_{min} = \lambda_{max} = 100$

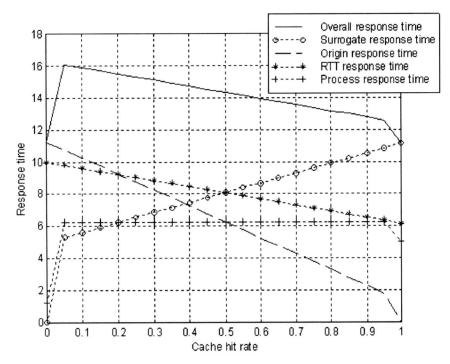

$$\overline{R}_p = \frac{1}{M} \sum_{i=1}^{M} \left\{ \sum_{j=1}^{P} \left(\frac{p_i^j}{\mu_p^j - \sum_{l=1}^{M} \lambda_l^j} \right) \right\}$$

$$= \frac{P}{(k-1) \cdot M \cdot \lambda}$$

(33)

The discontinuity effect is less perceivable in the graph, as the relative reduction is lower for p=1 than for p=0. Figure 10 shows the same CDN scenario but with a reduced value of the capacity factor k. This value supposes working at extreme capacity conditions, which is not a real case. However, it clearly shows the discontinuities at p=0 and p=1. Similar graphs could also be obtained for different values of M, P and λ.

From previous expressions it is easy to obtain response times associated with contacting just the surrogates and contacting just the origin server, in order to observe in both cases the linear depen-

dency between response time and caching hit ratio.

$$\overline{R}_{srrgt} = p \cdot N \cdot \tau_p^* + \frac{P}{(k-1) \cdot M \cdot \lambda}$$

(34)

$$\overline{R}_{origin} = (1-p) \cdot N \cdot \tau_0 + \frac{1}{(k-1) \cdot M \cdot \lambda}$$

(35)

A fixed capacity factor k does not realistically represent server load status, as capacity always increments by the same factor – independently of the traffic rate that is being supported, which is not the real case. Though this feature has helped us by simplifying the global expression into interesting partial conclusions, it leads to working scenarios where the response time associated with the server process remains practically constant,

Figure 11. Response times for M =100, P =50, N=5, α=0.7, k=1.1, hit_ratio=0..1, τ_0^{min} =0.3 sec, τ_0^{max} = 0.5 sec, τ_d^{min} =0.3 sec τ_d^{max} =0.4 sec, λ_{min}=50, λ_{max} = 100

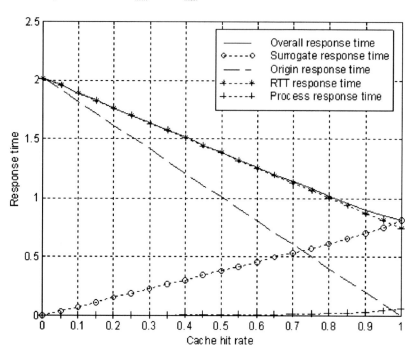

independently of other parameters in a possibly real CDN environment.

Real servers have a limited capacity that cannot be increased dynamically. The greater the number of requests supported then the longer the required process time, until a limit of overload is reached where packets may be discarded. On the contrary, a fixed value of k in our model supposes that a huge traffic arrival rate will result in a reduced process response time, as

$$R_p = \frac{1}{\mu - \lambda} = \frac{1}{\lambda \cdot (k-1)} \qquad (36)$$

To correct this drawback, a fixed capacity must be fixed to all the servers. A worst-case dimensioning will be utilized here. For the origin server, the worst case takes place when the hit ratio p is 0, and therefore it must support all the traffic. So it follows for the origin service rate (μ_s):

$$\mu_s = k \cdot \sum_{i=1}^{M} \lambda_i \qquad (37)$$

For the surrogates, the worst case appears when p=1, so clients send all traffic to surrogates. As there are certain weights for the communication, as well as different traffic rates per client, each surrogate has a different perceived arrival rate, which will result in a different capacity. So we can construct a vector for the surrogate service rates such as:

$$\vec{\mu}_p = P_w^T \cdot \vec{\lambda} \qquad (38)$$

where P_w^T is the transposed probability-weight matrix and $\vec{\lambda}$ is a vector containing the traffic rate of each client (a random number between λ_{min} and λ_{max}). Note that the matrix dimensions (PxM and Mx1) enable the use of the matrix multiplica-

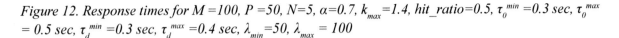

Figure 12. Response times for M =100, P =50, N=5, α=0.7, k_{max}=1.4, hit_ratio=0.5, τ_0^{min} =0.3 sec, τ_0^{max} = 0.5 sec, τ_d^{min} =0.3 sec, τ_d^{max} =0.4 sec, λ_{min}=50, λ_{max} = 100

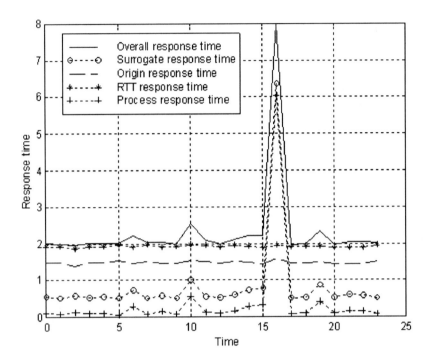

tion, and so resulting in a new vector with dimension Px1.

Figure 11 depicts a new CDN scenario where server capacity has been previously fixed using the previous considerations commented before.

It can be seen that process time is very reduced, so overall response time is mostly affected by roundtrip time. This is because the servers are over-dimensioned as a consequence of worst-case design. In fact, this is realistic if the traffic rates of the clients (or the perceived arrival rate at the surrogates) can be estimated. For a CDN that uses Internet as a communication infrastructure, the number of requesting clients is unpredictable. This becomes a problem when flash crowds events occur, which could be simulated in a simplified way through a very reduced value of k. The independent variable for the flash-crowd simulation should be the time, and not the caching hit probability. Figure 12 depicts a possible simulation where the effective capacity factor k is a random

variable, but always bigger than the traffic arrival rate in order to comply with the stability factor. Its variability margins are between a very reduced value (1.001) and the given value of k (k_{max}). Besides, flash crowds affect network link speed, as networks become more congested. This normally supposes that distances (in terms of latency) between clients and surrogates increase, and probably some packets are discarded at an intermediate node. For simplicity, this effect will be simulated through a variability of the variable N (between its given value and the double) that represents the necessary number of retransmissions required to satisfy a request. Figure 12 shows a possible flash crowd that appears at four o'clock in the afternoon. The reduced absolute value of the response time is not important here, but the relative increment from the mean response time over the whole time interval is important. For this CDN scenario, server overload has mostly determined the mean response time, whereas link

Figure 13. Response times for M =100, P =50, N=5, α=0.7, k_{max} =1.3, hit_ratio=0.5, τ_0^{min} =0.3 sec, τ_0^{max} = 0.5 sec, τ_d^{min} =0.3 sec, τ_d^{max} =0.4 sec, λ_{min}=50, λ_{max} = 100

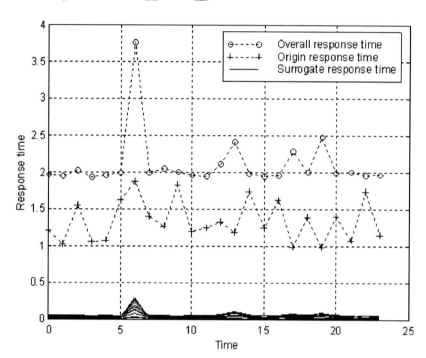

bandwidth has hardly varied during the simulation. However, it could have been the other way round.

Some other considerations about the graph must be made. A flash crowd can be local to a certain zone, or global over whole content distribution network. The former can be successfully managed, at least partially, by the CDN provider redirecting clients to other distant surrogates, but this would supply low response times by avoiding either congested paths or server overload. A global flash crowd affects the whole system and very little can be done as congestion and overload conditions are everywhere and balancing mechanisms are less successful. While Figure 12 shows mean response times obtained from multiple surrogates, Figure 13 depicts a CDN scenario where response time is represented for each surrogate and origin server, as well as the mean response time experienced by a client. Note that, as each client contacts different surrogates and origin servers, it is not easy to obtain the mean response

time graph from the other functions, as the probability weights must also be taken into account.

CONCLUSION AND FUTURE RESEARCH DIRECTIONS

Content Delivery Networks deal with a communication process where network latency and server capacity are decisive parameters in the response time perceived by the user, as well as the system's client redirection ability to match each client with a suitable nearby surrogate. Performance studies have been made by the research community both in empirical and analytical approaches. This article focuses on the latter approach, starting from previous work where a simple model of a CDN is presented. The work we present here tries to introduce a more realistic model of a CDN, where clients and surrogates are dispersed throughout the world with different link latencies and traffic rates. Server redirection behaviour is better characterized when each client contacts various nearby surrogates with different probability weights based on distance in terms of latency. We have come to the following conclusions:

- It is desirable to offload all the content to the surrogates from the point of view of the roundtrip time, as they are located closer to clients than the origin server. Moreover, the roundtrip time follows under reasonable conditions a linear function dependent on the caching hit rate with a negative slope. This corroborates the previous statement.

- If the servers are dimensioned with a capacity value dependent on just the traffic arrival rate, the caching hit rate does not have any effect on the process time. Under this assumption it is necessary to discriminate in the analysis when the content is served by the origin site (no CDN), only surrogates (100% hit rate), or a mixture of both. If the dimensioning factor is the same for all servers, serving all the content from the origin server produces a lower response from the point of view of the process time.

- Real cases suppose a limited server capacity, selected at design phase on the expected client population. This implies a greater value for process time when the caching hit ratio increases, so the total offload of content is undesirable from this perspective. Therefore, a trade-off between roundtrip time and process time determines the scenario for optimum values of total response time inside a caching hit range.

- Flash crowd effect can be caused by network congestion, server overload, or both. All these scenarios can be simulated through large retransmission values, factor N and roundtrip times τ (for network congestion), and capacity factor k and traffic arrival rate λ (for overload conditions). As the variables are assigned per surrogate,

origin server, and client, the flash crowd can be reproduced either locally (only on a few nodes of the network) or globally (on the whole CDN).

The results presented in this chapter are related to web content and how this content is treated by the origin and surrogates. Streaming media, though presented in the CDN reference architecture, requires a different treatment as it should not be modeled in the same way as web content, both in terms of disk space and bandwidth consumed. This has a direct impact on the way caching and the caching hit ratio is treated in the model as well as the way it is delivered to the client. Anyway the presented model should just be extended to include the streaming features through new complementary parameters.

REFERENCES

Agrawal, D., Giles, J., & Verma, D. (2001). On the use of content distribution networks. *Proceedings International Symposium on Performance Evaluation of Computer and Telecommunication Systems*, (pp.221-229). Orlando, FL.

Akamai. (2011). *Website*. Retrieved May 11, 2011, from: http://www.akamai.com.

Androutsellis-Theotokis, S., & Spinellis, D. (2004). A survey of peer-to-peer content distribution technologies. *ACM Computing Surveys*, *36*(4), 335–371. doi:10.1145/1041680.1041681

Calo, S., Verma, D., Agrawal, D., & Giles, J. (2002). On the effectiveness of content distribution networks. *Proceedings International Symposium on Performance Evaluation of Computer and Telecommunication Systems*, (pp. 331-338). San Diego, CA.

Cardellini, V., Colajanni, M., & Yu, P. S. (2003). Request redirection algorithms for distributed web systems. *IEEE Transactions on Parallel and Distributed Systems, 14*(4), 355–368. doi:10.1109/TPDS.2003.1195408

Caviglione, L., & Cervellera, C. (2011). Design, optimization and performance evaluation of a content distribution overlay for streaming. *Computer Communications, 34*(12), 1497–1509. doi:10.1016/j.comcom.2010.04.047

Clarke, I., Sandberg, O., Wiley, B., & Hong, T. (2001). Freenet: A distributed anonymous information storage and retrieval system. In H. Federrath (Ed.), *Proceedings of Designing Privacy Enhancing Technologies: International Workshop on Design Issues in Anonymity and Unobservability*, (pp. 46-66). Berkeley, CA.

Cranor, C. D., Green, M., Kalmanek, C., Shur, D., Sibal, S., Van der Merwe, J. E., & Sreenan, C. J. (2001). Enhanced streaming services in a content distribution network. *IEEE Internet Computing, 5*(4), 66–75. doi:10.1109/4236.939452

Dilley, J., Maggs, B., Parikh, J., Prokop, H., Sitaram, R., & Weihl, B. (2002). Globally distributed content delivery. *IEEE Internet Computing, 6*(5), 50–58. doi:10.1109/MIC.2002.1036038

Doyle, R. P., Chase, J. S., Gadde, S., & Vahdat, A. M. (2002). The trickle-down effect: web caching and server request distribution. *Computer Communications, 25*(4), 345–356. doi:10.1016/S0140-3664(01)00406-6

Dutta, A., Das, S., Chen, W., McAuley, A., Schulzrinne, H. A., & Altintas, O. (2002). MarconiNet supporting streaming media over localized wireless multicast. *Proceedings of the 2nd International Workshop on Mobile Commerce*, (pp. 61-69). Atlanta, GA

Fei, Z. (2001). A novel approach to managing consistency in content distribution networks. *Proceedings of the 6th International Workshop on Web Caching and Content Distribution*, (pp.77-86), Boston, MA.

Gadde, S., Chase, J., & Rabinovich, M. (2000). Web caching and content distribution: A view from the interior. *Proceedings of the 5th International Workshop on Web Caching and Content Distribution*, (pp.1-12), Lisbon, Portugal.

Johnson, K. L., Carr, J. F., Day, M. S., & Kaashoek, M. F. (2000). The measured performance of content distribution networks. *Proceedings of the 5th International Workshop on Web Caching and Content Distribution*, (pp.1-12), Lisbon, Portugal.

Karbhari, P., Rabinovich, M., Xiao, Z., & Douglis, F. (2002). ACDN: A content delivery network for applications. *Proceedings of the 2002 ACM SIGMOD International Conference on Management of Data*, (p. 619). Madison, WI.

Khan, S. U., & Ahmad, I. (2008). Comparison and analysis of ten static heuristics-based Internet data replication techniques. *Journal of Parallel and Distributed Computing, 68*(2), 113–136. doi:10.1016/j.jpdc.2007.06.009

Kleinrock, L., & Gail, R. (1996). *Queueing systems: Problems and solutions*. New York, NY: John Wiley & Sons.

Krishnamurthy, B., Wills, C., & Zhang, Y. (2001). On the use and performance of content delivery networks. *Proceedings of the 1st ACM SIGCOMM Workshop on Internet Measurement*, (pp.169-182), New York, NY

Li, B., Golin, M., Italiano, F., Deng, X., & Sohrabi, K. (1999). On the optimal placement of web proxies on the internet. *Proceedings - IEEE INFOCOM*, 1282–1290.

Liben-Nowell, D., Balakrishnan, H., & Karger, D. (2002). Analysis of the evolution of peer-to-peer systems. *Proceedings of the 21ˢᵗ Annual Symposium on Principles of Distributed Computing*, (pp.233-242), Monterey, CA.

Limelight Networks. (2011). retrieved May 11, 2011, from http://www.limelightnetworks.com

Mao, Z., Cranor, C., Douglis, F., & Rabinovich, M. (2002). A precise and efficient evaluation of the proximity of web clients and their local DNS servers. *Proceedings USENIX 2002 Annual Technical Conference* (USENIX'02), (pp.229-242), Monterey, CA

Masa, M., & Parravicini, E. (2003). Impact of request routing algorithms on the delivery performance of content delivery networks. *Proceedings 22ⁿᵈ IEEE International Performance Computing and Communications Conference*, (pp.5-12), Phoenix, AZ

Mendonça, N. C., Silva, J. A. F., & Anido, R. O. (2008). Client-side selection of replicated web services: An empirical assessment. *Journal of Systems and Software*, *81*(8), 1346–1363. doi:10.1016/j.jss.2007.11.002

Molina, B., Palau, C., Esteve, M., Alonso, I., & Ruiz, V. (2006). On content delivery network implementation. *Computer Communications*, *29*(12), 396–412.

NETLI. (2011). Retrieved May 11, 2011, from http://www.akamai.com/html/about/press/releases/2007/press_020507.html

Pallis, G., & Vakali, A. (2006). Insight and perspectives for content delivery networks. *Communications of the ACM*, *49*(1), 101–106. doi:10.1145/1107458.1107462

Park, K., Pai, V. S., Peterson, L., & Wang, Z. (2004). CoDNS: Improving DNS performance and reliability via cooperative lookups. *Proceedings of the 6ᵗʰ Symposium on Operating Systems Design and Implementation* (OSDI '04), (p. 14). San Francisco, CA

Peng, G. (2003). *CDN: Content distribution network*. Technical Report TR-125, Experimental Computer Systems Lab, Department of Computer Science, State University of New York, Stony Brook, NY.

Pierre, G., & van Steen, M. (2006). Globule: A collaborative content delivery network. *IEEE Communications Magazine*, *44*(8), 127–132. doi:10.1109/MCOM.2006.1678120

PlanetLab. (2011). Retrieved May 11, 2011, from http://www.planet-lab.org/

Qiu, L., Padmanabhan, V. N., & Voelker, G. M. (2001). On the placement of web server replicas. *Proceedings - IEEE INFOCOM*, 1587–1596.

Rodriguez, P., & Sibal, S. (2000). SPREAD: Scalable platform for reliable and efficient automated distribution. *Proceedings of the 9ᵗʰ World Wide Web Conference*, Amsterdam (The Netherlands).

Roy, S., Covell, M., Ankcorn, J., Wee, S., & Yoshimura, T. (2003). A system architecture for managing mobile streaming media service. *Proceedings International Conference on Distributed Computing Systems* (ICDCS'03), (pp. 408-413). Providence, RI

Sariou, S., Gummadi, K. P., Dunn, R., Gribble, S., & Levi, H. M. (2002). An analysis on Internet content delivery systems. *Proceedings 5ᵗʰ Symposium on Operating Systems Design and Implementation*, (pp. 315-327). Boston, MA.

Shaikh, A., Tewari, R., Agrawal, M., Center, I., & Heights, Y. (2001). On the effectiveness of DNS-based server selection. *Proceedings - IEEE INFOCOM*, 1801–1810.

SINOCDN. (2011). Retrieved May 11, 2011, from http://www.sinocdn.com

Turaga, D. S., van der Schaar, M., & Ratakonda, K. (2005). Enterprise multimedia streaming: Issues, background and new developments. *Proceedings of IEEE International Conference on Multimedia and Expo* (ICME'05), (pp.1-6). Amsterdam (The Netherlands).

Vakali, A., & Pallis, G. (2003). Content delivery networks: Status and trends. *IEEE Internet Computing*, 7(6), 68–74. doi:10.1109/MIC.2003.1250586

Verma, D. (2002). *Content distribution networks: An engineering approach*. New York, NY: John Wiley & Sons. doi:10.1002/047122457X

Verma, D., Calo, S., & Amiri, K. (2002). Policy based management of content distribution networks. *IEEE Network*, 15(3), 34–39. doi:10.1109/65.993221

Voddler. (2011). Retrieved May 11, 2011, from: http://www.voddler.com

Wang, L., Pai, V. S., & Peterson, L. (2002). The effectiveness of request redirection on CDN robustness. *Proceedings of 5th Symposium on Operating Systems Design and Implementation*, (pp. 345-360). Boston, MA.

Wee, S., Apostolopoulos, J., Tan, W., & Roy, S. (2003). Research and design of a mobile streaming media content delivery network. *Proceedings of IEEE International Conference on Multimedia and Expo* (ICME'03), (pp. 5-8). Baltimore, MD.

Wu, J. J., Shih, S., Liu, P., & Chung, Y. (2011). Optimizing server placement in distributed systems in the presence of competition. *Journal of Parallel and Distributed Computing*, 71(1), 62–76. doi:10.1016/j.jpdc.2010.08.008

Yoshida, N. (2008). Dynamic CDN against flash crowds. In Buyya, R., Pathan, M., & Vakali, A. (Eds.), *Content delivery networks* (pp. 275–296). Springer. doi:10.1007/978-3-540-77887-5_11

ADDITIONAL READING

Aalto, S., Aaltonen, J., & Karvo, J. (2006). Quantitative performance comparison of different content distribution modes. *Performance Evaluation*, 63(4), 395–442. doi:10.1016/j.peva.2005.03.003

Amble, M. M., Parag, P., Shakkottai, S., & Ying, L. (2011). Content-aware caching and traffic management in content distribution networks. *Proceedings - IEEE INFOCOM*, 2858–2866. doi:10.1109/INFCOM.2011.5935123

Ardaiz, O., Freitag, F., & Navarro, L. (2001). Improving the service time of web clients using server redirection. *ACM SIGMETRICS Performance Evaluation Review*, 29(2), 39–44. doi:10.1145/572317.572324

Bakiras, S. (2005). Approximate server selection algorithms in content distribution networks. *IEEE International Conference on Communications* (ICC'05), (pp. 1490- 1494). Seoul, Korea.

Bektas, T., Oguz, O., & Ouveysi, I. (2008). Designing cost-effective content distribution networks. *Computers & Operations Research*, 34(8), 2436–2449. doi:10.1016/j.cor.2005.09.013

Beloued, A., Gilliot, J.-M., Segarra, M. T., & André, F. (2005). Dynamic data replication and consistency in mobile environments. *Proceedings of the 2nd international doctoral symposium on Middleware*, (pp. 1-5), Grenoble (France)

Biliris, A., Cranor, C., Douglis, F., Rabinovich, M., Sibal, S., Spatcheck, O., & Sturm, W. (2002). CDN brokering. *Computer Communications*, 25(4), 393–402. doi:10.1016/S0140-3664(01)00411-X

Cahill, A. J., & Sreenan, C. J. (2004). An efficient CDN placement algorithm for the delivery of high-quality TV content. *Proceedings of ACM Multimedia Conference, Doctoral Symposium*, (pp. 975-976). New York, NY.

Cameron, C., Low, S., & Wei, D. (2002). High-density model for server allocation and placement. *Proceedings of ACM SIGMETRICS '02*, (pp. 152-159). Marina del Rey, CA.

Chen, Y., Katz, R. H., & Kubiatowicz, J. D. (2002). Dynamic replica placement for scalable content delivery. *Proceedings of International Workshop on Peer-to-Peer Systems*, (pp. 306-318). Cambridge, MA.

Dilley, J., Maggs, B. M., Parikh, J., Prokop, H., Sitaraman, R. K., & Weihl, W. E. (2002). Globally distributed content delivery. *IEEE Internet Computing*, 6(5), 50–58. doi:10.1109/MIC.2002.1036038

Dutta, A., Schulzrinne, H., & Yemini, Y. (1999). MarconiNet: An architecture for Internet radio and TV networks. *Proceedings of Network and Operating System Support for Digital Audio and Video* (NOSSDAV'99), Basking Ridge, NJ.

Han, S. C., & Xia, Y. (2009). Network load-aware content distribution in overlay networks. *Computer Communications*, 32(1), 51–61. doi:10.1016/j.comcom.2008.09.021

Jung, J., Krishnamurthy, B., & Rabinovich, M. (2002). Flash crowds and denial of service attacks: Characterization and implications for CDNs and web sites. *Proceedings of the 11th International Conference of WWW*, (pp. 293-304). Honolulu, HI.

Kangasharju, J., Ross, K. W., & Roberts, J. W. (2000). Performance evaluation of redirection schemes in content distribution networks. *Proceedings of the 5th International Workshop on Web Caching and Content Distribution*, (pp. 1-11). Lisbon, Portugal.

Lee, S. Y., Choi, C. Y., & Song, H. Y. (2007). Hybrid architecture for efficient mobile streaming service. *Proceedings of the 2nd IEEE International Conference on Innovative Computing, Information and Control* (ICICIC '07), (p. 204). Kumamoto, Japan.

Lloret, J., Esteve, M., & Palau, C. E. (2008). Structuring connections between content delivery servers groups. *Future Generation Computer Systems*, 25(4), 191–201. doi:10.1016/j.future.2007.06.008

Loulloudes, N., Pallis, G., & Dikaiakos, M. D. (2008). Information dissemination in mobile CDNs. In Buyya, R., Pathan, M., & Vakali, A. (Eds.), *Content delivery networks* (pp. 343–366). Springer. doi:10.1007/978-3-540-77887-5_14

Manal, D. E., Pacitti, E., Akbarinia, R., & Kemme, B. (2011). Building a peer-to-peer content distribution network with high performance, scalability and robustness. *Information Systems*, 36(2), 222–247. doi:10.1016/j.is.2010.08.007

Pan, J., Hou, Y. T., & Li, B. (2003). An overview of DNS-based server selections in content distribution networks. *Computer Networks*, 43(6), 695–711. doi:10.1016/S1389-1286(03)00293-7

Pathan, M., & Buyya, R. (2009). Resource discovery and request-redirection for dynamic load sharing in multi-provider peering content delivery networks. *Journal of Network and Computer Applications*, 32(5), 976–990. doi:10.1016/j.jnca.2009.03.003

Pathan, M., Vecchiola, C., & Buyya, R. (2008). Load and proximity aware request-redirection for dynamic load distribution in peering CDNs. *Proceedings of the OTM 2008 Confederated International Conferences*, (pp. 62-81). Brussels, Belgium.

Pierre, G., & van Steen, M. (2003). Design and implementation of a user-centered content delivery network. *Proceedings of the 3rd IEEE Workshop on Internet Applications*, (pp. 42-49). San Jose, CA.

Sayal, P. S. M., & Vingralek, P. (1998). Selection algorithms for replicated web servers. *ACM SIGMETRICS Performance Evaluation Review*, 26(3), 44–50. doi:10.1145/306225.306238

Shen, J., Li, J., & Wang, X. (2010). SCDN: Stable content distribution network based on demands. *Journal of Parallel and Distributed Computing, 70*(9), 880–888. doi:10.1016/j.jpdc.2010.05.010

Sivasubramanian, S., Szymaniak, M., Pierre, G., & van Steen, M. (2004). Replication for web hosting systems. *ACM Computing Surveys, 36*(3), 291–334. doi:10.1145/1035570.1035573

Sivasubramanian, S. M., Pierre, G., & van Steen, M. (2006). Towards autonomic hosting of multi-tier internet applications. *Proceedings of the First IEEE International Conference on Hot Topics in Autonomic Computing,* (p. 5). Dublin, Ireland.

Tse, S. S. H. (2005). Approximate algorithms for document placement in distributed web servers. *IEEE Transactions on Parallel and Distributed Systems, 16*(6), 489–496. doi:10.1109/TPDS.2005.63

Xu, Z., Hu, Y., & Bhuyan, L. (2006). Efficient server cooperation mechanism in content delivery network. *Proceedings of 25th IEEE International Performance, Computing, and Communications Conference,* (p. 440). Mesa, AZ.

KEY TERMS AND DEFINITIONS

Content Distribution Network: A content distribution network is a set of dedicated servers distributed among a subnet or even the Internet that collaborate within an overlay network in order to deliver web and media content to sparse users. There is a global redirection mechanism that transparently associates a user request to a nearby server in order to reduce the response time and improve the overall scalability of the system.

Flashcrowd: A flash crowd corresponds to a sudden huge amount of request in a short period of time. The traffic peak experienced can load the server supporting the requests severely if no measurements are taken to avoid it.

Hit Ratio: Hit ratio or caching hit ratio refers to the percentage of accesses that are served directly by a cache without contacting the origin server. This implies having the requested content available and fresh.

Load Balancing: Load balancing refers to the process of offloading single servers by distributing the computational load among two or more servers. For example a server farm is a group of servers where user requests are received by a front end load balancer, which redirects user among the servers.

P2P: Peer-to-peer communication refers to a communication paradigm where a node may behave both as server and as client. The model is different to the traditional client-model communication, where a powerful server serves thin clients. In P2P, mostly all nodes are considered equal and enough powerful, and may potentially perform any task in the discovery or delivery phase.

Request Redirection: Process of redirecting a user to another location. This process is typically perfomed natively by the communication protocols and the user does not perceive it. Typical redirection codes in the HTTP protocol are the 3XX codes.

Surrogate: A surrogate is also called a replica and refers to a server within a content distribution network (CDN). Surrogates typically replicate content from an origin server (content provider) and serve as transparent proxies providing the same content with fewer response times.

Video Streaming: Video streaming is a special way of delivering media content to users while it is being played without any previous download. The mechanism includes communication buffers and flow control protocols to ensure that the playback is smoothly. Common protocols are MMS and RTP.

Chapter 2
On the Performance of Content Delivery Clouds

Mukaddim Pathan
Commonwealth Scientific and Industrial Research Organization (CSIRO), Australia

James Broberg
University of Melbourne, Australia

Rajkumar Buyya
University of Melbourne, Australia

ABSTRACT

Extending the traditional Content Delivery Network (CDN) model to use Cloud Computing is highly appealing. It allows developing a truly on-demand CDN architecture based upon standards designed to ease interoperability, scalability, performance, and flexibility. To better understand the system model, necessity, and perceived advantages of Cloud-based CDNs, this chapter provides an extensive coverage and comparative analysis of the state of the art. It also provides a case study on the MetaCDN Content Delivery Cloud, along with highlights of empirical performance observations from its world-wide distributed platform.

INTRODUCTION

Content Delivery Networks (CDNs) (Buyya, et al., 2008; Pallis & Vakali, 2006) are designed to improve Web access performance, in terms of *response time* and *system throughput*, while delivering content to Internet end-users through multiple, geographically distributed replica servers. The CDN industry, i.e. content delivery, consumption and monetization, has been undergo-

ing rapid changes. The multi-dimensional surge in content delivery from end-users has lead to an explosion of new content, formats as well as an exponential increase in the size and complexity of the digital content supply chain. These changes have been accelerated by economic downturn in that the content providers are under increasing pressure to reduce costs while increasing revenue.

With the traditional model of content delivery, a content provider is locked-in for a particular period of time under specific Service Level Agreements (SLAs) with a high monthly/yearly fees and excess

DOI: 10.4018/978-1-4666-1794-0.ch002

data charges (Hosanagar, et al., 2008). Thus, far from democratizing content delivery, most CDN services are often priced out of reach for all but large enterprise customers (Rayburn, 2009). On the other hand, a commercial CDN provider realizes high operational cost and even monetary penalization if it fails to meet the SLA-bound commitments to provide high quality of service to end-users. Thus, it suffers from—spiraling ownership costs; resource wastage for maintaining infrastructure; inability to grow or to profit from economics of scale; inability to fully monetize new or long tail content—to leave lucrative business deals on the table and forfeit profits.

Furthermore, the main value proposition for CDN services has shifted over time. Initially, the focus was on improving end-user perceived experience by decreasing response time, especially when the customer Web site experiences unexpected traffic surges. Nowadays, CDN services are treated by content providers as a way to use a shared infrastructure to handle their peak capacity requirements, thus allowing reduced investment cost in their own Web site infrastructure. Moreover, recent trends in CDNs indicate a large paradigm shift towards a utility computing model (Canali, et al., 2004), which allows customers to exploit advanced content delivery services without having to build a dedicated infrastructure (Gayek, et al., 2004; Subramanya & Yi, 2005). To break through these barriers, a more efficient content delivery solution is required—a truly on-demand architecture based upon standards designed to ease interoperability, scalability, performance, and flexibility.

One approach to address these issues is to exploit the recent emergence of "Cloud Computing" (Buyya, et al., 2009), a recent technology trend that moves computing and data away from desktop and portable PCs into computational resources such as large Data Centers ("Computing") and make them accessible as scalable, on-demand services over a network (the "Cloud"). The main technical underpinnings of Cloud Computing infrastructures and services include virtualization, service-orientation, elasticity, multi-tenancy, power efficiency, and economics of scale. The perceived advantages for Cloud-service clients include the ability to add more capacity at peak demand, reduce cost, experiment with new services, and to remove unneeded capacity.

Extending the traditional CDN model to use clouds for content delivery, i.e. a Content Delivery Cloud (Cohen, 2008), is highly appealing as cloud providers, e.g. Amazon Simple Storage Service (S3), Mosso Cloud Files, and Nirvanix Storage Delivery Network (SDN), charge customers for their utilization of storage and transfer of content (*pay-as-you-go*), typically in order of cents per gigabyte. Cloud providers, on the face value, offer SLA-backed performance and uptime guarantees for their services. Moreover, they can rapidly and cheaply scale-out during flash crowds (Arlitt & Jin, 2000) and anticipated increases in demand. By exploiting the power of Cloud computing, CDN providers endeavor to improve cost efficiency, accelerate innovations, attain faster time-to-market, and achieve application scalability (Leighton, 2009). There are a number of major players in this domain that are providing cloud-based content delivery services on a commercial basis, either by themselves or by partnering with an existing CDN, such as Amazon CloudFront, VoxCAST CDN, and Akamai Cloud Optimizer.

An example research initiative in this context is MetaCDN (Broberg, et al., 2009; Pathan, et al., 2009), an integrated overlay network that leverages resources from existing storage clouds to provide content delivery services. The main goals of the MetaCDN system is to provide economics of scale and high content delivery performance through its simple yet general purpose, reusable, and reliable geographically distributed framework. MetaCDN delivers high performance content delivery via an on-demand cloud service, eliminating costly capital expenditures or infrastructure upgrades. MetaCDN can be deployed as a fully outsourced, end-to-end services platform or as a complement to a CDN provider's existing infrastructure. Thus, it provides flexibility to CDN providers and their customers (content providers) to tailor a solution to meet their unique needs.

A vital component for MetaCDN is a request-redirection technique for directing end-user requests to optimal replica servers according to performance requirements. A suitable request-redirection mechanism extends the system's reach and scale and can alleviate the problems with overloaded servers and congested networks to maintain high accessibility (Barbir, et al., 2003). Therefore, it is desired to devise a redirection mechanism that exhibit the following properties—scalability, transparency, geographic load sharing, and high user perceived performance, to name a few. Towards this end, this chapter addresses the problem of designing request-redirection mechanisms for MetaCDN. It also presents empirical results from a *proof-of-concept* study to evaluate candidate redirection techniques that are implemented within the MetaCDN Content Delivery Cloud.

THE MetaCDN OVERLAY

MetaCDN is developed as a simple, general purpose, and reusable overlay network in the face of daunting challenges faced by content providers to exploit multiple cloud providers' resources. It provides a platform to harness content delivery services, by hiding the complexity of using unique Web services or programmer APIs coupled with each cloud provider. End-users experience little of the complex technologies associated with MetaCDN. Content providers interact with the service in a limited number of ways, such as enabling their content to be served, viewing traffic reports, and receiving usage-based billing.

Overview

MetaCDN has opened up opportunities for content providers and end-users to reap rewards through low-cost, high performance and easy to use distributed CDN. Figure 1 provides an illustration of the MetaCDN system. It is coupled with each storage cloud via *connectors*, which provide an abstraction an abstraction to conceal different access methodologies to heterogeneous providers. These connectors (cloud provider specific; and FTP, SSH/SCP or WebDAV for shared or private hosts) provide basic operations for creation, deletion, rename and listing of replicated content. End-users can access the MetaCDN overlay either through a Web portal or via RESTful Web services. In the first case, the Web portal acts as an entry point to the system and performs application level load balancing for end-users who intend to download content that has been deployed through MetaCDN. Content providers can sign up for an account on the MetaCDN system and enter credentials for any storage cloud providers that have an account with. Upon authentication, they can utilize MetaCDN functionalities to intelligently deploy content over geographically spanned replicas from multiple storage clouds, according to their performance requirements and budget limitations.

A distributed MetaCDN gateway (middleware entity) provides the logic and management required to encapsulate the functionality of upstream storage cloud providers with a number of core components. The *MetaCDN allocator* performs optimal provider selection and physical content deployment using four options, namely, *maximize-coverage*, *geolocation-based*, *cost-optimized*, and *QoS-optimized* deployment. The *MetaCDN QoS monitor* tracks the current and historical performance of participating storage providers. The *MetaCDN Manager* has authority on each user's current deployment and performs various housekeeping tasks. The *MetaCDN Database* stores crucial information, such as user accounts and deployments, and the capabilities, pricing and historical performance of providers. Finally, the *MetaCDN Load Redirector* is charged with different redirection policies and is responsible for directing end-users to the most appropriate rep-

Figure 1. Components of the MetaCDN overlay system

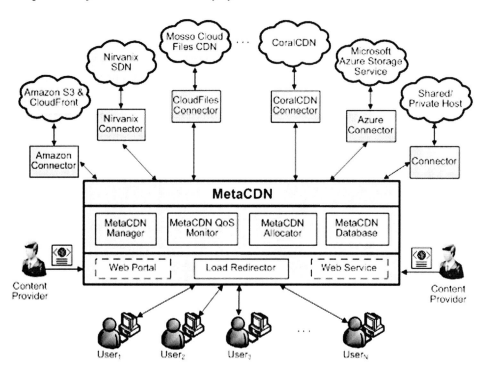

lica according to performance requirements. Further details on the critical functionalities of MetaCDN along with full architectural description and development methodology can be found in a prior work (Broberg, et al., 2009).

System Characteristics

MetaCDN is a smart, agile and flexible approach for content delivery that is willing to break with tradition. Specifically, the following set of attributes can be used to characterize it:

- *Multi-tenancy.* MetaCDN provides content delivery services for many content providers and end-users on the same distributed infrastructure for different content types. With a cloud-based model, all resources and costs are shared among a large pool of users, enabling genuine savings and economics of scale.

- *Elasticity.* It is able to support diverse range of performance requirements from content providers and end-users. This characteristic allows it to quickly and gracefully respond to high request rates at reasonable response time.

- *Scalability.* MetaCDN resources are dynamically scalable to handle workload variations with growing number of content providers and end-users, thus enabling optimum resource utilization.

- *Load sharing.* It offers automatic and totally transparent load balancing on end-user requests. It enables faster absorption of load spikes with the aid of different load balancing and redirection policies.

- *Global availability and reliability.* MetaCDN is a truely on-demand service to provide content delivery functionalities to all authorized users from any-where on the Internet natively. It has the ability to automatically avoid failed replicas or replicas without desired content. In particular, its tolerance to high failure rate ensures that end-users suffer from little to no outages (i.e. rare in-frequent downtime), such as server or network failures.

- *Ease of use/operability.* It can be accessed through a simple Web interface that mimics the look and feel of familiar consumer Web applications, making it extremely intuitive and easy to operate.

- *Reusability and cost of development.* The low development cost of using sto-rage clouds for MetaCDN ensures significantly reduced upfront costs. It is implemented by means of reusable simple APIs exposed by the storage cloud providers, while avoiding too many parameters that must be tuned in order to perceive good performance for diverse content providers and their end-users.

- *Metered services.* By using the third-party content delivery services of the MetaCDN system, content providers have to pay only for the capacity that they use from upstream cloud providers. Usage information for each replica (e.g. download count and last access) is recorded in order to track the cost in-curred for specific content from a content provider.

- *Security.* It addresses crucial security concerns, as content providers use their own credentials for any cloud storage or other provider they have an account with. Thus, it allows content providers to entrust their content to MetaCDN for processing, rest assuring that it will be protected from theft, loss or corruption.

A COMPARATIVE ANALYSIS

Interconnecting multi-provider content delivery services, i.e. CDN peering or CDN internetworking (Amini, et al., 2004; Buyya, et al., 2006;

Day, et al., 2003; Pathan, et al., 2008; Pathan & Buyya, 2009b), is a new, flexible and effective way to harness multi-provider capabilities. The aims are to improve performance for end-users, and to achieve pervasive geographical coverage and increased capacity for a provider. These aims are achieved through the deployment of proper request-redirection policies. MetaCDN complements such initiatives by providing an end-to-end cloud-based solution, coupled with on-demand intelligent request-redirection. In this section, we first ascertain MetaCDN's feasibility and position it as a distributed CDN by presenting a comparative study with related systems. Then we study existing redirection mechanisms available in literature and used in practice to endorse MetaCDN's novelty and uniqueness.

MetaCDN and Related Systems

The Content Distribution Internetworking (CDI) (Day, et al., 2003) model lays the foundation for interconnecting providers. Following the footsteps of the CDI initiative, several research efforts explore the benefits of internetworking/peering of CDN providers, content providers, Peer-to-Peer (P2P) networks, and overlays with main focus on offering increased capacity, intelligent server selection, reduced cost, and improved fault tolerance. Examples include CDI protocol architecture (Turrini, 2004; Turrini & Panzieri, 2002), multi-provider peering (Amini, et al., 2004), Synergy overlay internetworking (Kwon & Fahmy, 2005), peer-assisted content delivery (Tran & Tavanapong, 2005), group-based content delivery (Lloret, et al., 2009), provisioning content delivery over shared infrastructure (Nguyen, et al., 2003), use of emerging technologies for the development of enhanced content delivery service (Fortino & Russo, 2008), resource management in a Grid-based CDN (Di Stefano & Santoro, 2008), capacity provisioning networks (Geng, et al., 2003), open CDN implementation (Molina, et al., 2006), and CDN peering (Pathan & Buyya, 2009a, 2009b).

In contrast, MetaCDN assumes no cooperation or peering. Rather it follows a brokering-based approach as in CDN brokering (Biliris, et al., 2002), which is a content delivery brokerage system deployed on the Internet on a provisional basis. MetaCDN differs in that it functions as a Content Delivery Cloud (Cohen, 2008; Pathan, 2010; Pathan, et al., 2009), replicating content over its distributed infrastructure spanning multiple continents, and providing content delivery services to far flung end-users. It has demonstrated improved content delivery performance, and enumerate its content-serving utility and content provider's benefits from using it (Broberg, et al., 2009; Pathan, et al., 2009). While MetaCDN is comparable to the collaborative CDNs, such as CoDeeN (Wang, et al., 2004), CoralCDN (M. Freedman, 2010; M. J. Freedman, et al., 2004), and Globule (Pierre & van Steen, 2001, 2006), it is significantly different as it integrates storage cloud resources spanning the globe to provide content delivery services.

Many Websites have utilized individual storage clouds to deliver some or all of their content (Elson & Howell, 2008), most notably the New York Times (Gottfrid, 2007) and SmugMug (MacAskill, 2007). On the contrary, MetaCDN provides general purpose reusable content delivery services by interacting and leveraging multiple cloud providers. MetaCDN is positioned as a logical fit in the industry initiatives to couple content delivery capabilities with existing cloud deployments, such as Amazon S3 and CloudFront; Silverlining and VoxCAST CDN; Mosso Cloud Files; Nirvanix SDN, which partners with CDNet-works for content delivery; TinyCDN, which leverages Amazon Web services and cloud computing; and Edge Content Network (ECN) from Microsoft, which is re-ported to partner with Limelight Networks for content delivery (Miller, 2008). However, as these systems use centralized or a small number of datacenters, they may suffer from deteriorated end-user experience due to network congestions, peering point congestion, routing inefficiencies,

and other bottlenecks of the Internet middle mile (Leighton, 2009). On the contrary, MetaCDN is attributed with a distributed CDN infrastructure to overcome the challenges posed by the Internet's middle mile and ensure that end-user performance does not fall short of expectations. The MetaCDN approach is analogous to the Akamai cloud computing initiative (Leighton, 2009), which provides cloud optimization services for its highly distributed EdgePlatform. However, unlike Akamai it endeavors to achieve true economics of scale by exploiting the pay-as-you-go model of upstream cloud providers.

Recent innovations such as P4P (Xie, et al., 2008) and its companion traffic engineering models (Jiang, et al., 2008) enable P2P to communicate with network providers through a portal for cooperative content delivery. Such proactive network provider participation optimizes global peer-to-peer connections as it saves significant user costs, and by using local connections also speeds up download times for P2P downloaders by 45%. MetaCDN endorses them in the sense that it assists toward a systematic understanding and practical realization of the interactions between storage clouds, which provide an operational storage network and content delivery resources, and content providers, who generate and distribute content.

Table 1 summarizes the comparative analysis between MetaCDN and other related systems in terms of distinctive features and system characteristics. This analysis of existing cloud-based content delivery services assists to separate the performance-wise superiority of representative systems.

Request-Redirection Techniques

Request-redirection is an indispensible enabling cornerstone for CDNs. It is generally used to direct end-user requests to replica servers based on various policies and a possible set of metrics, such as network proximity, user perceived latency,

Table 1. Feature comparison

Feature[a]	Amazon (S3 & CloudFront)	Rackspace (Mosso Cloud Files)	Voxel (VoxCAST, Silverlining)	Nirvanix (CloudNAS)	Microsoft (Windows Azure CDN)	Akamai (Cloud Optimizer)	MetaCDN (integrates storage clouds)
Storage & content delivery	S3 Storage services; CloudFront content delivery	Mosso storage services; content delivery via Limelight	Silverlining cloud services; VoxCAST CDN	Storage services; content delivery via CDNetworks	Azure storage services; content delivery via Limelight	NetStorage services; EdgePlatform content delivery	**Services by leveraging upstream cloud providers**
Service type	On-demand storage in multiple datacenters; on-demand content delivery	On-premises storage	Managed hosting; On-demand content delivery	Managed cloud storage services	On-demand managed hosting in datacenters	On-demand storage and content delivery	**Storage in multiple cloud providers; on-demand content delivery**
Performance	Comparable latency with customer-owned data centers. Sparsely reported performance problem due to outages	Twice more latency than S3 & CloudFront. Reported stability and performance issues for increased traffic	Reported consistent performance on par with competitors such as Akamai and Limelight	Storage functions 222% faster and 2 MB sample file transfer is nearly 300% faster than Amazon S3	Best performance obtained from CDN edge caching by delivering blobs less than 10 GB in size	Up to 400% improvement and at least twice faster application response time than Amazon EC2	**Comparable perceived latency and throughput with upstream providers with little overhead due to load redirection**
Availability & reliability	Availability zones to enable resiliency in case of single location failure, and redundancy	Subject to single point of failure	All time availability as it fails safe against origin server outages	Customizable availability against unplanned outages and redundancy	Service deployment, update and failure management to maintain availability	No single point of failure, automatic failover and redundancy	**Harness the state-of-the-art availability and reliability features of cloud providers**
Geographic distribution	Datacenters at 14 edge locations in three continents (North America, Europe & Asia)	Partnership with Limelight Networks for coverage at 60 locations	POPs at 17 locations in Asia, North America, and Europe	Storage nodes at 5 locations in North America, Europe & Asia	22 physical nodes available globally	48000 servers in 1000 networks world-wide	**Footprint in six continents (Asia, North & South America, Europe, Australia, Africa)**
Multi-tenancy	Yes	Yes	Yes (also dedicated mode)	Yes	Yes	Yes	**Yes**
Load balancing	Listed in future investments	Apache as load balancer	Yes (server switching)	Yes (global and dynamic)	Yes (built-in hardware)	Yes (global and dynamic)	**Yes (automatic and transparent)**
On-demand scalability	Yes	No	Yes	Yes	Yes	Yes	**Partial (work in progress)**
Accessibility	Amazon Web Services API or management console	Browser-based control panel or programmatic API	VoxCAST Web-based portal	Web-based Nirvanix management portal	Azure Services Management Tools	Akamai Edge-Control	**Yes (Web interface)**

continued on following page

Table 1. Continued

Feature[a]	Amazon (S3 & CloudFront)	Rackspace (Mosso Cloud Files)	Voxel (VoxCAST, Silverlining)	Nirvanix (CloudNAS)	Microsoft (Windows Azure CDN)	Akamai (Cloud Optimizer)	MetaCDN (integrates storage clouds)
Automatic replication	S3: No; CloudFront: Yes	Yes	Yes	Yes	No	Yes	**Yes**
SLA (%)	99-99.9	99.9	100	99.9	99.95	100	**Provider specific**
Developer API	Yes (Amazon Web services)	Yes (Cloud Servers API)	Yes (Hosting API)	Yes (Web services API)	Yes (Azure SDK API)	Yes (EdgeScape API)	**Connectors for integration**
Economic model and pricing	Pay-as-you-go	Pay-as-you-go	Progressive universal scale billing upon usage	Pay-as-you-go	Consumption-based pricing model	Volume-based pricing; pay-par-use model for NetStorage	**Built on pay-as-you-go model**
Security	Protection for DDoS attacks, access control list and firewalls	Data protection, DDoS migration services, firewalls	Secure authentication, firewalls	Secure authentication, transmission via SSL	Intrusion prevention, .net security, firewalls	Protection for DDoS attacks and application firewall	**Secure authentication to reap provider's security measures**

[a]The facts presented in this table are based on existing literature including industry-specific Website, data sheet, whitepaper, and professional news blogs.

bandwidth, content availability and replica server load. There exist multiple request-redirection mechanisms, which can be categorized in a number of ways according to different performance objectives.

Barbir et al. (Barbir, et al., 2003) categorize the known request-redirection techniques in CDNs into *DNS-based, transport-layer* and *application-layer* redirection. In DNS-based techniques, a specialized DNS server is augmented in the name resolution process to return different server addresses to end-users. They are the most common due to the ubiquity of the DNS system as a directory service. The performance and effectiveness of DNS-based redirection techniques have been studied in a number of recent studies (Biliris, et al., 2002; Mao, et al., 2002; Shaikh, et al., 2001). Despite its wide usage, DNS-based approaches are found to suffer from the following drawbacks: (a) actual end-user request is not redirected, rather its Local DNS (LDNS), assuming that end-users are near to their LDNS; (b) browser's request is cached due to the hierarchical organization of the DNS service; (c) the DNS system is not designed for very dynamic changes in the mapping between hostnames and IP addresses; and (d) most significantly DNS cannot be relied upon as it can have control over as little as 5% of incoming requests in many instances (Cardellini, et al., 2002). In transport-layer redirection, the information available in the first packet of the end-user request, in combination with user-defined policies and other metrics are used to take redirection decision. Several research (Liston & Zegura, 2001; Pai, et al., 1998; Yang & Luo, 1999) report using this approach for redirection. In general, this approach is used in combination with DNS-based techniques. While this approach is suitable for steering end-users away from overloaded replica servers, the associated overhead limits its usage for long-lived sessions such as FTP and RTSP. Finally, application-layer redirection involves deeper examination of end-user request packet to provide fine-grain redirection. However, this approach may suffer from the lack of transparency and additional latency. URL rewriting and HTTP 302 redirection are the examples of techniques using this approach. In the context of MetaCDN, the system exploits a combination of DNS-based and application-layer techniques for request-redirection. Specifically, name resolution for the base MetaCDN URL is performed using DNS-redirection and end-user request for specific content (Web object) is serviced using application-layer redirection.

With the objective to minimize Web access latency, request-redirection can be partitioned into client and server-side techniques. Client-side redirections in CDNs (Conti, et al., 2001; Kangasharju, et al., 2001; Rangarajan, et al., 2003; Wang, et al., 2002) are based on the premise that the network is the primary bottleneck. They tend not to rely on any centralization as redirections occur independently. Server-side techniques perform URL redirection using HTTP status code. They direct all incoming requests to a set of clustered hosts based on load characteristics. These techniques are mainly application specific and more suited for clustered servers. There also exist significant research (Cardellini, et al., 2000, 2003; Karaul, et al., 2000; Rabinovich, et al., 2003) combining client and server-side redirection. This hybrid approach works well when the bottleneck is not clearly identified or varying over time. According to this categorization, MetaCDN complements the hybrid request-redirection technique; by performing server-side gateway redirection and client-side HTTP 302 redirection for content requests.

In terms of content retrieval, request-redirection techniques can be divided into full and selective (or partial) redirection. In full redirection, the DNS server is modified in such a way that all end-user requests are directed to a replica server. This scheme requires that either replica servers hold all the content from the origin server, or that they act as surrogate proxies for the origin server. On the other hand, in selective redirection, a content provider modifies its content so that links to specific embedded Web objects have host names in a domain for which the CDN provider is authoritative. Thus, the base HTML page is retrieved from the origin server, while embedded objects are retrieved from CDN replica servers. While full replication has dynamic adaptability to new hot-spots, it is not feasible considering the on-going increase in Web objects size. A selective redirection works better in the sense that it reduces load on the origin server and on the Web site's content generation infrastructure. Moreover, if the embedded content changes infrequently, it exhibits better performance. While it is possible to use the MetaCDN replica infrastructure to enable full redirection, we limit our work for selective redirection by storing only embedded Web content into replicas and directing end-user requests to them.

Request-redirection mechanisms are governed by policies that outline the actual redirection algorithm on how to perform server selection in response to an end-user request. These policies can be either adaptive or non-adaptive. Adaptive policies consider the current system condition, whereas non-adaptive policies use some heuristics in order to perform target server selection. The literature on re-quest-redirection policies is too vast to cite here (see the survey by Sivasubramanian et al. (Sivasubramanian, et al., 2004) and the references therein for initial pointers for redirection policies in CDN context). MetaCDN deploys adaptive redirection with the ability to cope with degenerated load situations. In particular, it strives to demonstrate high system robustness in the face of unanticipated events, e.g. flash crowds.

There exist significant research efforts (Amini, et al., 2003; Erçetin & Tassiulas, 2003; Presti, et al., 2005; Ranjan, et al., 2004) that model request-redirection as a mathematical problem. They attempt to find a solution from an operations research perspective by modeling redirection as a graph theory, optimization, delay constrained routing, or server assignment problem. Most of these work use simulations to evaluate the performance of their approach. On the contrary, the MetaCDN redirection is evaluated through a proof-of-concept implementation on its distributed infrastructure.

The request-redirection techniques employed within MetaCDN also draw similarity with those used in the collaborative CDNs, such as CoDeeN (Wang, et al., 2004), CoralCDN (M. Freedman, 2010; M. J. Freedman, et al., 2004), Globule (Pierre & van Steen, 2001, 2006), and PRSync (Shah, et al., 2008), which perform overlay redirection by exploiting request locality, network measurement, topology, and AS-based proximity. Similarly, MetaCDN's request-redirection techniques are based on metrics such as geographic proximity, cost, request traffic, and QoS metrics (response time, throughput, HTTP response code). The uniqueness lies in adding the capability for quantifying traffic activities using a network utility metric within MetaCDN while intelligently redirecting user requests.

REQUEST-REDIRECTION DESIGN

An efficient request-redirection technique is vital to extend the reach and scale of MetaCDN. In this section, we analyze the design space of competent request-redirection techniques and describe MetaCDN redirection logic along with the candidate techniques.

Design Space

Designing a request-redirection strategy that does not sacrifice the scalability, transparency, availability and performance benefits of a content delivery cloud, i.e. MetaCDN, is a challenging task. A candidate redirection technique should have the following properties:

- *Scalability.* It should be responsive to changing circumstances. It should aid the system with the ability to gracefully scale and expand its network reach in order to

handle new and large number of data, end-user requests, and transactions without any significant decline in performance.

- *Load balancing.* With the aid of the redirection technique, MetaCDN as a service provider should be able to effectively react to overload conditions by selecting least loaded optimal server(s) for serving content requests. The load balancing decisions should ensure that end-users experience reasonable con-tent delivery performance.

- *Distributed redirection.* It should not rely on any centralization and all redi-rectors (i.e. MetaCDN gateway) should operate independently. It should also accommodate any dynamic changes in network performance and incoming request traffic.

- *Transparent name resolution.* DNS mapping during redirection should be transparent to end-users. In order to transparently contact a replica server for desired content, redirection should ensure a one-to-many mapping from the hostname to one of the IP addresses of distributed replicas.

- *Fault transparency.* It should ensure that unresponsive replicas are detected, by-passed and end-users are unaware of the redirection to other replicas. Moreover, previously failed replicas that become available again should be incorporated quickly.

- *Flexibility.* There should be provision to accommodate different request-redir- ection techniques to provide options to content providers and its users with varied objectives. In addition, a candidate request-redirection technique should improve the usefulness of distributed replicas.

- *Server decoupling.* The redirection logic should be implemented without any change of the existing client or server code, conforming to existing standards. It should also be possible to deploy the devised re-direction scheme easily, pre-ferrably as a

Figure 2. MetaCDN request-redirection

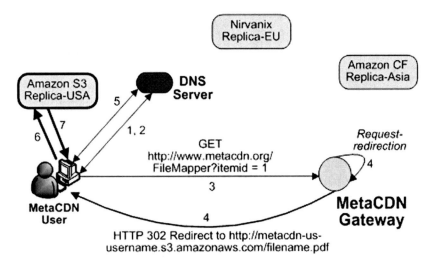

plug-in to the server, with minimum effort. Thus, it should be ensured that the implementation overhead of a given request-redirection technique is minimal.

MetaCDN Request-Redirection Logic

Request-redirection in MetaCDN takes place under the governance of the MetaCDN gateways, which resemble distributed request-redirectors to forward end-user content requests to appropriate replica server. The MetaCDN gateway is capable of utilizing any request-redirection technique that is plugged into the MetaCDN Load Redirection module. Integrating a new request-redirection scheme does not require any changes to the server or client-side.

As shown in Figure 2, the sequence of steps for an end-user in the East Coast of the USA to retrieve content through MetaCDN is as follows:

1. The end-user issues an HTTP request for a content that has been deployed by the MetaCDN Allocator using one of the content deployment options available. The browser attempts to resolve the base hostname (http://www.metacdn.org) for the MetaCDN URL

http://www.metacdn.org/ *FileMapper?itemid=XX*, where XX in the URL format is a unique key associated with the deployed content.

2. The Local DNS (LDNS) of the end-user contacts the authoritative DNS (ADNS) for that domain to resolve this request to the IP address of the closest MetaCDN gateway, e.g. http://us.metacdn.org.

3. The end-user (or its browser) then makes an HTTP GET request for the desired content on the MetaCDN gateway.

4. Depending on the utilized request-redirection scheme, the MetaCDN Load Redirector is triggered to select the optimal replica that conforms to the specified service requirements. At this point, the MetaCDN gateway returns an HTTP redirect request with the URL of the selected replica.

5. Upon receiving the URL of the selected replica, the DNS resolves its domain name and returns the associated IP address to the end-user.

6. The user sends request for the content to the selected replica.

7. The selected replica satisfies the user request by serving the desired content.

In order to ensure that the best replica is selected for serving user requests, the following tests are performed during the request-redirection process:

- Is there a content replica available within required response time threshold?
- Is the throughput of the target replica within tolerance?
- Is the end-user located in the same geographical region as the target replica?
- Is the replica utility the highest among all target sites?
- Is one of the target replicas preferred, according to user requirements or any administrative settings?

If it is assumed that all candidate replicas are available and have capacity, i.e. response time and throughput thresholds are met, the MetaCDN system checks for the continent/geographic location and administrative preference (an indicative flag used by MetaCDN manager to manually prefer or avoid a replica). MetaCDN achieves transparency as end-user browsers automatically access the redirection service, being redirected by the MetaCDN gateway. End-users have least possible to do to take benefit of request-redirection. They see only MetaCDN URL and they have no way for discovering the address of a replica when using the redirection service and accessing the replica server directly. Thus, an end-user is prevented to keep an explicit reference to a replica, which may cause dangling pointers during the downtime of the replica.

While MetaCDN Load Redirector ensures directing users to the best responding replica, an extra feature is realized through its ability to automatically avoid failed replicas or replicas without the desired content. Bypassing occurs in the following two ways. Firstly, if a replica has the desired content, but shows limited serving capacity due to network congestions, it is reflected in its measured network utility metric, exhibiting a low value. As a consequence, the replica

is not considered as a candidate for redirection. Secondly, if the replica does not have the desired content, it can not serve end-user requests and thus leads to an insignificant utility value. Hence, it is automatically discarded to be considered as a candidate replica. In addition, a secondary level of internal redirection enabled by an individual cloud provider ensures that request-redirection does not overload any particular replica.

Candidate Techniques

Representative request-redirection techniques used for experimentation and evaluation of the MetaCDN system are:

- *Random redirection.* It is a simple baseline policy where each content request is sent to a randomly picked replica. This scheme can be used for comparison purpose to determine a reasonable level of performance, since an effective redirection technique is expected to scale with the increasing number of clients and MetaCDN replicas, and to not exhibit any pathological behavior due to the assignment patterns. The drawback of this approach is to often increase latency by not picking up the most appropriate replica. Moreover, adding more servers does not reduce the working set of each server.
- *Geolocation-based redirection.* It exploits the request locality by taking into account end-user preferences and directing the user to the closest physical replica in the specified region(s). For this purpose, a geolocation service is utilized that finds the geographic location (latitude and longitude) of the end-user and measures their distance from each matching replica using a simple spherical law of cosines, or a more accurate approach such as the Vincenty formula for distance between two latitude/longitude points (Vincenty, 1975), to find the clos-

Figure 3. Experiment testbed

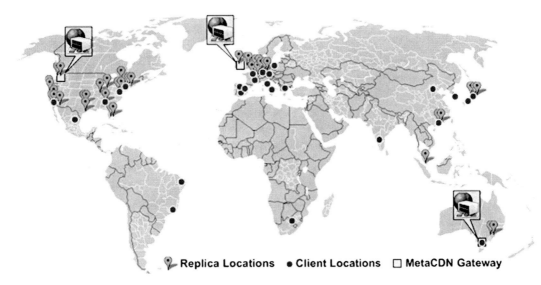

est replica. Although there exists a strong correlation between the performance experienced by end-users and their locality to replicas (Broberg, et al., 2009), there is no guarantee that the closest replica is always the best choice, due to cyclical and transient load fluctuations in the network path.

- *Utility-redirection.* In this scheme, end-users are directed to the highest utility optimal replica that conforms to the specified service requirements. If there is more than one candidate target replica exhibiting the highest utility, the one with the fastest response time is chosen to redirect user requests. For this purpose, utility is measured quantitatively based on MetaCDN's traffic activities. It is expressed with a value in the range [0, 1], quantifying the relation between the number of bytes of the served content against the number of bytes of the replicated content (Pathan, et al., 2009). The measured utility metric represents the usefulness of MetaCDN replicas in terms of data circulation in its distributed network. It is vital as system wellness greatly affects the content delivery performance to end-users. Although utility-based request-redirection outcomes sensible replica selection in terms of response time, it may not provide a high throughput performance to end-users. Nevertheless, being it is focused on maximizing the utility of the MetaCDN system; it results in high utility for content delivery to end-users.

PERFORMANCE EVALUATION

This section presents the outcome of a proof-of-concept testbed experiment to determine the performance of MetaCDN content delivery cloud, by measuring the user perceived response time and throughput. Figure 3 provides a schematic representation of the experimental testbed and Table 2 provides a summary of the conducted experiment. The global MetaCDN testbed spans six continents with distributed clients at different institutions; replicas from multiple storage cloud providers; and MetaCDN gateways, hosted on the Amazon Elastic Computing Cloud (EC2) and a cluster at the University of Melbourne, Australia. All client locations, except in Africa, South America and

Table 2. Summary of the experiment

	Category	Value	Provider	Locations
Experiment Testbed	Number of MetaCDN gateways	3	Amazon EC2 and own cluster	Asia/Australia, Europe, and North America
	Number of replicas	40	Amazon, Mosso and Nirvanix	Asia, Australia, Europe, and North America
	Number of clients (end-user nodes)	26	Voluntary	Asia, Australia, Europe, North and South America, and Africa

	Category	Description
Experiment Details	Total experiment time	48 hours
	Duration of an epoch	2 hours
	Maximum user requests/epoch	30 requests from each client
	Service timeout for each request	30 seconds
	Test file size	1 KB and 5 MB
	Content Deployment	Maximize-coverage deployment
	Request-redirection policies	Random, Geo, and Utility

	Category	Distribution	PMF	Parameters
End-user Request Modeling	Session inter-arrival time (Floyd & Paxson, 2001)	Exponential	$\lambda e^{-\lambda x}$	$\lambda = 0.05$
	Content requests per session (Arlitt & Jin, 2000)	Inverse Gaussian	$\sqrt{\dfrac{\lambda}{2\pi x^3}}e^{\frac{-\lambda(x-\mu)^2}{2\mu^2 x}}$	$\mu = 3.86$ $\lambda = 9.46$
	User think time (Barford & Crovella, 1999)	Pareto	$\alpha k^{\alpha} x^{-\alpha-1}$	$\alpha = 1.4, k = 1$

South Asia, have high speed connectivity to major Internet backbones to minimize the client being the bottleneck during experiments.

Methodology

The experiment was run simultaneously at each client location over a period of 48 hours, during the middle of the week in May 2009. As it spans two days, localized peak times (time-of-day) is experienced in each geographical region. Two test files of size 1KB and 5MB have been deployed by the MetaCDN Allocator module, which was instructed to maximize coverage and performance, and consequently the test files were deployed in all available replica locations of the storage cloud providers integrated to MetaCDN. While these file sizes are appropriate for the conducted experiment, a few constraints restrict the use varied and/or even larger sized files. Firstly, the experiments generate heavy network traffic consuming significant network bandwidth, thus larger file trafficking would impose more strain and network congestions on the voluntary clients, which some clients may not be able to handle. Moreover, at some client locations, e.g. India and South Africa, Internet is at a premium and there are checks regarding Internet traffic so that other users in the client domain accessing the Internet are not affected.

The workload to drive the experiment incorporates recent results on Web characterization

Table 3. List of performance indices

Performance Index	Description
Response time	The time experienced by an end-user to get serviced
Throughput	Transfer speed to download a test file by an end-user
Utility	Content-serving ability, ranges in [0, 1]
Probability(Utility achieved)	The probability or the fraction of time that the system achieves the given utility
Content provider's benefit (Surplus)	Surplus from using MetaCDN, expressed as a percentage

(Arlitt & Jin, 2000; Barford & Crovella, 1999; Floyd & Paxson, 2001). The high variability and self-similar nature of Web access load is modeled through heavy-tailed distributions. The experiment time comprises epochs of 2 hours, with each epoch consisting of a set of user sessions. Each session opens a persistent HTTP connection to MetaCDN and each client generates requests to it to download each test files, with a timeout of 30 seconds. Between two requests, a user waits for a think time before the next request is generated. The mean think time, together with number of users defines the mean request arrival rate to MetaCDN. For statistical significance, each client is bounded to generate a maximum number of 30 requests in each epoch. The files are downloaded using the UNIX utility, wget, with the --no-cache and --no-dns-cache options to ensure that a fresh copy of the content is downloaded each time (not from any intermediary cache) and that the DNS lookup is not cached either.

The *response time* and *throughput* obtained from each client location were measured. The first performance metric captures the end-to-end performance for end-users when downloading a 1 KB test file from MetaCDN. Due to the negligible file size, the response time is dominated by DNS lookup and HTTP connection establishment time. Lower value of response time indicates fast serviced content. The latter metric shows the transfer speed obtained when the 5 MB test file is downloaded by users from the MetaCDN replicas. It provides an indication of consistency and variability of throughput over time.

The *utility* of MetaCDN is measured according to a quantitative expression, capturing the true traffic activities, in terms of the number of bytes transferred during content replication and servicing (Pathan, et al., 2009). A high utility value shows the content-serving ability of the system, and signifies its durability under highly variable traffic activities. To emphasize the impact of request-redirection on the measured utility, the *probability* that MetaCDN achieves a given level of utility as the performance metric. Finally, based on the measured observations, we determine the benefits of a content provider (surplus) from using the MetaCDN system. Table 3 summarizes the performance indices used in the experimental evaluation.

EMPIRICAL RESULTS

To avoid redundancy, we present average of the results from the following eight representative client locations in five continents—Paris (France), Innsbruck (Austria), and Poznan (Poland) in Europe; Beijing (China) and Melbourne (Australia) in Asia/Australia; Atlanta, GA, and Irvine, CA (USA) in North America, and Rio de Janeiro (Brazil) in South America. Detailed results in each locations for the full experiment duration can be found in another work (Pathan, et al., 2009).

Table 4. Average response time observations (in seconds) at client locations

End-user location	Random	Geo	Utility
Paris	0.92	0.78	0.99
Innsbruck	0.75	0.71	0.70
Poznan	1.59	1.53	1.48
Beijing	4.16	4.03	3.61
Melbourne	1.73	1.26	1.52
Atlanta	0.81	0.74	0.72
Irvine	0.90	0.90	0.77
Rio de Janeiro	1.67	1.63	1.20

Response Time

Table 4 shows the end-to-end response time experienced by end-users when downloading the 1 KB test file over a period of 48 hours. The measure of the response time depends on the network proximity, congestions in network path and traffic load on the target replica server. It provides an indication of the responsiveness of the replica infrastructure and the network conditions in the path between the client and the target replica which serves the end-user. A general trend is observed that the clients experience mostly consistent end-to-end response time. For all the request-redirection policies, the average response time in all the client locations except Beijing is just over 1 second, with a few exceptions. Notably the users in Beijing experience close to 4 seconds average response time from the MetaCDN infrastructure. This exception originates as a consequence of firewall policies applied by the Chinese government. Similar observations have been reported in a previous measurement study (Rahul, et al., 2006), which demonstrates that the failure characteristics on the Internet path to the edge nodes in China are remarkably different than the Internet paths to the edge nodes in other part of the world.

At several time instances during the experiment, end-users experience increased response time. The resulting spikes are due to the sudden increases in request traffic, imposing strain on the

MetaCDN replicas. Under traffic surges, the MetaCDN Load Redirector module activates to handle peak loads. As a consequence, end-user requests are often redirected to a target replica outside its authoritative domain and/or are served from an optimal distant proximity server, thereby, contributing to the increased response time. However, MetaCDN handles peak loads well to provide satisfactory service responsiveness to end-users. This phenomenon of increased response time is more visible for random-redirection. As it makes a random choice, often the target replica selection is not optimized, thus leading to highly variable response time. Especially, at several occasions, users observe more than 30 seconds response time, thus leading to service timeout. Geo-redirection directs user requests to the closest proximity server, understandably producing low response time. On the contrary, utility-redirection chooses the highest utility replica, which may not be in close proximity to an individual client location. Nevertheless, there is no clear winner between them in terms of response time, as they exhibit changeable performance at different client locations. As for instance, end-users in Paris enjoy better average response time (0.77 seconds) with geo-redirection, due to their close proximity to the Amazon, Mosso and Nirvanix nodes in Frankfurt (Germany), Dublin (Ireland), and London (UK). For Melbourne, the reason behind better performance of geo-redirection is the existence

Table 5. Average throughput observations (in KBs) at client locations

End-user location	Random	Geo	Utility
Paris	1486.46	2146.75	475.39
Innsbruck	2020.76	2178.03	518.67
Poznan	7551.53	9012.28	1795.80
Beijing	229.32	269.15	206.54
Melbourne	3625.26	6519.39	413.15
Atlanta	6137.11	6448.30	3349.39
Irvine	4412.62	2757.73	504.74
Rio de Janeiro	838.94	521.30	1138.14

of the Mosso node in Sydney. For both of these two clients, utility-redirection policy directs requests to a distant replica than the closest one and results in increased response time.

Throughput

Table 5 shows the average throughput obtained per two hours, when downloading content (5MB file) via MetaCDN. At all the client locations, consistent throughput was observed during the experiment. As expected, we observe that in almost all the client locations, geo-redirection results in highest throughput as the users get serviced from the closest proximity replica. However, it performs worse than random-redirection for the Irvine client. The reason is that random-redirection decision in this location most of the time selects close proximity Amazon replica(s) with better network path than that of geo-redirection, which chooses Mosso replica. Moreover, the service capability from these two replicas and the network path between the replica and client also contribute to the observed throughput variations.

For most of the clients, except Rio de Janeiro, utility redirection performs much worse than geo-redirection. The reason is understandable, as utility-redirection emphasizes maximizing MetaCDN's utility rather than serving an individual user, thus sacrificing end-user perceived performance. For Rio de Janeiro, geo-redirection

leads to the closest Mosso node in the USA, whereas utility-redirection results in more utility-aware replica, which is the Amazon node(s) in the USA. It could be presumed that Amazon node supersedes the Mosso node in terms of its service capability, better network path, internal overlay routing, and less request traffic strain.

It is observed that users in Poznan enjoy the best average throughput, which is 9MB/s for geo-redirection. The reason is that the client machine is in a MAN net-work, which is connected to the country-wide Polish optical network PIONEER with high capacity channels dedicated to the content delivery traffic (Kusmierek, et al., 2007). Another client location with high throughput is Atlanta, which achieves speeds of approximately 6.2 MB/s for geo-redirection and 3.3 MB/s for utility-redirection, due to the existence of better network path between the client and the MetaCDN replica infrastructure. This reasoning is deemed valid, since there are Mosso nodes in the same location.

Alike response time, end-users in China achieves the lowest throughput among all the client locations. The underlying reason is again checks on the request traffic and bandwidth constraints due to firewall policies. We put more emphasis on the results from Melbourne, which is of interest as Australia is not as highly connected as Europe or North America, depending on a small number of expensive international links to major data centers in Europe and the USA. We observe that due to the existence of a nearby Mosso node in Sydney, the users in Melbourne experience 6.5 MB/s of throughput with geo-redirection and 3.6 MB/s for random-redirection. However, for utility-redirection the replica selections result in the Amazon node(s) in the USA, thus leading to a lower but consistent average throughput of 410 KB/s.

From these observations, the following decisive conclusions can be reached. Although utility-redirection outcomes sensible replica selection in terms of response time, it may not provide a high throughput performance to end-users. Nevertheless, being focused on maximizing the utility of the MetaCDN system; it results in high utility for content delivery. Sufficient results to support this claim are presented in the next section.

MetaCDN Utility

Figure 4 shows how MetaCDN utility is varied during the testbed experiment upon replica selection for incoming content requests. The shown utility values in the figure are averaged over three deployed MetaCDN gateways in Asia/Australia, Europe and North America. It is observed that utility-redirection produces the highest utility in the system by selecting the most active replicas to serve users. It also improves the traffic activities and contributes to uplifting MetaCDN's content-serving ability. It should be noted that there is a warm-up phase at the beginning of the 48 hours experiment during which the replicas are populated with content requests, resulting in low utility values. This is visible during the initial hours for utility and geo-redirection.

To emphasize the content-serving ability of MetaCDN, Figure 4 presents the probability (or the fraction of time) that the system observes a utility above a certain utility level during the experiment. The intention is to show to what extent the system can maximize its own profit. The higher the probability, the more likely it is

Figure 4. Probability of achieving specified utility

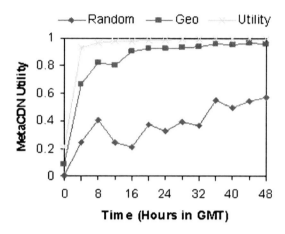

that the specified utility level could be achieved. From the figure, it is noticeable that utility-redirection outperforms other alternatives, as it often produces over 0.95 utility for MetaCDN with a 0.85 probability. Geo-redirection performs well as it has a 0.77 probability that it can achieve 0.9 utility. Finally, random-redirection performs the worst and it can only achieve close to 0.56 utility for MetaCDN with a probability of 0.23. Therefore, a MetaCDN administrator may utilize a request-redirection policy apart from random, in order to maximize the system's content-serving ability.

FUTURE RESEARCH DIRECTIONS

A number of future research directions in relation to Cloud-based content delivery systems can be devised. In this section, an indicative list is populated, realizing the awaited technological innovations in this area in the coming years. While elaborating on the future research topics, pointers to existing literature are provided so as to lay out a comprehensive research roadmap to the CDN community.

A Cooperative Architecture for Dynamic Replication

The "time-shifted" nature of the dynamic content defies the existing content delivery architectures and increases the overall traffic loads and bandwidth demands by orders of magnitude. To overcome the problems of resource over-provisioning, performance degradation, and adverse business impact, it is required to develop a light-weight cooperative architecture, potentially taking advantage of the Cloud systems, where CDN servers are grouped into clusters of neighbor surrogates, cooperatively replicate and deliver the user-requested content. A solution towards this end can extend the existing architecture (Amini, et al., 2004; Buyya, et al., 2006; Day, et al., 2003; Pathan, et al., 2008) that allow resource sharing among multiple Cloud-based content delivery services.

On the Economics of Cooperation

There is the need to incentivize CDN providers to keep motivated for contributing resources to allow replication in the cooperative domain content delivery clouds. To ensure sustained resource sharing, sufficient incentives should be provided to all parties (Pathan & Buyya, 2007). Use of economics principles in this context represents a dynamic scenario and makes the system more manageable through regulating and analyzing the emergent marketplace behavior. In this context, an economic model can be developed to consider a CDN as an independent economic agent for buying and selling content. It is significant to emphasize the QoS-oriented aspects of provider selection and analyze the sensitivity of different performance metrics such as cost, net benefit, value and popularity of the content, and transport cost. Future research in this direction will focus on the development of dynamic pricing policies for Cloud systems and CDNs (Anandasivam & Premm, 2009; Pueschel, et al., 2009); study of the interaction between different pricing approaches

(Hosanagar, et al., 2008); and investigation of the impact of competition in the CDN industry on CDN pricing (Christin & Chuang, 2004, 2005; Christin, et al., 2008).

Replication to Consider Mobility in the Cooperative Domain

CDNs offer an exciting playground to exploit the emerging technological advances of mobile computing. To deliver content to a large number of highly dynamic users, it is required to take into account the mobility notion. The variations in mobile user requests are caused not only by changes in content popularity, but also by user mobility. Each user request is characterized by the requested content, the time of the request, and the location of the user. The concept of caching "hot" content is not new, but in the context of mobility for content delivery in the Cloud-based cooperative domain, there are significant competing considerations. It is required to develop dynamic, scalable, and efficient replication mechanisms that cache content on demand with respect to the locality of requests, focusing on regions where specific content is needed most (Chen, et al., 2003; Fortino, et al., 2009). In this context, developed solutions should include a mobility model, geolocation-oriented services, a monitoring mechanism and a service delivery protocol for CDNs (Loulloudes, et al., 2008). Future research in this direction will focus on potentially considering user location context, navigational behavior, and very high spatial and temporal demand variations to dynamically reconfigure the system, and minimize the total traffic over the network backbone.

Replica Placement, Consistency, and Ranking

There are a number of research issues to be resolved for replica management, such as how many replicas of various objects to have, where in the network to place them, how to manage the replicas, and how they are to be ranked for efficient request distribution (Cameron, et al., 2002; Chen, et al., 2002; Presti, et al., 2005). In this context, existing approaches will be extended for cooperative content delivery in Cloud-based CDNs. It is crucial to decide on the use of static or dynamic approach, granularity of replication and handling of failed replicas. In order to guarantee that the requested users are not serviced with stale objects, a proper replica consistency technique is to be devised. An appropriate technique for ranking replicas can also be developed by using a combination of metrics such as Web server load, latency, geographical proximity and network distance (Bakiras & Loukopoulos, 2005).

Energy-Aware Request-Redirection

Energy-awareness in computing is an emerging research area. Large-scale distributed systems such as CDNs consume huge amount of electricity, thus leading to high energy cost (Qureshi, et al., 2009). Conventionally, the approach to reduce energy cost is to decrease the amount of the consumed energy. Request-redirection to optimal replicas can aid to cut down the energy cost by decreasing the amount of the consumed energy during cooperative content delivery in Cloud-based CDNs. While energy-aware content delivery is economically beneficial for commercial CDNs, there are also benefits for a third-party Cloud-based CDN system, e.g. MetaCDN (Broberg, et al., 2009; Pathan, et al., 2009), which may be interested in attaining social welfare by reducing the environmental impact of high energy consumption. Therefore, it is required to develop schemes to reduce the energy consumption and carbon footprint of CDNs. These energy-aware request-routing techniques will consider end-user's geographical proximity, energy usage and cost, and incoming traffic load for directing users to the most cost-effective replica.

Enhancement for Cloud-based CDNs

Extension of traditional CDNs model to Cloud-based CDNs enhances capabilities to deliver services that are not only limited to Web applications, but also include storage, raw computing or access to any number of specialized services. It initiates potential research that focuses on identifying necessary application requirements, enhancing scalability, system robustness, usability and access performance, low cost, data durability, and support for security and privacy. For instance, as an advancement of previous work with the MetaCDN system, future research can develop active measurement approaches for QoS-based and probabilistic request-redirection, autonomic scaling of infrastructure, and a security framework that spans the integrated storage cloud providers.

CONCLUSION

MetaCDN, characterized as a Content Delivery Cloud, provides a cost-effective solution for responsive, scalable, and transparent content delivery services by harnessing the resources of multiple storage cloud providers. It provides sensible performance and availability benefits without requiring the content providers to build or manage complex content delivery infrastructure themselves. This chapter presented a performance study of MetaCDN, based on conducted *proof-of-concept* experiments on a global testbed. An indicative list of future research directions is also presented, including the development of advanced request-redirection techniques and pricing policies for Content Delivery Clouds; and on-demand autonomic management (expansion/contraction) of replica deployment. From the results obtained, it can be concluded that the utility of MetaCDN is maximized by using utility-based request-redirection to provide sensible replica selection and consistent average response time; however, with the cost of lower throughput in comparison to other candidate request-redirection policies. In contrast, a content provider's benefit is enhanced with improvement of the perceived throughput through MetaCDN.

REFERENCES

Amini, L., Shaikh, A., & Schulzrinne, H. (2003). Modeling redirection in geographically diverse server sets. *Proceedings 12th International Conference on World Wide Web (WWW'03)*, (pp. 472-481).

Amini, L., Shaikh, A., Schulzrinne, H., Res, I. B. M., & Hawthorne, N. Y. (2004). Effective peering for multi-provider content delivery services. *Proceedings - IEEE INFOCOM, 04*, 850–861.

Anandasivam, A., & Premm, M. (2009). Bid price control and dynamic pricing in clouds. *Proceedings 17th European Conference on Information Systems (ECIS'09)*.

Arlitt, M., & Jin, T. (2000). A workload characterization study of the 1998 World Cup Web site. *IEEE Network, 14*(3), 30–37. doi:10.1109/65.844498

Bakiras, S., & Loukopoulos, T. (2005). Combining replica placement and caching techniques in content distribution networks. *Computer Communications, 28*(9), 1062–1073. doi:10.1016/j.comcom.2005.01.012

Barbir, A., Cain, B., Nair, R., & Spatscheck, O. (2003). Known content network (CN) request-routing mechanisms. *Internet Engineering Task Force RFC 3568*.

Barford, P., & Crovella, M. (1999). A performance evaluation of hyper text transfer protocols. *ACM SIGMETRICS Performance Evaluation Review, 27*(1), 188–197. doi:10.1145/301464.301560

Biliris, A., Cranor, C., Douglis, F., Rabinovich, M., Sibal, S., Spatscheck, O., & Sturm, W. (2002). CDN brokering. *Computer Communications, 25*(4), 393–402. doi:10.1016/S0140-3664(01)00411-X

Broberg, J., Buyya, R., & Tari, Z. (2009). MetaCDN: Harnessing 'storage clouds' for high performance content delivery. *Journal of Network and Computer Applications, 32*(5), 1012–1022. doi:10.1016/j.jnca.2009.03.004

Buyya, R., Pathan, M., & Vakali (Eds.), A. (2008). *Content delivery networks* (Vol. 9). Springer, Germany.

Buyya, R., Pathan, M., Broberg, J., & Tari, Z. (2006). A case for peering of content delivery networks. *IEEE Distributed Systems Online, 7*(10), 3. doi:10.1109/MDSO.2006.57

Buyya, R., Yeo, C. S., Venugopal, S., Broberg, J., & Brandic, I. (2009). Cloud computing and emerging IT platforms: Vision, hype, and reality for delivering computing as the 5th utility. *Future Generation Computer Systems, 25*(6), 599–616. doi:10.1016/j.future.2008.12.001

Cameron, C. W., Low, S. H., & Wei, D. X. (2002). High-density model for server allocation and placement. *Proceedings ACM SIGMETRICS, 02*, 152–159. doi:10.1145/511399.511354

Canali, C., Rabinovich, M., & Xiao, Z. (2004). Utility computing for Internet applications. In Tang, X., Xu, J., & Chanson, S. T. (Eds.), *Web content delivery* (pp. 131–151). Springer.

Cardellini, V., Casalicchio, E., Colajanni, M., & Yu, P. S. (2002). The state of the art in locally distributed Web-server systems. *ACM Computing Surveys, 34*(2), 263–311. doi:10.1145/508352.508355

Cardellini, V., Colajanni, M., & Yu, P. S. (2000). Geographic load balancing for scalable distributed Web systems. *Proceedings International Symposium on Modeling, Analysis and Simulation of Computer and Telecommunication Systems (MASCOTS'00)*.

Cardellini, V., Colajanni, M., & Yu, P. S. (2003). Request redirection algorithms for distributed Web systems. *IEEE Transactions on Parallel and Distributed Systems, 14*(4), 355–368. doi:10.1109/TPDS.2003.1195408

Chen, Y., Katz, R. H., & Kubiatowicz, J. (2002). Dynamic replica placement for scalable content delivery. *Lecture Notes in Computer Science, Peer-to-Peer Systems: Revised Papers of 1st International Workshop on Peer-to-Peer Systems (IPTPS'02), 2429*, (pp. 306–318).

Chen, Y., Qiu, L., Chen, W., Nguyen, L., & Katz, R. H. (2003). Efficient and adaptive Web replication using content clustering. *IEEE Journal on Selected Areas in Communications, 21*(6), 979–994. doi:10.1109/JSAC.2003.814608

Christin, N., & Chuang, J. (2004). On the cost of participating in a peer-to-peer network. *Lecture Notes in Computer Science, Peer-to-Peer Systems III: Revised paper of 4th International Workshop on Peer-to-Peer Systems (IPTPS'04), 3279*, (pp. 22-32).

Christin, N., & Chuang, J. (2005). A cost-based analysis of overlay routing geometrics. *Proceedings IEEE INFOCOM'05, 4*, (pp. 2566-2577).

Christin, N., Chuang, J., & Grossklags, J. (2008). Economics-informed design of CDNs. In Buyya, R., Pathan, A.-M. K., & Vakali, A. (Eds.), *Content delivery networks* (pp. 183–210). Germany: Springer-Verlag. doi:10.1007/978-3-540-77887-5_7

Cohen, R. (2008). Content delivery cloud (CDC). *Elastic Vapor: Life in the Cloud*.

Conti, M., Gregori, E., & Panzieri, F. (2001). QoS-based architectures for geographically replicated Web servers. *Cluster Computing, 4*(2), 109–120. doi:10.1023/A:1011412830658

Day, M., Cain, B., Tomlinson, G., & Rzewski, P. (2003). A model for content internetworking (CDI). *Internet Engineering Task Force RFC 3466*.

Di Stefano, A., & Santoro, C. (2008). An economic model for resource management in a Grid-based content distribution network. *Future Generation Computer Systems, 24*(3), 202–212. doi:10.1016/j.future.2007.07.014

Elson, J., & Howell, J. (2008). Handling flash crowds from your garage. *Proceedings USENIX 2008 Annual Technical Conference (USENIX'08)*, (pp. 171-184).

Erçetin, O., & Tassiulas, L. (2003). *Request routing in content distribution networks*. (Technical Report). Retrieved from http://digital.sabanciuniv.edu/elitfulltext/3011800000049.pdf

Floyd, S., & Paxson, V. (2001). Difficulties in simulating the Internet. *IEEE/ACM Transactions on Networking, 9*(4), 392–403. doi:10.1109/90.944338

Fortino, G., Garro, A., Mascillaro, S., Russo, W., & Vaccaro, M. (2009). Distributed architectures for surrogate clustering in CDNs: A simulation-based analysis. *UPGRADE-CN'09, Proceedings 18th IEEE International Symposium on High Performance Distributed Computing (HPDC'09) Workshops*, (pp. 3-10).

Fortino, G., & Russo, W. (2008). Using P2P, GRID and agent technologies for the development of content distribution networks. *Future Generation Computer Systems, 24*(3), 180–190. doi:10.1016/j.future.2007.06.007

Freedman, M. (2010). Experiences with CoralCDN: A five-year operational view. *Proceedings 7th USENIX Symposium on Network Design and Implementation (NSDI '10)*.

Freedman, M. J., Freudenthal, E., & Mazieres, D. (2004). Democratizing content publication with Coral. *Proceedings 1st USENIX/ACM Symposium on Networked Systems Design and Implementation (NSDI'04)*, (pp. 239-252).

Gayek, P., Nesbitt, R., Pearthree, H., Shaikh, A., & Snitzer, B. (2004). A Web content serving utility. *IBM Systems Journal, 43*(1), 43–63. doi:10.1147/sj.431.0043

Geng, X., Gopal, R. D., Ramesh, R., & Whinston, A. B. (2003). Scaling Web services with capacity provision networks. *IEEE Computer, 36*(11), 64–72. doi:10.1109/MC.2003.1244537

Gottfrid, D. (2007). Self-service, prorated super computing fun! *The New York Times*.

Hosanagar, K., Chuang, J., Krishnan, R., & Smith, M. D. (2008). Service adoption and pricing of content delivery network (CDN) services. *Management Science, 54*(9), 1579–1593. doi:10.1287/mnsc.1080.0875

Jiang, W., Zhang-Shen, R., Rexford, J., & Chiang, M. (2008). Cooperative content distribution and traffic engineering. *Proceedings Workshop on the Economics of Networks, Systems, and Computation (NetEcon'08)*, (pp. 7-12).

Kangasharju, J., Ross, K. W., & Roberts, J. W. (2001). Performance evaluation of redirection schemes in content distribution networks. *Computer Communications, 24*(2), 207–214. doi:10.1016/S0140-3664(00)00316-9

Karaul, M., Korilis, Y. A., & Orda, A. (2000). A market-based architecture for management of geographically dispersed, replicated Web servers. *Decision Support Systems, 28*(1-2), 191–204. doi:10.1016/S0167-9236(99)00068-8

Kusmierek, E., Czyrnek, M., Mazurek, C., & Stroinski, M. (2007). iTVP: Large-scale content distribution for live and on-demand video services. *Proceedings SPIE'07*.

Kwon, M., & Fahmy, S. (2005). Synergy: An overlay internetworking architecture. *Proceedings 14th International Conference on Computer Communications and Networks (ICCCN'05)*, (pp. 401-406).

Leighton, T. (2009). *Akamai and cloud computing: A perspective from the edge of the cloud* (No. White Paper). Akamai Technologies, Inc. Retrieved from http://www.akamai.com/cloud

Liston, R., & Zegura, E. (2001). Using a proxy to measure client-side web performance. *Proceedings Intlernational Web Content Caching and Distribution Workshop (WCW'01)*.

Lloret, J., Garcia, M., Bri, D., & Diaz, J. R. (2009). Study and performance of a group-based content delivery network. *Journal of Network and Computer Applications, 32*(5), 991–999. doi:10.1016/j.jnca.2009.03.008

Loulloudes, N., Pallis, G., & Dikaiakos, M. D. (2008). Information dissemination in mobile CDNs. In Buyya, R., Pathan, A.-M. K., & Vakali, A. (Eds.), *Content delivery networks* (pp. 343–366). Germany: Springer-Verlag. doi:10.1007/978-3-540-77887-5_14

MacAskill, D. (2007). *Scalability: Set Amazon's servers on fire, not yours*. O'Reilly Emerging Technology Conference (ETech'07).

Mao, Z. M., Cranor, C. D., Douglis, F., Rabinovich, M., Spatscheck, O., & Wang, J. (2002). A precise and efficient evaluation of the proximity between Web clients and their local DNS servers. *Proceedings USENIX 2002 Annual Technical Conference (USENIX'02)*, (pp. 229-242).

Miller, R. (2008). *Microsoft building own CDN network*. Data Center Knowledge.

Molina, B., Palau Salvador, C. E., Esteve Domingo, M., Alonso Peña, I., & Ruiz Extremera, V. (2006). On content delivery network implementation. *Computer Communications, 29*(12), 2396–2412. doi:10.1016/j.comcom.2006.02.016

Nguyen, T. V., Chou, C. T., & Boustead, P. (2003). Provisioning content distribution networks over shared infrastructure. *Proceedings 11th IEEE International Conference on Networks (ICON'03)*, (pp. 119-124).

Pai, V. S., Aron, M., Banga, G., Svendsen, M., Druschel, P., Zwaenepoel, W., & Nahum, E. (1998). Locality-aware request distribution in cluster-based network servers. *ACM SIGPLAN Notices*, *33*(11), 205–216. doi:10.1145/291006.291048

Pallis, G., & Vakali, A. (2006). Insight and perspectives for content delivery networks. *Communications of the ACM*, *49*(1), 101–106. doi:10.1145/1107458.1107462

Pathan, M. (2010). *Content delivery networks (CDNs) research directory.*

Pathan, M., Broberg, J., & Buyya, R. (2008). Internetworking of CDNs. In Buyya, R., Pathan, A.-M. K., & Vakali, A. (Eds.), *Content delivery networks* (pp. 389–413). Germany: Springer-Verlag. doi:10.1007/978-3-540-77887-5_16

Pathan, M., Broberg, J., & Buyya, R. (2009). Maximizing utility for content delivery clouds. *Lecture Notes in Computer Science, Proceedings 10th International Conference on Web Information Systems Engineering (WISE'09), 5802,* (pp. 13-28).

Pathan, M., & Buyya, R. (2007). Economy-based content replication for peering content delivery networks. *TCSC Doctoral Symposium, Proceedings 7th IEEE International Symposium on Cluster Computing and the Grid (CCGrid'07),* (pp. 887-892).

Pathan, M., & Buyya, R. (2009a). Architecture and performance models for QoS-driven effective peering of content delivery networks. *Multiagent and Grid Systems, 5*(2), 165–195.

Pathan, M., & Buyya, R. (2009b). Resource discovery and request-redirection for dynamic load sharing in multi-provider peering content delivery networks. *Journal of Network and Computer Applications, 32*(5), 976–990. doi:10.1016/j.jnca.2009.03.003

Pierre, G., & van Steen, M. (2001). Globule: A platform for self-replicating Web documents. *Lecture Notes in Computer Science, Proceedings 6th International Conference on Protocols for Multimedia Systems (PROMS'01), 2213,* (pp. 1-11).

Pierre, G., & van Steen, M. (2006). Globule: A collaborative content delivery network. *IEEE Communications Magazine, 44*(8), 127–133. doi:10.1109/MCOM.2006.1678120

Presti, F. L., Bartolini, N., & Petrioli, C. (2005). Dynamic replica placement and user request redirection in content delivery networks. *Proceedings International Conference on Communications (ICC'05),* (pp. 1495-1501).

Pueschel, T., Anandasivam, A., Buschek, S., & Neumann, D. (2009). Making money with clouds: Revenue optimization through automated policy decisions. *Proceedings 17th European Conference on Information Systems (ECIS'09).*

Qureshi, A., Weber, R., Balakrishnan, H., Guttag, J., & Maggs, B. (2009). Cutting the electric bill for Internet-scale systems. *Proceedings ACM SIGCOMM'09.*

Rabinovich, M., Xiao, Z., & Aggarwal, A. (2003). Computing on the edge: A platform for replicating internet applications. *Proceedings 8th International Workshop on Web Content Caching and Distribution (WCW'03).*

Rahul, H., Kasbekar, M., Sitaraman, R., & Berger, A. (2006). Towards realizing the performance and availability benefits of a global overlay network *Proceedings 7th International Conference on Passive and Active Network Measurement (PAM'06).*

Rangarajan, S., Mukherjee, S., & Rodriguez, P. (2003). A technique for user specific request redirection in a content delivery network. *Proceedings 8th International Web Content Caching and Distribution Workshop (WCW'03)*.

Ranjan, S., Karrer, R., & Knightly, E. (2004). Wide area redirection of dynamic content by internet data centers. *Proceedings IEEE INFOCOM'04*.

Rayburn, D. (2009). CDN research data: Market sizing and pricing trends. *Streaming Media West: The Business and Technology of Online Video*.

Shah, P., Pâris, J. F., Morgan, J., Schettino, J., & Venkatraman, C. (2008). A P2P-based architecture for secure software delivery using volunteer assistance. *Proceedings International Conference on Peer-to-Peer Networks (P2P'08)*.

Shaikh, A., Tewari, R., Agrawal, M., Center, I., & Heights, Y. (2001). On the effectiveness of DNS-based server selection. *Proceedings - IEEE INFOCOM, 01*, 1801–1810.

Sivasubramanian, S., Szymaniak, M., Pierre, G., & Van Steen, M. (2004). Replication for Web hosting systems. *ACM Computing Surveys, 36*(3), 291–334. doi:10.1145/1035570.1035573

Subramanya, S. R., & Yi, B. K. (2005). Utility model for on-demand digital content. *IEEE Computer, 38*(6), 95–98. doi:10.1109/MC.2005.206

Tran, M., & Tavanapong, W. (2005). Peers-assisted dynamic content distribution networks. *Proceedings 30th IEEE International Conference on Local Computer Networks (LCN'05)*, (pp. 123-131).

Turrini, E. (2004). *An architecture for content distribution internetworking*. (Technical Report UBLCS-2004-2). University of Bologna, Italy.

Turrini, E., & Panzieri, F. (2002). Using P2P techniques for content distribution internetworking: A research proposal. *Proceedings International Conference on Peer-to-Peer Computing (P2P'02)*.

Vincenty, T. (1975). Direct and inverse solutions of geodesics on the ellipsoid with application of nested equations. *Survey Review, 22*(176), 88–93.

Wang, L., Pai, V., & Peterson, L. (2002). The effectiveness of request redirection on CDN robustness. *ACM SIGOPS Operating Systems Review, 36*, 345–360. doi:10.1145/844128.844160

Wang, L., Park, K. S., Pang, R., Pai, V., & Peterson, L. (2004). Reliability and security in the CoDeeN content distribution network. *Proceedings USENIX 2004 Annual Technical Conference (USENIX'04)*.

Xie, H., Yang, Y. R., Krishnamurthy, A., Liu, Y., & Silberschatz, A. (2008). P4P: Provider portal for (P2P) applications. *Proceedings ACM SIGCOMM'08*.

Yang, C.-S., & Luo, M.-Y. (1999). An effective mechanism for supporting content-based routing in scalable Web server clusters. *Proceedings International Workshop on Parallel Processing (ICPP'99)*, (pp. 240-245).

KEY TERMS AND DEFINITIONS

Cloud Computing: It is a recent technology trend that moves computing and data away from desktop and portable PCs into computational resources such as large Data Centers ("Computing") and make them accessible as scalable, on-demand services over a network (the "Cloud"). The main technical underpinnings of Cloud Computing infrastructures and services include virtualization, service-orientation, elasticity, multi-tenancy, power efficiency, and economics of scale.

Content Delivery Cloud: It extends the traditional CDN model to harness the power of Cloud computing to deliver cost-effective and high performance content delivery to Internet end-users. Alike the Cloud computing paradigm, content delivery cloud follows a pay-per-usage model to charge the customers for using the storage and bandwidth used to deliver content.

Content Delivery Network (CDN): Content Delivery Networks (CDN), evolved first in 1998, replicate contents over several mirrored web servers (i.e. surrogate servers) strategically placed at various locations to deal with the flash crowds. Geographically distributing the web servers' facilities is a method commonly used by service providers to improve performance and scalability. A CDN has some combination of a content-delivery infrastructure, a request-routing infrastructure, a distribution infrastructure and an accounting infrastructure.

Overlay: An overlay network is built on top of another network. Overlay network nodes can be considered as being connected by virtual or logical links, each of which corresponds to a path, likely through many physical links, in the underlying computer network. Distributed systems such as Content Delivery Network, Content Delivery Cloud, Cloud computing infrastructure, Peer-to-Peer (P2P) networks are examples of overlay networks because their nodes run on top of the Internet.

Request-Redirection: It is a technique commonly used in the World Wide Web (WWW) and in particular in CDNs to direct end-user requests to surrogate replica servers in the face of peak loads. Request-redirection mechanisms are governed by policies that outline the actual redirection algorithm on how to perform server selection in response to an end-user request

Response Time: It refers to the time required for a system to react on a given input. In CDN context, response time is associated with the time for an end-user to be serviced, i.e. receive the requested content.

Throughput: It refers to the average message delivery over a communication channel. In CDN context, it is interpreted as the transfer speed to download/receive content from a CDN replica server.

Chapter 3
P2P Streaming Content Delivery Systems

Tieying Zhang
Institute of Computing Technology, Chinese Academy of Sciences, China

Xueqi Cheng
Institute of Computing Technology, Chinese Academy of Sciences, China

Weisong Shi
Tongji University, China & Wayne State University, USA

ABSTRACT

In recent years, Peer-to-Peer (P2P) streaming systems have attracted enormous attention from both industries and academia. P2P streaming technology not only improves system scalability but also enables resource aggregation. This chapter reviews the field of P2P streaming by summarizing the key concepts and giving an overview of the most important systems. Design and implementation issues of P2P streaming systems are analyzed in general, and then six case studies for P2P live streaming, P2P on-demand streaming, and P2P download-based streaming separately are discussed. This chapter will help people in the research community and industry understand the potential properties of P2P streaming. For people unfamiliar with the field, it provides a general overview. Comparison of P2P steaming designs with different architectures is intended for developers and researchers.

INTRODUCTION

With the rapid deployment of broadband access into household, online video streaming services have become one of the most popular Internet applications, such as Hulu (Hulu, 2010) and YouTube (YouTube, 2010). Such video streaming services are generally divided into two categories: 1) live

streaming 2) Video-on-Demand (VoD) streaming. However, due to its high bandwidth requirements, it is of extensive high-cost to provide the video streaming services online. For instance, YouTube, the most popular on-demand video-sharing service, has to pay more than one million dollars' worth of bandwidth a month for transmission. Moreover, YouTube has to be equipped with a supercomputer with 400 nodes and a 10 gigabit Ethernet connection to provide video service.

DOI: 10.4018/978-1-4666-1794-0.ch003

As Peer-to-peer (P2P) technologies have obtained enormous success in content delivery, more and more video streaming providers have paid attention to developing P2P streaming applications to reduce server costs and accelerate user downloading. In P2P architecture, clients' resources (bandwidth, CPU, storage) are used to power the P2P system while optimizing network resources utilization. As P2P networks do not require any special servers or routers, the cost of such solutions is appealing. P2P multicasting is an elegant alternative to CDN infrastructure which each end-host (peer) may act as a potential server for other peers. This avoids dedicated replication servers altogether. The approach is self-scaling, as the number of peer "servers" and peer clients increases at the same rate, hence it avoids the bottleneck of a central server (or dedicated replication server). The approach, in principle, would allow a highly dynamic support of changing multicast demand at very low cost.

P2P streaming focuses on real-time video streaming applications, which include both live and on-demand streaming. These systems are harder to deploy due to the real-time playback requirement at the receiver end.

Many technologies exist for real-time video delivery. Broadcast video as used in TV is very good for delivering a limited number of streams to a very large audience. Point-to-point delivery is currently used for VoD and interactive video, as well as much of Internet video streaming, and can support a small audience with a large number of streams. The middle ground is covered by multicast delivery. Multicast delivery is very flexible and can enable a large number of senders to deliver content to any number of receivers.

IP multicast was the first solution to provide multicast functionality in the Internet. It put forth an ambitious vision to support all multicast functionality within the routers in the network and proposed a powerful abstraction to applications where a group address identifies a multicast group and any host can send a message to a group by simply sending to the group address. However, due to many technical and marketing reasons, it is still far from being widely deployed.

More recently, application layer multicast or overlay multicast has been proposed as an alternate architecture to provide multicast functionality in the Internet. In this type of multicast architecture, group membership, multicast delivery structure construction, and data forwarding are solely controlled by participating end hosts, thus no such functionality is required within routers in the network.

The application layer multicast systems can be grouped into tree-based and non-tree-based classes. Tree-based classes can be extended to single tree, multiple trees and mesh structures. It is a logical tree rooted at the source, where all nodes are hosts and each link in the tree is a network path, and the data is always delivered from the source to the parents then to the children. Constructing and maintaining an efficient distribution tee among the peers is a key challenge for tree-based systems. Mesh-based protocols are popular in treeless P2P systems. They achieve operation decentralization via gossip, i.e. delivering data and/or control messages to peers randomly. The following sections will describe examples of tree-based and mesh-based structures in details.

It is noted that tree or non-tree based structure are constructed at the application layer, while at the substrate layer, either structured or non-structured substrate can be used. Structured schemes leverage Distributed Hash Table (DHT) based substrate and build multicast forwarding trees on top of this structured substrate. In most of the Internet based implementations described in the following sections, non-structure substrate is used, while the nodes participate in a random manner, and the content location is independent of the nodes.

This chapter presents an overview of the fast growing Peer-to-Peer streaming that is competing with the traditional TV and Internet services. We analyze P2P streaming by dividing this field into P2P-live, P2P-VoD and P2P download-based streaming with discussing several typical case studies.

In section 2, we first introduce the development of P2P live streaming. Then, we divide live steaming system into tree-based and mesh-based architecture and discuss some popular system accordingly.

Then, in section 3, we present the emerging Internet Video-on-Demand services and also distinguish tree-based overlay from mesh-based structure. After looking at the introduction of P2P-VoD streaming, we also briefly look at its key concept. Again, we discuss some important P2P-VoD system, such as P2Cast, P2VoD, HON and PPLive.

In section 4, we mainly discuss an important P2P streaming application - download-based steaming and present a popular download streaming system, CoolFish. CoolFish is not only a download-based streaming system but also an integrated steaming platform providing both live and VoD services.

Section 5 summarizes the chapter based on the previous sections, and proposes some technical and research topic which may be useful for further studies.

This chapter is intended for people new to the field of P2P streaming as well as for experts. It is also intended for developers, researchers and the readers interested in P2P streaming and video content delivery.

P2P LIVE STREAMING

Overview

P2P live streaming application has attracted the interest of numerous researchers around the world in the last few years. Hundreds of papers have been published on this subject. Most of the proposals rely on the Application Layer Multicast approach. And in the last two years, some of these academic research projects have been turned into Internet based implementations, and it is now getting into commercial phase. Although most of the research proposals were initiated in the U.S., most of the recent activities are concentrated in Asia, and small start-up companies are emerging in Asia and Europe. A few popular examples are PPlive, PPStream, etc. The initial Internet based services offered by these companies have attracted users globally due to its low cost (mostly free) and number of available content, and these companies are potentially facing the copyright issues, and they are actively improving the quality of their service, adding new content, improving the relationships with content providers and network operators, and are in search for the valid business models to move forward.

Tree-Based Systems

Introduction

The idea of employing P2P networks to convey live streaming started attracting the attention of researchers a few years ago.

The first applicative scenario introduced was the large-scale distribution of non-interactive content. The most significant research papers date back to 2000, with the proposal of the Overcast (Cisco) (John Jannotti, David K. Gifford, Kirk L. Johnson, M. Frans Kaashoek, & James W. O'Toole, Jr., 2000) and Scattercast (UC Berkeley) (Yatin Dilip Chawathe, 2000). architectures, which both employ a two-tiered infrastructure (the actual p2p network is at the core of the system, the outer network, where the end-users reside, doesn't take an active part in the content distribution) to spread the load from a single server to a large pool of supporting nodes.

The other field of interest, which was also explored around year 2000, was small-scale, multiple source video distribution in cooperative environments with a certain aim at intra-company conferencing and media broadcasting. Good results have been achieved by the Narada (CMU)

(Yang-hua Chu, Sanjay G. Rao & Hui Zhang, 2000). and Yoid (USC) (P. Francis, 2010). Narada is a commercial product, which uses a mesh-based architecture. Yoid's structure is a mix of mesh and tree.

In the following years, since 2001, the research started focusing on completely distributed systems for media streaming, relying on application layer multicast. The three main branches of this field are summarized in below:

- Several studies have been proposed which rely on single application layer multicast trees, like SpreadIt (Stanford) (Hrishikesh Deshpande, Mayank Bawa & Hector Garcia-Molina, 2001), PeerCast (Stanford) (Mayank Bawa, Hrishikesh Deshpande & Hector Garcia-Molina, 2003, p107), ESM (CMU) (Yang hua Chu, Aditya Ganjam, T.S. Eugene Ng, Sanjay G. Rao, Kunwadee Sripanidkulchai, Jibin Zhan & Hui Zhang, 2004) and NICE (U. of Maryland) (Bobby Bhattacharjee, 2010).

- Other projects have explored approaches based on multiple application layer multicast trees - to obtain a better resiliency to node failures, and appropriate data encodings, to protect the playback quality in case of packet losses - like Splitstream (Microsoft) (Miguel Castro, Peter Druschel, Anne marie Kermarrec, Animesh Nandi, Antony Rowstron & Atul Singh, 2003), CoopNet (Microsoft) (Venkata N. Padmanabhan & Kunwadee Sripanidkulchai, 2002, p178. Venkata N. Padmanabhan, Helen J. Wang, Philip A. Chou & Kunwadee Sripanidkulchai, 2002, p177) and P2PCast (NYU) (Antonio Nicolosi, 2003).

- Improved single-tree based solutions have been proposed by Zigzag (U. of Central Florida) (K. Hua D. Tran & S. Sheu, 2003) and Bullet (Duke) (Dejan Kosti´c, Adolfo Rodriguez, Jeannie Albrecht & Amin Vahdat, 2003, p282).

There are numerous research papers being published in tree-based P2P live streaming, mostly proposed by the researchers in U.S. Universities. But most of these projects stayed at the research stage, did not move on to the implementation stage. Among a few of them that have been implemented over the Internet, ESM is a well-known one, it is currently operational, usually serves at the academic conferences, and can support thousands of users at the same time.

Case Study I: ESM

System Overview

End System Multicast (ESM) is a proposal made by the CS department of Carnegie Mellon University. The aim of the project is creating a readily deployable and easy to operate unreliable multicast infrastructure. The authors' concerns are more about using readily-available technologies (e.g., traditional delay-optimized single-rooted overlay tree, use of standard codecs for the media streams) and overcoming the large-scale connectivity problems (e.g., firewall and NAT), rather than developing theoretical models and crafting improved algorithms.

ESM is currently an operational Internet broadcast system hosted by CMU. It can be used for any event that requires broadcasting high quality video to as few as one or two people, or as many as hundreds or thousands. ESM has been used for over 30 different events by the project members, and by over 10,000 users across the world, in home, academic and commercial environments. This section gives the system overview and protocol introduction. Some of the content is adapted from (Jibin Zhan & Hui Zhang, 2004).

Figure 1 (adapted from (Jibin Zhan et al., 2004)) presents a high-level overview of the ESM broadcast system.

The encoder takes the multimedia signal from the camera, converts into audio and video streams, and sends to the broadcast source. The streams are disseminated along the overlay from broadcast

Figure 1. ESM system overview

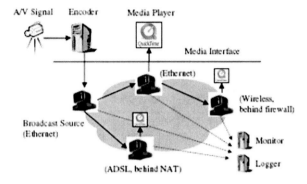

Figure 2. ESM software architecture

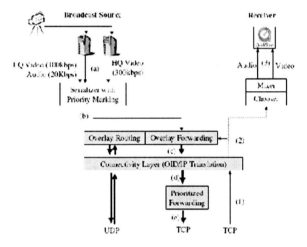

source to the receivers. Using multicast protocol, each receiver gets the broadcast stream, and forwards it to the local media player.

Figure 2 (adapted from (PPLive, 2010)) describes the detailed software architecture at the source and the receiver.

Tracing the data flow,

- The broadcast source encodes the media signal into audio and multiple video packet streams
- Marks the packets with priority bits, and sends them to the overlay models (shaded blocks)

- The overlay modules replicate packets to all of its children.
- Packets are translated from Overlay ID (OID) to IP addresses
- Packets are forwarded to each child using prioritization semantics

Once a child receives packets,

- it translates IP addresses back to OIDs
- selects the best video stream, adjusts the RTP/RTCP headers
- forwards to the media player

Protocol

ESM is based on a single tree (single-sourced) architecture, where the protocol builds an tree overlay based on distributed maintenance. The overlay is designed primarily for bandwidth optimization. Because ESM is a tree-based system, the optimization of delay is also considered.

Group Management. New hosts join the broadcast by contacting the source and retrieving a random list of hosts that are currently in the group. It then selects one of these members as its parent using the parent selection algorithm. Each member maintains a partial list of members, including the hosts on the path from the source and a random set of members, which can help if all members on the path are saturated. To learn about members, ESM uses a gossip protocol. Each host A periodically picks one member (B) at random, and sends B a subset of group members (8 members) that A knows, along with the last timestamp it has heard for each member. When B receives a membership message, it updates its list of known members. Finally, members are deleted if its state has not been refreshed in a period.

Performance-Aware Adaptation. ESM considers three dynamic network metrics: available bandwidth, latency and loss. There are two main components to this adaptation process: (1) detecting poor performance from the current parent, or identifying that a host must switch parents, (2) choosing a new parent.

Parent Selection. When a host (A) joins the broadcast, or needs to make a parent change, it probes a random subset of hosts it knows (e.g. 30). The probing is biased toward members that have not been probed or have low delay. Each host B that responds to the probe provides information about: (1) the performance (application throughput in the recent 5 seconds, and delay) it is receiving (2) whether it is degree-saturated or not, and (3) whether it is a descendant of A to prevent routing loops. The probe also enables A to determine the round trip time to B. A waits for responses for

1 second, then eliminates those members that are saturated, or who is its descendant. It then evaluates the performance (throughput and delay) of the remaining hosts if it were to choose them as parents.

A switches to the parent B either if the estimated application throughput is high enough for A to receive a higher quality stream or if B maintains the same bandwidth level as A's current parent, but improves delay. This heuristic attempts to increase the tree efficiency by making hosts move closer to one another.

In order to assess the number of children a parent can support, ESM asks the user to choose whether or not it has at least a 10 Mbps up-link to the Internet. If so, ESM assigns such hosts a degree bound of 6, to support up that many number of children. Otherwise, ESM assigns a degree bound of 0 so that the host does not support any children.

Much of the ESM deployments use TCP as the congestion control protocol, and also incorporated TFRC, a UDP-based congestion control protocol, into the system.

Case Study II: Peercast

System Overview

Peercast is a live streaming tool which can be used to multicast audio (Ogg Vorbis, Mp3, WMA) or video (Ogg Theora, Nullsoft Video, or WMV), or any other stream of data, over the internet. It is an open source software used as a streaming media tool for individual to broadcast their personal videos.

Peercast is designed using P2P overlay network to minimize the upload bandwidth for the original broadcaster. Peercast is released under the GPL license and is available for Linux, Windows, and Mac. It is currently being developed by a single developer (Giles), and is always in need of new help.

The technology Peercast used is presented in "Streaming live media over peers" whose writer is M. Bawa in Stanford University.

Peercast has the features listed below:

- Support for MP3, OGG Theora and Vorbis, WMA, WMV and NSV.
- HTML (Linux/Windows) and Windows task-bar icon interface.
- Remote configuration via any web browser.
- Extremely low memory footprint and CPU load.
- One click streaming - click on any peercast:// URL to start listening.
- Direct streaming - PeerCast can act as a standard streaming server such as Shoutcast/Icecast to provide both direct and P2P streaming.
- Multiple broadcasting - use mount points to broadcast multiple channels from the same server.
- Anonymous broadcasting - clients do not tell each other if they are the source or just listening.
- Remote broadcasting - broadcast to a client located on another machine anywhere on the Internet.
- I c e c a s t / I c e c a s t 2 / S H O U T c a s t / WindowMedia streaming support including relaying from external sources.
- Support for all popular media players, WinAmp, XMMS etc.
- Fully decentralized - any PeerCast client can be used to setup a private relay or provide connection bases to the main network.
- Security settings to control access rights for Connections/Broadcasting/Admin etc.
- IP address filtering and banning.
- Custom settings to limit bandwidth and the number of connections in/out.
- Does not require incoming ports to be configured.

- Full support for ICY-Metadata (MP3) and OGG Vorbis comment headers for title/artist/song display.
- One-click play for any channel straight from the Taskbar icon.
- Favorite channels list allowing almost instant reconnection to your channels.
- Freeware, not ad/spy ware.
- Open source.
- Now includes OggCap - Video broadcasting tool.

Architecture

In Peercast, the peers are organized as tree architecture to provide the multicast service. The tree overlay is self-organized, source-specific that is maintained as nodes join and leave. The group members are arranged at different levels of a multicast tree rooted at the sources. Each node n (including source s) forwards the stream to all its immediate children (if any). Effectively each node acts as a multicast router, replicating and forwarding packets. Note that the resulting topology is a tree overlay: the actual forwarding paths in the underlying physical network may not be a tree, as shown in Figure 3 (adapted from (Mayank Bawa et al., 2003).

In Peercast, a basic P2P infrastructure layer, called peering layer, is introduced between the application and the transport layers for streaming. All communication between application and transport layers passes through the peering layer, as shown in Figure 4 (adapted from (Mayank Bawa et al., 2003)). The peering layer exists below the end application and is a placeholder for policies that govern topology maintenance.

There are two kinds of sessions in Peercast, data transfer session and application session. **Data transfer sessions** are established between two peers in the peering layers. Such two peers are identified by their IP-addresses, ports, and stream URL. IP-address and port identify the transport peers involved in the session. Stream URL serves

Figure 3. Multicast tree overlay

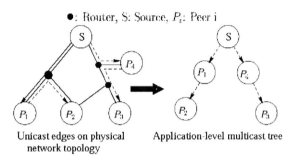

Figure 4. Peercast architecture

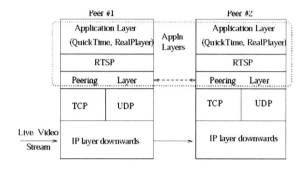

to identify the specific stream data is intended for. **Application sessions** are established between the peering layer and the upper application layer. Intuitively, the application layer is the software application interface, that notifies the peering layer to obtain which stream, through a "get-stream" message. Then, the peering layer lookups a peer which can provide the stream, and establishes a data-transfer session with the peer. To prevent session failure, Peercast locates some other peers for data feed. If an alternate peer cannot be found, an error is returned to the application layer.

Development Information

PeerCast is licensed under the terms of the GPL license, users are free to download, modify and distribute it as long as they agree to the terms of the GPL.

- The latest development version of PeerCast (The latest trunk version may not be in a working state) can be accessed via an anonymous read-only SubVersion repository: svn://peercast.org/peercast/trunk
- Older versions are available here: svn:// peercast.org/peercast/tags

Mesh-Based Systems

Introduction

As mentioned above, to send live media from a source to a large population of users, IP multicast is probably the most efficient way. However it is not deployed for large-scale implementation due to practical and political issues. Then, researchers resort to application-level multicast solutions.

Mesh-based network is regarded as an improvement of tree-based overlay. While this kind of network works well with dedicated infrastructure routers as in IP multicast, it often mismatches an application-level overlay with dynamic peers. As the overlay peers can easily crash or leave at any time, a tree structure is highly vulnerable, which is further aggravated with streaming applications that have high bandwidth and stringent continuity demands. Therefore, researchers have paid more attention to sophisticated structures like mesh and forest, which can partially solve the problem in tree overlay.

In the more recent years, gossip-based (mesh-based) solutions have been proposed for P2P live streaming. In a mesh-based approach, there is no pre-defined structure of the nodes such as trees, no pre-defined role such as parent or child, and the path of the data delivery is not based on the hierarchical order, but are decided on real-time, based on the data availability.

Compared with tree-based approaches, there are less research papers available on gossip based approaches, but on the implementation side, gossip-based approaches are more active. For example, there are more than 10 P2P based Internet TV systems have been developed and deployed by the small start-ups in China, e.g. CoolStreaming (Xinyan Zhang, Jiangchuan Liu, Bo Li & Tak shing Peter Yum, 2005), PPLive (Yan Huang, Tom Z. J. Fu, Dah-ming Chiu, John C. S. Lui & Cheng Huang, 2008. PPLive, 2010), PPStream (PPStream, 2010), etc. Most of them adopted the gossip type of approaches.

Most of the above implementations are based on proprietary systems, and not too much public information is available, the following section will use CoolStreaming as an example to describe this family of implementations in general.

Case Study III: CoolStreaming

System Overview

CoolStreaming was mainly designed by Xinyan Zhang, from The Chinese University of Hong Kong, and several others as a research project, named DONet - A Data-driven Overlay Network for live media streaming. On May 30, 2004, an Internet-based DONet implementation, called CoolStreaming was released for large-scale tests. This was the first successful implementation of P2P Internet TV, which has attracted over 30,000 distinct users with more than 4000 simultaneous use at some peak times. Unfortunately, due to copyright infringement issues, this service was shut down on June 10, 2005.

For the technical reasons with the IP multicast and the tree-based Application Layer Multicast, designers of CoolStreaming system have employed a Data-driven Overlay Network for live streaming media streaming. It does not maintain an explicit overlay structure, but adaptively forwards data according to data availability and demanding information. There are no prescribed roles like

Figure 5. A generic system diagram for a Cool-Streaming node

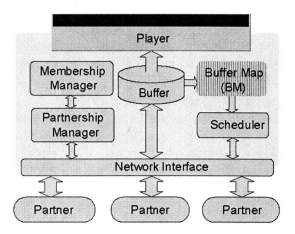

parent/child, internal/external, and upstreaming/downstreaming, etc.

The core operations in CoolStreaming are simple, every peer (node) periodically exchanges data information with a number of partners. Then partners are acquainted with the status of each other and can retrieve unavailable data from some partners.

CoolStreaming adopted the gossiping protocol for control message delivery and organize its mesh-based overlay. However, using gossip protocol might cause some problems for streaming service because its random push may cause significant redundancy. CoolStreaming addresses these problems with a smart partner selection mechanism and a low-overhead scheduling algorithm to intelligently pull data from multiple partners, which greatly reduces redundancy. Besides, membership and partnership management is also proposed to cooperate with scheduling and partner membership. All of these two algorithms are described below.

Figure 5 (adapted from (Xinyan Zhang et al., 2005)) depicts the system diagram of a Cool-Streaming node. There are four key modules:

- Membership manager - helps the node maintain a partial view of other overlay nodes
- Partnership manager - establishes and maintains the partnership with other nodes
- Buffer Map (BM) - a video stream is divided into segments of uniform length, and the availability of the segments in the buffer of a node is represented by BM
- Scheduler - schedules the transmission of video data

Protocol

Membership Management. Each node maintains a membership cache (mCache) containing a partial list of the other active node. A key practical task in CoolStreaming is how to create and update its mCache. To accommodate overlay dynamics, each node periodically generates/distributes a membership message to the others to announce its existence, based on the Scalable Gossip Membership protocol (SCAM). Upon receiving the membership message, the receiving node updates its mCache entry for the sending node, or creates the new entry it not existing.

Partnership Management. Based on gossip protocol, each node periodically establishes new partnerships with nodes, which are randomly selected from the mCache. Thus the partnership list is always a subset of the membership list.

Node Joining Mechanism. In CoolStreaming joining mechanism, a newly joined node first contacts the origin node. This origin node randomly selects a deputy node from its mCache and redirects the new node to the deputy. The new node can then obtain a list of candidates from the deputy and contacts these candidates to establish its partners.

Node Departure Algorithm. There are two kinds of node departure, graceful departure and node failure. **Graceful departure**: the departing node issues a departure message. **Node failure:**

By checking the status of each partner when a message arriving, it is easy to detect the failures and replace the failure nodes through ordinary gossip messages or searching some new nodes.

Data Delivery. As mentioned before, neither the partnerships nor the data transmission directions are fixed in CoolStreaming. Specifically, a video stream is divided into several segments of uniform length. The availability of the segments of a node can be represented by a Buffer Map (BM) which is represented by 0/1. Each node continuously exchanges its BM with its partners, and then decides which segment should to be scheduled.

Scheduling Algorithm. CoolStreaming's scheduling algorithm strikes to meet the requirement of the playback continuity, which is based on two constrains: the deadline for each segment and the heterogeneous streaming bandwidth from the partners.

CoolStreaming's algorithm first calculates the number of potential suppliers for each segment, and among the multiple potential suppliers, the one with the highest bandwidth and enough available time is selected.

In CoolStreaming, the segments to be fetched from the same supplier are marked in a BM-like bit sequence. These segments are then delivered in order through a real-time transport protocol. CoolStreaming does not specify a particular protocol, in its implementation, it adopted the TCP-Friendly Rate Control (TFRC) protocol.

Deployment

CoolStreaming application contains 2000 lines of Python source codes. It streams Real Video and Windows Media formats, but can accommodate other streaming formats as long as they are supported by user-side players. Furthermore, its implementation is platform-independent, and thus can be used under Unix, Windows, or other OS supporting Python and the corresponding video decoder.

CoolStreaming has broadcasted live sports programs (450Kbps - 755Kbps RealVideo/Windows Media format) over the Internet, and the source is a free video server. The capacity of the server is very limited. Using the traditional Client-Server setup, this server cannot support many users and will get over-loaded easily. But by utilizing CoolStreaming's P2P architecture, it supported more than 4000 users simultaneously during some peak time. If the server were directly serving these users, it would require a 3Gbps outbound bandwidth, which is unbelievably difficult for state-of-art access technologies.

CoolStreaming has observed some interesting facts from their deployment experiences:

- The current Internet has enough available bandwidth to support TV-quality streaming (>= 450 kbps)
- It confirms their speculation that the limited processing capabilities and outbound bandwidths of video servers, while not necessarily the backbone network, are slowing down the deployment of streaming services over the Internet.
- The larger the data-driven overlay is, the better the streaming quality it delivers CoolStreaming speculate that it is because the degree of cooperation increase with larger overlays, as each node has more flexibilities to locate better partners using their partner refinement algorithm.

Roadmap. In 2005, CoolStreaming planned to add the VoD functions, according to them, in a data-driven design, the data availability information can effectively help a node locate the appropriate partners for such VCR functions as fast-forward, backward, or random-seek. Embedding these functions in CoolStreaming thus could be easier than in a structure-based overlay.

CoolStreaming also was working on simplifying the membership management and the scheduling algorithms, to reduce the overhead.

Another roadmap item is to improve the robustness and adaptability of the system by splitting the streaming into several sub-streams.

Additional Information. CoolStreaming started as an academic research project, and was successfully implemented over the Internet, but it was later shut down due to copyright infringement issues. Since then, CoolStreaming has worked on transitioning into a commercial model.

In June 2005, Roxbeam Media Network Corp. was formed, after receiving funding from Softbank, the chief researcher of CoolStreaming become CTO of Roxbeam, CoolStreaming was officially turned into commercial.

Roxbeam currently provides its P2P technology to operators and content providers in Japan (Softbank BB, Yahoo BB) and U.S. (Comcast). It has also created a web2.0 type of on-line community for users to share their multimedia experiences (video, music, picture, etc.).

P2P VIDEO-ON-DEMAND STREAMING

Overview

A near-VOD capability would enable the users to watch the video right away, and have the flexibility to watch the video at any arbitrary time, i.e., users do not need to synchronize their viewing times as in live media content distribution. Also, the users can watch any part of the video, i.e., they will be able to perform operations like rewind and fast-forward on the video file.

Compared with the progress made in the P2P live streaming domain, the technology advancement in the P2P on-demand streaming area is relatively slower. This is due to the high complexity of the system design to achieve the VOD requirements: The user will be able to watch the video right away, and the users will have the flexibility to watch the video at any arbitrary time, i.e., users do not need to synchronize their viewing times as in live media content distribution. Also, the users can watch any part of the video, i.e., they will be able to perform operations like rewind and fast-forward on the video file.

A few early proposals were made by the researchers in the U.S. Universities: GnuStream (Purdue U.) (Xuxian Jiang, Yu Dong, Dongyan Xu & B. Bhargava, 2003, p325), P2Cast (U. of Mass. at Amherst) (Yang Guo, Kyoungwon Suh, Jim Kurose & Don Towsley, 2003, p301), PROMISE/CollectCast (Purdue U.) (Mohamed Hefeeda, Ahsan Habib, Boyan Botev, Dongyan Xu & Bharat Bhargava, 2003, p45), P2VoD (U. of Central Florida) (Tai T. Do, 2004, p1467), oStream (U. of Illinois, Urbana) (Yi Cui, Baochun Li & K. Nahrstedt, 2004), etc. Most of these projects are at research stage, there is no large scale implementation.

Most of these proposals are similar to P2P live streaming, relying on application layer multicast. But since in on-demand streaming, the nodes can join at any time, at the beginning, during the middle, or at the end of a program, and the user should be able to capture the missing initial portion of the video. This means the buffering capability of each node becomes very important.

Starting this year, some Internet based P2P VoD implementations are emerging from China, a few examples are Dragoncast, Girdcast (Bin Cheng, Lex Stein, Hai Jin, Xiaofei Liao & Zheng Zhang, 2008), etc. Currently most of these systems are still at the experiment stage, and most of the implementations are proprietary. It is unknown whether these systems are similar to the university research proposals that are listed above.

The following sections will give a few examples of P2P on-demand streaming university research projects.

Tree-Based Systems

Case Study IV: P2Cast

System Overview

In order to meet the challenge of providing VoD service over the Internet in a scalable way, Yang Guo and a few others at Dept. of Computer Science, University of Massachusetts at Amherst proposed the P2Cast architecture. It uses a peer-to-peer approach to cooperatively stream video using patching techniques. It is an extension of Patching, with the exception that a late client can get a patch not only from the server (as in original Patching) but also from other clients.

Traditional VoD service uses client-server architecture and employs unicast model. Each client sets up connection with the server to establish a unicast channel. As the video popularity increases, the server soon becomes the bottleneck. The question of how to best provide VoD service to a large number of clients in a scalable manner remains to be solved.

Some approaches have been proposed in the past for VoD service to accommodate the scalability issues. IP multicast has been explored to enhance the efficiency of one-to-many and many-to-many communication over the Internet. Then, a series of IP Multicast-based schemes, such as Patching, Periodic Broadcast, and Stream Merging, have been developed that can drastically decrease the aggregate bandwidth requirement at the server by leveraging the native IP multicast. Unfortunately, as mentioned above, IP multicast has not been widely deployed due to practical and political issues. On the other hand, in P2P network, individual uses bring computation and storage resources into the system, which reduces the workload on the server and thereby increases the overall scalability.

Whether Patching and P2P can be integrated to tackle the scalability issue faced by the VoD service is an intriguing technical question. P2Cast

Figure 6. An example of P2Cast

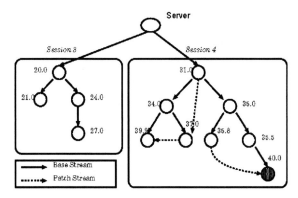

tries to answer that question. In P2Cast, clients (peers) arriving close in time (within a threshold) form a session. **For each session**, the server, together with the clients, form an application-level multicast tree. This tree overlay is built on the unicast-only network. The entire video steam is delivered over the application-level multicast tree, so that it can be shared among peers. For peers who arrive later than the first peer in the session and thus miss the initial part of the video, the missing part can be retrieved from the server or other peers that have already cached the initial part. The peers in P2Cast are "active" in the sense that they can forward the video stream to other peers, and also serve the initial part of the video to other peers. Every P2Cast peer actively contributes its bandwidth and storage space to the P2Cast system while taking advantage of the resources from other peers.

P2Cast is not a simple extension of patching mechanism. The following issues need to be properly addressed before patching can be successfully applied.

- Constructing the application overlay appropriate for streaming. An application-level multicast tree having sufficient bandwidth to transmit the stream must be constructed. In addition, when a new client arrives, P2Cast needs to select a patch server that can serve the missing initial part of the video.

- Providing continuous stream playback (without glitches) in the face of disruption from departing clients. When clients leave the application overlay, P2Cast needs to overcome disruptions due to early departures by restructuring the application overlay.

In P2Cast, the peers not only receive the requested stream, but also contribute to the overall VoD service by forwarding the stream to other peers and serving the initial part of the stream. P2Cast peers arriving within a time threshold constitute a session. Together with the server, peers belonging to the same session form an application-level multicast tree, denoted as the base tree. The server delivers the entire video steam over the base tree. This complete video stream is denoted as the base stream. When a new peer joins the session, it joins the base tree and retrieves the base stream from it. Meanwhile, the new peer must obtain a "patch" - the initial part of the video from the start of the session to the time it joined the base tree. The new peer obtains the patch from the server or another peer. P2Cast peers provide the following two functions:

- Base Stream Forwarding. P2Cast clients need to be able to forward the received base stream to other clients so that clients and the server can form an application-level multicast tree over which the base stream is transmitted.
- Patch Serving. P2Cast clients need to have sufficient storage to cache the initial part of the video. A P2Cast client can then serve the patch to other clients

Figure 6 (adapted from (Yang Guo et al., 2003, p301)) illustrates an example of P2Cast. It illustrates a snapshot of P2Cast at time 40.

It shows two sessions, session 3 and session 4, starting at time 20.0 and 31.0, respectively, with the threshold equal to 10.

The server and the peers in a session form an application-level multicast tree to deliver the base video stream. At time 40, all peers in session 3 have finished the patch retrieval while three peers in session 4 are still in the process of receiving the patch stream. The peers belonging to different sessions are independent of each other.

Protocol

New client admission. A new peer first contacts the server, which allows the VoD service provider to keep track of the peers. All peers arriving within the time threshold form a session. A new peer that cannot join the most recent session starts a new session. The server deliveries the entire video stream to this new peer.

If the new peer belongs to an already existing session, it tries to join this session's base tree. Meanwhile, the new peer tries to select a patch server in its session that can deliver the patch to it. If the new peer successfully joins the base tree and selects a patch server, it is admitted.

Tree construction. P2Cast employs the tree structure to construct its overlay. For a new peer, the joining process mentioned above starts with the server. Streaming media service requires a minimum amount of available bandwidth from a parent node to a child node. The server measures the available bandwidth from itself to the new peer, and decides whether this peer can be its child node. If the server admits the new peer, this peer joins the base tree and receives the base stream from the server. Otherwise, the server redirects the new client to one of its existing child peers, denoted as candidate peer. The candidate peer makes its own decision as to whether to admit this new peer to be its child node. If not, the new peer further re-directed to its child node. The process continues recursively until the peer successfully joins the tree overlay, or is rejected.

Patch server selection. A patch server serves the patch to a new peer. Except for the first client in a session who receives the entire video (base stream) from the server, all other peers who miss the initial part of the video and will require a patch. A new peer needs to select a patch server who can unicast the patch to it.

Failure Recovery. P2Cast provides two types of failure recovery: *base stream recovery* and *patch recovery.*

In terms of base stream recovery, suppose peer A is disrupted by a failure. Due to the tree structure, all peers rooting from A are affected by the failure. For the sake of simplicity and to prevent the server from receiving a large number of recovery messages, P2Cast only allows peer A to contact the server to perform recovery. The recovery process is similar to that of a new peer joining system except that only the base stream is required.

Simulation experiments show that P2Cast scales much better than traditional client-server unicast VoD service, and generally out-performs the multicast-based patching if clients can cache more than 10% of stream's initial part.

Other Examples

P2VoD

P2VoD (peer-to-peer approach for VoD streaming) is a proposal made by a few researchers at University of Central Florida.

In P2VoD, asynchronous requests of peers are handled by utilizing the peers' resources. Each P2VoD peer has a FIFO buffer to cache the most recent content of the video stream it receives. Existing peers can forward the video stream to a new peer as long as they have enough out-bound bandwidth and still hold the first block of the video file in the buffer. The concepts of generation and a novel caching scheme are introduced to deal effectively with failures.

P2VoD is similar to P2Cast, but is different in a couple of ways. First, peers in P2VoD always cache the most recent content of the video stream, while P2Cast peers only cache the initial part of the video. Furthermore, only one stream from an early peer is needed to serve a late peer in P2VoD, while two such streams in P2Cast. Besides, P2Cast has to get the source involved whenever a failure occurs, thus vulnerable to disruption due to server bottleneck at the source. In addition, orphaned peers reconnect by using the join algorithm resulting in long blocking time before their service can resume. On the contrary, in P2VoD, failures are handled locally and most of the times without involvement of the source.

HON

HON (Ming Zhou & Jiangchuan Liu, 2005, p1309), A Hybrid Overlay Network is a proposal made by researchers at Simon Fraser University in Canada.

It constructs and maintains two overlays, a tree overlay and a gossip overlay, which collectively deliver video contents to clients of asynchronous demands. In particular, most data segments are delivered through the gossip overlay, only if a node fails to receive a data segment till certain deadline, will it resort to the tree overlay to fetch the segment from its parent. Intelligent and efficient overlay construction and data scheduling algorithms are designed to facilitate streaming in this hybrid system.

HON has combined the best features of tree structure and gossip's random message dissemination: low delay with a regular tree topology, and robust delivery with random switching among multiple paths, which makes effective use of the available bandwidth in the network.

Mesh-Based Systems

Case Study V: PPLive

System Overview

PPLive is a peer-to-peer streaming video network created in China. PPLive was born from a University project in 12/2004, and the first version of Internet shareware was made available online in 01/2005. PPLive has a strong partnership with Synacast, which is a commercial company. Originally, PPLive is only for live streaming, especially online TV programs. With PPLive, everyone can become a broadcaster without the cost of traditional streaming infrastructure. The more users are online, the faster the TV programs can start. PPLive can download stream data from different connection nodes and can automatically find the nearest nodes for downloading stream data. PPlive supports various stream data: mms, asf. TV channels are usually encoded at 400 kbps and up to 800 kbps.

Sine the fall of 2007, P2P-VoD service has been built and deployed by PPLive. By the end of November 2007, about 2.2 million independent users had tried the VoD service of PPLive. A total of 3900 movies has been published at the end of 2007, with around 500 movies on-line simultaneously. In late January 2008, the number of simultaneous users reached over 150,000 and was still growing.

Protocol

Piece Size. For a P2P system, a fundamental decision is to divide a video into several piece for transition. However, how to decide the suitable size of a segment is still a hot topic and challenge due to the conflicting requirements of overhead and schedule. According to the practical experience, PPLive designs three levels of segmentation of a video:

- Chunk: 2MB (unit for storage and advertisement)
- Piece:16KB (unit for playback)
- Sub-piece: 1KB (unit for transmission)

The size of piece is dictated by the media player and a size of 16KB is chosen. PPLive uses the WMV format for video encoding. In such format, as long as the source rate is less than 1.4 Mbps, 16KB segment will contain a viewable piece. However, the size of piece is still large for efficient scheduling of transmission. Therefore, sub-piece is used with the size of 1KB.

Piece selection. In PPLive, a peer uses *pull* method to download chunks from other peers and integrate two piece selection strategies:

- Sequential: select the piece which is just contiguous to the current piece.
- Rarest first: select the piece that is the rarest, which is clearly explained in BitTorrent protocol (BitTorrent, 2010. BitTorrentSpecification, 2010).

PPlive gives the first priority to sequential, then rarest-first. Actually, there is another popular piece selection mechanism: anchor-based which selects the closest anchor point if the piece for the jump location is missing. But PPLive does not use this method in the current deployment.

Cache Mechanism. There are two important storage or cache mechanisms named SVC (single-video cache) and MVC (multi-video cache). SVC means a peer only caches the current viewing video on the disk, while MVC can also cache multiple videos which have been watched before. PPLive uses MVC as its basic cache mechanism due to the flexibility of MVC. When the disk cache is full, how to remove the content which has been stored is the next consideration. In PPLive, once a movie has been chosen as the next one to view, all the chunks of the movie immediately become candidates for removal one by one. Doing it at a chunk level would incur more overheads (for

collecting necessary information about different chunks). How is the next video picked? The favorite choices by many caching algorithms are least recently used (LRU) or least frequently used (LFU). LRU is the original choice in PPLive VoD. After further studies, the simple LRU is replaced by a weight-based evaluation process.

DOWNLOAD-BASED STREAMING

Overview

Downloadable video is available on the Internet of both industrial and research producers of video content. There are numerous online services that allow users to download video content to a computer hard disk for viewing on a personal computer, television, or mobile video device. In October 2005, Disney's ABC and Apple's iTunes entered into a deal to offer current and past season episodes of ABC and Disney Channel television shows for download from Apple's iTunes Music Store for viewing on a PC or iPod video player. Another example, Movielink, a joint venture of Metro-Goldwyn-Mayer Studios, Paramount Pictures, Sony Pictures Entertainment, Universal Studios, and Warner Bros. Studios, offers movies, television shows, and other popular videos for download on a rental or purchase basis. Some other companies are planning to offer content distribution via the Internet as independent content producers. Akimbo (Akimbo, 2010), Google (GoogleTV, 2010), and Hulu (Hulu, 2010) provide an Internet-based distribution interface for content producers of all sizes.

Some content producers are offering their services directly to the users via Internet. For example, Strandvenice (Strandvenice, 2010) is an online reality channel which offers a 50-minute series episode for free and charges 99 cents for future 30-minute. Akimbo has partnered with producers and distributed videos directly to a subscriber's television using high-speed network. Its service is built on IP set-top box generating an on-screen guide which enables the subscriber to choose programming from a library of video selections.

Unlike memory cache streaming services, video download services enable user to view any video content downloaded in the disk and share more data with other devices or their community.

Actually, Download-based Streaming mainly focuses on Video-on-Demand (VoD) application, because VoD needs more data for schedule and viewing. We discuss this kind of streaming due to its different properties, especially storage mechanism and data schedule.

Case Study VI: CoolFish

System Overview

CoolFish (CoolFish, 2011) is a hybrid streaming system integrating both live streaming and VoD services in one platform. For live streaming service, CoolFish uses memory cache mechanism, which is similar to the traditional cache and replacement methods (LRU). As for VoD service, CoolFish designs download-based steaming (viewing as downloading). To simplify the cache system, CoolFish do not restrict the cache capacity in CoolFish. Which video should be deleted is totally decided by user himself.

CoolFish is mainly deployed in China Science and Technology Network (CSTNet), a nationwide network connecting about 200 research institutes of the Chinese Academy of Sciences and four campuses with more than 58,000 students. It has been very popular since released in CSTNet for most communication traffic locates in the same ISP according to our observation. From Oct. 2008 to Mar. 2010, there have been over 4.2 million user visits and the number of recent daily visits has exceeded 7000. Its users mainly come from 4 ISPs in China: CSTNet, CERNet, Telecom and Netcom. Our measurements show that 80% users come from CSTNet and CERNet. The remaining 20% users belong to Telecom and Netcom. At hot

Table 1. CoolFish system statistics from Oct. 2008 to Jun. 2010

Parameter	Value
Total number of visited users	≈4,800,000
Peak number of online users	>700
Server upload bandwidth	100 Mbps
Number of videos	>1000
Average video bit rate	700 Kbps
Average video length	1.2 hours
Average disk space contribution per peer	3 GB
Percentage of CSTNet and CERNet users	80%
Percentage of NAT users	22%

time, there are over 700 simultaneous viewers. CoolFish is able to support an average video bit rate of 700Kbps, which is about 50% higher than that of most commercial P2P-VoD systems with a video bit rate less than 450Kbps (PPStream, 2010. Zimu Liu, Chuan Wu, Baochun Li & Shuqiao Zhao, 2009). Table 1 presents the detailed log statistics of the system.

CoolFish is a mesh-based network just like BitTorrent system with over 80,000 lines of C++ codes in total. Figure 7 represents the general architecture of the CoolFish system. The whole system includes a set of servers and peers (end users). The function of each component can be understood by following the operation procedures (the numberings labeled from 1 to 7 in Figure 7) below.

Step 1: Peers report their programs (movies) information to Program Server, including video name, viewing progress, jump and pause position, startup and jump latency, and so on.

Step 2: Program Server writes the information into Database.

Step 3: Web Server reads the portal information from Database, shows the program list and online peers on the web site.

Figure 7. CoolFish architecture. The numberings of the operation procedures labeled from 1 to 7 are explained in the text.

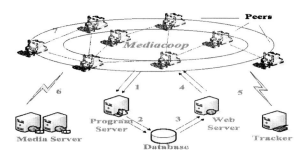

Figure 8. CoolFish user distribution in China (from Google analytics)

Step 4: Peers access the Web Server to browse the video information.

Step 5: Peers register themselves to the Tracker and gets the peer list.

Step 6: Media Server holds the full content of all the videos and provides them to the peers.

Step 7: Peers conduct content lookup using Mediacoop.

To guarantee the QoS (Quality of Services), a media content server is deployed in CoolFish to provide more than 1,500 videos. A peer will require data from content server if it can not get the data from other peers. When a peer joins the system, it can also share its local videos. There is another server in the system, Tracker, which is responsible for the control messages reported from peers every two minutes. The peers are distributed over 28 provinces in China, shown in Figure 8 from Google Analytics report (Google Analytics, 2010).

Protocol

Content Discovery

Besides the traditional tracker server, CoolFish designs a distributed content discovery method (called Mediacoop) combining both content and quality match to provide random jump service for P2P-VoD service. In this book, we mainly discuss this distributed method. Essentially, a distributed lookup is built on the P2P network overlay, which indexes the peers using routing information. Then, the lookup operation can be performed along the network overlay. Therefore, *how to construct an*

Figure 9. An example of playpoint overlay in CoolFish

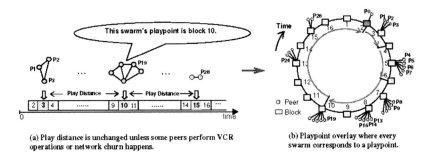

(a) Play distance is unchanged unless some peers perform VCR operations or network churn happens.

(b) Playpoint overlay where every swarm corresponds to a playpoint.

efficient overlay is the key fundamental framework for providing lookup service.

The lookup process in CoolFish is divided into two stages. In the first stage, CoolFish uses *unchanged playpoint distance* to locate the candidate suppliers with the required data block. Here *unchanged* means the viewers of the same video are expected to playback continuously and thus their playpoint distances do not change. The content of a video is segmented into *M* blocks and each block corresponds to a playpoint. CoolFish groups peers with the same playpoint into one swarm (see Figure 9 (a). Adapted from (Tieying Zhang, Jianming Lv & Xueqi Cheng, 2009, p486)). In view of the fact that the distance of playpoints is unchanged due to the constant playback rate for a given movie, CoolFish utilizes the distance of playpoints to index all swarms on a ring, called playpoint overlay (Figure 9(b)). Therefore, every swarm is acquainted with the status of each other even though they are moving on. A requester can easily find peers according to a Chord-like structured overlay (Ion Stoica, Robert Morris, David Karger, M. Frans Kaashoek & Hari Balakrishnan, 2001, p149). The difference is that CoolFish uses the distance of playpoint rather than hash value, and the unchanged distance leads to no requirement for state update messages, which reduces huge communication overhead. If one viewer performs VCR operations (e.g., jump, stop, pause) or network churn happens, new playpoint updates will be triggered.

In the second stage, the candidates are indexed into a novel tree-like sub-overlay. Refined search is performed within the sub-overlay to efficiently find the "best" suppliers. Specifically, the results of the first stage are a series of *seed* peers, from which our goal is to find some peers who have low delay with the requester (*quality match*). Inspired by the delay detection approach which can get the AS level or IP prefix level delay table (Shansi Ren, Lei Guo & Xiaodong Zhang, 2006, p70), in the second stage, CoolFish index all the peers in the target swarm using their IP prefixes as a sub-overlay. Then CoolFish can find the peers with target IP prefix along the sub-overlay assisted by a delay table. The details about how to get the delay table without ISPs' help will be explained in the following section.

Storage and Schedule

Currently, a common practice in P2P-VoD is to use Single-Task Downloading (STD). In STD, as shown in Figure 10(a) (adapted from (Tieying Zhang, Sun Xianghui Li, Zhenhua & Xueqi Cheng, 2010)), only one video (task) is being downloaded at any time, where the downloading task is also the current viewing video. Intuitively, STD is a natural idea to download the viewing video. However, measurements have indicated that STD has long startup and jump delay which are typically on the order of 10 - 60 seconds. Particularly, a user always wants to watch some popular movies consecutively. For example, the

Figure 10. STD vs. MTD

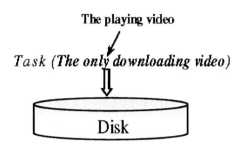

(a). Single-Task Downloading (STD)

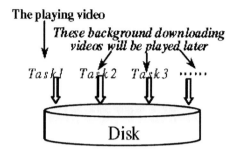

(b). Multi-Task Downloading (MTD)

top 3 popular movies are all the favorites for a user and he will watch them all. The switch delay of 10 - 60 seconds is certainly unacceptable, as users are used to the delays of less than 3 seconds when switching videos and channels.

Furthermore, lot of bandwidth is idle in STD. Only one downloading video usually can not make full use of peer download and upload bandwidth to share media data. Taking the home network ADSL for example (which is referred as low-bandwidth network), the download bandwidth is usually 2 - 4 Mbit/s (Mbps) and the bit rate of a video is 350 Kbps - 500 Kbps for most P2P-VoD systems. Therefore, only one video being downloaded can only take about 1/12 - 1/10 of download bandwidth. The "bandwidth waste" is more serious in high-bandwidth network, such as ADSL2+ and campus network. ADSL2+ is widely deployed throughout Europe and North America, and some other countries in the world. It can be as high as 24 Mbps downstream and 3.5 Mbps upstream bandwidth. As for the video bit rate of 500 Kbps, it is only about 1/50 of the download bandwidth and 1/7 of the upload bandwidth. That is to say, most of the bandwidth has been wasted in STD.

CoolFish proposes a cross-video downloading scheme, which is referred to as Multi-Task Downloading (MTD). MTD allows the user to download other videos (tasks) in parallel with his current viewing video, shown in Figure 10(b). The so-called "other" tasks are totally decided by the user himself, so they are also the candidate videos to be played sooner or later. When a peer switches from the current viewing to the background task, the startup content has been downloaded on the disk, so the new video can often be played at once. This advantage significantly decreasing the startup delays when switching videos.

This mechanism can also improve the jump latency and playback continuity. Assume that if the video has been totally downloaded, any jump latency is 0 second. In MTD, when a user starts to watch the background video, the video data has been totally or partially cached on the disk. When this user jumps to a new position in the video, the data is likely to be cached. Therefore, MTD can decrease the jump latency to some extent and the already prefetched data can also improve the playback continuity.

Multi-Task Downloading is a natural idea to utilize the free bandwidth. In MTD, besides the current viewing video, a user can also select candidate videos downloading in the background. As shown in Figure 10(b), task 1 is the current playing video, and the other tasks being downloaded in the background are selected by the user.

Some people might ask what videos are selected for background download. The most favorable way is to predict which video a user will pick next.

However, such prediction is difficult when there are many channels (videos). Instead, in CoolFish, the background tasks are totally decided by user himself. It is imaginable that these background tasks are selected according to the user's interest. Thus, these videos will be played sooner or later. When the user switches video, because the data is already prefetched, it can be played immediately without delay.

DISCUSSION OF FUTURE WORK

P2P media streaming applications enables a source to distribute real-time video to a large population of hosts by making use of their forwarding capacity rather than relaying on dedicated media servers, which is typically useful for large content distribution events, such as live streaming, Video-on-Demand service, etc.

However, it is an open question whether P2P technologies are suitable for video streaming services. The major challenge is the complete lack of performance guarantees in the P2P network. Peers might be turned off or disconnected at any time without prior notice, while other peers join or re-join. Such a highly unreliable network fabric poses a major difficulty for media streaming. Furthermore, the application requirement of streaming is different with that of file sharing. For example, in a VoD system, peers are in different parts of a video at the same time, which dilutes their ability to help each other and offload the server. Additionally, the random access and jump also make it harder to be optimized than the traditional content delivery systems due to the difficulty of peer lookup. Especially for the ISPs who provide paid IPTV service, the QoS (Quality of Services) of the video is significantly important. Whether using P2P streaming approach is able to guarantee the QoS for the ISP's requirement is not sure according to the current studies. Some measurements have show that P2P streaming suffers from long startup delays usually on the order of 1-2 minutes, instability, and their streaming quality is not yet a threat to standard definition TV. Such delays are certainly unacceptable, as users are used to the delays of less than 3 seconds when starting and switching videos and channels.

Therefore, how to design an efficient P2P streaming mechanism to match the high quality QoS requirement is vitally important, especially for its practicability for the ISP's implementation. Generally, the key design issues of P2P streaming involve three fold: peer lookup, data schedule and content store. 1) Peer lookup. The essential difference between P2P and the traditional client/server is that a requester obtains data from other peers instead of the server. Therefore how to efficiently find the good supplying peers is the fundamental requirement. Here "good" means the supplying peers should meet not only content match but also network quality match. 2) Data schedule. After obtaining the good supplying peers, how to efficiently exchange data is the next key issue, which we refer as data schedule. Data schedule in P2P network is a typically distributed scheme. It involves supplying peers selection and data request. Especially for P2P streaming application, its high real-time property requires peers should obtain data as soon as possible. 3) Content store. This issue is not a new topic in the field of distributed computing. However, it is challenging to design a good content store approach for P2P steaming due to its high dynamic and real-time property. For example, we might only need to consider data backup in CDN network which is based on stable servers; but such design is not enough in P2P streaming systems because the service provider can not control the peers' behavior. Content is the basis for peer lookup and data schedule. Therefore, a good content store design is very useful for P2P streaming systems.

REFERENCES

Akimbo. (2010). Retrieved from http://www. akimbo.ca/

Bawa, M., Deshpande, H., & Garcia-Molina, H. (2003). Transience of peers & streaming media. *SIGCOMM Computer Communication Review, 33*(1), 107–112. doi:10.1145/774763.774780

Bhattacharjee, B. (2010). *NICE.* Retrieved from http://www.cs.umd.edu/projects/nice/

BitTorrent. (2010). Retrieved from http://www. bittorrent.com

BitTorrent Specification. (2010). Retrieved from http://wiki.theory.org/bittorrentspecification

Castro, M., Druschel, P., Kermarrec, A. M., Nandi, A., Rowstron, A., & Singh, A. (2003). High-bandwidth content distribution in a cooperative environment. In *IEEE IPTPS'03.* Splitstream. doi:10.1007/978-3-540-45172-3_27

Chawathe, Y. D. (2000). *Scattercast: An architecture for internet broadcast distribution as an infrastructure service.* PhD thesis.

Cheng, B., Stein, L., Jin, H., Liao, X., & Zhang, Z. (2008). Gridcast: Improving peer sharing for p2p VOD. *ACM Transactions on Multimedia Computing and Communication Applications, 4*(4), 1–31. doi:10.1145/1412196.1412199

Chu, Y. H., Ganjam, A., Ng, T. S., Rao, S. G., Sripanidkulchai, K., Zhan, J., & Zhang, H. (2004). *Early experience with an internet broadcast system based on overlay multicast.* In USENIX Annual Technical Conference.

Chu, Y. H., Rao, S. G., & Zhang, H. (2000). A case for end system multicast. In *SIGMETRICS '00: Proceedings of the 2000 ACM SIGMETRICS International Conference on Measurement and Modeling of Computer Systems,* (pp. 1–12). New York, NY: ACM.

CoolFish. (2011). Retrieved from http://www. cool-fish.org

Cui, Y., Li, B., & Nahrstedt, K. (2004). Ostream: Asynchronous streaming multicast in application-layer overlay networks. *IEEE Journal on Selected Areas in Communications, 22*(1), 91–106. doi:10.1109/JSAC.2003.818799

Deshpande, H., Bawa, M., & Garcia-Molina, H. (2001). *Streaming live media over a peer-to-peer network.* Technical Report 2001-30, Stanford InfoLab.

Do, T. T. (2004). P2vod: Providing fault tolerant video-on-demand streaming in peer-to-peer environment. In *IEEE International Conference on Communications 2004,* (pp. 1467–1472).

Francis, P. (2010). *YOID.* Retrieved from http://www.isi.edu/div7/yoid/

Google Analytics. (2010). Retrieved from http://www.google.com/analytics

Google TV. (2010). Retrieved from http://www. google.com/tv/

Guo, Y., Suh, K., Kurose, J., & Towsley, D. (2003). P2cast: Peer-to-peer patching scheme for VOD service. In *WWW '03* (pp. 301–309). New York, NY: ACM. doi:10.1145/775152.775195

Hefeeda, M., Habib, A., Botev, B., Xu, D., & Bhargava, B. (2003). Promise: Peer-to-peer media streaming using collectcast. In *MULTIMEDIA '03* (pp. 45–54). New York, NY: ACM.

Hua, K., Tran, D., & Sheu, S. (2003). Zigzag: An efficient peer-to-peer scheme for media streaming. In *INFOCOM 2003.* IEEE.

Huang, Y., Fu, T. Z. J., Chiu, D.-M., Lui, J. C. S., & Huang, C. (2008). Challenges, design and analysis of a large-scale p2p-VOD system. *ACM SIGCOMM Computer Communication Review, 38*(4), 375–388. doi:10.1145/1402946.1403001

Hulu. (2010). Retrieved from http://www.hulu. com

Jannotti, J., Gifford, D. K., Johnson, K. L., Kaashoek, M. F., & O'Toole, J. F., Jr. (2000). Overcast: Reliable multicasting with an overlay network. In *OSDI'00: Proceedings of the 4th conference on Symposium on Operating System Design & Implementation*, Berkeley, CA, USA, USENIX Association.

Jiang, X., Dong, Y., Xu, D., & Bhargava, B. (2003). Gnustream: A p2p media streaming system prototype. In *ICME '03: Proceedings of the 2003 International Conference on Multimedia and Expo*, (pp. 325–328). Washington, DC: IEEE Computer Society.

Kostic, D., Rodriguez, A., Albrecht, J., & Vahdat, A. (2003). Bullet: High bandwidth data dissemination using an overlay mesh. *SIGOPS Operation Systems Review*, 37(5), 282–297.

Liu, Z., Wu, C., Li, B., & Zhao, S. (2009). *Distilling superior peers in large-scale P2P streaming systems*. In IEEE INFOCOM 2009. Nicolosi, A. (2003). *P2pcast: A peer-to-peer multicast scheme for streaming data*. In 1st IRIS Student Workshop (ISW03).

Padmanabhan, V. N., & Sripanidkulchai, K. (2002). The case for cooperative networking. In *IPTPS '01: Revised Papers from the First International Workshop on Peer-to-Peer Systems*, (pp. 178–190). London, UK: Springer-Verlag.

Padmanabhan, V. N., Wang, H. J., Chou, P. A., & Sripanidkulchai, K. (2002). Distributing streaming media content using cooperative networking. In *NOSSDAV'02: Proceedings of the 12th International Workshop on Network and Operating Systems Support for Digital Audio and Video*, (pp. 177–186). New York, NY: ACM.

PPLive. (2010). Retrieved from http://www.pplive.com

PPStream. (2010). Retrieved from http://www.ppstream.com

Ren, S., Guo, L., & Zhang, X. (2006). ASAP: An as-aware peer-relay protocol for high quality VOIP. In *ICDCS '06* (p. 70). Washington, DC: IEEE Computer Society.

Stoica, I., Morris, R., Karger, D., Kaashoek, M. F., & Balakrishnan, H. (2001). Chord: A scalable peer-to-peer lookup service for internet applications. In *SIGCOMM '01* (pp. 149–160). New York, NY: ACM. doi:10.1145/383059.383071

StrandVenice. (2010). Retrieved from http://www.strandvenice.com/

YouTube. (2010). Retrieved from http://www.youtube.com

Zhang, T., Lv, J., & Cheng, X. (2009). Mediacoop: Hierarchical lookup for p2p-vod services. In *ICPP '09: Proceedings of the International Conference on Parallel Processing*, (pp. 486–493). Washington, DC: IEEE Computer Society.

Zhang, T., Xianghui, S., Li, Z., & Cheng, X. (2010). Multi-task downloading for p2p-vod: An empirical perspective. In *ICPADS'10: Proceedings of the 2010 International Conference on Parallel and Distributed Systems*, Shanghai, China. IEEE Computer Society.

Zhang, X., Liu, J., Li, B., & Yum, T. S. (2005). *Coolstreaming/donet: A data-driven overlay network for peer-to-peer live media streaming*. In IEEE Infocom'05.

Zhou, M., & Liu, J. (2005). A hybrid overlay network for video-on demand. In *IEEE International Conference on Communications*, Vol. 2, (pp. 1309 – 1313).

Chapter 4
Wireless Multimedia Content Distribution Architecture

Israel Pérez-Llopis
Universitat Politecnica de Valencia, Spain

Carlos E. Palau
Universitat Politecnica de Valencia, Spain

Manuel Esteve
Universitat Politecnica de Valencia, Spain

ABSTRACT

Wireless video streaming, and specifically IPTV, has been a key challenge during the last decade, including the provision of access to users on an always best connected basis using different wireless access networks, including continuous seamless mobility. There are different proposals including IP based video streaming, DVB-H, or MediaFLO to carry out IPTV and video streaming on demand to users in a wireless environment, but one of the most relevant elements is the architecture of the service, with all the components of the delivery process. In this work the authors propose an alternative architecture based on a wireless Content Delivery Network, optimized to distribute video to mobile terminals in order to create a triple screen platform; considering that the main available wireless access networks are WiFi, WiMAX, and 3G, this work focuses on the last two. Surrogates within the CDN architecture act as video streaming servers, while the origin servers in the content providers carry out the transcoding process in order to be compliant with individual client requirements.

INTRODUCTION

There is an increasing demand for mobile users to access to live videos of sport events; TV programs; User Generated Content (UGC) or even movies through their handheld terminals (e.g. smartphones or tablet PC). However, since mobile terminals are diverse in resource and quality, ie: they have different screen sizes, computation powers, battery, and available network bandwidths, it is difficult to stream live video to those diverse mobile terminals efficiently in terms of provider's and user's benefits. For efficient live video streaming to heterogeneous mobile terminals, it is required

DOI: 10.4018/978-1-4666-1794-0.ch004

that each mobile terminal receives streamed video with the best quality within its capabilities and in the video format to easily play back the video with the most adequate QoS/QoE that could be provided(Ahmed, et. al., 2005).

3G wireless systems and WMAN WiMAX networks have been designed for advanced multimedia communications that can be enhanced with high quality voice, images and video. UMTS is among the first 3G mobile systems to offer wireless wideband multimedia communications over IP, used by different services (Agilent, 2006). Mobile IPTV is a technology that enables users to transmit and receive multimedia traffic including, video, audio, text and graphic services over core IP networks and heterogeneous wireless access networks with support for Quality of Service/Quality of Experience (QoS/QoE), security, mobility, and interactive functions, including mobile and nomadic users (Bonastre, O, 2009).

Wireless IPTV aims to make the traditional IPTV and related services available to users anywhere, anytime, on any device, and through any network. This goal requires advanced technology where networks, services, and content are highly adaptive, and thus able to respond to the needs of consumers in different use situations, accounting user's preferences and the limitations in capabilities of the mobile devices and networks. Additionally, there are usually no QoS guarantees available in currently used IP networks, which can cause big variations in the transmission capability of the network. In fixed networks this problem can be taken care of by over provisioning, but in wireless networks this is difficult. Also the mobility of the terminals affects the connection, especially if it includes switching from one network technology to another or between networks belonging to different administrative domains. (Braet et al, 2008; Cha, et al, 2006).

Basic components for adaptive media transmission over wireless networks are a source encoder, transmission unit, transport network, network monitoring mechanism, client and feedback or

control channel. The active parts in wireless IPTV service are (Cha et al, 2008; Etoh et al, 2005):

- The clients: The one choosing the program through a certain interface and receiving the media streams.
- The content providers: that can deliver the media either on demand or not
- The NOP: this entity is usually separate from the content providers. Its task is mainly co-ordination, control and charging.

Heterogeneous broadband networks, wired and wireless enable seamless mobility and multimedia session continuity to achieve the paradigm of Always-Best-Connected, e.g. with the interaction defined in IEEE 802.21 standard. Video streaming and particularly TV is becoming the service that justifies the deployment of more broadband networks as there could be revenue: operators may define new business models in order to deploy mobile video streaming TV (e.g. link between IPTV and social networks). (Taniuchi et al 2009; Monpetit et al 2009)

Media streaming over wireless links is a challenging problem due to both the unreliable, time-varying nature of the wireless channel and the stringent delivery requirements of media traffic. Recent advances in video compression and streaming as well as in wireless networking technologies (next-generation cellular networks and high-throughput wireless LANs), are rapidly opening up opportunities for media streaming over wireless links. However, the erratic and time-varying nature of a wireless channel is still a serious challenge for the support of high-quality media applications. To deal with these problems, different protocol architectures have been proposed (Li et al 2008). These proposals focus on the use of content distribution mechanisms adapted to wireless networks, trying to overcome the time-variations of the wireless channels, mobility, handovers, reduces bandwidth and mainly the non-multicast nature of certain IP networks. Web caching and

CDN are two of the main proposals available to such a system, and have proved in some previous works the improvement in performance.

In this chapter we propose such architecture in order to deploy a video streaming service which could be used to distribute Mobile IPTV, over heterogeneous wireless networks: 3G (UMTS and HDSPA) and different WLAN/WMAN network technologies like WiMax (IEEE 802.16) and WiFi (IEEE 802.11). The work analyses the possibility of using multihomed terminals to switch from one network to another in order to reduce cost of communications and improve bandwidth from 3G to WLAN (Braet et al, 2008; Lazaro et al, 2007). The architecture is based in the use of a CDN, with surrogates in the different access networks available, considering that independently of the technology the access network could belong to the same network operator, so they will share the same core IP network, or that they belong to different operators, using different core IP networks, different IP addresses prefixes and making mandatory the use of BGP as external gateway protocol, routing streams from one access network to another in case of roaming. (Molina et al, 2009).

BACKGROUND

Previous Work

IPTV provides digital television services over IP networks for residential and business users at a lower cost, as a convergence of communication, computing and content, as well as an integration of broadcasting and telecommunication. IPTV has a two-way interactive communications between operators and users, e.g. streaming control functions such as pause, forward, rewind, and so on, which traditional cable television services do not provide. Triple play is a package provided by service operators; it includes voice, video, and data, and is defined as quadruple play if mobility is considered. Video in MPEG2 or MPEG4 format

is delivered via IP unicast or multicast depending on the availability, other coding mechanisms like H.263 or H.264 are used in mobile networks, the main drawbacks are related with bandwidth and terminal capability, although both parameters are fast improving.(Ahmed et al, 2005)(European Commission, 2007) Current quality of IPTV does not yet approach that of cable TV services, but the gap will shrink as bandwidth increases and video codecs improve. In 2005, there were about four million homes in the world that already had IPTV, with Asia in the forefront.

Different companies like Microsoft or HP have developed IPTV products and distribution architectures, and operators like AT&T and Verizon in the US or HomeChoice (UK), Telefonica/Imagenio (Spain), France Telecom/ Maligne system and Neuf Telecom/Free (France), T-Home or Alice Home/Handsenet (Germany) are other proposals of IPTV systems recently announced. All these companies are making significant investments to deliver IPTV channels to residential customers, integrating heterogeneous content providers and operators with different infrastructures and back-office systems. Some challenges are related with long term stability and matching cable providers' quality of service (QoS). (Fortino et al, 2007) IPTV can be incorporated with high-speed DSL access technologies, including the emerging high throughput IEEE 802.11n WLAN and of course streaming in 3G and WiMAX networks (which is the main goal o this chapter) or the alternative of DVB-H. (Fröjdh et al,2006)

Another approach to IPTV, different from the infrastructure-based scheme introduced previously, is P2P-TV, in which each peer is potentially an additional server, multicasting received content to other peers. In a P2P IPTV system, users serve as peers and participate in video data sharing. Examples of P2P IPTV are PPLive, Joost, Zatoo, or BBC iPlayer. (Fröjdh et al,2006; Davies et al, 2009)

Regarding mobile IPTV, it has become increasingly popular in recent years. To support such systems, there are several mobile video

Figure 1. Architectures for mobile streaming content distribution

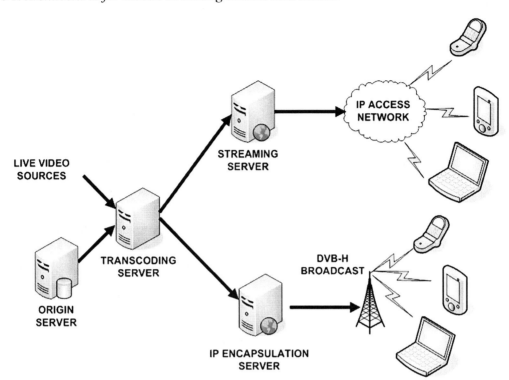

technologies using mainly versions of existing digital television broadcast formats. An alternative is the use of separate RF spectrum in next generation phones with a second radio receiver. The two existing alternatives are MediaFLO developed by Qualcomm and used in Verizon VCast, and DVB-H, supported by an alliance, including Motorola, Nokia and device manufacturers such as Intel, are the most popular, and more supported in Europe, with several deployed pilots. DVB-H was supported by traditional 3G vendors from the start, aiming at creating a technology that could be supported by many carriers and device vendors, as an adaptation of the DVB standard. (Ahmed et al, 2005)

Mobile video streaming using RTP/RTSP directly over IP can provide interoperability of terminals between 3G and WLAN/WMAN. Video streaming over 3G networks related technologies are H.264, MPEG4 SP and H.263 for Video and HE-ACC, AAC and AMR for audio. Figure 1 represents the main differences between mobile streaming and broadcast (e.g.DVB-H). For the latter a second radio receiver is needed. Different commercial products already exist like Darwin, Helix or Envivio. The IP Multimedia Subsystem) IMS has been used to develop IPTV architectures. IPTV functions have to be adapted to be supported by the IMS subsystem and employ these functions to allow reused IMS functions and also make service initiation and control based on SIP, (Hjelm, 2008)(ITU, 2009).

The proposed video streaming architecture is developed with COTS technology, based on a CDN structure in order to provide the best performance to the clients providing a three screen transmission system (mobile, fixed IPTV and InternetTV), simply transcoding the original video signal. The developed system can evolve to an IMS based system and even use other broadband wireless networks like WiMAX.(ITU, 2009)

Standardization

The background and related work of a mobile video streaming system, applicable to IPTV would not be complete without a review of the standardization efforts. There are several research and engineering organizations working in this area, like existing work of the ITU study groups, as well as standards-developing organizations, forum, and consortia; ITU formed the Focus Group on IPTV (FG-IPTV) in July 2006. The mission of FG-IPTV includes the study of the QoE/QoS aspects of IPTV. This has been assigned to Working Group 2 (WG2) of FG-IPTV, which is currently developing the following four documents for standardization in ITU-T: (FFMPEG, 2008; Jain, 2005)

- Quality of experience requirements for IPTV.
- Traffic management mechanism for the support of IPTV services.
- Application layer reliability solutions for IPTV.
- Performance monitoring for IPTV.

Recently there is a new ITU-T recommendation ITU-T H.770 about "Mechanisms for service discovery and selection for IPTV". The new recommendation, still under consent, deepens in the mechanisms for service provider discovery, service discovery and selection. Services such as linear TV and video-on-demand are addressed, with metadata that describes programming and delivery protocols detailed (Mas et al, 2007). This new recommendation expands the way a new service sharing and UGC culture evolving IPTV to a more cooperative and complex idea, stressed in the last years by the use of smartphones and tablet PC.

The development of Mobile IPTV specification is in an early stage. Currently, ITU-T FG IPTV is collecting requirements regarding mobility and wireless characteristics. (Alliance for Telecommunications Industry Solutions) ATIS has not shown any interest in mobility support yet. In the Open IPTV Forum, mobility service entirely based on IMS (IP Multimedia Subsystem) which is a set of specification from 3GPP for delivering IP multimedia to mobile users will be forthcoming. Open Mobile Alliance (OMA) BCAST is working for IP based mobile broadcasting networks, trying to define an end-to-end framework for mobile broadcast and compile the set of necessary enablers. Its features are bearer agnostic, which means any Broadcast Distribution Network can be adopted as its transport means, which is directly linked with the proposal of this work. (Jenkac et al, 2006) (Xiao et al, 2007)

Video streaming requires compatibility so as efficiency, so codecs are a key component. The most commonly used multimedia codecs in today's mobile TV services are H.264/AVC (Advanced Video Coding) MPEG-4 for video and High-Efficiency Advanced Audio Coding (HE-AAC)/MPEG-4 for audio. H.264 video provides notable quality and compression improvements over the previous mobile profiles in MPEG-4. Many standards use the MPEG-2 transport stream as a way to add service streams into a single carrier frequency. For example, the DVB, ISDB, and DMB families use this multiplexing technique. H.264/MPEG4 was recently standardized by the International Telecommunications Union-Telecommunication (ITU-T), and is designed to packetize the video data into real-time transport protocol (RTP), such that a substantial improvement over MPEG-2 performance, especially for both HDTV and VoD contents, can be obtained. The latest video coding schemes enable the same content to be encoded once while supporting heterogeneous transport conditions and end-user devices that allow the same content to be subscribed by home and mobile users at the same time with different types of device/communication media. (Zhao et al, 2009)

ADVANCES IN MOBILE VIDEO STREAMING CONTENT DISTRIBUTION

The convergence of television and mobile technology is an up-to-date topic in specialized literature as well on media. Opinions regarding the possible success of mobile television are rather opposite. Some authors see Mobile TV as a new media, very flexible highlighting the individual personal experience; others are less enthusiastic emphasizing the existence of competing standards with different leading vendors (e.g. DVB-H vs MediaFLO); high costs of network investments and licenses; the absence of clear insight into the customer demands and the advertisement strategies of the business model. (Agilent, 2006)

Mobile TV is only one of the modern technological trends expected to radically change conventional provisioning of broadcast services, where the client experience has been passive, but recently the content-consumption experience has moved toward increasing interactivity and active participation (e.g. mobile messaging or SetTopBoxes connected to the Internet). The use of advanced telecommunications technologies, mobile devices, social networking on the Web, and networked and electronic content for nomadic use emphasizes the consumers' role in the TV experience. (Zhou et al, 2009).

Mobile IPTV using mobile video streaming considers the advantages and also minimizes the highlighted disadvantages. The system proposed in this paper is one of the latter. Mobile television distinguishes three major alternatives: mobile TV broadcast, mobile TV streaming and Video-on-Demand. VoD is already on its way to define the adequate business model; while mobile TV broadcast and streaming are currently under deployment the first under a licensed procedure and the second unlicensed but with the main drawback of the cost of bandwidth consumption by the users.

The possible success of Mobile TV in any of its forms will be content availability and attractiveness. Content has been the key success factor of other media so, its influence in the success of Mobile TV has to be considered. Currently Mobile TV content is the same as for fixed TV or IPTV, while users of Mobile TV will use the system less time (e.g. short clips or sit-coms).

Mobile TV is still in the early stages of its use, systems and usage costs are still too expensive, use is still not too much spread, and there are usually problems depending on Telco facilities. Commercial-off-the-Shelf (COTS) low-cost system available for content providers and media companies are still not too much used. Triple screen systems are not currently deployed. The system proposed in this paper is a COTS IPTV streaming system, for fixed and mobile environments, considering different access networks like WLAN/WMAN or 3G. The system consider the existence of different terminals (PDA, phones, tablet PC, portable PC,…). There is a clear idea that scalable architectures to support video streaming distribution in mobile environments are needed, due to the increase in connected clients and multimedia content consumption rate, different proposals exist in the literature, including P2P and CDN based architectures.

WIRELESS CONTENT DISTRIBUTION NETWORK ARCHITECTURE

Mobile IP video streaming systems provide video services through the all-IP networks. Use of multicast in the access network, from the surrogates to the client, could improve performance and bandwidth saving. Usually the core IP networks do not provide multicast so connection from the production centers to the surrogates will mainly be unicast, additionally if two access networks are used BGPv4 routing protocol has to be used in order to achieve inter-domain multicast.

The proposed mobile media streaming platform (could be applied for IPTV systems) shown in Figure 2 consists in a media/transcoding server,

Figure 2. Basic mobile media streaming platform architecture

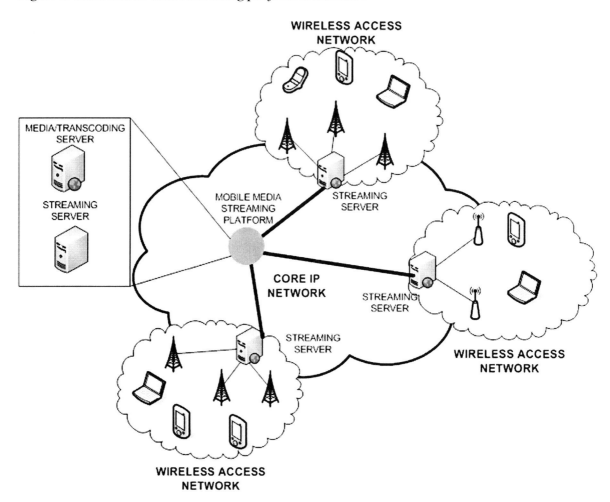

a video streaming server, core IP network, access networks, mobility management mechanisms, and video clients for different devices. The platform is built using off-the-shelf and custom components, but instead of being a static structure, new technologies such as applications, codecs, and protocols can be easily integrated into the platform. Delivering media to large numbers of mobile users presents challenges due to the stringent requirements of streaming media, mobility, wireless, and scaling to support large numbers of users. We propose a link between wireless networks and multimedia CDN technology in order to improve performance of the streaming system for mobile

users, having content closer improves latency and jitter. Mobile video streaming features include:

- Selection (users are able to select their TV programs with fast channel selection and short channel changing time), so as select video on demand reproductions.
- Storage (TV programs are stored in local storage devices so that users can watch them anytime; in mobile system storage facilities are limited).
- QoS/QoE (both must be guaranteed; a definition is limited by available bandwidth and screen size), these parameters are highly restrictive in wireless networks,

Figure 3. Functional diagram of the mobile streaming IPTV system

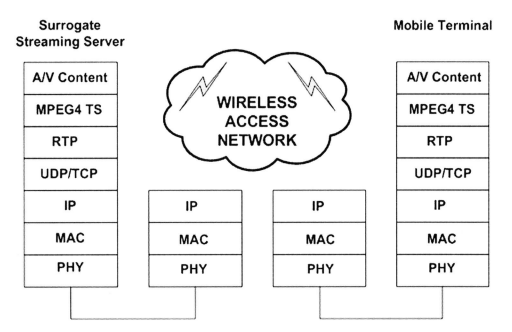

mainly if they are operated by a public network operator; this is the main reason to include a transcoding server in such a system.

- Low cost, due to COTS elements integration in the system

Functional block diagram of a mobile streaming system is illustrated in Figure 3. Video servers/encoders store audio/video (A/V) content which are encoded and compressed from live and pre-recorded programs. Video servers/encoders are either centralized or distributed in core networks, as we will present in the following section.

In such a system, A/V content from the source is formatted, compressed (e.g. MPEG-4 encoding) (Kerpez et al, 2006) and is encapsulated as real time transport protocol (RTP), compression and transport mechanisms vary more in mobile streaming systems due to bandwidth and screen size restrictions. This payload is transported as either user datagram protocol (UDP) in almost all multimedia traffic or transmission control protocol (TCP) datagram which in turn becomes the pay-

load for internet protocol (IP),and used in those systems as a transaction or control transport protocol, for service searching or contracting. The IP payload is encapsulated in the corresponding MAC layer protocol. The reversed process through said layers delivers A/V content for example to IPTV ready STB, PCs or handheld devices. One of the drawbacks of packet based video streaming is the overheads associated with each layer. (Kothari et al, 2005)

The architecture of the system is based in the utilization in a CDN-like architecture. Surrogates form a network overlay consisting of overlay servers on top of the existing network; these overlay servers are control points that facilitate end-to-end media delivery and mid-network media services, and they act as streaming servers to the clients. The mobile video streaming system is based on modular components that interact with one another (Figure 4). This modularity allows the system to be deployed incrementally over time in a manner that adapts to user, network, and system load, as new access networks are connected (Larribeau, 2006)(Lázaro et al, 2007).

Figure 4. Block diagram of components of the proposed streaming system

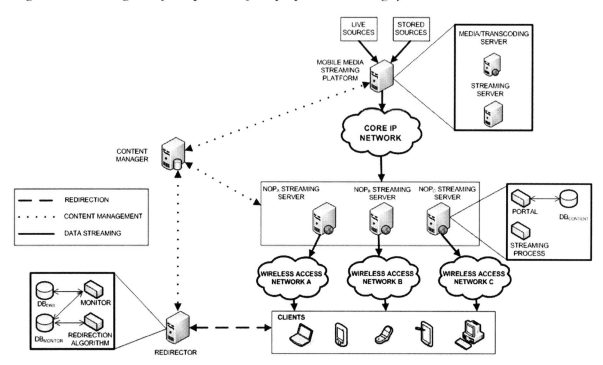

An end-to-end media delivery system must satisfy a number of system requirements. First, a system must be interoperable with existing infrastructure not adding more problems than solving old ones. Also, it must be flexible to allow customization for different system requirements (e.g. using a transcoding server in order to meet QoS requirements). Then, systems can be deployed incrementally, and adapted for evolving user and system usage patterns. Such flexibility is typically accomplished through modular design. Finally, it must be self-manageable or manageable to allow monitoring of system performance by network operators and users.

The main components of the architecture are the following:

- Media/Transcoding Server, included in the mobile media streaming cluster/platform.
- Streaming servers/surrogates, are the servers closer to the clients, the mobile media platform requires at least one to stream

content to the surrogates, it acts as the origin server in a CDN.

- Core IP network, is the distribution network, in Figure 4 it has been represented as belonging to one operator, but two core IP networks of several operator can be interconnected using the adequate routing protocols
- Access networks, typically they have been wired, but in the proposed architecture they are wireless and support mobility.
- Management servers, the most relevant are the redirector, which selects the most adequate streaming server for each request and the content manager which is in charge of controlling the stored contents

Media/Transcoding Server

This server is in charge of the capture and encoding of the media input e.g. a DVB receiver, external video camera, media file, or a network stream, it is

Table 1. Model of multimedia service profile

MULTIMEDIA SERVICE PROFILE: Static, Mobile, Pocket
-Service: Description of the multimedia service
-Video codec: H263,H264,MPEG-2,Xvid, etc.
-Video Bitrate: 50,100,200, 500, 1000, Variable
-Image Size: 177x144,320x240,352x288,640x480, etc.
-Frame Rate: 5,10, 15, 20, 25,30
-Audio codec: MP3,AAC,AMR, etc.
-Sample rate: 8000,16000,32000,etc.
-Audio Bitrate: 16,32,64,128, etc.
-Transmission: UMTS, HDSPA, ETHERNET,802.16x,802.11x,WAN
-QoS application level associated: 0,1,2,3

typically located in the origin server, but other alternatives like outsourcing are possible depending on the business model applied. The media server includes several codecs such as MPEG-2, Xvid, MPEG-4, H.263 or H.264 expanding the spectrum of the media purposes. For example, MPEG-2, Xvid.or some implementations of MPEG-4 would be suitable for video storing, broadcasting or VoD and a moderate access bandwidth, but not for real video sessions or current 3G networks, where H263 or h264 are more proper options. Hence, we can use real-time transcoding to change the coding parameters of the video stream, adjust spatial or temporal resolution, or change the video format. Furthermore, the media server includes an interface for controlling data by initializing and adjusting the video encoder parameters during the encoding. Transcoding is a CPU intensive operation; if there are several content providers more servers should be deployed. At the same time on transcoding server serves several Streaming Servers with the same content, establishing multicast or unicast links with them.

These servers will be connected to the media servers, which will be the ones who will serve requests from the clients, reducing consumed bandwidth. A key strategy for the architecture in order of keeping the best QoS and QoE possible for the wide range technologies the system is prepared

to is to implement several quality and codification profiles. One first approaching to this strategy is to define three archetypical profiles (Table 1):

- Static: designed for wired broadband access and tough networks
- Mobile: for WiFi and WiMAX, in devices like laptops and netbooks and finally
- Pocket: for personal devices with UMTS and HDSPA access (PDA, MP4 player, phones, and other PAN devices).

The goal is to generate simultaneously the profiles, transmitting them separately through the core IP network to the streaming servers obtaining redundancy, and better levels of QoS and QoE. Those profiles are, indeed, subject of on the fly adjusts of bit rate, frame rate and resolution, the transcoding server is in charge of this task.

Model presented define summarily the characteristics of the streams that are intended to broadcast. The main idea is design models accurately for the specific scenarios it is previewed to have and set a mechanisms of dynamic dialog between the media server and the streaming server to calibrate this profiles according the IP core network conditions (the way those elements are connected), and furthermore provide, with those profiles, a strong basis for make automatic stream handover

Table 2. QoS level of application table

QoS Level	Description
Level 0	Best effort, there is no QoS control in the transmission. Typically common Internet context
Level 1	Low loaded wireless (802.11x) networks, or broadband mobile networks (HDSPA,WiMAX) with QoS Mechanisms (Differentiated services, queuing techniques, topology proximity, etc.)
Level 2:	Wired, low loaded and over dimensioned networks
Level 3:	Wired private or corporative LAN with active QoS mechanisms (Differentiated services, queuing techniques, topology proximity, etc.

maximizing clients experience. There will be as many unicast connections between these servers and the streaming servers as available profiles.

The application levels of QoS of the table are indicative criteria of the expected state of the access network. Those states are working levels inside the protocol, considered for making decisions about the calibrations of the models and the stream handover in the streaming server. A clear example is that you won't use profiles whit QoS level 3 in a UMTS access network, because the main parameters of this profile will exceed its capabilities. Table 2 summarizes the available QoS levels.

Streaming Server/Surrogates

The streaming server supports several protocols such as RTP, HTTP, TCP, UDP or IPv6. The server streams the videos to the end users by using either unicast or multicast communication, where possible and available. The server receives the video streams from the media platform after being transcoded and distributes it to the different clients. The streaming server can be located at the same network as the transcoding server or can be deployed following a CDN structure in the different access networks in order to improve performance and reduce latency to the users. The Streaming server has different functional blocks; the two main components are the portal and the video streaming server. These two processes work in direct link with the data base of files.

Different Streaming Servers could rely on one Media Server, receiving the video streams coded with same coding parameters or different, depending on the QoS parameters of the network and the specific characteristics of the clients. The system consider one Streaming Server, acting as surrogate in each NOP Access Network, if one NOP had an increasing traffic new streaming servers could be included. Media Streaming involves the delivery of long continuous media streams, and desires highly predictable bandwidths, low delay, and preferably no losses. In particular, mid-stream disruption of a streaming session can be highly distracting.

Another key problem is supporting popular events via multicast or one-to-many communication. IP Multicast is currently not supported in the Internet, but other alternatives like ALM could be used, diverse clients requiring different bit rate versions of the same content can he supported by using scalable coding and sending different layers on different multicast trees if needed, although the proposed architecture does not include layered coding, on the contrary is supported by the transcoding servers. A use case of the mobile media streaming platform would allow unicast transmission over the core IP network using unicast and distributing through the wireless access network IPTV channels using multicast with clients joining the desired groups, this alternative is possible in WiFi, WiMAX and in 3G networks using MBMS.

Core IP Network

It connects the access networks to customer premises/origin servers it should be managed by a single entity for simplicity, but also exists the possibility of several interconnected core IP networks. Managed content is usually centralized and processed at the content provider premises before being delivered to different access networks. This network can be inexistent if the transcoding server is placed directly in the access network.

This is the proposal of our architecture, in order to reduce latency between the clients and the streaming servers and reduce the restriction of QoS experienced in these IP networks. When the streaming path involves both wired and wireless links the packet delivery time increases. The long round-trip delay and jitter reduces the efficiency of a number of end-to-end error control mechanisms. Additionally there is a high difficulty in inferring network conditions from end-to-end measurements, making difficult to deploy network selection algorithms and global monitoring tools. However, a wider range of choices for the unmanaged content by other content providers can be made, and the unmanaged content is fed into the national distribution network to the customers through the Internet.

The proposed architecture will avoid high bandwidth consumption in core IP network, Streaming Servers will be deployed closer to the users, so the Core IP Network will only support the transcoded video streams from the Media Servers to the Streaming Servers.

Access Networks

These is the critical part of the transport network and are used to reach each individual customer at his or her home through the STB or mobile terminal, in this work we focus on the latter. The most extended technologies available today are mainly wired like xDSL and coaxial hybrid fiber cable (HFC) or fiber techniques such as fiber-to-

the-node (FTTN), to extend the reach to customer communities before xDSL or cable wiring. But as technology improves, and deployment of new wireless networks provides more coverage WiMAX, High Speed WiFi and 3G are available options.

As access networks bandwidth uses to be limited, to cater to all of the customers for simultaneous access of the video streams, multicast has been widely adopted to enable a scalable delivery of video data streams, because it keeps bandwidth and minimize unnecessary packet duplication. A single transmission of each unique video data is shared among a group of clients who demand the same live content. Data is replicated only at appropriate branching locations, such as a regional edge router when it is necessary to fork another substream to reach another group of customers or an individual customer. Multicasting is mandatory in the access networks, multicasting in 3G networks can be provided by using the MBMS system, with a small modification in the UMTS/GSM networks.

The developed platform considers different access networks connecting the client devices to the Streaming Servers. These technologies are: IEEE 802.11g and pre-standard IEEE 802.11n wireless LANs, cellular 3G/HSDPA, and IEEE 802.16d and IEEE 802.16. Due to the restrictions in QoS and the deployment required for the system in a real environment the platform is focused on 3G networks as are intended to provide a global mobility with wide range of services including telephony, paging, messaging, Internet and broadband data.

Management Servers

The mobile streaming platform requires management in order to coordinate content location, distribution and access from the clients. Two management servers have been considered:

- Content Manager, which in charge of feeding the portals of the Media Servers with information related of the events and the new contents, available from the Origin Servers (live or stored). This server interacts with the Redirector in order to feed the surrogate selection algorithm.

- Redirector, which will provide the clients with the address of the most adequate Streaming Server for the request. If there is only one in an Access Network the response will be that, but if there are more than one, load balancing mechanisms should be used. The two main components of the redirector are the monitor which gathers information from surrogates and network components and the modified DNS server fed by the monitor, in order to provide the best response to each client request.

Clients

The client applications receive and display the video stream. The system has considered several video clients for different devices, for instance the VLC media player on PCs and PDAs, and different clients compatible with RTSP to mobile phones of different brands in order to make easy the use of the system to the users. Currently many portable multimedia devices such as iPhone, iPod, iPad, BlackBerry, as well as powerful cell phones and PDA with different OS (e.g. Android), are already on the shelf to support mobile video streaming. Many of these multimedia handheld devices provide a video streaming playback client in the equipment, mainly RealVideo or Microsoft Media Player. Provisions of links and parameters to access the channel have to be announced by the content producers. The clients will be able to:

- Start the playback of the chosen program or video stream right away or at a specific time, selecting QoS and the access network to be used.

- Skip or pause the media currently playing and go to the next one
- Stop the playback
- Additionally the client needs to be able to interact and manage the platform to record, delete recorded material and other operations.

If different access networks are available for the user he will be able to select the more convenient one. In order to support mobility, the platform has been analyzed to support the mobility and multihoming using NEMO, and detailed reference about its performance can be obtained in (Lee, Yong-Ju et al., 2005). This allows us to analyze the effects of experimenting with multihoming which allows a terminal to be concurrently connected via several access networks so that for example different data flows to be transported via different networks. Terminals need to be multimodal, i.e. including two different radio access interfaces.

PRACTICAL USES OF WIRELESS ACCESS NETWORKS FOR VIDEO STREAMING

Main alternatives as wireless access networks to support a video streaming service are: IEEE 802.11, IEEE 802.16d and IEEE 802.16e and 3G networks. IEEE 802.11 only could be considered if the n standard is used or in small hotspots connected by a broadband wired or wireless network like WiMAX. To complete the main goal of this paper we focus on WiMAX and 3G networks as access technologies in combination with the CDN architecture to improve efficiency.

As an alternative to the conventional wired access network technologies, WiMAX offers the ease of deployment similar to other wireless technologies, but with larger service coverage and more bandwidth. The cost for infrastructure deployment and for service provision can be dramatically reduced. Delivering IPTV services over WiMAX to complement the current IPTV deployment can provide better accessibility to the same pool of video content for mobile users as other technologies. WiMAX provides two versions IEEE 802.16d (fixed) and IEEE 802.16e (mobile), both provide a multicast communication paradigm as all IEEE standards, providing security management as in unicast connections. A Streaming Server of the CDN architecture installed in each BS or cluster of BS would improve the performance as has been indicated in the architecture of the previous section.

3G networks are increasingly being used for internet access, the service is mainly unicast. To provide video streaming even IPTV services via cellular networks, the 3rd Generation Partnership Project (3GPP) and 3GPP2, have developed the MBMS and Broadcast and Multicast Service (BCMCS) standards. While these standards don't make changes to the underlying cellular network, they are designed to create hybrid multicast and broadcast configurations that use advanced communication service components. This hybrid solution enables coexistence of unicast, multicast, and broadcast configurations in the same network infrastructure.

UMTS and better HDSPA offers bearer services, which provide the capability for information transfer between access points. It is possible to negotiate the characteristics of a bearer service at session or connection establishment and re-negotiate them during the session or connection. UMTS/HDSPA network services have different QoS classes for four types of traffic:

- Conversational class (voice, video telephony, video gaming).
- Streaming class (multimedia, video on demand, webcast).
- Interactive class (web browsing, network gaming, database access).
- Background class (email, SMS, downloading).

Offered data rate targets are: 144 Kbps for satellite and rural outdoor, 384 Kbps for urban outdoor, and 2048 Kbps, indoor and low range outdoor, for HDSPA values suffer a great improvement, achieving values from 1.8 to 4 Mbps in common urban scenarios and up to 1 Mbps indoor and low range outdoor. These are the maximum theoretical values in each environment for downlink speeds. The actual data rates may vary from 32-128 Kbps, for a single voice channel, to 768 Kbps-1.4 Mbps in urban low speed connections depending always on the class of service supported. (Vanhastel, S. et al., 2008)

The 3GPP developed MBMS to efficiently enable one-to-many data-distribution services—that is, broadcasting and multicasting services—via existing Global System for Mobile Communications (GSM) and Universal Mobile Telecommunications System (UMTS) cellular networks. Within the UMTS radio-access network, MBMS integrates both point-to-multipoint bearers for broadcast in cells with a high number of group members and point-to-point bearers for unicast. Meanwhile, to support user interactivity, MBMS employs an additional uplink channel for each user. Following the same evolution path of GSM and UMTS, MBMS provides backward compatibility to end users, which means that terminals not supporting MBMS service can work well in MBMS networks. For this purpose, MBMS doesn't interfere with existing GSM and UMTS services; it merely adds some additional components in the original GSM and UMTS architecture. (Zhou et al, 2009)

Comparing both technologies it could be found the following advantages and disadvantages when deployed to support video streaming service in an IPTV deployed system:

- To provide the same service WiMAX requires 6 times more cells than 3G networks with the current available devices. WiMAX in combination with WiFi hotspots could be comparable.

Table 3. WiMAX vs 3G parameters

Parameter	802.16-2004	802.16e-2005	WCDMA (HDSPA)
Downlink speed	<75Mbps	Up to 46Mbps (with 10MHz channel)	1.8-14.4 Mbps
Uplink speed	<10Mbps	Up to 7.8 (with 10MHz channel)	Up to 5.8 Mbps
System technology	OFDM	MIMO-SOFDMA	CDMA/FDD CDMA/FDD/MIMO
Typical cell radius	LoS 10-50Km NLoS 1-9Km	2-5Km	<0.1Km <1Km <20Km
Channel BW	1.25-10 Mhz	5,7,8.75,10 MHz	5MHz
Uplink Modulation	QPSK/16QAM	QPSK/16QAM	BPSK/QPSK
Download Modulation	QPSK/16QAM/64QAM	QPSK/16QAM/64QAM	QPSK/16QAM
Handoff Capability	--	Network optimized Handoff	Network initiated handoff

- Currently there are no WiMAX chipset installed in PDA or laptops, 3G connections are available in any of these devices.
- Coverage of WiMAX networks is not very broad, so WiMAX devices will need to work with multimode enabled roaming to 3G networks when needed.
- Multicast is not fully available in 3G networks, so WiMAX provides here a very interesting advantage.
- There are more 3G vendors rather than WiMAX vendors, there are more than 100 device and nearly 30 infrastructure 3G manufactures. (Qualcomm, 2009)
- 3G offers fixed, mobile and nomadic services. Regarding WiMAX operators offers fixed and nomadic, and although the standard for mobile already exists, there are not many implementations (e.g. WiBRO in Korea).
- WiMAX and 3G need licensing, and operation of both networks is rather complex.
- Regarding performance, WiMAX provides better QoS possibilities for video streaming rather than 3G in its current state of development and deployment by the operators.

As conclusion we can state that WiMAX will provide better performance for video streaming and explicitly for IPTV, regarding the inherent multicast nature of the network; the design with security from its early stages and the QoS management provided by the BS. But currently the most secure option due to its coverage for a mobile TV access network is 3G, with the support of MBMS, although it is not available in every network, multicast can be used. The developed system has been tested with 3G and WiMAX (see Table 3).

PERFORMANCE EVALUATION

Video streaming (e.g. for VoD and IPTV) systems relay on the use of adequate codec, WiMAX is still not widely deployed and 3G networks do not provide always as much bandwidth as needed due to losses, scalability and available technology, so we have evaluated the performance of some of this video streaming transcoding facilities over wireless networks. To evaluate the performance of a video streaming system, there are a large and diverse number of variables that must be taken into consideration (see Figure 5 for the testbed structure).

Figure 5. Testbed structure for video streaming analysis

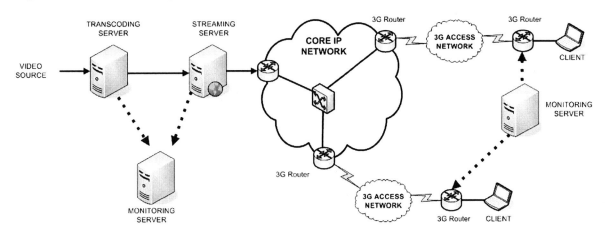

- The actual content and complexity of the content being streamed which in turn affects the efficiency of the encoder to compress the stream.
- The compression scheme being used, that is, different compression schemes have differing levels of efficiency.
- The encoding configuration. There could be any number of possible encoding configurations possible such as the error resilience, frame rate, the I-frame rate, the quantization parameter, the target bit rate (if any) supplied and target stream type i.e. VBR, CBR or near CBR.
- If the file to be streamed is .MP4 or .3gp, then a hint track must be prepared that indicates to the server how the content should be streamed.
- The streaming server being used, the rate control adaptation algorithm being used, and the methods of bit rate adaptation used by the server.

When the streaming path involves both wired and wireless links, some additional challenges evolve, e.g. much longer packet delivery time and jitter with the addition of a wireless link and the difficulty in inferring network conditions from end-to-end measurements.

In wired networks, packet corruption is rare so packet loss is an indication of network congestion, the proper reaction of which is congestion control. In wireless networks, however, packet losses may occur due to corruption in the packet. In the future we will have access to different mobile terminals with a wide range of display sizes and capabilities. In addition, different radio-access networks will make multiple maximum-access link speeds available. Due to the physical characteristics of cellular radio networks, the quality and, thus, the data rate of an ongoing connection will also vary, contributing to the heterogeneity problem. A related problem is to efficiently deliver streamed multimedia content over various radio-access networks with different transmission conditions. This is achievable if the media transport protocols incorporate the specific characteristics of wireless links.

Performance evaluation analyses two aspects, video coding in mobile handheld devices, and improvement of load balancing when video streaming/surrogate servers are introduced in the streaming CDN based architecture. The Mobile Streaming System has been evaluated in a controlled testbed, with just one streaming server and some basic entities including content servers with pre-encoded content, live multicodec encoder server and a streaming server.

Table 4. Performance evaluation for different frame sizes

	QCIF: 176x144		SIF: 320x240	
Frame Rate	Average BW	CPU Used	Average BW	CPU Used
10	54.4 Kbps	6%	58.8 Kbps	3%
20	60 Kbps	3.3%	62.2 Kbps	2.9%
30	67 Kbps	13%	70 Kbps	12.3%

The clients were connected to the streaming server by means several access networks (3G and WiMAX), using routers. Clients were executed on laptops with a playback application installed (e.g. VLC). The system included a COTS monitoring system. The testbed provided data corresponding to coding procedures. For 3G we have used two Spanish 3G operator (the two, out of four, with better performance were selected) and for WiMAX we have used a SS and a HiperMax BS from AirSpan vendor. (AirSpan, 2009)

The selected parameters for the performance evaluation, corresponds with an approach to a system with an intense mobile activity and deep live broadcast usage. The usual situation of use in 3G or 3.5G access implies PDA and mobile phones which have common resolution of QCIF (177x144) and SIF (320x240). The results of this performance tests become useful for establishing the criteria of stream control and multimedia profile and making decisions at the media and streaming servers. Performance evaluation has been done using H.263 and Xvid (MPEG4-ASP) encoders. Table 4 represents H.263 performance for different parameters, we used different bandwidths in order to check CPU usage, for different frame rates. Regarding CPU usage the results indicate that as more raw video streams have to be compressed or transcoded, more increases the CPU usage, so in the coding block of the Mobile streaming system several codecs or a cluster of them need to be placed. The second result is related with image size and bandwidth needed. In these tests the media source used provided an output of video raw with 575 effective lines and 20fps, data

tests made at this frame rate present better CPU usage. It is important also that bandwidth results have been taken from a variable bitrate criteria around the reference of 50kbps, it means the codification algorithm will try to not go far than this threshold, it is indeed, an average measurement. Transcoding results improve those presented in (Braet et al, 2008) and (Fortino et al, 2007).

As has been explained in the previous section, different profiles have been considered. For these tests we used the POCKET multimedia service profile; it, actually, should only specify one value per field, the following values summarize the profile options usable for this performance evaluation

- Service: Real Video 3GPP streaming
- Video codec: H263
- Video Bitrate: 50
- Image Size: 177x144/320x240
- Frame Rate: 10,20,30
- Audio codec: AAC
- Sample rate: 8000
- Audio Bitrate: 16
- Transmission: UMTS
- QoS application level associated: 0

H.263 is a required video codec in ETSI 3GPP technical specifications for IP Multimedia Subsystem (IMS), Multimedia Messaging Service (MMS) and transparent end-to-end Packet-switched Streaming Service. In 3GPP specifications is H.263 video usually used in 3GP container format. Due to this context, it is only evaluated here

Table 5. Xvid average bandwidth performance evaluation for different frame sizes

QCIF: 176x144	Fixed Bitrate			SIF 320x240	Fixed Bitrate		
Frame Rate	50	100	200	Frame Rate	50	100	200
5 fps	X	109	209,4	5 fps	57,7	124,5	238
10 fps	63,2	111	232	10 fps	58	110	212,4
20 fps	68	120	220	20 fps	56	109,7	214,8
30 fps	58	99,3	190,4	30 fps	69	102	184

(H263) with a very low bitrate, embraced for 3G access purposes. The proposed POCKET profile

Xvid is a codec library that follows the MPEG-4 standard, specifically MPEG-4 Part 2 Advanced Simple Profile (ASP). Following figures represent the results for "on the fly" codification of media with Xvid codec, regarding "Mobile" or "Pocket" profile and medium loaded networks. It would be also used and tuned depending on network status.

Observing the data results, the first impression that would be taken, is the significant increment of CPU consumption with the Xvid library. As it was briefly commented previously, the main use of Xvid codec corresponds with digital video broadcast and storage, acting as a serious free COTS alternative to DivX codec. Hence, the relevance of CPU consumption was not the priority at the design. As a result of the new multimedia conceptions and the improvement of networking and computing devices, it is also proposed here for the use at broadband and/or low loaded networks with a higher bitrate (up to 500kbps or better), some example scenarios would be corporate LAN and WiMAX low or medium loaded connections. (Bektas et al, 2008)

Like for H.263 encoder the profile used was, the MOBILE multimedia service profile with the following parameters:

- Service: Videoconferencing, VoD
- Video codec: Xvid
- Video Bitrate: 50/100/200
- Image Size: 177x144/320x240
- Frame Rate: 10,20,30

- Audio codec: MP3
- Sample rate: 8000
- Audio Bitrate: 16
- Transmission: WiMAX
- QoS application level associated: 1

Table 5 shows the convergence to theoretical values of bitrate as the frame rate becomes higher, and the better the higher the bitrate threshold is. That behavior is predictable using Xvid, which is a library codec, as it is commented previously, not oriented to live video encoding; even it would be used for not critical applications as VoD or common use videoconferencing at broadband networks. Note that there is no value for 5fps and 50kbps, because the video stream obtained did not offer acceptable quality. Regarding CPU consumption, Table 6 presents a clear increment against de binomial H263/ffmpeg, that are specifically designed for those scopes, low bitrate taxes and very low transcoding time.

Redirection to Video Streaming Servers

The proposed architecture defined in section 4, includes video streaming servers in each of the access networks. The main aim of these video streaming servers is load reduction measured at the mobile media streaming platform; in the Core IP Network and in the access networks. The streaming servers gather the streams from the sources and multicast it in the corresponding access network. These servers act as surrogates

Table 6. Xvid % CPU usage performance evaluation for different frame sizes

QCIF: 176x144	Fixed Bitrate			SIF 320x240	Fixed Bitrate		
Frame Rate	50	100	200	Frame Rate	50	100	200
5 fps	14,60%	11,50%	12,00%	5 fps	7,00%	10,00%	16,00%
10 fps	23,00%	18,00%	26,00%	10 fps	21,00%	22,00%	24,00%
20 fps	34,00%	31,00%	37,00%	20 fps	36,00%	34,00%	35,00%
30 fps	30,00%	41,00%	41,00%	30 fps	47,00%	41,00%	45,00%

of the CDN. Additionally, each origin server, represented as the mobile media platform counts with a streaming server as highest node of the hierarchy. The testbed used is presented in Figure 6 and includes three access networks, each one with its own streaming server. The three client clusters generate enough sessions to increase the load in the streaming server. The redirector is in charge of assigning the right streaming server to each request from the clients. The algorithm in order to assign the surrogate/streaming server was defined for a wired network in Molina et al, 2006.

This scenario proofs that requests are directed by the content manager to the most adequate streaming server in the corresponding access network in order to leverage load in the IP core network, usually a non-multicast network and in the video codec of the content provider. In the testbed of figure every request is served by the only streaming server, but in testbed of Figure 6, requests are balanced and when the content manager detects the access network origin of a client the request is sent to the corresponding streaming server.

In this test scenario, the origin server transmits a unicast stream to each streaming server, and the streaming server multicasts it (if multicast is available as in WiMAX or 3G with MBMS) or unicasts it to each client. In order to present the load and sessions in each streaming server we have used unicast in all cases, and we present sessions as TCP connections used by the video streaming application.

Figure 7 illustrates the redirection behavior with regard to the client clusters without any streaming server fault in a monitoring period of 600 seconds, showing to which streaming server the requests issued by the workload generator of each client cluster are redirected (workload is generated following a predefined pattern). The workload generated by each client cluster varies slightly and independently, and the probability of redirection to each of the steaming servers varies according to this workload as passive TCP connections and CPU usage.

The evolution of the scenario goes through different phases, with three increases in streams requests from the cluster clients. The idea is to proof that requests are mainly assigned to the local streaming server in the wireless access network:

1. At the beginning, the load generated by the three client clusters is very low, so every client request is redirected to the access network streaming server. This leads to an equally distributed redirection probability. Figure 7 reports the graphs of the two key parameters in the execution of the redirection algorithm, the TCP passive connections and the CPU usage, during the selected monitoring period.

2. [120 seconds], the workload generated by client cluster 1 increase, leading to an increase in the number of TCP passive connections and the CPU usage in streaming server 1. As no other load has been generated by clients

Figure 6. Testbed for streaming server selection

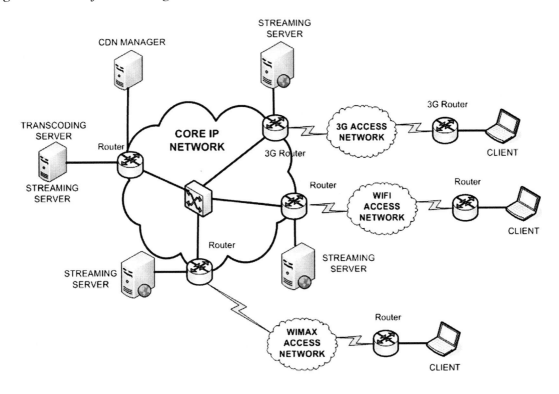

Figure 7. Streaming server requests of service

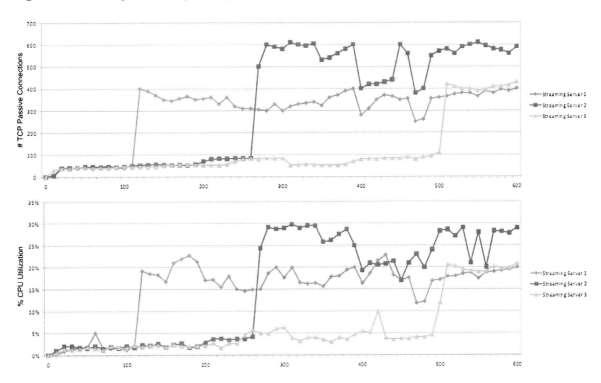

2 and 3, the load on the other two servers remains low and some requests from client 1 could be redirected to streaming servers 2 and 3, increasing the traffic in the core network but not significantly. This redirection to a non-subnet streaming server reflects the load balancing strategies of the CDN redirection algorithm, due to the execution of the defined heuristics. (Molina et al, 2006)

3. [270 seconds] the workload generated by cluster client 2 increases, while the load generated by cluster client 1 does not decrease. This triggers a similar effect in the parameters of streaming server 2. As streaming server 3 is the least loaded at this time, it absorbs not only requests generated by cluster client 1, but also those issued by cluster client 2.

4. Finally at time [500 seconds] the workload of cluster client 3 is raised in order to equal the others, so more or less the traffic served by each client is equivalent.

The main conclusion of this testbed, is that during the increase in requests the load in the core IP network is kept in the same minimum values. The performance of the system would be improved if multicast is used, being able to support even more clients in the system. When load increases in an access network the load in the streaming server increases, but at the same time load in nearby streaming servers in other wireless access networks may also increase because for some requests it could be more convenient to serve content from this streaming servers rather than from the local one. Although the streaming servers support heavier loads, the clients are served in a faster and secure way rather than with a centralized architecture without streaming servers deployed as surrogates in the wireless access networks.

CONCLUSION AND FUTURE WORK

The chapter outlines a proposed solution to develop a mobile video streaming platform; this solution is fully operative since July 2008, and has been used to distribute live events and sit-coms. The system has proved that COTS video streaming for mobile TV and VoD is an easy and non-expensive solution rather than DVB-H and other broadcast solutions. Main contribution is the introduction of a CDN architecture to deploy one video streaming server in each wireless access network. This solution reduces the bandwidth consumption and QoS restriction introduced by the IP core network, as has been indicated in the performance evaluation section. In wireless networks, the radio resource is limited mainly at the cell borders by low Signal to Noise and Interference Ratios (SNIR). For example, in the HSDPA technology, the radio rate varies from 12 Mb/s at the cell center, down to 0.4 Mb/s at the border. The proposed CDN solution provides an uninterrupted video session by taking advantage of bandwidth availability. This delivery mode optimizes the radio resource usage by the network. An improvement of the system could be achieved by a hybrid architecture P2P-CDN so the terminals could become servers within the wireless access network.

Current trends indicate service providers are headed toward delivering quadruple services (TV, telephony, Internet, and wireless). The use of heterogeneous networks enables the quadruple services to be adapted to any all-IP network. Given this trend, we believe future work in mobile video streaming will involve:

*   Bearer-independent quadruple service delivery.
*   Quadruple-service delivery over 3G and 4G networks
*   Quadruple-service delivery over P2P Session Initiation Protocol.
*   Web 2.0-enhanced quadruple-service delivery.

Different standards do not allow interoperability, neither vertical handover, IEEE 802.21 standard for Media Independent Handover could solve this problem. Research in bearer-independent, quadruple-service delivery aims to provide a common system for mobile video streaming applied to TV distribution, at least above IP transport, so that the same service-layer functionalities can be used for mobile TV and VoD services over different broadcast and access networks (e.g. DVB-H, MBMS, IPTV, and P2PTV). The strong motivation for 3G network operators is driven by the goal of providing TV service to as many mobile devices as possible. Incorporating IP Multimedia Subsystem into the technologies that facilitate mobile TV is part of the vision for evolving mobile networks beyond GSM. Research into quadruple-service delivery over 3G networks aims to provide TV services to users, regardless of location or access technology

On the basis of these findings, current research efforts are under way to define and analyze an improved system based on CDN to integrate IMS and optimize mobile media streaming delivery and deploy new interactive services on this platform. IMS in the scope of Mobile TV has been used in sever EC, US and other nations projects, being Asian nations the ones who have invested more in this line.

REFERENCES

Agilent. (2006). *IPTV QoE: Understanding and interpreting MDI values.* Retrieved January 11, 2006, from http://www.agilent.com

Ahmed, T. (2005). Adaptive packet video streaming over IP networks: A cross-layer approach. *IEEE Journal on Selected Areas in Communications, 23*(2), 385–401. doi:10.1109/JSAC.2004.839425

AirSpan. (2011). Retrieved May 21, 2011, from http://www.airspan.com

Bektas, T., Oguz, O., & Ouveysi, I. (2008). Designing cost-effective content distribution networks. *Computers & Operations Research, 34*(8), 2436–2449. doi:10.1016/j.cor.2005.09.013

Bonastre, O. (2009). Quality models for IPTV content distribution. In O. Bonastre (Ed.), *10th Conference on Telecommunications,* (pp.100-101). Zagreb, Croatia: IEEE Press.

Braet, O., & Ballon, P. (2008). Cooperation models for mobile television in Europe. *Telematics and Informatics, 25*(3), 216–236. doi:10.1016/j.tele.2007.03.003

Cha, M., Choudhury, G., Yates, J., Shaikh, A., & Moon, S. (2006). Resilient backbone network design for IPTV services. *Proceedings of International Workshop on IPTV Services over World Wide Web,* Edinburgh, UK.

Cha, M., Rodriguez, P., Moon, S., & Crowcroft, J. (2008). On next-generation telco-managed P2P TV architectures. In *Proceedings of International Workshop on Peer-To-Peer Systems* (IPTPS), Toronto, Canada.

Davis, A. G., Bayart, D., & Hands, D. S. (2006). Quality assurance for IPTV. *IEEE International Symposium on Broadband Multimedia Systems and Broadcasting* (BMSB '09), (pp. 1-7). Bilbao, Spain.

Etoh, M. (2005). Advances in wireless video delivery. *Proceedings of the IEEE, 93*(1), 111–122. doi:10.1109/JPROC.2004.839605

European Commission. (2007). *Future Internet of creative media: Workshop report.* Brussels 26-27/11/2007, organized by "Networked Media Systems Unit" DG INFSO, EC.

FFMPEG. (2008). *FFMPEG multimedia system.* Retrieved March 1, 2008, from http://ffmpeg.sourceforge.net/index.php

Fortino, G., Russo, W., Mastroianni, C., Palau, C., & Esteve, M. (2007). CDN-supported collaborative media streaming control. *IEEE MultiMedia, 14*(2), 60–71. doi:10.1109/MMUL.2007.29

Fröjdh, P., Horn, U., Kampmann, M., Nohlgren, A., & Westerlund, M. (2006). Adaptive streaming within the 3GPP packet-switched streaming service. *IEEE Network Magazine, 20*(2), 34–40. doi:10.1109/MNET.2006.1607894

Hei, X., et al. (2006). Insight into PPLive: Measurement study of a large scale P2P IPTV system. *Proceedings of WWW Conference*, Edinburgh, UK.

Hjelm, J. (2008). *Why IPTV? Interactivity, Technologies and Services*. J. Wiley & Sons, Inc.

ITU. (2009), *Mechanisms for service discovery and selection for IPTV*, retrieved October 9, 2009, from: http://www.itu.int/md/T09-SG16-090626-TD-WP2-0168/en

Jain, R. (2005). I want my IPTV. *IEEE MultiMedia, 12*(3), 95–96. doi:10.1109/MMUL.2005.47

Jenkac, H., Stockhammer, T., & Xu, W. (2006). Asynchronous and reliable on-demand media broadcast. *IEEE Network Magazine, Special Issue on Multimedia over Wireless Broadband Networks, 20*(2), 14-20.

Kerpez, K. (2006). IPTV service assurance. *IEEE Communications Magazine, 44*(9), 166–172. doi:10.1109/MCOM.2006.1705994

Kothari, R., & Ganz, A. (2005). Archies: An end-to-end architecture for adaptive live MPEG-4 video streaming over wireless networks. *Proceedings of IEEE International Conference on Wireless and Mobile Computing, Networking and Communications*, (pp. 181-188). Amherst, MA: IEEE Press.

Larribeau, B. (2006). *2006 IPTV standards survey report — Summary, streaming media whitepapers*. Internet Streaming Media Alliance. Retrieved May 30, 2006, from http://www.isma.tv

Lázaro, O., et al. (2007). MULTINET: Enabler for next generation pervasive wireless services. *Proceedings 16th IST Mobile and Wireless Communications Summit,* Budapest, Hungary.

Lee, Y.-J., Min, O.-G., & Kim, H.-Y. (2005). Performance evaluation technique of the RTSP based streaming server. *Proceedings of the 4th Annual ACIS International Conference on Computer and Information Science* (pp. 414-417). Washington, DC.

Li, Y., Markopoulou, A., Apostolopoulos, J., & Bambos, N. (2008). Content-aware playout and packet scheduling for video streaming over wireless links. *IEEE Transactions on Multimedia, 10*(5), 885–895. doi:10.1109/TMM.2008.922860

Mas, I. (2007). IMS-TV: An IMS-based architecture for interactive, personalized IPTV. *IEEE Communications Magazine, 46*(11), 156–163. doi:10.1109/MCOM.2008.4689259

Molina, B., Palau, C., Esteve, M., Alonso, I., & Ruiz, V. (2006). On content delivery network implementation. *Computer Communications, 29*(12), 396–412.

Molina, B., Pileggi, F., Esteve, M., & Palau, C. (2009). A negotiation framework for content distribution in mobile transient networks. *Journal of Network and Computer Applications, 32*(5), 1000–1011. doi:10.1016/j.jnca.2009.03.007

Montpetit, M. J., Klym, N., & Dain, E. (2009). The future of mobile TV: When mobile TV meets social networking. In Cereijo-Roibas, A. (Ed.), *Mobile TV: Customizing content and experience* (pp. 305–326). Springer. doi:10.1007/978-1-84882-701-1_21

Qualcomm. (2009). *WiMAX vs 3G whitepaper*. Retrieved January 11, 2009, from http://www.qualcomm.com

Retnasothie, F. E., et al. (2006). Wireless IPTV over WiMAX: Challenges and applications. *Proceeding IEEE Annual Wireless and Microwave Technology Conference* (WAMICON), (pp. 1-5). Clearwater, FL: IEEE Press.

Schatz, R., & Egger, S. (2008). Social interaction features for mobile TV services. *Proceedings IEEE International Symposium on Broadband Multimedia Systems and Broadcasting*, (pp. 1-6). Las Vegas, NV. IEEE Press.

Schorr, A., Kassler, A., & Petrovic, G. (2004). Adaptive media streaming in heterogeneous wireless networks. *Proceedings IEEE Multimedia Signal Processing Conference*, (pp. 506-509). Siena, Italy. IEEE Press.

Sentinelli, A., Marfia, G., Gerla, M., Kleinrock, L., & Tewari, S. (2007). Will IPTV ride the peer-to-peer stream? *IEEE Communications Magazine*, *45*(6), 86–92. doi:10.1109/MCOM.2007.374424

She, J., Hou, F., Ho, P.-H., & Xie, L.-L. (2007). IPTV over WiMAX: Key success factors, challenges, and solutions. *IEEE Communications Magazine*, *45*(8), 87–93. doi:10.1109/MCOM.2007.4290319

Taniuchi, K., Ohba, Y., Fajardo, V., Das, S., Tauil, M., & Cheng, Y. H. (2009). IEEE 802.21: Media independent handover: Features, applicability, and realization. *IEEE Communications Magazine*, *47*(1), 112–120. doi:10.1109/MCOM.2009.4752687

Vanhastel, S. (2008). Enabling IPTV: What's needed in the access network. *IEEE Communications Magazine*, *46*(8), 90–95. doi:10.1109/MCOM.2008.4597110

Vassiliou, V., Antoniou, P., Giannakou, I., & Pitsillides, A. (2006). Requirements for the transmission of streaming video in mobile wireless networks. *Proceedings of ICANN 2006*, Athens, Greece.

Wales, C., Kim, S., Leuenberger, D., Watts, W., & Weinroth, O. (2005). *IPTV - The revolution is here*. White paper. Retrieved June 11, 2011, from http://www.cs.berkeley.edu/~binetude/course/eng298a_2

Wiegand, T., Sullivan, G. J., Bjontegaard, G., & Luthra, A. (2003). Overview of the H.264/AVC video coding standard. *IEEE Transactions on Circuits and Systems for Video Technology*, *13*(7), 560–576. doi:10.1109/TCSVT.2003.815165

Xiao, Y. (2007). Internet protocol television (IPTV): The killer application for the next-generation internet. *IEEE Communications Magazine*, *45*(11), 126–134. doi:10.1109/MCOM.2007.4378332

Yeun, C. Y. (2007). Mobile TV technologies. In *Proceedings 5th International Conference on Information and Communications Technology* (ICICT), (pp. 2-9). Daejeon, S. Korea.

Zhou, J., Ou, Z., Rautiainen, M., Koskela, T., & Ylianttila, M. (2009). Digital television for mobile devices. *IEEE MultiMedia*, *12*(1), 60–71. doi:10.1109/MMUL.2009.7

ADDITIONAL READING

Aioffi, W. M., Mateus, G. R., Almeida, J. M., & Loureiro, A. A. F. (2005). Dynamic content distribution for mobile enterprise networks. *IEEE Journal on Selected Areas in Communications*, *23*(10), 2022–2031. doi:10.1109/JSAC.2005.854126

Apostolopoulos, J. G., Wee, S., & Tan, W. (2002). Performance of a multiple description streaming media content delivery network. *Proceedings of the International Conference on Image Processing* (ICIP 2002), (pp.189-192). Rochester, NY.

Bartolini, F. L. P., & Petrioli, C. (2003). Optimal dynamic replica placement in content delivery networks. *Proceedings of the 11ᵗʰ IEEE International Conference on Networks* (ICON 2003), (pp. 125-130). Sydney, Australia.

Beloued, A., Gilliot, J.-M., Segarra, M. T., & André, F. (2005). Dynamic data replication and consistency in mobile environments. *Proceedings of the 2nd International Doctoral Symposium on Middleware*, (pp. 1-5). Grenoble, France.

Chae, M., & Kim, J. (2003). What's so different about the mobile internet? *Communications of the ACM, 46*(12), 240–247. doi:10.1145/953460.953506

Challenger, J., Dantzig, P., Iyengar, A., & Witting, K. (2005). A fragment-based approach for efficiently creating dynamic web content. *ACM Transactions on Internet Technology, 5*(2), 359–389. doi:10.1145/1064340.1064343

Chand, N., Joshi, R. C., & Misra, M. (2007). Cooperative caching in mobile ad hoc networks based on data utility. *Mobile Information Systems, 3*(1), 19–37.

Chen, Y., Katz, R. H., & Kubiatowicz, J. D. (2002). Dynamic replica placement for scalable content delivery. *Proceedings of International Workshop on Peer-to-Peer Systems*, (pp. 306-318). Cambridge, MA.

Dikaiakos, M. D. (2004). Intermediary infrastructures for the world wide web. *Computer Networks, 45*(4), 421–447. doi:10.1016/j.comnet.2004.02.008

Dilley, J., Maggs, B. M., Parikh, J., Prokop, H., Sitaraman, R. K., & Weihl, W. E. (2002). Globally distributed content delivery. *IEEE Internet Computing, 6*(5), 50–58. doi:10.1109/MIC.2002.1036038

Han, S. C., & Xia, Y. (2009). Network load-aware content distribution in overlay networks. *Computer Communications, 32*(1), 51–61. doi:10.1016/j.comcom.2008.09.021

Hara, T. (2003). Replica allocation methods in ad-hoc networks with data update. *Mobile Networks and Applications, 8*(4), 343–354. doi:10.1023/A:1024523411884

Pallis, G., & Vakali, A. (2006). Insight and perspectives for content delivery networks. *Communications of the ACM, 49*(1), 101–106. doi:10.1145/1107458.1107462

Pathan, M., & Buyya, R. (2009). Resource discovery and request-redirection for dynamic load sharing in multi-provider peering content delivery networks. *Journal of Network and Computer Applications, 32*(5), 976–990. doi:10.1016/j.jnca.2009.03.003

Presti, F. L., Petrioli, C., & Vicari, C. (2005). Dynamic replica placement in content delivery networks. *Proceedings of the 13ᵗʰ International Symposium on Modeling, Analysis, and Simulation of Computer and Telecommunication Systems* (MASCOTS 2005), (pp.357-360), Atlanta, GA.

Rabinovich, M., & Spatscheck, O. (2002). *Web caching and replication*. Addison Wesley.

Rilling, L., Sivasubramanian, S., & Pierre, G. (2007). High availability and scalability support for web applications. *Proceedings of the 2007 International Symposium on Applications and the Internet* (SAINT), (p. 5). Washington, DC.

Roy, S., Ankcorn, J., & Wee, S. (2003). Architecture of a modular streaming media server for content delivery networks. *Proceedings of the 2003 International Conference on Multimedia and Expo* (ICME '03), (pp.569-572). Baltimore, MD.

Sidiropoulos, A., Pallis, G., Katsaros, D., Stamos, K., Vakali, A., & Manolopoulos, Y. (2008). Prefetching in content distribution networks via web communities identification and outsourcing. *World Wide Web (Bussum)*, *11*(1), 39–70. doi:10.1007/s11280-007-0027-8

Sivasubramanian, S., Pierre, G., van Steen, M., & Alonso, G. (2007). Analysis of caching and replication strategies for web applications. *IEEE Internet Computing*, *11*(1), 60–66. doi:10.1109/MIC.2007.3

Tse, S. S. H. (2005). Approximate algorithms for document placement in distributed web servers. *IEEE Transactions on Parallel and Distributed Systems*, *16*(6), 489–496. doi:10.1109/TPDS.2005.63

Turaga, D. S., el Al, A. A., Venkatramani, C., & Verscheure, O. (2005). Adaptive live streaming over enterprise networks. *Proceedings of International Conference on Multimedia and Exposition*, (pp. 974-979). Amsterdam, The Netherlands.

Wu, T., & Dixit, S. (2003). The content driven mobile internet. *Wireless Personal Communications: An International Journal*, *26*(2-3), 135–147. doi:10.1023/A:1025570318413

Xu, Z., Guo, X., Wang, Z., & Pang, Y. (2005). The dynamic cache algorithm of proxy for streaming media. *Proceedings of the International Conference on Intelligent Computing* (ICIC 2005), (pp. 1065-1074), Hefei, China.

Zhuo, L., Wang, C. L., & Lau, F. C. M. (2002). Load balancing in distributed web server systems with partial document replication. *Proceedings of the 31st International Conference on Parallel Processing* (ICPP), (p. 305). Vancouver, Canada.

KEY TERMS AND DEFINITIONS

3G: It refers to the third generation of mobile telephony (that is, cellular) technology. The International Telecommunications Union (ITU) defined the third generation (3G) of mobile telephony standards IMT-2000 to facilitate growth, increase bandwidth, and support more diverse applications. For example, GSM could deliver not only voice, but also circuit-switched data at speeds up to 14.4 Kbps. But to support mobile multimedia applications, 3G had to deliver packet-switched data with better spectral efficiency, at far greater speeds.

Content Distribution Network: A content distribution network is a set of dedicated servers distributed among a subnet or even the Internet that collaborate within an overlay network in order to deliver web and media content to sparse users. There is a global redirection mechanism that transparently associates a user request to a nearby server in order to reduce the response time and improve the overall scalability of the system.

IPTV: It refers to the delivery of TV content through IP networks. The main goal is the usage of IP networks as broadcast channel for TV. Typically IPTV is restricted to autonomous domains (and not the Internet) where native features can be used in order to improve the delivery efficiency, such as IP multicast.

Nomadic Terminal: A nomadic terminal is considered as a fixed host whose location may move, but not during a communication session. Whenever a session starts, the terminal does not move from its current location. For example, a laptop is considered a nomadic terminal, as one uses it either as home or at work, but not in between.

Redirection: Process of redirecting a user to another location. This process is typically perfomed natively by the communication protocols and the user does not perceive it. Typical redirection codes in the HTTP protocol are the 3XX codes.

Seamless Mobility: It is a mechanism that allows a user to move freely while keeping his/her ongoing communication sessions. The user does not perceive any significant communication cut even if a handover is taken place.

Transcoding: It is the process of changing the encoding of an input source preserving the same content. Typical reasons for transcoding are related for supporting device constraints (resolution, encoding formats) or communication bandwidth variability.

Video Streaming: Video streaming is a special way of delivering media content to users while it is being played without any previous download. The mechanism includes communication buffers and flow control protocols to ensure that the playback is smoothly. Common protocols are MMS and RTP.

WiMAX: WiMAX is a wireless communications standard designed for creating metropolitan area networks (MANs). It is similar to the Wi-Fi standard, but supports a far greater range of coverage. While a Wi-Fi signal can cover a radius of several hundred feet, a fixed WiMAX station can cover a range of up to 30 miles. Mobile WiMAX stations can broadcast up to 10 miles.

Chapter 5
Robust Broadcasting of Media Content in Urban Environments

Giancarlo Fortino
DEIS – University of Calabria, Italy

Carlos Calafate
DISCA – Universitat Politècnica de València, Spain

Pietro Manzoni
DISCA – Universitat Politècnica de València, Spain

ABSTRACT

In this work, the authors apply raptor codes to obtain a reliable broadcast system of non-time critical contents, such as multimedia advertisement and entertainment files, in urban environments. Vehicles in urban environments are characterized by a variable speed and by the fact that the propagation of the radio signal is constrained by the configuration of the city structure. Through real experiments, the authors demonstrate that raptor codes are the best option among the available Forward Error Correction techniques to achieve their purpose. Moreover, the system proposed uses traffic control techniques for classification and filtering of information. These techniques allow assigning different priorities to contents in order to receive firstly the most important ones from broadcasting antennas. In particular, as vehicle speed and/or distance from the broadcasting antenna increase, performance results highlight that these techniques are the only choice for a reliable data content delivery.

INTRODUCTION

Content-based information dissemination has a potential number of applications in vehicular networking, including advertising, entertainment, traffic and emergency announcements. In this work we focus on the use of a wireless vehicular communication system where corporate business servers push multimedia-based advertisement information (e.g. daily offers) to passing-by vehicles in urban environments (Fiore, Cassetti & Chiasserini 2005; Härri, Filali & Bonnet 2007).

Wireless vehicular communication systems include Vehicle-to-Vehicle (V2V) and Vehicle-to-Infrastructure (V2I) communications schemes. In terms of technologies, a single standard is

DOI: 10.4018/978-1-4666-1794-0.ch005

being developed specifically targeting vehicular environments, and supporting both V2I and V2V communication modes. This standard, known as IEEE 802.11p (Martinez, Cano & Manzoni 2009) is an enhancement of the original IEEE 802.11 standard that basically combines the IEEE 802.11a (operation in the 5 GHz band) and the IEEE 802.11e (MAC-level QoS support) annexes. In particular, the band of frequencies reserved for the operation of IEEE 802.11p is defined at 5.9 GHz, although there is still not a worldwide consensus on the use of this band.

Cars in urban environments are characterized by a variable speed and by the fact that the propagation of the signal is constrained by the configuration of the city structure (Giannoulis, Fiore & Knightly 2008). If a road side unit (RSU) wants to propagate a block of information to a passing by vehicle, the most basic approach would be to periodically rebroadcast the same content. This approach has fundamentally two limitations, namely: data synchronization and car speed. The first issue stands in the fact that, if the car starts receiving the block of information when the cycle has already began, it will have to wait for the next cycle to get the whole of the information. The second issue refers to the fact that, depending on the car speed and on the configuration of the city layout, the car will be reached by the information sent by the specific RSU during a limited interval of time.

In this work we propose an optimized solution for the broadcast-based delivery of small-size multimedia contents such as advertisements and news to moving vehicles using IEEE 802.11p. The objective is to reduce the problems due both to content synchronization and to the limited size of the transmission window. With this purpose we adopt raptor codes, which are an extension of LT-codes with linear time encoding and decoding. LT-codes (Luby Transform) are a new class of codes introduced by Luby for the purpose of scalable and fault-tolerant distribution of data over computer networks (Shokrollahi 2006). Moreover, we use

also flow control techniques based on filtering and classification of information in order to privilege the most important information for the user.

The rest of this paper is organized as follows. The *Background* section briefly describes the FEC schemes and the flow control techniques used in this work. In the section *A Robust Broadcast-based Content Delivery System*, we present the developed system for robust broadcasting of content to mobile users/vehicles. The performance evaluation of our system is discussed in the *Performance Evaluation* section. Finally, after delineating future research directions, conclusions are drawn.

BACKGROUND

In this section we introduce some background concepts about FEC and control flow techniques that are exploited in the broadcasting multimedia system proposed in this chapter.

Forward Error Correction Techniques

Forward Error Correction (FEC) is a transmission control system where the transmitter adds redundant data, called Error Correction Code (Luby & Vicisano 2004), to identify and possibly correct an error in the transmission without requiring the transmitter's intervention.

XOR is one of the simplest FEC schemes for error handling, being designed to ensure protection against the loss of a single packet in the presence of low error rates (Peltotalo, Peltotalo & Roca 2004). Its aim is to partition each source block using a fixed source symbol length, and then to add redundant symbols built as the XOR sum of all Source Symbols. This process is called Encoding $(k+1, k)$, where k is the number of Source Symbols.

Reed-Solomon (R-S) (Lacan & others 2009) is a much more sophisticated FEC scheme that assumes an RS(N, K) code, which results in N codewords of length N symbols, each storing K symbols of data, that are then sent over an erasure channel. Any combination of K codewords received at the other end is enough to reconstruct all of the N codewords. N is usually 2K, meaning that at least half of all the codewords sent must be received in order to reconstruct all of the codewords sent. Reed-Solomon is used in a series of commercial applications, mainly CDs and DVDs (to ensure their reading even with minor scratches) and broadcasting satellite, DSL, WiMax, as well digital Terrestrial TV (DVB-T).

More recently, RAPTOR encoding has emerged as the most efficient FEC technique currently available. The RAPTOR acronym stands for Rapid Tornado, and represents an evolution of the first types of "Erasure Codes". The technique was invented by Amin Shokrollahi in 2001 (Shokrollahi 2006), and is based on the concept of Luby Transform, which uses a parity array, being considered the first efficient method for encoding a block of n symbols in O(n) time. RAPTOR has a high efficiency because it uses multiple levels of encoding (and decoding): in the first level it performs a "pre-coding" on Source Blocks, thus generating intermediate symbols; although different pre-coding algorithms may be used, the most widely adopted is generally the LDPC (Low Density Parity Check). Afterwards, intermediate symbols are processed using LT-Codes (Luby Transform) to generate the final encoded symbols (Repair Symbols). A big advantage is that, with the Luby Transform, an unlimited number of Repair Symbols can be generated; this offers great flexibility to transmission systems.

Flow Control Techniques

In a context like vehicular networks, the time variable plays a fundamental role because car drivers and/or occupants would receive only essential information (through filtering techniques) and, among such information, they would receive only the one with higher priority (through classification techniques).

Thus, two operations are needed to fulfill such objectives:

- Filtering of the essential information;
- Classification of the information.

By means of queuing disciplines (hereafter called *qdisc*), it is possible to change the way to transmit and receive information, so allowing a flexible management of bandwidth.

There are two types of *qdisc*:

- Classless queuing disciplines, which typically use rescheduling, delay and eliminations of packets;
- Classful queuing disciplines, which allow the discrimination of the information through the classification of packets using filtering rules.

Each class can include other sub-classes or another queue, generating this way a tree structure of queues.

The analyzed Classless and Classful queuing disciplines are the following:

- *First In First Out* (FIFO). It is the simplest *qdisc*. There is no special treatment for packets but simply the packets that arrive first will be transmitted first.
- *Token Bucket Filter* (TBF). It is used to shape the traffic on the initial configured set-up. TBF is not suitable for the system considering that it can only apply shaping techniques. The Classful version is called Hierarchy Token Bucket (HTB).
- *Stochastic Fairness Queuing* (SFQ). The traffic is sent in a round robin fashion, giving each session the chance to send data in turn.
- *Random Early Detection* (RED). It is a queuing technique used at backbone networks, often involving megabit bandwidths (>100), which require an approach

different from normal LANs. For this reason, it will not be widely analyzed. In order to cope with transient congestion on links (Zang & others 2007), backbone routers will often implement large queues. RED statistically drops packets from flows before it reaches its hard limit. This causes a congested backbone link to slow more gracefully, and prevents retransmit synchronization. This also helps TCP find its 'fair' speed faster by allowing some packets to get dropped sooner, so keeping queue sizes low and latency under control. The probability of a packet being dropped from a particular connection is proportional to its bandwidth usage rather than the number of packets it transmits.

- *Priority Queuing* (PQ) The PQ *qdisc* does not actually shape, it only subdivides traffic based on how filters are configured. When a packet is enqueued into the *PQ qdisc*, a class is chosen based on the filter commands set up. Each class has a priority and the packet belonging to the higher priority will be sent out before the others. It is not suitable because it is limited only for prioritizing packets but not for the partitioning of the link bandwidth.

- *Hierarchical Token Bucket* (HTB). It is based on the technique of the Token Bucket. HTB is an implementation of the Weighted Fair Queuing. The *HTB qdisc* distributes bandwidth between its classes using the weighted round robin scheme.

- *Class Based Queuing* (CBQ). It is like the HTB *qdisc* and contains classes into which arbitrary *qdisc*s can be plugged. All classes that have sufficient demand will get bandwidth proportional to the weights associated with the classes. It is complex and does not seem optimized for some typical situations. Its hierarchical approach is well suited for set-ups where a fixed amount of bandwidth should be divided for different purposes, giving each purpose a guaranteed bandwidth, with the possibility of specifying how much bandwidth can be borrowed.

A ROBUST BROADCAST-BASED CONTENT DELIVERY SYSTEM

The developed system combines the functionality of the FLUTE (File Delivery over Unidirectional Transport) (Paila & others 2005) protocol with the features of the FEC schemes to provide more robustness and reliability to content delivery in wireless urban environments (Luby & others 2007), as well as file transfer time minimization. In particular, the system is intended for the delivery of small-size multimedia files (named *multimedia pills*), mainly related to advertisement and news.

FLUTE is a protocol specifically defined for broadcasting (or multicasting) data. It does not require bidirectional communication between sender and receiver, thus working with any network supporting unidirectional communications (Internet, satellite, WiFi, etc). In particular, it builds upon the ALC (Asynchronous Layered Coding) standard (Luby & others 2002), thus allowing to obtain great scalability in multicast-based environments.

The layered architecture of the proposed system is shown in Figure 1. The application layer is organized into two applications according to the data push model: the broadcaster, located at the static base station side, and the receiver, located at the mobile client side. Both applications are based on the FLUTE protocol, and may rely on different FEC schemes (XOR, Reed-Solomon, RAPTOR) to make data transfer more robust, reliable, and fast.

Figure 1. System architecture

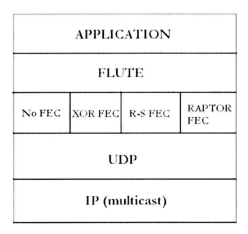

Figure 2. Schema of the broadcaster/receiver activity flow

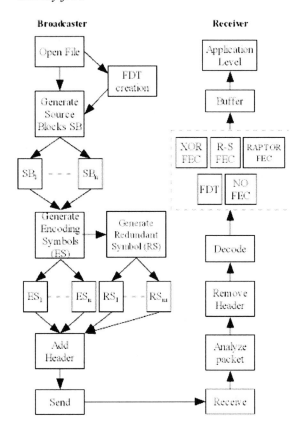

The broadcaster performs the following operations (Figure 2):

1. Opening the file to-be-transmitted in binary mode.
2. Data characterization and creation of the FDT (File Delivery Table). FDT instances, together with FLUTE header fields, give the necessary parameters to identify, locate and restore the files at the receiver.
3. Decomposition in source blocks. In particular, the decomposition FLUTE algorithm works as follows: computation of a source block structure so that all source blocks are as close to being of equal length as possible; all source blocks in the first group share a same larger length, while the second source blocks group is associated with a smaller length.
4. Decomposition in encoding symbols (only source symbols).
5. Addition of redundancy through FEC, if enabled. The integrated FEC schemes are XOR, R-S and RAPTOR (see section 2). Thus, the encoded symbols will be the source symbols plus the redundancy symbols.
6. Construction and transmission of the FLUTE packets.

The receiver carries out the inverse operations of the broadcaster (Figure 2):

1. Waiting for the FDT.
2. Parsing the FDT and saving the related parameters.
3. Waiting for data packets.
4. Analysis of the received packets.
5. Data decoding and buffering.
6. Passing the file to the application level as soon as it is fully received.

The system is fully implemented in C under Linux (Debian) and extends the FLUTE library mad-fcl 1.7 (FLUTE 2010), which already provides Compact No-Code, XOR, and R-S FEC schemes, to achieve integration with the RAPTOR encoder/decoder library (RAPTOR 2010) too.

System Enhancement for Composite Multimedia Objects Delivery

The proposed system broadcasts multimedia pills without taking into account the content inside the pills. If pills are composed of multiple multimedia objects, each object can have different dimensions and/or priorities so that delivery of such composite objects could be carried out either according to priorities or by shaping dimension differences so delivering objects at the same time.

The use of queuing disciplines (see *Background* section), specifically rate control techniques, allow to choose which packets are important for the user in order to transmit them with higher priority. Two criteria can be used to assign a weight for each object (or flow) to allow for:

1. Receiving all the flows at the same time;
2. Receiving one of the flows according to a higher priority.

In the first case, the weight to assign is proportional to the dimension of the flow. In general, given a composite multimedia object $O=<o_1, o_2, ..., o_n>$ each flow o_i is coded by Raptor code (or another FEC scheme) and assigned a weight for the WFQ (see *Background* section) to establish the flow bandwidth.

It is possible to combine both criteria in order to get only one weight matching each flow starting from two initial weights. In particular, p_u is the weight related to the priority of the user, and p_t is the weight related to the dimension of the file. The following convex combination allow combining both weights:

$$p_f = \alpha \cdot p_u + (1 - \alpha) \cdot p_t \qquad (1)$$

where p_f is the final weight and α is the importance of p_u with respect to p_t.

The main problem is related to the calculation of the α value, but it is simple to see that α has to be as higher as p_u becomes more important. So, for priority p_u to be important, it is necessary that among the weights p_{ui} of each file f_i there will be a great difference. In this way, α can be calculated by a distance measure between the weights of the files.

In a more formal way, we can say that, given n files: $f_i : p_{u_i}, p_{t_i}$ with $i = 1, 2, ..., n$; and the following constraints:

$$\sum_{i=1}^{n} p_{u_i} = 1 \sum_{i=1}^{n} p_{t_i} = 1 \qquad (2)$$

The convex combinations can be described through the following linear system:

$$
\begin{matrix}
f_1 \\ f_2 \\ \cdot \\ f_i \\ \cdot \\ \cdot \\ f_n
\end{matrix}
\begin{pmatrix}
p_{u_1} & p_{t_1} \\
p_{u_2} & p_{t_2} \\
\cdot & \cdot \\
p_{u_i} & p_{t_i} \\
\cdot & \cdot \\
\cdot & \cdot \\
p_{u_n} & p_{t_n}
\end{pmatrix}
\cdot \begin{pmatrix} \alpha \\ 1-\alpha \end{pmatrix}
= \begin{pmatrix}
p_{f_1} \\ p_{f_2} \\ \cdot \\ p_{f_i} \\ \cdot \\ \cdot \\ p_{f_n}
\end{pmatrix} \qquad (3)
$$

Specifically, α can be calculated by the sums of absolute difference between the weights:

$$\alpha_u = \sum_{i=1}^{n-1} \sum_{j=2}^{n} \left| p_{u_i} - p_{u_j} \right| \qquad (4)$$

$$\alpha_t = \sum_{i=1}^{n-1} \sum_{j=2}^{n} \left| p_{t_i} - p_{t_j} \right| \qquad (5)$$

So, the final α is calculated by normalization:

Figure 3. Example of tree structure of a composite multimedia object

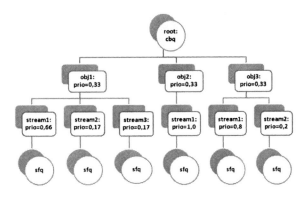

$$\alpha = \frac{\alpha_u}{\alpha_u + \alpha_l} \qquad (6)$$

The antenna can transmit much information with no correlation and, in many cases, not all the transmitted information is of interest to the user. So, it is more important to receive a little of complete information than a lot of partial information. To achieve it, the system uses, on the user-side, a technique based on information filtering.

There are two XML files used to manage the multimedia contents, namely *resources.xml* and *preferences.xml*.

The *resources.xml* file is an advertisement file broadcasted by the system to inform all vehicles about the available contents that can be received. Each element in this file represents a composite multimedia object and contains:

- Name of the information;
- Information type (e.g. weather, traffic, advertisement);
- Information description;
- Possibly various *stream* elements representing the flows of information; each of them contains:
  ○ Path of the flow;
  ○ Priority to assign;
  ○ Port of transmission;
  ○ Type (audio, video, text/html, etc).

The *preferences.xml* file contains information about user preferences. Its objective is to allow the user not to worry about the information he will receive while driving, thereby reducing possible distractions of drivers. This file contains *preferences* elements, and each of them contains:

- Type of preference (weather, traffic, advertisements, etc)
- Possibly various *stream* elements representing the flows of information desired by the user; each of them contains:
  ○ Type (audio, video, text/html, etc)

The broadcast system for the delivery of composite multimedia objects is enhanced with two modules: *cmo_sender* and *cmo_receiver*. The *cmo_sender* module reads the *resources.xml* file to select the files needed to be transmitted and to configure the *qdisc* (Graf & others 2010), setting the weight of each flow. In particular, the *cmo_sender* automatically creates a CBQ (Class Based Queuing) queuing and adds a class for each composite object. Then, for each class created, *cmo_sender* creates sub-classes according to the flow assigned to the object and calculates the final weights, getting the user weights from the *resources* file and the dimension weights from the file system, through the aforementioned procedure. Every leaf node of the tree structure of queues cannot be a class but only a queue. Therefore, for

Figure 4. Transmitter side of the broadcast system

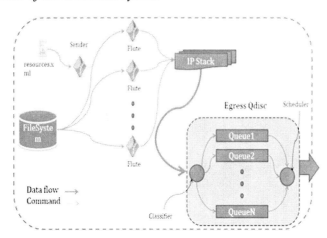

each sub-class, *cmo_sender* appends another SFQ queue. An example of a tree structure is shown in the Figure 3. Moreover, for each flow, a filter rule is created so that the classifier can move the packets of the flow to the proper queue.

Once the configuration is completed, *cmo_ sender* starts the *Flute* application for each flow, using the port contained in the *resources* file and setting the Raptor code for the corresponding FEC technique. The packets will reach the IP stack, so as to be managed by the Ingress Qdisc system (Graf & others 2010; see Figure 4).

Figure 5 shows the receiver side (in the vehicle) of the broadcast system. The *cmo_receiver* component waits for the reception of the *resources* file by using the *Flute* application component. Once *cmo_receiver* gets the file, it compares the *resources.xml* and *preferences.xml* files. In particular, the system compares the type of information in the *resources* file with the type of preferences in preferences file, to filter the favorite type of information. Furthermore, it is possible to filter information according to the format of flow comparing the type of transmitted stream with the type of favorite stream. Finally, *cmo_receiver* gets the ports of the favorite streams and starts the *Flute* application component for each flow.

PERFORMANCE EVALUATION

Performance evaluation was carried out with the aim of measuring a *multimedia pill* transfer time under different static and mobile conditions of the receiver with respect to the broadcaster, and through different FEC codes incorporated in the system. In particular, the experiments were run on two laptops communicating direct through WiFi 802.11g, one used as antenna and executing the broadcaster, and the other one used as user device and executing the receiver. All tests were based on the following common parameters: Broadcast transmission rate = 1 Mbps, size of the *multimedia pill* to be transmitted = 254 KB, which can be considered an average size for the delivered *multimedia pills*, and the code overhead for the RAPTOR encoding is unbounded since we are supposing the transmission process is in an infinite loop. Concerning the packet loss ratio, it will depend on the transmitter-receiver channel conditions, which are mostly related to the distance in the presence of Line-of-Sight (LoS) communications.

Two kinds of experiments were set up: (i) almost static receiver; (ii) mobile receiver.

In the first type of experiment, the broadcasting laptop was positioned at 15m from the ground, whereas the receiver laptop was located at different

Figure 5. Receiver side of the broadcast system

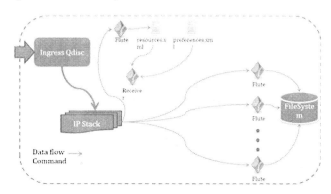

Figure 6. Multimedia pill (file) transfer time for almost static receivers by varying distance and FEC scheme type

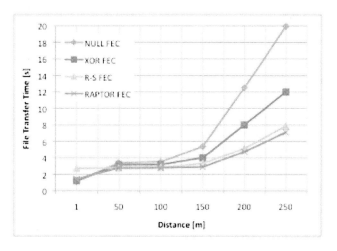

distances {1m, 50m, 100m, 150m, 200m, 250m} from the broadcaster (the first three distance values were set up with line-of-sight between broadcaster and receiver, while the last three distances had no line-of-sight). The receiver was either static or subject to human walking speed. The obtained results are reported in Figure 3. Obviously, at a distance of 1m, which is just a reference distance and not a possible value in a real context, the best results are provided by the NULL FEC, i.e., the option with no redundancy and computational complexity, since losses are null. Between 50 m and 100 m there is no significant difference among the 4 schemes. RAPTOR and R-S perform on average better than the NULL FEC and XOR FEC

by about 23% and 13%, respectively. However, from 100 m to 250 m, the use of FEC schemes leads to a considerable improvement with respect to the non-exploitation of a FEC scheme. As can be seen, RAPTOR is always the best performing scheme. In particular, at 250m, RAPTOR outperforms the NULL FEC, XOR and R-S by about 180%, 69% and, 11%, respectively. Moreover, it is worth noting that, even when relying only on XOR, the simplest FEC scheme, we obtain performance improvements of about 66% with respect to NULL FEC. This suggests that at least the XOR FEC scheme should be "mandatorily" used to reduce multimedia pill transfer time.

Figure 7. Multimedia pill (file) transfer time for mobile receivers by varying speed and FEC scheme type

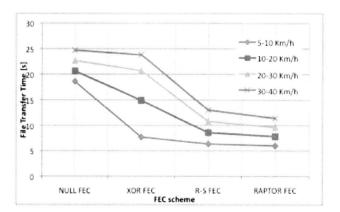

In the second type of experiment, the broadcasting laptop was positioned in such a way to fully cover an area of 100m x 100m containing a road between two roundabouts, and the receiver laptop was located inside a car that circulated through this road at different speeds {5-10 Km/h, 10-20 Km/h, 20-30 Km/h, 30-40 Km/h}. The obtained results are reported in Figure 7. They confirm the same trend as the ones obtained in the first experiment. RAPTOR is the FEC scheme providing the highest performance. At a speed of 30-40 Km/h the multimedia pill transfer time is on the average of 12s, so the mobile receiver can even travel straight for about 117m at an average speed of 35 Km/h without stopping, being timely served by the broadcaster. It is worth noting that, as soon as the speed increases, the performance percentage gain of the XOR scheme with respect to the NULL FEC scheme is reduced. This implies that it may be unsuitable for urban environments in which mobile receivers can travel at a speed higher than 5-10 Km/h.

Performance Evaluation of the Composite Multimedia Objects Delivery

In this section we evaluate several aspects of the delivery of composite multimedia objects, including the most suitable queuing discipline and the system performance for static and mobile receivers.

The first type of experiment carried out concerns a simulation to detect which queuing discipline was more suitable to be used in the broadcast system. In particular, the considered queuing techniques were: FIFO, SFQ, HTB and CBQ. The broadcasting laptop sends three image files {o_1, o_2, o_3} with the same size, so the weight for the dimension p_t is the same for all. Figure 8 shows the reception time for each flow.

The FIFO and SFQ disciplines do not give priority to the different flows, and so that the reception time is the same for all. The results obtained for the HTB and CBQ disciplines differ since these use a weighted queuing technique to privilege flows. In every case the CBQ appears to be the best choice.

The second type of experiments involved a simulation with the complete system using the configuration of the Egress Qdisc and filtering of information. So, in this case, the broadcasting laptop sends more than one flow since there are many composite multimedia objects that the sender has to transmit to the receiver laptop.

As for the evaluation of the basic system (see above), two kinds of experiments were set up: (i) almost static receiver; (ii) mobile receiver.

Figure 8. Reception time for each flow with different queuing disciplines

QDISC	Trx(o1) (sec)	Trx(o2) (sec)	Trx(o3) (sec)
FIFO	50,124	51,121	53,144
SFQ	56,278	55,823	57,699
HTB	42,538 (50%) 61,033 (33%)	64,569 (30%) 57,032 (33%)	103,628 (20%) 57,034 (33%)
CBQ	34,051 (50%) 51,527 (33%)	56,522 (30%) 51,534 (33%)	85,068 (20%) 53,028 (33%)

We suppose that the sender laptop sends only one composite multimedia object containing meteorological information with the following files:

- f_1 (html), dimension 1052768 bytes ;
- f_2 (jpg), dimension 518232 bytes;
- f_3 (avi), dimension 1165329 bytes.

Overall, the sender transmits 2.60 Mbytes, and we suppose that the receiver will receive all the files sent.

In a first phase we analyzed the best way to assign priorities to each flow in order to get a total reception time as low as possible. It is easy to see that assigning high priority to small files produces a great waste of bandwidth. In Figure 9 the obtained results are shown.

The best condition are obtained with p_1=0.45; p_2=0.1; p_3=0.45 because, as we referred above, it is better to assign the highest priority value to the flow with greatest dimension. The other solutions can be good for users when they want to privilege some file by assigning it a higher priority. In all cases, the total time increases as function of the distance between the two laptops. It is possible to reduce the reception time by tuning the loss parameter in the Raptor scheme. In particular, we can choose a good trade-off in order to increase the number of redundant packets according to the distance without congesting the network.

In the second type of experiment, we considered the mobility of the receiver along the road near the broadcaster. The distance between mobile receiver and broadcaster was set to 20 meters. Moreover, we set the RAPTOR parameters as follows: loss percentage = 20% and code overhead = 3%. This is a good tradeoff in function of the distance between the mobile receiver and the broadcaster.

Of course, in Figure 10, the solution labeled by (p_1=0.45, p_2=0.1, p_3=0.45) appears to be the best when we want to reduce the total reception time. During the experiment it was possible to see that in some cases not all files could be received by the receiving laptop. In particular, in the Figure 11 we show the percentage of information received by the receiver in the case of a great quantity of information transmitted.

The tests with the mobile receiver were difficult to carry out due to frequent disconnections; moreover a mobility analysis at distances greater than 20 meters was impossible. This was caused by the use of the IEEE 802.11g protocol. In particular, this protocol allows for good transmission performance when delivering multiple media flows to static receivers, but it is not suitable for mobile receivers.

Figure 9. Total reception time vs. the distance with different priority distribution

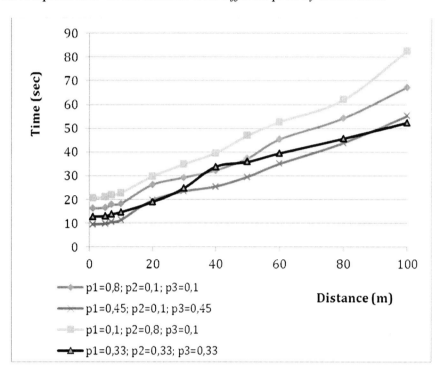

Figure 10. Total reception time vs. the velocity with different priority distribution and with a fixed distance of 20 meters

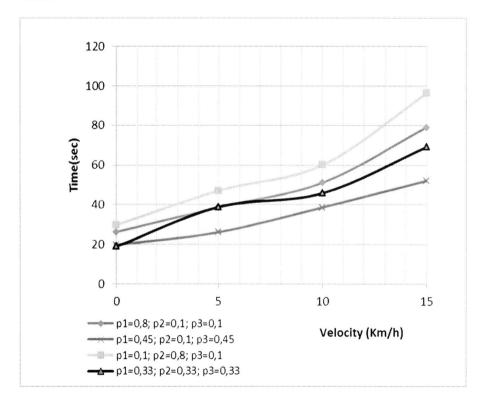

Figure 11. Percentage information received vs. the velocity with a dimension of the multimedia object of 7MB, different priority distributions and with a fixed distance of 20 meters

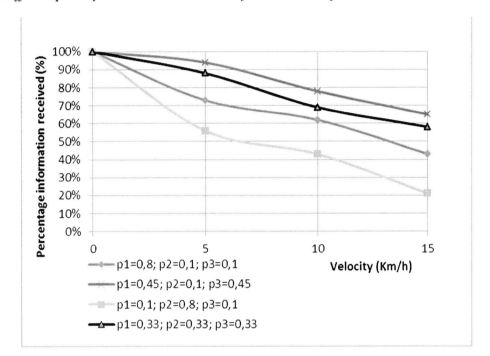

FUTURE RESEARCH DIRECTIONS

Media broadcasting architectures deployed in urban and non-urban environment are expected to be composed of a given number of broadcasting points that deliver contents of all sorts to users. New architectures and techniques are required to coordinate content delivery across multiple points to maximize the success probability of media delivery to mobile vehicles. Innovative cooperative multimedia multicast systems (Fortino & Nigro 1998, Fortino & Nigro 2000a; Fortino & Nigro 2000a; Fortino & Nigro 2003) and CDN architectures (Fortino & others 2007; Fortino & Russo, 2008; Fortino, Mastroianni & Russo 2005; Fortino, Mastroianni & Russo 2009) developed in recent years could be reused to this purpose. Additionally, novel solutions specific to vehicular environments (Calafate & others 2012) are required to seamlessly switch between different technologies depending on factors such as availability, congestion, costs, etc. Combined with vehicle-to-vehicle communications, such forthcoming communication paradigms are expected to address the multiple challenges of vehicular networks, while assuring that security, privacy and even anonymity issues are respected.

CONCLUSION

Wireless content delivery infrastructures in urban environments are emerging to provide a wide range of contents (e.g. advertising, entertainment, traffic and emergency announcements) to moving vehicles as well as roaming people.

In this paper we proposed a robust content broadcasting system for the delivery of multimedia-based advertisement and news information, under the form of *multimedia pills*, to passing-by vehicles and people in urban environments. The system integrates the FLUTE protocol and FEC schemes (XOR, R-S, and RAPTOR) to make content distribution more robust, reliable and fast for the filtering and classification of information.

Our system is composed by delivery techniques based on queuing disciplines (e.g. FIFO, stochastic fairness queuing, hierarchy token bucket, class based queuing) and FEC scheme parameter tuning for prioritized delivery. Prioritized delivery allows transmitting contents according to their mutual priority to improve file transfer time and/or reliability of higher priority contents. In particular, the user can choose his favorite flow by giving it higher priority. Experimental results show that the best solution for the packet queuing is to use a CBQ queuing discipline in order to receive the flow transmitted by the sender laptop.

The system performance evaluation was carried out in two different urban environment scenarios: one related to roaming people and the other one related to moving vehicles. The obtained results show that the RAPTOR FEC scheme offers the best performance. Moreover, it is quite evident that the use of a FEC code, even the simplest one like the XOR FEC scheme, should be adopted as it allows improving performance by about 66% with respect to the non-exploitation of FEC schemes. In fact, if vehicles travel at speeds in the range of 30-40 Km/h (typical of urban scenarios), the R-S and RAPTOR schemes represent the only viable choice.

Performance evaluation results of the complete composite multimedia objects transmission system show that different priority distributions have a clear impact on the total reception time. The mobility experiments have also highlighted that the use of 802.11g should be avoided due to frequent network disconnections.

Current work is aimed at experimenting the development of a system based on IEEE 802.11p protocol to fully support receiver device mobility. Moreover, a further extension is the development of a synchronized reception of atomic and composite multimedia objects that would allow the receiver to collect a set of time-related contents of different dimensions at the scheduled time.

REFERENCES

Calafate, C. T., Fortino, G., Fritsch, S., Monteiro, J., Cano, J. C., & Manzoni, P. (2012). An efficient and robust content delivery solution for IEEE 802.11p vehicular environments. *Journal of Network and Computer Applications*, *35*(2), 753–762. doi:10.1016/j.jnca.2011.11.008

Digital Fountain. (2010). *DF Raptor R11 encoder/decoder 2.2.1 software development kit.*

Fiore, M., Casetti, C., & Chiasserini, C. (2005). On-demand content delivery in vehicular wireless networks. *Proceedings of the 8th ACM International Symposium on Modeling, Analysis and Simulation of Wireless and Mobile Systems*, Montréal, Canada, October 10-13, (pp. 87-94). New York, NY: ACM.

Fortino, G., Mastroianni, C., & Russo, W. (2005). Cooperative control of multicast-based streaming on-demand systems. *Future Generation Computer Systems*, *21*(5), 823–839. doi:10.1016/j.future.2004.08.002

Fortino, G., Mastroianni, C., & Russo, W. (2009). A hierarchical control protocol for group-oriented playbacks supported by content distribution networks. *Journal of Network and Computer Applications*, *32*(1), 135–157. doi:10.1016/j.jnca.2008.04.001

Fortino, G., & Nigro, L. (1998). QoS centred Java and actor based framework for real/virtual teleconferences. *Proceedings of SCS EuroMedia*, (pp. 4-6).

Fortino, G., & Nigro, L. (2000a). ViCRO: An interactive and cooperative video recording on-demand system over MBone. *Informatica (Slovenia)*, *24*(1).

Fortino, G., & Nigro, L. (2000b). A cooperative playback system for on-demand multimedia sessions over Internet. *Proceedings of IEEE Multimedia and Expo (ICME 2000)*, (pp. 41-44).

Fortino, G., & Nigro, L. (2003). Collaborative learning on-demand on the internet MBone. In Ghaoui, C. (Ed.), *Usability evaluation of online learning programs. Hershey, PA: Idea Publishing Group*. USA. doi:10.4018/978-1-59140-105-6. ch003

Fortino, G., & Russo, W. (2008). Using P2P, GRID and agent technologies for the development of content distribution networks. *Future Generation Computer Systems, 24*(3), 180–190. doi:10.1016/j. future.2007.06.007

Fortino, G., Russo, W., & Mastroianni, C. (2007). CDN-supported collaborative media streaming control. *IEEE MultiMedia, 14*(2), 60–71. doi:10.1109/MMUL.2007.29

Giannoulis, A., Fiore, M., & Knightly, E. W. (2008). Supporting vehicular mobility in urban multi-hop wireless networks. *In Proceedings of the 6th International Conference on Mobile Systems, Applications, and Services*, Breckenridge, CO, USA, June 17-20, (pp. 54-66). New York, NY: ACM Press.

Graf, T., Maxwell, G., van Mook, R., van Oosterhout, M., Schroeder, P. B., Spaans, J., & Larroy, P. (2010). *Linux advanced routing & traffic control*. Retrieved April 15, 2010, from http://lartc.org/

Härri, J., Filali, F., & Bonnet, C. (2007). *Mobility models for vehicular ad hoc networks: A survey and taxonomy*. Research Report RR-06-168, Institut Eurecom, March.

Lacan, J., Roca, V., Peltotalo, J., & Peltotalo, S. (2009*). Reed Solomon error correction scheme*. (IETF RMT Working Group, RFC 5510 Standards Track/Proposed Standard), April.

Luby, M., Gasiba, T., Stockhammer, T., & Watson, M. (2007). Reliable multimedia download delivery in cellular broadcast networks. *IEEE Transactions on Broadcasting, 53*(1), 235–246. doi:10.1109/TBC.2007.891703

Luby, M., Gemmell, J., Vicisano, L., Rizzo, L., & Crowcroft, J. (2002). *Asynchronous layered coding (ALC) protocol instantiation*. IETF RFC 3450, December.

Luby, M., & Vicisano, L. (2004). *Compact forward error correction (FEC) schemes*. RFC 3695, February.

Martinez, F. J., Cano, J.-C., Calafate, C. T., & Manzoni, P. (2009). A performance evaluation of warning message dissemination in 802.11p based VANETs. In *Proceedings of the 34th IEEE Conference on Local Computer Networks*, Zürich, Switzerland, October 20-23, (pp. 221-224). IEEE Computer Society.

Paila, T., Luby, M., Lehtonen, R., Roca, V., & Walsh, R. (2005). *FLUTE – File delivery over unidirectional transport*. IETF RFC 3926, October.

Peltotalo, S., Peltotalo, J., & Roca, V. (2004). *Simple XOR, Reed-Solomon, and parity check matrix-based FEC schemes*. IETF RMT Working Group, draft-peltotalo-rmt-bb-fec-supp-xor-pcm-rs-00.txt (Work in Progress), June.

Project, M. A. D. (2010). *FLUTE implementation*. Retrieved May 2, 2010, from http://mad.cs.tut.fi/

Shokrollahi, A. (2006). Raptor codes. *IEEE Transactions on Information Theory, 52*, 2551–2567. doi:10.1109/TIT.2006.874390

Zang, Y., Stibor, L., Cheng, X., Reumerman, H.-J., Paruzel, A., & Barroso, A. (2007). Congestion control in wireless networks for vehicular safety applications. In *Proceedings of the 8th European Wireless Conference*, April, Paris, France, (p. 7)

KEY TERMS AND DEFINITIONS

FLUTE: FLUTE is a protocol specifically defined for broadcasting (or multicasting) data. It does not require bidirectional communication between sender and receiver, thus working with any network supporting unidirectional communications (Internet, satellite, WiFi, etc). In particular, it builds upon the ALC (Asynchronous Layered Coding) standard thus allowing to obtain great scalability in multicast-based environments.

Forward Error Correction: Forward Error Correction (FEC) is a transmission control system where the transmitter adds redundant data, called Error Correction Code to identify and possibly correct an error in the transmission without requiring the transmitter's intervention. Well-known FEC schemes are XOR, Reed-Solomon and RAPTOR.

IEEE 802.11p: IEEE 802.11p is an enhancement of the original IEEE 802.11 standard that basically combines the IEEE 802.11a (operation in the 5 GHz band) and the IEEE 802.11e (MAC-level QoS support) annexes. In particular, the band of frequencies reserved for the operation of IEEE 802.11p is defined at 5.9 GHz, although there is still not a worldwide consensus on the use of this band.

Multimedia Pills: Multimedia pills are small-size multimedia files mainly related to advertisement and news. Indeed, pills can be composed of multiple synchronized multimedia objects.

Queuing Discipline: Queuing disciplines (qdisc) allow changing the way to transmit and receive information for a more flexible management of bandwidth. There are two types of qdisc: (i) Classless queuing disciplines, which typically use rescheduling, delay and eliminations of packets; (ii) Classful queuing disciplines, which allow the discrimination of the information through the classification of packets using filtering rules.

Vehicle-to-Infrastructure (V2I): V2I allows connecting vehicle to a back-end infrastructure to be able to retrieve/push information (e.g. diagnostics data, news, advertisement) from/to the vehicle or to allow vehicle to access network resources.

Vehicle-to-Vehicle (V2V): V2V allows connecting vehicles to each other and with the infrastructure allows them to share and exchange information and sensor data among each other and among them and the infrastructure (e.g. for entertainment, diagnostics, safety, probe data collection, wireless payments, toll collection).

Chapter 6
Quality Guaranteed Media Delivery over Advanced Network

Zhiming Zhao
University of Amsterdam, The Netherlands

Paola Grosso
University of Amsterdam, The Netherlands

Jeroen van der Ham
University of Amsterdam, The Netherlands

Cees de Laat
University of Amsterdam, The Netherlands

ABSTRACT

Moving large quantities of data between distributed parties is a frequently invoked process in data intensive applications, such as collaborative digital media development. These transfers often have high quality requirements on the network services, especially when they involve user interactions or require real time processing on large volumes of data. The best effort services provided by IP-routed networks give limited guarantee on the delivery performance. Advanced networks such as hybrid networks make it feasible for high level applications, such as workflows, to request network paths and service provisioning. However, the quality of network services has so far rarely been considered in composing and executing workflow processes; applications tune the execution quality selecting only optimal software services and computing resources, and neglecting the network components. In this chapter, the authors provide an overview on this research domain, and introduce a system called NEtWork QoS Planner (NEWQoSPlanner) to provide support for including network services in high level workflow applications.

DOI: 10.4018/978-1-4666-1794-0.ch006

1. INTRODUCTION

The development of a large multi-media application involves raw material acquired from different sources and is often a collaborative effort among several parties. Moving large quantities of semi-finished material between distributed locations is a frequently invoked process during the development phase. IP-routed paths in the Internet are not the most suitable way to transfer high-quality digital media. Streaming content in 4K-format (4096 pixels of horizontal resolutions) or higher formats has two basic requirements: sufficient network capacity and quality of experience for the end user. Uncompressed 4K content requires a network bandwidth of more than 7Gbps. This can be accomplished by ensuring that the whole end-to-end path, from source to destination, is provisioned over a 10Gbps channel. Nowadays this is technically feasible, but it cannot be a priori guaranteed in the Internet where there is very limited control over the segments the data will be routed through. Furthermore, packet loss, reordering and varying jitter cannot be avoided in a best-effort environment as the Internet. These performance hiccups cause severe degradation of the viewing performance.

To investigate solutions to these problems, several research initiatives have started. Notably, a group of researchers and industrial partners started in 2006 the CineGrid collaboration (http://www.cinegrid.org). CineGrid is a non-profit organization whose members form an interdisciplinary community focused on the research, development, and demonstration of networked collaborative tools to enable the production, use and exchange of very-high-quality digital media over photonic networks. The basic idea of CineGrid is that network circuits implemented over photonic networks provide the proper guarantees of bandwidth and quality of service for media delivery applications. A challenge is to integrate the network in the overall delivery framework, where also computing nodes and many types of software components play an important role. The techniques used for digital content delivery are easily ported to support content-delivery networks (CDNs), such as (Fortino, Russo, Mastroianni, Palau, & Esteve, 2007). It is our opinion that these types of networks could fully utilize the advanced network services exposed by the network providers and that they could integrate the workflow planning techniques in their optimizations.

We shall highlight our research focuses: modeling the meta information of network resources and media material, managing operation sequences of data access and movement sequences, and using advanced network infrastructure to provide quality guaranteed connections for moving large quantity data. Workflows are the natural way to address this resource selection and composition problem and they are playing an important role in the daily operations and use of grid and cloud infrastructures. Particularly, in the scientific community workflow systems have gained popularity among researchers to support complex experiments (Zhao, Belloum, & Bubak, 2009). Still the application of workflows to media delivery scenarios is fairly new. The inclusion of network information in the workflow planning phase and the use of a continuous feedback regarding the current status of the network resources during workflow execution are the two main novel aspects of our work.

This chapter is about using these technologies in digital content delivery. First, we will introduce the background for our work, and review the state of the art. We then introduce a system called NEWQoSPlanner, and we discuss how it can be used to enhance the resource description, discovery, network path selection and provisioning for content delivery.

2. BACKGROUND

Advanced network architectures can provide quality guaranteed services for data intensive applications, such as content delivery, which have a high requirement on the data delivery and on the data operations. We will focus in this section on the technologies involved in developing such kind of new (network) infrastructures.

2.1 Data Intensive Applications over Grid

Grids, and nowadays clouds, provide a suitable environment for the execution of data intensive applications. Data can be processed in parallel at different locations and later on transported back to a single place where the final computation is performed. Data Grids provide also support for distributed storage, allowing users to leverage the infrastructures present in multiple data centers (Maassen, Verstoep, Bal, Grosso, & de Laat, 2009; Venugopal, Buyya, & Ramamohanarao, 2006). The combination of computing Grids and advanced network services, as the ones offered by many Research and Education Networks, has enabled the support of applications from various scientific fields, e.g. high-energy physics, geosciences, bioinformatics, ecology, astronomy. In particular high-definition video and digital-cinema streaming, high performance computing, visualization and virtual reality applications fully exploit this type of infrastructures.

A very illustrative example is the plethora of applications that already in 2005 were showcased during the iGrid2005 conference (Smarr, Brown, de Fanti, & de Laat, 2006). Participants could witness a full range of working demonstrations in the area of visualization and video streaming. Cosmic ray data collected in Tibet was sent to Beijing and later on to all projects partners that needed to process it, using *lightpaths services* (Nan, Ma, Zhang, & Chen, 2006); a high-quality collaborative environment that used HD video provided an enhanced video conferencing system to participants around the globe (Holub et al., 2006); interactive 3D video streams were transported over 10Gbit/s intercontinental dedicated connections (Jo et al., 2006); video transcoding, from high-

resolution broadcast video into MPEG_2 format, in order to reduce file size and resolution, made use of remote computers connected by on-demand paths (Grasa et al., 2006). iGrid2005 also showed for the first time a real-time, international transmission of 4K digital cinema and 4K Super High Definition digital video between Japan and the USA west coast (Shimizu et al., 2006).

Several data intensive applications were also presented, in particular in the area of computational astrophysics and astronomy. For example; 797GB astronomical data from the Sloan Digital Sky Survey was sent to computing centers across the world (Grossman et al., 2006); or, the electronic long base interferometry (e-VLBI) application (Sobieski et al., 2006), which can provide ultra-high resolution images of faint and distant objects in the universe, required the creation of a single computational environment allowing data coming on the network links to many radio telescopes around the globe.

One very interesting use case that well high-lighted the fruitful symbiosis of grids and advanced networks was the seamless migration of virtual machines over the wide area network (Travostino et al., 2006). A live virtual machine could be moved from Amsterdam (NL) to San Diego (USA) with just 1-2s of application downtime. Balancing the work load across data centers and disaster recovery are among the most important motivations for this advanced use of grids and networks, and in general to support data intensive applications over lambda grids.

2.2 Advanced Network Services for Data Intensive Applications

The Internet, based on the TCP/IP architecture, has been designed as a best-efforts service, where the intelligence is in the end nodes at the edges. The functionalities related to problems occurred during communication on the networks, such as for example the reordering of packets due to the erroneous order of packets arrival or the detection of duplicates, are all function of the Transport Layer, *i.e.* the Transmission Control Protocol (TCP). In the core of the Internet the Internet Protocol (IP) *'limits'* itself to perform fast and efficient delivery.

Quality of Service can be defined as the statistical performance guarantees that a network system can make in terms of throughput, delay, jitter and loss. The Internet treats everybody, *i.e.* all packets, as equal. But applications are not equal as they differ in the sensitivity to delays, and the mission critical value of the data being transported.

There are four principles that govern the implementation of Quality of Service (QoS) in the Internet. All of these principles have led to the development of protocols and techniques to mitigate and solve the original design flaw of TCP/IP:

1.   Marking (packet classification) allows routers to distinguish between different classes of packets; and router policies to treat packets accordingly;
2.   Isolation (scheduling and policing) provides protection for one class from other classes; it ensures sources adhere to bandwidth requirements; scheduling and policing are QoS functions performed at the edges of the network.
3.   High resource utilization. While providing isolation, it is desirable to use resources as efficiently as possible.
4.   Call admission (signaling) prevents that traffic is ingested in the network beyond link capacity. Application flows need to declare their needs, and the network may block calls if it cannot satisfy the requests.

Packet marking has relied on the use of the Type of Service (ToS) field in the IP packets. The Integrated Services (Intserv) architecture provides QoS guarantees in IP networks for individual application sessions. It was defined in 1994 in RFC 1633 (Braden, Clark, & Shenker, 1994). Its main characteristics are 1) the support for resource reservation, as routers maintain state info of allocated resources and QoS requests and 2) the possibility to admit/deny new call setup requests. IntServ does not scale well, because maintaining per-flow router state with large number of flows is difficult.

In 1998 RFC 2474 (Nichols, Blake, Baker, & Black, 1998) and RFC 2475 (Blake et al., 1998) defined the Differentiated Services (DiffServ) protocol. DiffServ provides simple functions in the network core, and relatively complex functions at edge routers (or hosts). It does not define service classes, but it provides the functional components to build such service classes. DiffServ supersedes the ToS field in IPv4 to make per-hop behavior (PHB) decisions about packet classification and traffic conditioning functions. The PHB results in a different observable (measurable) forwarding performance behavior, but it does not specify what mechanisms to use to ensure required PHB performance behavior. DiffServ marks packets using the IPv4 ToS and the Traffic Class field in IPv6. Six bits are used for Differentiated Service Code Point (DSCP) and to determine PHB that the packet will receive, while 2 bits are unused. DiffServ has replaced IntServ as the protocol of choice to provide different level of services in the Internet. Still DiffServ fails to guarantee a specified service level, as there is no guarantee that packets marked will receive the expected service. This limitation has led to look for different ways to provide applications with the proper guarantees in terms of throughput, delay, jitter and loss.

The idea of providing data intensive applications with deterministic point-to-point connections was fostered by a community of research networks, later organized in the Global Lambda Integrated Facility (GLIF). This community provides a global network to support data-intensive scientific research, and also supports middleware development for optical networking. The ideas in this community led to the concept of *hybrid networking*, the offering of packet switched (IP)

Figure 1. Visualization techniques shown during the iGrid2005 workshop: high-definition passive stereo displays (bottom right), auto-stereoscopic displays (top right), ultra-high definition tiled projection and LCD displays (left top and bottom)

services and circuit switched connections over the same physical network infrastructure (de Laat, Radius, & Wallace, 2003).

Since most data intensive applications operate in a large-scale environment, with collaborators at different locations, the networks required for these applications are nearly always multi-domain networks. De Laat estimated in 2000 that a typical network connection for a physics experiment crosses seven domains (de Laat & Blom, 2000). To achieve inter-domain operations, the different networks have to collaborate. For dedicated network connections, this collaboration is done in the GLIF community. In few years time a number of international network connections have been established to provide the inter-domain

connectivity. Figure 2 shows a collection of the interconnections provided by partners in the GLIF community as of May 2011.

The GLIF community is working hard at improving the lightpath provisioning process by exchanging experiences, documenting processes and developing middleware. In the meantime, the available speeds of lightpaths keep growing. While 10Gbit/sec links were introduced only a few years ago, 40Gbit/sec links are now becoming available to application developers and 100Gbit/sec hardware is just becoming available (Dumitru, Koning, & de Laat, 2010). These kinds of links provide unique opportunities for the transport of high-quality media and the construction of CDN architectures.

Figure 2. GLIF world map of May 2011, with all network connections offered by its participants [1]

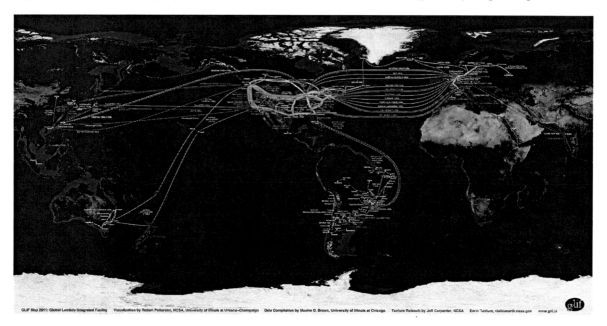

2.3 Information Model of Advanced Network Infrastructures

Automatic path finding and provisioning of inter-domain lightpaths is important to facilitate the usage of the advanced network infrastructures mentioned in 2.2. Figure 3 shows the steps that currently need to be taken to establish a network connection for any high level application, in this example between a cluster and a display. If we examine this procedure in more detail, we see that it is broken up in the following underlying steps:

1. The user formulates the requirements, including the end points and the network characteristics like bandwidth, latency, jitter, minimum packet size (if applicable), reliability, etc.
2. These requirements must be communicated to their upstream network provider. The network provider must gather information about available resources, including the resources in other networks, as the two end-points are typically in different networks.
3. The network provider must, in collaboration with the other network providers, determine a valid path that uses available resources, and is within the specs of the user. The resources needed for the path must be reserved in all networks involved.
4. Once the reservations are all confirmed, the reserved resources must be configured in the networks. The end-to-end path must be tested, and in case of faults the faults must be examined and resolved. The network provider informs the user, and the user must configure the end nodes (e.g. configure the IP addresses and set the routing table).
5. The user runs the applications.

Currently, this whole process of acquiring a (working) lightpath across multiple domains can take several weeks, a lot of emails and phone calls and extensive testing. It is clear that the whole process needs to be improved and automated in order to scale.

The example described in Figure 3 shows that the intermediate steps by the network operators

Figure 3. Steps to set up a network connection between a cluster and a display

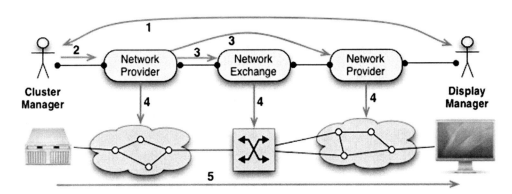

involve a lot of communication. In order to determine the path, they have to exchange topology and capability information. Once a path has been determined an operator must communicate the specifics to the other operators involved. There are several information models available to describe network topologies. However, these information models are either aimed at a knowledgeable single network operator, since they are mostly suitable for describing monitoring, diagnostics and configuration information, such as SNMP (Case, Mundy, Partain, & Stewart, 2002), NetConf (IETF, 2011) or CIM (DMTF, 2011).

Other network information models are aimed more at describing topologies such as the Network Measurements-WG (Nsi-Wg, 2011) model or G.805 (International Telecommunications Union, March 2000), however these models are not intended to publish topology information to other domains. Another very complete network information model is GMPLS (Farrel & Bryskin, 2006); however, that model is squarely aimed at networking devices, and is not suitable for publishing outside the domain, or for extension to other applications.

Based on the existing work, a Network Description Language (NDL) (Ham, Dijkstra, Travostino, Andree, & de Laat, 2005) has been developed to model the network information, which uses the Resource Description Framework (W3C, 2010) as

its basis. NDL provides generic globally unique identifiers, so that different domains can publish and share network descriptions. In the next section, we will have more discussion on NDL.

2.4 QoS and Workflow Systems in Data Intensive Applications

Delivering large quantity data over advanced networks involves several steps in setting up networks and needs invocation of different services to perform the data movement and processing. Scientific workflow systems are suitable in this context to hide low-level integration details and to automate the management of delivering and sharing digital contents in the applications. But it also requires workflow systems to meet the performance requirements on the data operations.

The development of scientific workflow can be roughly divided into four phases (Deelman, Gannon, Shields, & Taylor, 2009): composition, enactment, execution, and post analysis. Service oriented architecture plays a key role in decomposing workflow processes and in integrating them. The Quality of Services needs to be included in each phase of the workflow lifecycle to optimize the global performance of the application to meet the user's requirements. In the following sections we briefly review the existing work from four aspects: workflow composition, service selection, execution control and provenance.

A workflow composition process that is QoS-aware must: 1) compose a service of the highest quality and 2) determine the quality of the composition process itself. The first goal is achieved by computing the global quality starting from the QoS attributes of constituting services (Lecue & Mehandjiev, 2009). Graph reduction is a widely used approach (Cardoso, Miller, Sheth, & Arnold, 2002); a pre-defined set of logic patterns defines certain reduction rules which can be used to simplify the logical dependencies among constituting services. From the reduction rules, the quality parameters are computed; for instance the computing time of two sequentially connected services is computed as the sum of the quality of each of them, the computing time of two parallel services is computed as the maximal one. The second goal requires modeling the quality attributes of the semantic links between services, the composition quality of the workflow can then be evaluated by the semantic fit and the reliability of the selected service in the workflow.

Searching for suitable services from available resources is a basic procedure in composing a workflow. QoS aware service selection implies two steps: properly formulating the requirements and selecting resources that meet these requirements. Rosenberg proposed a QoS enabled description language, the Vienna composition language (VCL) (Rosenberg, Leitner, Michlmayr, Celikovic, & Dustdar, 2009), to specify an abstract flow for workflow composition. VCL defines an abstract workflow as four parts: feature definition, feature constraints, global constraints and the business protocol (the desired workflow language). The feature constraints and global constraints include both functional constraints and QoS attributes. The problem of resource selection has been formulated differently. A commonly used formulation is *shortest path finding in a weighted graph*, in which the available services are represented as a directed graph according to the service types, and

the graph nodes are labeled by the quality attributes of the service (Li, Chen, Wen, & Sun, 2008). Well known shortest path finding algorithms include Bellman-Ford and Dijkstra's. These algorithms exhibit optimal performance because of their greedy search strategy and avoid backtracking operations during the search; however, the minimal cost path found by the algorithms is often not the most optimal solution if there are multiple constraints on the quality attributes. Therefore, the problem has also been formulated as a multi constraint optimal path problem (Yu, Kirley, & Buyya, 2007), or multi objective optimization problem. Ant colony optimization (ACO) is a meta heuristic search approach proposed in (Li & Xu, 2003; Alaya, Solnon, & Ghdira, 2007) for discovering minimum cost path in a graph, and for solving NP-hard combinatorial optimization problems. Fang, Peng, Liu and Hu (2009) applied ACO in service selection and proposed a multi objective ACO approach that can simultaneously optimize several objectives. Genetic algorithms in searching optimal paths, and constraint programming or Integer programming methods are also widely used for the multi objective optimization problem.

Workflow execution is the mapping of workflow processes onto underlying computing resources and the scheduling of the execution sequence. Task based scheduling is a straightforward approach, in which the workflow tasks are submitted to the local manager of the computing infrastructure. Several researchers have instead proposed a workflow level scheduling that takes into account future task performance (Harada, Ushio, & Nakamoto, 2007); this approach will achieve higher performance and better resource utilization than only using local resource managers. Multi objective optimizations are widely used to formulate the problem of QoS aware scheduling. Avanes and Freytag (2008) proposed a constraint programming based approach to search for the best match between workflow requirements and the available computing resources. The basic idea is to describe the quality requirements and resource dependencies as constraints by partitioning the workflow into different parts based on the patterns and QoS requirements. One of the contributions from Avanes work is that the network dynamics has been also included in the procedure of constraint resolving. Resource provision plays an important role to improve the fault tolerance and the performance of the workflow (Juve & Deelman, 2008). Basically, provisioning can be either static or dynamic. Advance reservation is a typical static provisioning mechanism, and several batch based schedulers support it. Based on the quality requirements, the workflow engine reserves computing resources and time slots from the Grid resource manager. One of the disadvantages of static provisioning is its overhead on the total cost for computing the workflow. To improve this, Raicu, Zhao, Dumitrescu, Foster and Wilde (2007) proposed multi level scheduling strategies, in which the application level scheduler is able to interact with the low level resource manager to tune the requirements at runtime. This approach introduces a dynamic component in the provisioning process.

The provenance service tracks the events occurred in the workflow execution, and allows scientists to trace the evolution of data computed in the workflow and to obtain insights in the experiment processes. Moreover, provenance data can also be used to debug errors of the workflow execution and optimize the workflow design. The Open Provenance Model (OPM) (Moreau et al., 2008) emerges as a standard model to represent workflow provenance information. Including QoS information of the workflow processes and the execution in the provenance model allows scientists to analyze the quality of the services and the workflow scheduling. Michlmayr, Rosenberg, Leitner and Dustdar (2009) provide the provenance service using a QoS aware middleware, which records the changes of the service quality as events. Evaluating trust and reliability of the

provenance data itself has also been discussed in the literature (Rajbhandari, Contes, Rana, Deora, & Wootten, 2006). However, research on the provenance model which includes the QoS information of the workflow processes is still in its very early stage.

The above technologies contribute necessary building blocks to enable the delivery of large quantity digital content over distributed environments. However, putting them all together and providing quality guarantee for overall applications in terms of high quality of both media content and the delivery is not trivial; not only the network QoS is not directly included the scheduling loop of high level workflow systems, but also optimizing the usage of network services require real time monitoring of network infrastructures is not an easy task. In the next section, we will formulate the problem and propose an agent based solution to enable quality guarantee for workflows that handle content delivery over advanced network.

3. NETWORK QoS AWARE WORKFLOW PLANNING

In the previous section, we reviewed different technologies involved in delivering content over network, and we argued that including network QoS in high level applications is essential to enable global quality guarantee on applications. In this section, we will discuss an agent based solution for this problem. Our focus is on improving existing workflow systems by adding an extra planner.

We had two alternatives when we looked at the inclusions of QoS aware functionalities in scientific workflow systems: 1) re-engineer the functional components of existing systems to include the QoS support, or 2) consider existing systems as legacy systems, and provide QoS support as plugable components to the systems. Each alternative has advantages and disadvantages, we chose ultimately the second approach.

3.1 Design Requirements

Network QoS support can be applied to: QoS aware resource selection, resource provisioning and quality assured workflow execution. The designed system thus needs to meet the following functional requirements:

1. The system must include QoS aware resource discovery and selection of network resources. To support this we must have descriptions of the network resources and their quality attributes, we must provide a search tool that checks the suitable resources based on the input requirements.
2. The system should be able to generate a resource provisioning plan for the selected resources based on the input requirements. The plan is made based on the provisioning services that the available network infrastructure provides.
3. The system should be able to generate workflows that handle large data movement between network resources with guaranteed data transfer quality, and wrap the generated workflow as a service, which can be executed standalone or included in a third party workflow.
4. At runtime, the system should provide monitoring services to track the actual state of the network resources. It should also provide interfaces for third party workflows to invoke during their provenance procedure to record the runtime information.

The Agent Oriented (AO) methodology complements the object and component oriented methods with knowledge related notions to manage system complexity (Massonet, Deville, & Neve, 2002), and emerges as an important modeling and engineering approach for constructing complex systems, such as workflow management systems. The concept of *agents* originated in the mid-1950s as *a 'soft robot' living and doing its business within the computer's world* (Kay, 1984). Wooldridge distinguished three types of agent architectures: deliberative, reactive and hybrid (Wooldridge & Jenings, 1995). The difference between the deliberative and reactive architectures is that the former incorporates a detailed and accurate symbolic description of the external world and uses sophisticated logic to reason about the activities, while the latter one only implements a stimulus-reaction scheme. Reactive architectures are easier to implement but lack a subtle reasoning capability. Hybrids of the two schemes are commonly used. During the past two decades, agent based models, in particular reactive models, have been applied as an advanced technology in modeling and constructing complex systems. Agent frameworks, such as FIPA (Bellifemine, Poggi, & Rimassa, 2001), abstract the structure of basic agents and define standardized communication languages to represent interactions between agents, which facilitate the implementation of agent-based applications.

JADE (Java Agent DEvelopment Framework) is a free software and distributed by Telecom Italy (Case et al., 2002). Fully implemented in Java, JADE realizes a FIPA compliant multi agent middleware. In our project, we choose JADE as the implementation framework. Firstly, the JADE platform can be distributed across machines and the configuration can be controlled via a remote GUI; the Java language makes the development portable; the JADE framework allows agents move from one machine to another at runtime. Moreover, being compliant to the FIPA protocol, JADE provides a standard architecture for scheduling agent activities, which makes the inclusion of high level functionality easy, e.g., adding a Prolog module for activity reasoning. Finally, the ontology enabled agent communication between agents promotes seamless integration among the semantic network description, QoS aware searching modules, underlying models of workflow descriptions, and other necessary functional components of our system.

Figure 4. The basic architecture of the NEtWork QoS planner

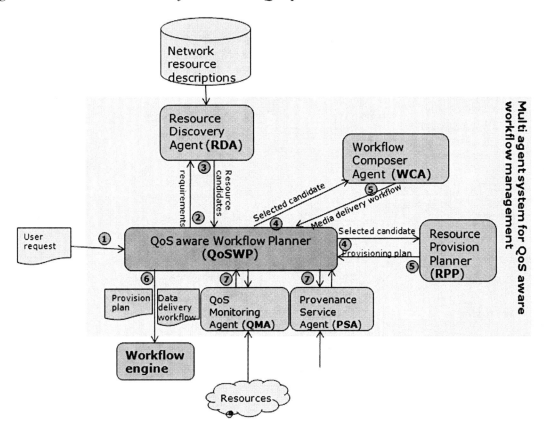

3.2 An Agent Based QoS Workflow Planner

We propose an agent based architecture, composed of a *QoS aware workflow planner (QoSWP)* and five more agents: *a Resource Discovery Agent (RDA), a Workflow Composition Agent (WCA), a Resource Provisioning Planner (RPP), a QoS Monitor Agent (QMA)* and *a Provenance Service Agent (PSA)*. Figure 3 provides a conceptual schema of our agent system.

The QoSWP coordinates the other agents to select suitable services, to propose optimal network connections between the services, and to create the necessary scripts for the workflow engine to invoke the requested services. A typical use case scenario will illustrate the role of each component (see Figure1). The QoSWP receives the request for data process services and the service requirements

from the user (step1). After that, the RDA reads the description of the resources and the network topologies from the registry, and searches suitable data sources and destinations, and network paths between them (step2). The RDA returns a list of qualified candidates, and sorts them based on the quality metrics of each candidate (step3). From the candidates, the QoSWP selects the best one, and requests WCA and RPP to generate a resource provisioning plan and a data transfer workflow (step4 and step5), both of which will be executed by the workflow engine (step6). At run time, the QMA monitors the actual state of the resources and checks whether the global quality required by the workflow is satisfied (step7). Based on the states updated by the QMA, the QoSWP decides if the resources of the workflow should be adapted. The provenance service records events in the resources provisioning, allocation, and combine

Figure 5. The concept schema of network description language

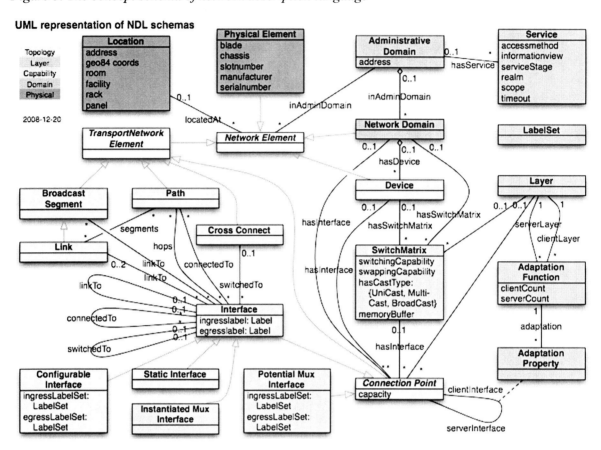

the actual state of the quality attributes with the log data (step7).

In the rest of the section, we will discuss the detailed design issues.

3.3 Semantic Network Description

Semantic web technologies (Berners-Lee, Hendler, & Lassila, 2001) provide suitable solutions to describe network topologies, devices, and the QoS requirements for data *and network resource*. We have developed two ontologies for describing CineGrid services and network topologies respectively. The CineGrid Description Language (CDL) describes the services and resources available on top of the network infrastructure. The Network Description Language (NDL) models the different levels of a network infrastructure:

physical, domain, capability, layer and topology (Ham et al., 2008).

NDL (see: http://www.science.uva.nl/research/sne/ndl) comprises of a series of RDF schemas that categorize information for network topologies, network technology layers, network device configurations, capabilities, and network topology aggregations. The main use cases so far have been generation of network maps, lightweight offline path finding and more recently multi-layer path finding, and network topology information exchange. NDL has been used primarily in the research community in the Netherlands: UvA, SARA and SURFnet (SURFnet, 2002). It also has been applied to the GLIF Optical Lightpath Exchanges (see: http://www.glif.is).

NDL chooses RDF because 1) RDF allows easier exchange of information between independent domains and 2) it is easily extendible and it allows integration of independent data models developed in other fields, by other researchers. Several tools that consume RDF data are publicly available and make the use of this syntax straightforward. NDL is a modular set of schemata, defining an ontology to describe computer networks. Figure 5 shows the UML diagram of the NDL schemas.

1. The topology schema describes devices, interfaces and connections between them on a single layer. The classes and properties in the topology schema describe the topology of a hybrid network, without detailed information on the technical aspects of the connections and their operating layer. Through this lightweight schema NDL provides an easy toolset for basic information exchange and path finding.
2. The layer schema describes generic properties of network technologies, and the relation between network layers. The topology schema defines network topologies on a single layer. The NDL layer schema allows applications to describe multi-layer networks, like hybrid networks. The NDL layer schema is based on a formal model, which uses ITU-T G.805 functional elements (see: http://www.itu.int/rec/T-REC-G.805/en) and the concept of labels as described in GMPLS (see: http://www.ietf.org/rfc/rfc3945.txt).
3. The capability schema describes device capabilities.
4. The domain schema describes administrative domains, services within a domain, and how to give an aggregated view of the network in a domain. It allows network operators to provide an aggregated view of their domain to neighboring domains, rather than the full topology. An important concept in the domain schema is that of Service Descriptions.
5. Service descriptions allow domains to point applications to the (web) services they of-

fer. The idea is that domains publish static information in NDL, and provide a web service for dynamic information or more confidential data, like reservation requests. Furthermore, different domains will have different opinions on what is "static" and "non-sensitive"".
6. The physical schema describes the physical aspects of network elements.

The CineGrid Description Language (CDL) defines an ontology for describing CineGrid resources. CDL consists of two parts, an infrastructure ontology and a service ontology. The service ontology describes the tasks a device can perform for the users of the CineGrid Exchange. Devices in the Exchange nodes perform multiple types of tasks, possibly at the same time. We map these tasks into services; and the user of the ontology deals directly with services.

In order to do resource planning the service ontology had to be mapped onto network infrastructure descriptions. The infrastructure part of the CDL provides a loosely mapped paradigm between the CDL and the underlying network description schemas. In this way, other network description schemas, for example the Network Markup Language currently under development in the OGF (OGF, 2011), can also be integrated with the CDL.

Figure 6 shows the classes used in CDL and their relations to each other. The classes related to the infrastructure are on the left side and the classes representing the different services are on the right side. Let's begin with the service ontology in the CDL. We have a generic Service class, which contains three sub classes: DisplayService, StorageService and StreamService. The DisplayService defines all the common properties needed for a display service; StorageService defines all the common properties needed by a storage service; and, StreamService defines all the common properties needed by a streaming service. We identify seven specific implementations of these

Figure 6. The concept schema of CineGrid description language (CDL)

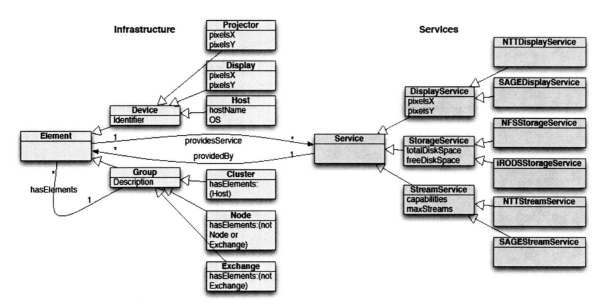

three main services. SAGEDisplayService is a service to display video on tiled panels running SAGE (Sage, 2010); this specific service inherits all the properties of DisplayService, which in turn inherits the properties of Service. We intend to extend the supported services with video manipulation and transcoding services in the near future. Users of CDL can also create their own services' descriptions, by simply inheriting from the general Service class. The infrastructure part defines the basic building blocks that reflect the hierarchical structure of the CineGrid Exchange. We define the Element class to describe the common characteristics of elements in the infrastructure. There are two classes which inherit directly from Element, and seven more specific classes that inherit from these two intermediate classes:

Device for single devices.

- **Projector** to represent stand alone video projection devices.
- **Display** to represent video display devices.
- **Host** to represent a single host.

Group to represent element groups.

- **Cluster** to represent computing clusters.
- **Node** to represent a collection of devices working as a single entity.
- **Exchange** to represent an exchange platform (e.g. the CineGrid Exchange).

Elements provide the services to the users. The cdl:providesService property links services to elements.

We map NDL to the CDL infrastructure ontology using the owl:sameAs property; this allows us to say that a certain object in one namespace is the same as an object in the other namespace. This has a very essential practical implication for the operation of the CineGrid Exchange. Network administrators can describe the network portion in NDL and CineGrid node administrators can link their device objects to the NDL objects, and do reasoning on both the CineGrid Exchange and the supporting network topology.

Figure 7. The abstract workflow process schema

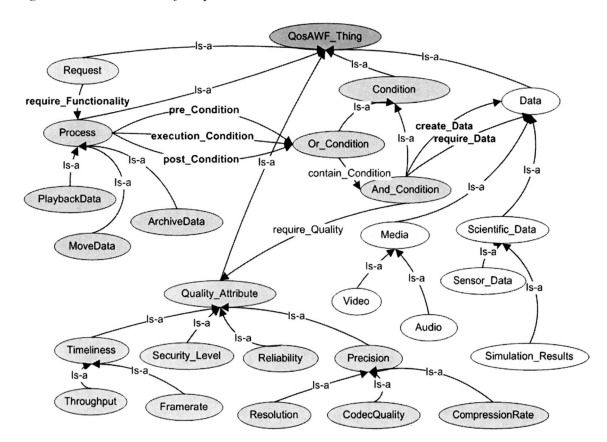

3.4 QoS Abstract Workflow Process Modeling

Based on early work (Caragea & Syeda-Mahmood, 2004; Klusch, Fries, & Sycara, 2006; Bubak, Gubala, Kapalka, Malawski, & Rycerz, 2005), we propose an ontology for describing abstract workflows (*qosawf. owl*). Figure 7 shows the graphical representation.

This ontology defines the basic concepts of workflow processes, pre/post/execution conditions of the process, media data, and quality attributes. A user's request is described as an object of the *Request* class, and a *Request* consists of one or more *Processes* which can be accessed via the *request Functionality* property. A *Process* class uses *pre Condition* and *post Condition* to indicate the requirements for *Data* the process requires

and generates, and the quality for the required data. The *Process* class also uses *execution Condition* to indicate the service quality for the process. In the current definition, *Data* contains two specific types: *Media* and *Scientific Data*. And the service quality is modeled as a set of *Quality Attributes*. Based on the QoS taxonomy defined in (Sabata, Chatterjee, Davis, Sydir, & Lawrence, 1997), *Quality attribute* can more specifically be *Precision*, *Timeliness*, *Reliability* and *Security Level*. In our case, where the pre and post conditions consist of requirements for data and the data quality, *and Condition* and *or Condition* are the two most important types. Using the above ontology, a user is able to formulate a request for obtaining and playing back specific video material with a minimal resolution and frame rate.

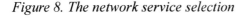

Figure 8. The network service selection

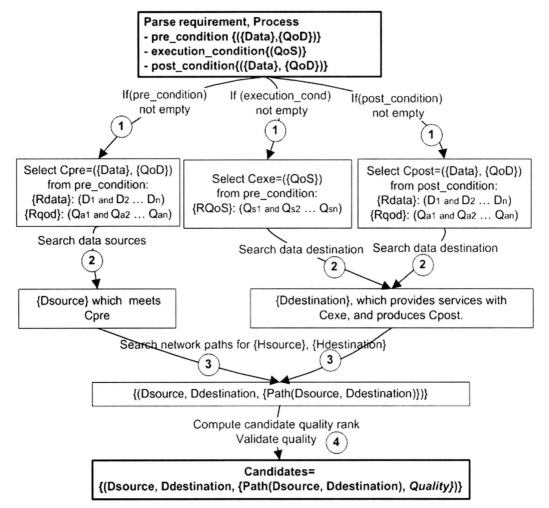

3.5 Resource Discovery

Figure 8 shows the basic procedures in the network resource selection process. The resource discovery agent 1) parses the input description, 2) searches suitable CineGrid resources which meet the requirements for being the data sources and destination, 3) looks for optimal network paths between them, and 4) computes the quality of resource candidates and proposes solutions, as shown in Figure 8.

1) Step 1: QoS requirement parsing. The input of RDA contains functional requirements for data operation (*Process*) and the quality requirement

for both the operation and the data. The current QoSAWF schema allows one input description to contain only one instance a *Process* concept. The parsing procedure obtains the pre/execution/post condition of the process. The *pre Condition* and *post Condition* of a process contains both requirements for data, such as data type and properties, and for the quality of the data, such as resolution if the data is a video file. The *execution Condition* gives QoS requirements for the process. For instance, the *pre Condition* contains both content and quality requirements for data, as follows:

$$C\,pre = \{Cpre_{data}\ and\ Cpre_{qod}\}$$

$$Cpre_{data} = \{Cpre_{d1}\ or\ Cpre_{d2}\ or\ldots\ Cpre_{dn}\}\ in\ which$$

$$Cpre_{di} = \{Cpred_{i1}\ and\ Cpred_{i2}\ and\ldots\ Cpre_{dim}\};$$

$$Cpre_{qod} = \{Cpre_{qod1}\ or\ Cpre_{qod2}\ or\ \ldots\ Cpre_{qodn}\}\ in\ which$$

$$Cpre_{qodi} = \{Cpre_{qodi1}\ and\ Cpre_{qodi2}\ and\ \ldots\ Cpre_{qodik}\}.$$

The RDA selects an element in the pre/execution/post condition, and uses it as the constraints for the resource search.

2) Step 2: data and the operation. From the data requirements derived from the step 1, the hosts that contain the required data, namely *data sources*, and the hosts that will consume or store the data, namely *data destinations*, are identified. From the resource description, the RDA derives the set of storage services that contains the *Data* instance that meets the required type, and quality. In CineGrid, each *Data* instance is associated with a *Meta data* object, which can be accessed via the property *hasMetadata*. Therefore, the sources of data are located by searching instances of *Data* which contain meta data meet the requirements abstracted from the *pre Condition*. Using the property of *cdl:providedby* and *owl:sameAs*, the actual host that stores data can then be derived.

The destination of the data is derived from the process types described in the requirement. As we mentioned above, based on the type of data operations, we abstract three basic process types: *MoveData*, *PlayData*, and *ArchiveData*. For the process of *PlayData*, *post Condition* can be empty, because the process does not generate data. The processes are linked to the actual services of CineGrid via property *implementedBy*. Therefore, the process destination of the data is determined by both the location of the implemented services

and the location of the data required in the *post condition*.

3) Step 3: network paths. The next step is to find all network paths between the data sources and destinations. Using NDL, a network path can be found using three properties: *link to*, *connect to* and *switch to*. The *link to* property indicates that two network devices are directly connected via a physical line, while *connect to* refers to a connection which might include unknown devices between the two end points of the path. The *connect to* property is mostly used in the situation where two devices belong to two different domains and the detailed physical connections between them is not clear or not open to public due to administration rules. The *switch to* property is only used in a switch device to indicate the connectivity between different ports in the device. The RDF triples defined in the network topology description give a suitable *graph* representation for finding network paths.

4) Step 4: quality ranking: The first three steps return resource candidates, which are represented as (*source, destination, path*). The quality of the resource can be evaluated at multiple levels: 1) the quality of data, 2) the quality of the storage/stream services, 3) quality of the hosts, which provide the services, and 4) the network connection between hosts. From the CDL and NDL ontology, the RDA can abstract the following quality attributes: 1) the quality of data, such as compressed ratio and resolution, from the data catalogue of resources 2) the properties of host, such as its CPU speed, memory size and the available storage space, 3) the network bandwidth of network connections. From the quality attributes and the quality requirements defined for the process, the RDA applies the following rules to filter unqualified candidates from the searched results:

1. The RDA first checks if the data and services meet the quality requirement.
2. Then compute the bandwidth of the candidate network paths, only the candidates that have

bandwidth meet the minimal data transfer rate are kept.

3. The RDA sorts all qualified candidates based on the quality of the hosts that provide data or visualization service, and the bandwidths of the network connections.

We have compared different options to realize the resource search mechanism; we have evaluated several Query languages (RQL, RDQL, N3, Versa, SeRQL, SPARQL) and Rule languages (SWRL, Prolog/RDF lib, JESS etc.). We have finally chosen the RDF library of SWI-Prolog; its triple based manipulation interface is flexible for the high level language we use to implement the agents (Java); it is also easy to access the runtime state of the triples. Finally, the Prolog language provides effective solutions to realize graph path findings. The FIPA (FIPA, 2011) standards provide a suitable architecture to implement distributed agents in our system. The Agent Communication Language (ACL) allows agents to exchange messages using an explicitly defined semantic schema, which allows seamless integration between agents and remote Ontology knowledge bases. In the current prototype, the RDA receives the URI of the user requirements and network resources from the QoSWP. The RDA parses the given abstract workflow and searches the resource description; it returns results in the form of (storage host, visualization host, path, quality rank).

3.6 Network Provisioning

The ultimate goal of our NEWQoSPlanner is to automatically find a quality optimal network path for delivering and processing media content. Provisioning a path in the network is an important step to make the network available to workflow. So far we have only integrated the NEWQoSPlanner in an ad hoc fashion with our network test bed. The planner can execute some scripts to create network paths in our experimental network. Obviously, such an approach does not scale to

larger networks. There will be problems with authentication and authorization, supporting different kinds of network equipment, compatibility with other systems, et cetera. An easier solution is to integrate with existing network management tools. This will allow the workflows to be used for intra-domain path selection in many more networks, or even inter-domain using the global GLIF network.

There are currently several network provisioning systems that allow integration with other applications. ESnet and Internet2, two large research and education networks in the USA, have developed the On-Demand Secure Circuits and Advance Reservation System (OSCARS) (Gridnets, 2006). This system allows users to create reservations for circuits in the ESnet and Internet2 network. The system can use either MPLS and RSVP to create connections, in the case of the ESnet network, or integrate with Internet2's Dynamic Circuit Network and provision VLANS on their national backbone network.

The OSCARS system allows users to specify different properties that a circuit reservation should fulfill, such as bandwidth, or a specific VLAN number. The OSCARS system also allows applications to use the web service interface for a more direct provisioning service. This kind of integration would be ideal for our NEWQoSPlanner.

Another system currently available is the OpenDRAC system (OpenDrac, 2011), originally developed by Nortel Networks. This provisioning system is currently in use on the SURFnet network in the Netherlands. The management system provides the network operator with the tools to manage and monitor the network, but also has an interface for users to request lightpaths. Depending on the access rights of the user he can request lightpaths from several locations with different capacities. OpenDRAC allows users to specify other attributes of the circuit as well, such as bandwidth, VLAN ID, etc., depending on the capabilities of the underlying network. The OpenDRAC system also features a web service interface, which allows for simple integration with other applications.

Currently, the different management systems such as OpenDRAC and OSCARS are not directly compatible, meaning that it is not possible to create a reservation that goes from a domain managed by OpenDRAC to an OSCARS managed domain or vice-versa. There currently is a demonstration project going, called Fenius, to implement a simple inter-domain interface between these provisioning systems to allow for the automatic set up of inter-domain circuits. This has been demonstrated successfully at the SuperComputing 2010 conference (Fenius, 2011). In the future this will converge to a standard currently in development in the Open Grid Forum, called the Network Service Interface (Nsi-Wg, 2011). This standard will allow provisioning systems to interact with each other to automatically create inter-domain circuits for the users and their applications.

4. A USE CASE

The system presented in section 3 was originally developed in the context of CineGrid. An important mission of the CineGrid project is to provide a dedicated network environment to connect distributed parties from different domains to share large quantities of very high quality digital media, such as the high definition video material used in the movie industry. The results reach beyond the workflow field, and they can be beneficial to understand how advanced network connections enhance the digital media delivery in the academic and education context. In this section, we will demonstrate how the designed architecture works in the following use case, and discuss the technical considerations to prototype the system.

4.1 Basic Scenario

We are focusing on a *digital media delivery on demand* use case: the goal is to retrieve media

material from the infrastructure, and request quality guaranteed connections to deliver the data to qualified nodes for further processing, such as playback or visualization. Using the proposed agent framework, the use case will be prototyped as follows:

1. The user uses the schema provided by the system to describe the name and properties of the media, and to specify the quality requirements for visualizing the data.
2. The QoSWP parses the user input and creates queries for the RDA to look for data sources of the media.
3. Based on the input requirements, the RDA looks for the data repositories that contain the required media, and the visualization devices that meet the required playback quality. Then the RDA looks for all possible network paths between the sources and the visualization devices.
4. The RDA returns a list of candidates in the form of (source, destination, path) triplets, and the candidates are ordered based on the quality they provide. The QoSWP selects the best candidate from the list and sends it to the RPP and WCA to make a resource provisioning plan, and to create a workflow that can deliver the media from the source to the visualization device, and to play it back in the visualization device.
5. To help RPP and WCA make the provision plan and the workflow compliant to a specific workflow engine, the QoSWP also explicitly tells the RPP and WCA what language of the third party engine will use.
6. After receiving the scripts generated by the RPP and WCA, the QoSWP sends them to the third party engine to execute the provisioning plan and the delivery plan.

Figure 9. The test bed of the use case and the screen snapshot of the user portal

4.2 Prototype

We are prototyping our ideas using a small portion of the CineGrid infrastructure as a test bed. Four locations in Amsterdam host CineGrid resources and are connected via dedicated and configurable circuits provided by SURFnet. Using the description languages presented in section 3.3, we have described the use case test bed. Four locations (UvA, SARA, De Waag and the Dutch Film and TV institute) in Amsterdam are connected with up to two dedicated switchable 1Gbit/s links, which can be dynamically changed between locations using the openDRAC network provisioning software used by SURFnet. In the use case, a portal is developed as the user front end to the NEWQoSPlanner. The portal allows a user to search a movie in two ways: browsing the entire media base by category, or searching a specific movie by providing relevant meta information. The user can also specify the quality requirements for playing back the movie. The Portal encodes all

the user input using the schema discussed in 3.4 and sends it to the QoSWP. The QoSWP returns the results as a list of ordered candidates based on their quality. The user can then select an optimal option and play it back. The use case has also been partially demonstrated in the Super Computing Conference 2010 (Zhao, Koning, Grosso, & de Laat, 2010). Figure 9 shows the screen snapshot and the test bed topology.

4.3 Discussion

The media delivery use case presented in the previous section demonstrates the feasibility of including network QoS in the resource planning of the high level data intensive applications. The planner extends the control loop of high level applications to tune the behavior of the network infrastructure. In our research we initially chose workflow as an application execution manager; however, our solution does not preclude its use in other systems that have control on the network behavior, *e.g.* clouds' front ends.

The planner currently assumes that all the infrastructure descriptions share NDL and CDL as the schema. Descriptions of a large scale environment are often composed and maintained by the different owners. Therefore, these descriptions do not always share the same level of details, and do not provide the same level of information to external parties due to different administrative policies. Often network administrators prefer not to publish the entire network topology description to minimize security risks. In such cases, the planner has to obtain the descriptions from all involved parties in order to do a resource query on the entire environment. Even then, the application might not have access to all the information needed, *e.g.* the quality attributes that applications require may not be explicitly stated in the collection of descriptions.

There is clearly a big gap between the requirements from high level applications and the availability of the semantic information provided by the distributed environments. On the one side, information from different infrastructure domains may be partially accessible and may have overlaps or conflicts on certain infrastructure due to evolution and or the delay of maintenance of the descriptions. On the other side, applications require different types of information from the descriptions to find suitable resources or to make decisions on resource allocations. To apply the planner in a large scale infrastructure, we plan to develop an information preprocessing framework that will ensure that the infrastructure descriptions meet the requirements of the planner.

5. FUTURE RESEARCH DIRECTIONS

In this chapter, we discussed how network QoS and workflow systems are used to optimize the data movement processes in the media delivery. The use of dedicated network paths, such as the ones described previously, certainly increases the QoS that can be offered to streaming applications. We believe this trend toward pay-per-use advanced network services will increase; as service provider will realize the earning potential of offering this guaranteed quality to specific applications. It is foreseeable that the same model will slowly trickle down to the single individual customers. Still we envision two main evolutions in the offering of these services: one related to increases in network bandwidths and one to a change in network provisioning model.

First, higher and higher bandwidths are in fact available to send data between end points and can certainly be used for streaming video; 40Gbit/s channels are now a reality (Dumitru et al., 2010) and they will increase the potential for remote collaborations on digital material editing and production. While certain quality of service aspects will automatically improve by the larger network pipes available, we believe the problem of selecting, configuring and matching resources at the edge of the networks will still require the same semantic based approach to workflow delivery we have started to develop.

Second, we are moving already towards the use of Next Generation Ethernet as the supporting technology for education and research networks; here individual applications use a QoS-enabled vLAN in the core infrastructure, created with the use of Provider Backbone Transport and Provider Link State Bridging technologies. This will require the proper evaluation of the semantic information that needs to be included in the network ontologies describing these networks, as proper path and resource selection will rely on smart and usable categorizations. It is now possible to combine semantic descriptions of the network, and the available media content on the network to provide a QoS aware workflow for media delivery. This is only the first step into making available all the relevant resources for generic workflows.

Third, workflow systems emerge as a key service to glue different levels of technologies and hide the underlying details from the high level applications. However, it also introduces new challenges in application development and the validation of workflow results. An important issue in our research agenda is to develop a suitable semantic model is needed for logging and querying workflow processes with the network QoS information. With this model, namely provenance model, the runtime information of the workflow and the network events will be recorded for the further querying for reproducing execution scenarios of the workflow. Furthermore, we also plan to extend the ontologies to other kinds of resources. This will make it possible to define any kind of computing workflow that can involve searching for content, computation, data transport and visualization.

6. CONCLUSION

Quality control at the network level is crucial for workflow applications in which large data movement is the performance bottleneck. Advanced network infrastructures provide guaranteed services for high level data intensive applications. To bridge workflow requirements and the services provided by the network we propose to use the semantic web technology. We developed the QoSAWF ontology to provide lightweight solution to describing QoS requirements for data operation related workflow processes.

Our network resource discovery agent provides a necessary service for tuning data transfer processes from the application level. The NEWQoSPlanner is the first step towards the direction of network quality adaptive workflow planner, and it can play a role in the development of CDNs based on the latest hybrid network architectures in place of a traditional internet fabric.

REFERENCES

W3C. (2010). *Resource description framework.* Retrieved from http://www.w3.org/RDF/

Alaya, I., Solnon, C., & Ghdira, K. (2007). Ant colony optimization for multi-objective optimization problems. In *Proceedings of IEEE International Conference on Tools with Artificial Intelligence*, (pp. 450–457).

Avanes, A., & Freytag, J. (2008). Adaptive workflow scheduling under resource allocation constraints and network dynamics. In *Proceedings of VLDB Endowment*, *1*(2), 1631–1637.

Bellifemine, F., Poggi, A., & Rimassa, G. (2001). JADE: A FIPA 2000 compliant agent development environment. In *Proceedings of the Fifth International Conference on Autonomous Agents*, (pp. 216–217). ACM Press.

Berners-Lee, T., Hendler, J., & Lassila, O. (2001). The Semantic Web. *Scientific American*, *284*, 34–43. doi:10.1038/scientificamerican0501-34

Blake, S., Black, D., Carlson, M., Davies, E., Wang, Z., & Weiss, W. (1998). *An architecture for differentiated service.* Request for Comments 2475, IETF. Retrieved June 10, 2011, from http://www.ietf.org/rfc/rfc2475.txt

Braden, R., Clark, D., & Shenker, S. (1994). *Integrated services in the internet architecture: An overview.* Request for Comments 1633, IETF. Retrieved June 10, 2011, from http://www.ietf.org/rfc/rfc1633.txt

Bubak, M., Gubala, T., Kapalka, M., Malawski, M., & Rycerz, K. (2005). Workflow composer and service registry for grid applications. *Future Generation Computer Systems*, *21*(1), 79–86. doi:10.1016/j.future.2004.09.021

Caragea, D., & Syeda-Mahmood, T. (2004). Semantic API matching for automatic service composition. In *WWW Alt. '04: Proceedings of the 13th international World Wide Web Conference on Alternate Track Papers & Posters*, (pp. 436–437). New York, NY, USA.

Case, J., Mundy, R., Partain, D., & Stewart, B. (2002). *Introduction and applicability statements for internet-standard management framework. RFC 3410*. Informational.

De Laat, C., & Blom, J. (2000). User-level performance monitoring program. *In Proceedings of TERENA Network Conference 2000,* Lisbon, Portugal.

De Laat, C., Radius, E., & Wallace, S. (2003). The rationale of the current optical networking initiatives. *3rd Biennial International Grid Applications-Driven Testbed Event. Future Generation Computer Systems, 19*(6), 999–1008. doi:10.1016/S0167-739X(03)00077-3

Deelman, E., Gannon, D., Shields, M., & Taylor, I. (2009). Workflows and e-Science: An overview of workflow system features and capabilities. *Future Generation Computer Systems, 25*(5), 528–540. doi:10.1016/j.future.2008.06.012

DMTF. (2011). *Common information model* (CIM). Retrieved from http://www.dmtf.org/standards/cim/

Dumitru, C., Koning, R., & de Laat, C. (2010). *ClearStream: End-to-end ultra fast transmission over a wide area 40Gbit/s Lambda.* Demo Supercomputing 2010.

Fang, Q., Peng, X., Liu, Q., & Hu, Y. (2009). *A global QOS optimizing Web services selection algorithm based on moaco for dynamic web service composition* (pp. 37–42). International Forum on Information Technology and Applications.

Farrel, A., & Bryskin, I. (2006). *GMPLS: Architecture and applications* (1st ed.). Morgan Kaufmann.

Fenius. (2011). Retrieved June 17, 2011, from http://code.google.com/p/fenius/

FIPA. (2011). *The Foundation for Intelligent Physical Agents*. Retrieved from www.fipa.org

Fortino, G., Russo, W., Mastroianni, C., Palau, C. E., & Esteve, M. (2007). CDN-supported collaborative media streaming control. *IEEE Multimedia Magazine, 14*(2), 60–71. doi:10.1109/MMUL.2007.29

Grasa, E., Figuerola, S., Recio, J., Lopez, A., Palol, M., & Ribes, L. (2006). Video transcoding in a Grid network with user controlled LightPaths. *Future Generation Computer Systems, 22*(8), 920–928. doi:10.1016/j.future.2006.03.003

Gridnets. (2006). Retrieved June 17, 2011 from https://oscars.es.net/OSCARS/docs/papers/gridnets.pdf

Grossman, R., Gu, Y., Hanley, D., Sabala, M., Mambretti, J., & Szalay, A. (2006). Data mining middleware for wide-area high-performance networks. *Future Generation Computer Systems, 22*(8), 940–948. doi:10.1016/j.future.2006.03.024

Ham, J., Dijkstra, F., Grosso, P., Pol, P., Toonk, A., & de Laat, C. (2008). A distributed topology information system for optical networks based on the semantic web. *Optical Switching and Networking, 5*(2–3), 85–93.

Ham, J., Dijkstra, F., Travostino, F., Andree, H., & de Laat, C. (2005). *Using RDF to describe networks.* Future Generation Computer Systems, Feature topic iGrid.

Harada, F., Ushio, T., & Nakamoto, Y. (2007). Adaptive resource allocation control for fair QoS management. *IEEE Transactions on Computers, 1*(56), 344–357. doi:10.1109/TC.2007.39

Holub, P., Matyska, L., Liska, M., Hejtmanek, L., Denemark, J., & Rebok, T. (2006). High-definition multimedia for multiparty low-latency interactive communication. *Future Generation Computer Systems, 22*(8), 856–861. doi:10.1016/j.future.2006.03.014

IETF. (2011). *Netconf working group.* Retrieved June 17, 2011, from http://www.ops.ietf.org/netconf/

International Telecommunications Union. (ITU) (March 2000). *Generic functional architecture for transport networks. Recommendation ITU-T G.805.* Retrieved June 17, 2011 from http://www.itu.int/rec/T-REC-G.805/

Jo, J., Hong, W., Lee, S., Kim, D., Kim, J., & Byeon, O. (2006). Interactive 3D HD video transport for e-science collaboration over UCLP-enabled GLORIAD lightpath. *Future Generation Computer Systems, 22*(8), 884–891. doi:10.1016/j.future.2006.03.006

Juve, G., & Deelman, E. (2008). Resource provisioning options for large-scale scientific workflows. In *Proceedings of ESCIENCE '08: The 2008 Fourth IEEE International Conference on eScience*, (pp 608– 613). Washington, DC: IEEE Computer Society.

Kay, A. (1984). Computer software. *Scientific American, 251*(3), 53–59. doi:10.1038/scientificamerican0984-52

Klusch, M., Fries, B., & Sycara, K. (2006). Automated semantic web service discovery with OWLS-MX. In *AAMAS '06: Proceedings of the Fifth International Joint Conference on Autonomous Agents and Multiagent Systems*, (pp. 915–922). New York, NY, USA.

Lecue, F., & Mehandjiev, N. (2009). Towards scalability of quality driven semantic web service composition. In *Proceedings of IEEE International Conference on Web Services*, (pp. 469–476).

Li, Y., Chen, M., Wen, T., & Sun, L. (2008). Quality driven web services composition based on an extended layered graph. In *Proceedings of International Conference on Computer Science and Software Engineering*, (pp. 53– 156).

Li, Y., & Xu, Z. (2003). An ant colony optimization heuristic for solving maximum independent set problems. In *Proceedings of International Conference on Computational Intelligence and Multimedia Applications.*

Maassen, J., Verstoep, K., Bal, H. E., Grosso, P., & de Laat, C. (2009). Assessing the impact of future reconfigurable optical networks on application performance. In Proceedings of *the 2009 IEEE International Symposium on Parallel & Distributed Processing*, (pp. 1-8).

Massonet, P., Deville, Y., & Neve, C. (2002). From AOSE methodology to agent implementation. In *Proceedings of the First International Joint Conference on Autonomous Agents and Multi Agent Systems*, (pp. 27–34). ACM Press.

Michlmayr, A., Rosenberg, F., Leitner, P., & Dustdar, S. (2009). Service provenance in QoS-aware web service runtimes. In *Proceedings of IEEE International Conference on Web Services*, (pp. 115–122).

Moreau, L., Freire, J., Futrelle, J., & Robert, E. Mcgrath, Myers, J., & Paulson, P. (2008). The open provenance model: An overview. *Provenance and Annotation of Data and Processes*, (pp. 323–326). Berlin, Germany: Springer-Verlag.

Nan, K., Ma, Y., Zhang, H., & Chen, G. (2006). Transfer, processing and distribution of cosmic ray data from Tibet. *Future Generation Computer Systems, 22*(8), 852–855. doi:10.1016/j.future.2006.03.015

Nichols, K., Blake, S., Baker, F., & Black, D. (1998). *Definition of the differentiated services field (DS Field) in the IPv4 and IPv6 headers.* Request for Comments 2474. Retrieved June 17, 2011, from http://www.ietf.org/rfc/rfc2474.txt

Nsi-Wg. (2011). Retrieved June 17, 2011, from http://forge.ogf.org/sf/projects/nsi-wg/

OGF. (2011). *Open Grid Forum homepage.* Retrieved June 17, 2011, from www.ogf.org

OpenDrac. (2011). *The open dynamic resource allocation controller.* Retrieved June 17, 2011, http://www.opendrac.org

Raicu, I., Zhao, Y., Dumitrescu, C., Foster, I., & Wilde, M. (2007). Falkon: A fast and light-weight task execution framework. In *SC '07: Proceedings of the 2007 ACM/IEEE Conference on Supercomputing*, (pp. 1–12). New York: ACM.

Rajbhandari, S., Contes, A. F., Rana, O., Deora, V., & Wootten, I. (2006). Trust assessment using provenance in service oriented applications. In *Proceedings of International Conference on Enterprise Distributed Object Computing Workshops.*

Rosenberg, F., Leitner, P., Michlmayr, A., Celikovic, P., & Dustdar, S. (2009). Towards composition as a service - a quality of service driven approach. In *Proceedings of International Conference on Data Engineering*, (pp. 1733–1740).

Sabata, B., Chatterjee, S., Davis, M., Sydir, J., & Lawrence, T. F. (1997). Taxonomy of QoS specifications. In *Proceedings of IEEE International Workshop on Object-Oriented Real-Time Dependable Systems*, (pp. 0-100). IEEE Computer Society.

Sage. (2010). *Scalable adaptive graphics environment.* Retrieved June 17, 2011, http://www.evl. uic.edu/cavern/sage/

Shimizu, T., Shirai, D., Takahashi, H., Murooka, T., Obana, K., & Tonomura, Y. (2006). International real-time streaming of 4K digital cinema. *Future Generation Computer Systems, 22*(8), 929–939. doi:10.1016/j.future.2006.04.001

Smarr, L., Brown, M., de Fanti, T., & de Laat, C. (2006). Special Issue on iGrid2005. *Future Generation Computer Systems, 22*(8).

Sobieski, J., Lehman, T., Jabbari, B., Ruszczyk, C., Summerhill, R., & Whitney, A. (2006). Dynamic provisioning of LightPath services for radio astronomy applications. *Future Generation Computer Systems, 22*(8), 984–992. doi:10.1016/j. future.2006.03.012

The SURFNet. (2002). *The surfnet homepage.* Retrieved June 17, 2011, http://www.surfnet.nl/

Travostino, F., Daspit, P., Gommans, L., Jog, C., de Laat, C., & Mambretti, J. (2006). Seamless live migration of virtual machines over the MAN/WAN. *Future Generation Computer Systems, 22*(8), 901–907. doi:10.1016/j.future.2006.03.007

Venugopal, S., Buyya, R., & Ramamohanarao, K. (2006). A taxonomy of data grids for distributed data sharing, management and processing. *ACM Computing Surveys, 38*(1), 1-53. ISSN 0360-0300

Wooldridge, M., & Jenings, N. (1995). Intelligent agents: Theory and practice. *The Knowledge Engineering Review, 10*(2), 115–152. doi:10.1017/S0269888900008122

Yu, J., Kirley, M., & Buyya, R. (2007). Multiobjective planning for workflow execution on grids, In *Proceedings of IEEE/ACM International Workshop on Grid Computing*, (pp. 10–17).

Zhao, Z., Belloum, A., & Bubak, M. (2009). Editorial: Special section on workflow systems and applications in e-Science. *Future Generation Computer Systems, 25*(5), 525–527. doi:10.1016/j. future.2008.10.011

Zhao, Z., Koning, R., Grosso, P., & de Laat, C. (2010). *Quality guaranteed media delivery on advanced network.* Demo in Supercomputing 2010.

ADDITIONAL READING

Braun, T., Diaz, M., Gabeiras, J., & Staub, T. (2008). *End to end quality of service over heterogeneous networks.* Springer Verlag.

KEY TERMS AND DEFINITIONS

Advanced Network: Networks that provide enhanced services to end users, in particular with focus on greater Quality of Service. Advanced networks often make use of the latest technologies, such as fully photonic or all optical devices to create circuits for transport of applications data.

Multi Agent System: A set of software agents that work together in a system. The agents may cooperate, compete, or both via some common infrastructure. A multi agent system is not simply a collection of disjoint set of autonomous agents.

Provisioning: The procedure of configuring network elements according to the user service requirements and make them ready for the customer to actually use the service.

Quality of Service (QoS): A measure of the ability that a service can provide to its consumers. In the network context, QoS refers to the performance attributes such as delay variation, bandwidth, and packet loss rate, which are also called QoS metric.

Scientific Workflows: The workflows used in scientific experiments.

Workflows: Sequences of steps or tasks defined in the business processes or scientific experiments. A workflow management system provides modeling mechanisms for describing workflow logics, automates the execution of workflow steps, and provides necessary support at different levels to allow users to interact with the execution.

ENDNOTE

[1] Acknowledgements - The Global Lambda Integrated Facility (GLIF) Map 2011 visualization was created by Robert Patterson of the Advanced Visualization Laboratory (AVL) at the National Center for Supercomputing Applications (NCSA) at the University of Illinois at Urbana-Champaign (UIUC), using an Earth image provided by NASA with texture retouching by Jeff Carpenter, NCSA. Data was compiled by Maxine D. Brown of the Electronic Visualization Laboratory (EVL) at the University of Illinois at Chicago (UIC). Support was provided by GLIF, NCSA/UIUC, the State of Illinois, and US National Science Foundation grants # OCI-0962997 to EVL/UIC. For more information on GLIF, see http://www.glif.is/. The GLIF map does not represent all the world's Research and Education optical networks, and does not show international capacity that is dedicated to production usage. The GLIF map only illustrates excess capacity that its participants are willing to share with international research teams for applications-driven and computer-system experiments, in full or in part, all or some of the time. GLIF does not provide any network services itself, and researchers should approach individual GLIF network resource providers to obtain lightpath services.

Chapter 7
Optimizing Content Delivery in QoS-Aware Multi-CDNs

Nadia Ranaldo
University of Sannio, Italy

Eugenio Zimeo
University of Sannio, Italy

ABSTRACT

Broadband network technologies have improved the bandwidth of the edge of the Internet, but its core is still a bottleneck for large file transfers. Content Delivery Networks (CDNs), built at the edge of the Internet, are able to reduce the workload of network backbones, but their scalability and network reach is often limited, especially in case of QoS-bound delivery services. By using the emerging CDN internetworking, a CDN can dynamically exploit resources of other cooperating CDNs to face peak loads and temporary malfunctions without violating QoS levels negotiated with content providers. In this chapter, after a wide discussion of the problem, the authors propose an architectural schema and an algorithm, based on the divisible load theory, which optimizes delivery of large data files by satisfying an SLA, agreed with a content provider, while respecting the maximum budget that the delivering CDN can pay to peer CDNs to ensure its revenue.

INTRODUCTION

The increasing desire of using rich media services is often not satisfied due to bandwidth limitations, high latency and low quality of service. In fact, even if broadband technologies are significantly improving the bandwidth of the edge of the Internet, backbones remain limited and congested because of the huge traffic generated by service providers for replying to user requests. Therefore, smarter infrastructures are necessary to improve quality, bandwidth availability and profitability by using edge technologies, such as Content Delivery Networks (CDNs) (Hofmann & Beaumont, 2005; Pallis & Vakali, 2006).

DOI: 10.4018/978-1-4666-1794-0.ch007

A CDN is a collection of cooperating servers, distributed across multiple locations, optimized to deliver content, such as static Web pages, applications files, stored multimedia objects and real-time audio/video. Content providers, such as large enterprises, Web service providers, media companies and news broadcasters, exploit CDN services to deliver content and applications with high performance and reliability to a wide and geographically distributed audience.

The basic idea of a CDN is to replicate contents on servers (called replica servers) and deliver them to end-users from "the best" server with the aim of minimizing user-perceived response time and of maximizing overall CDN performance with respect to some metrics, such as bandwidth consumption, server utilization and reliability. The redirection of the user's request to the best replica server is performed using a request routing mechanism, such as the Global Server Load Balancing (GSLB), DNS-based request routing, dynamic metafile generation and HTML rewriting (Pathan & Buyya, 2008a).

From a business point of view, deploying a large-scale CDN for Internet-wide available content is complex and requires high operation costs. It, in fact, involves the availability and management of distributed resources with large storage capacity connected among them by means of high throughput networks. Against sustained costs, CDNs obtain their revenues by service contracts stipulated with content providers, which typically define fees related to the amount of stored and of transferred content. Moreover, Service Level Agreements (SLAs) (Bouman, Trieneken, & van der Zwan, 1999), used to formally define a service contract, agreed between a customer and a service provider, are becoming more and more popular in the context of content delivery services. Commercial CDNs, in fact, are recently starting to adopt SLAs to agree a desired degree of quality of service (QoS) against a penalty to pay to the customer if an SLA is not satisfied; however, at our knowledge, only service availability is taken

into consideration by existing providers (Amazon Web Services, 2010).

CDNs could negotiate further QoS parameters for becoming more attractive to content providers, such as maximum response time for dynamic Web transactions or maximum download time for large multimedia data. However, satisfying SLAs for content delivery services introduces an additional complexity in CDN infrastructures management. This leads to further increase the economic investments against low revenue margins.

An approach that can be exploited to foster QoS-aware CDNs is *CDN internetworking*, also called *content peering* (Day, Cain, Tomlinson, & Rzewski, 2003). This emerging approach, based on interoperability and resource sharing mechanisms, allows a CDN to optimize its content delivery services by dynamically exploiting capabilities of other CDNs participating to the same virtual organization, called *multi-CDN*. Since content peering allows a CDN to expand beyond its borders and to deliver large-scale (eventually Internet-wide) services without huge economical investments, it is gaining popularity for improving scalability and network reach of CDN providers and to tear down the initial investment of new ones.

Content peering allows a CDN to avoid the violation of negotiated QoS levels with content providers by dynamically addressing unforeseen situations caused by malfunctions of CDN infrastructures or peak loads typically generated by global and limited-time interest events, such as worldwide sport competitions and historical significance actuality and political occurrences. As an example, in conjunction with the Soccer World Cup 2010, during which Akamai delivered live and on-demand Web content for 24 global broadcasters in 65 countries for one month, a peak of more than 20 million visitors per minute was registered on June 24th, over twice higher than the World Cup 2006 (Young & Faris, 2010).

In the context of a business multi-CDN, CDNs offer their content delivery services with fees to content providers negotiating SLAs with them. If a CDN encounters problems in satisfying negotiated SLAs, it tries to respect them employing with fee dynamically resources and services of other peer CDNs (Pathan & Buyya, 2009). A CDN participating to a multi-CDN, as a consequence, derives its revenues stipulating direct contracts not only with content providers but also with other CDNs. In such scenario, classical mechanisms adopted by single CDNs (related to issues such as replica placement, content updating, cache organization and request routing) require to be extended in order to take into account SLA-based cooperative policies among CDNs that are subject to business models.

With respect to replica placement, especially in a wide-area distributed system, it is necessary to adopt innovative strategies to avoid the placement of more replicas of the same content than necessary. Since the content transfer and updating from a CDN to other CDNs is subject to a payment (such as based on a per-byte pricing), such strategies promote cost reduction and content delivery services with high QoS levels and low prices. To this aim, efficient replica placement strategies among peer CDNs should adopt dynamic mechanisms to retain balanced resource consumption of the underlying infrastructure while respecting negotiated SLAs and should take into consideration variations in request frequency both for the same content and from the same user. As a consequence, content replication involving multiple CDNs should be performed in a pull-based (lazy) approach, that means only when the content is requested, and not in advance as proposed in the push-based (eager) approach (Kangasharju, Roberts, & Ross, 2002), which works effectively only if reliable predictive mechanisms are adopted.

To further enforce SLAs guarantees, especially for delivery of large files, such as software and multimedia data, content delivery can leverage *multi-source transfer*, also called *parallel download*, which allows for exploiting multiple simultaneous connections from a client to a pool of servers that are in charge of delivering different parts of the same content.

Multi-source transfer was originally proposed in the context of the Grid delivery technology (Zhihui, Yiping, Shiyong, & Jie, 2003). This technology addressed the issue of enhancing large rich content delivery exploiting emerging Grid technology (Foster, Kesselman, Nick, & Tuecke, 2002) for creating virtual dynamic organizations and using a set of open standards and protocols for the sharing and cooperation of geographically distributed resources.

Parallel download, after having a high utilization mainly in free peer-to-peer (P2P) systems for file sharing, such as the widespread BitTorrent (Izal, Urvoy-Keller, Biersack, Felber, Al Hamra, & Garcès-Erice, 2004) and Gnutella (Klingberg & Manfredi, 2002), has also gained popularity in the context of Data Grid, in which performance of data intensive applications can be increased reducing the delay caused by "waiting for input data" (Zhang, Lee, Tang, & Yeo, 2008). Also pay-per-use content delivery networks for distribution of large files, such as the P2P CDN Kontiki (Kontiki, Inc., 2011) and Velocix (Velocix, 2011) are recently introducing parallel download to improve delivery performance.

The adoption of parallel download in a multi-CDN can lead to substantial advantages in terms of both low user-perceived latency and load balancing of large-scale distributed resources, through the utilization of server capacity and bandwidth of under-exploited CDN servers distributed over the network. The approach, in fact, allows a CDN server, requiring content updating, to receive different portions of the content simultaneously from other servers belonging to the multi-CDN.

Even though this approach seems to be feasible to improve performance, it poses new challenges in the context of SLA-based interactions: server selection and file partitioning mechanisms have to take into account not only performance parameters, but also business exchanges among CDNs, that are typically monetary transactions in which a service ensures better QoS levels against larger prices.

While some research was dedicated to the definition and enhancement of parallel download protocols aiming to minimize user-perceived latency in the context of P2P systems (Xu, Xianliang, Mengshu, & Chuan, 2005), Data Grids (Bhuvaneswaran, Katayama, & Takahashi, 2007; Yang, Chi, & Fu, 2007) and single CDNs (Malli, Barakat, & Dabbous, 2005; Gkantisidis, Ammar, & Zegura, 2003; Rodriguez & Biersack, 2002), only few work has yet been conducted on QoS-aware parallel download mechanisms in a pay-per-use context (Hsu, Chu, & Chou, 2009).

In this chapter, we discuss the state of the art and propose a solution for optimizing content delivery of large files in an SLA-bound multi-CDN. In particular, our solution, called routing and parallel updating algorithm, handles content delivery requests in two main steps. In the first step, a request routing algorithm selects "the best" replica server that will directly transfer the required content to the end-user. The best replica server is selected among the ones belonging to all the peering CDNs in the same multi-CDN. The selection criteria are based on the best throughput reachable between the replica server and the end-user and on the best ratio throughput-cost. This mainly leads to the choice of a replica server around the outer edge of the entire network, placed close to the end-user. If the selected server does not own the required content in its local storage space (content miss), the parallel updating step is performed. It is based on a pay-per-use based parallel transfer algorithm aiming to maintain the user-perceived response time within limits negotiated between the delivering CDN and the content provider. The algorithm uses a heuristic which, assuming the adoption of mechanisms for granting minimum levels of service rates (i.e. reservation control or network traffic differentiation mechanisms), allows for minimizing the user-perceived latency without overcoming the maximum budget that

the delivering CDN can pay to other peer CDNs to ensure its revenue.

The rest of the chapter is organized as follows. The next section presents background and related work. The successive section describes a QoS-aware multi-CDN and details the architectural components tied to the proposed routing and parallel updating algorithm. Then, the problem of optimizing content delivery, adopting a pay-per-use based parallel transfer approach, is discussed. Hence, performance analysis shows the validity of the proposed approach and, finally, future research directions are presented.

BACKGROUND

CDN internetworking was originally introduced by the Content Distribution Internetworking (CDI) IETF work group as an Internet draft (Day, Cain, Tomlinson, & Rzewski, 2003). It defines standard protocols to allow separate CDNs, that typically use proprietary protocols, to cooperate among each other. Following this trend, the CDI brokering system (Biliris, Cranor, Douglis, & Rabinovich, 2002), based on a specialized DNS server to dynamically redirect the content request to a CDN, was implemented and actually deployed and experimented on the Internet. The main objective was to increase the capability of peering CDNs in performing transparent load-balancing of content delivery requests among available replica servers. On the other hand, the problem of content delivery satisfying QoS levels agreed between various CDNs and content providers, such as the user-perceived latency, was not taken into account.

Other interesting CDN peering systems are the multi-provider infrastructure in (Amini, Shaikh, Schulzrinne, & Res, 2004), which proposes a peering redirecting algorithm to minimize cost and to improve performance, and CoralCDN (Freedman, Freudenthal, & Mazières, 2004), which takes into account a free content delivery service that exploits a P2P DNS-like approach based on a best effort policy (there is no economic compensation to participating nodes). Both proposals do not take into account mechanisms to define QoS levels and policies among peering CDNs to grant their satisfaction.

The work presented in (Pathan & Buyya, 2008b) aims at defining a collaborative approach for the request redirection algorithm considering the satisfaction of QoS levels (such as the maximum response time for a service request) specified in a Service Level Agreement (SLA) signed between two CDNs. The work adopts a model of peering CDNs based on the queuing theory in which each CDN is modeled as a waiting queue of user requests, served with an equal mean service rate. It takes into account the decrease of the expected waiting time of a request to evaluate the increase of the CDN performance by adopting various peering redirection algorithms. The same model is adopted in another work of the same authors (Pathan & Buyya, 2009), who present a policy-based framework for SLA negotiation among peering CDNs in a virtual organization-based model. The QoS performance model does not take into account the influence of other performance parameters such as heterogeneous service rates of replica servers and the usage cost of such servers that, on the other hand, could dynamically affect the redirection process of each request.

An attempt to address the problem of granting latency bounds can be found in (Huang & Addelzaher, 2005). In this work, a content distribution algorithm for the optimal and dynamic selection of the replica server aiming to meet global latency bounds is formulated as a graph domination problem. On the other hand, the problem of cost usage of replica servers is not taken into account.

The approach presented in this chapter is similar, as concerning adaptivity, to the one adopted by Akamai (Dilley, Maggs, Parikh, Prokop, Sitaraman & Weihl, 2002) and to those proposed in (Andrews, Shepherd, Srinivasan, & Winkler, 2002) and in (Ardaiz, Ardaiz, Freitag, & Navarro, 2001). With respect to these approaches, however, we take into account the maximum user-perceived latency agreed between the content provider and the delivering CDN and the cost for replica server usage.

With respect to content updating required in case of content miss, pull-based approaches can be distinguished in non-cooperative and cooperative ones. Many commercial CDNs, such as Akamai (Dilley, Maggs, Parikh, Prokop, Sitaraman & Weihl, 2002) and Mirror Image (Mirror Image Internet, Inc., 2011), adopt a non-cooperative approach, in which the content is pulled directly from the origin server. On the other hand, this approach can limit the multi-CDN scalability. It, in fact, can face with SLAs violations due to congestion situations for high frequently requested contents to the same origin server and, at the same time, with the wasting of temporarily idle or under-exploited resources of other CDNs. To overcome this issue, the cooperative approach proposes to exploit replica servers that store the required content. CoralCDN (Freedman, Freudenthal, & Mazières, 2004) adopts a cooperative pull-based approach exploiting a distributed index. It efficiently retrieves the requested content from a nearby server, avoiding transfers among distant nodes and the overloading of the origin server. Unlike the CoralCDN approach, based on a single transfer, we propose a multi-source transfer involving a pool of replica servers belonging to different peer CDNs. Such servers are selected by an updating algorithm that aims to maintain the user-perceived response time within limits negotiated between the delivering CDN and the content provider without overcoming the maximum budget that the CDN, in charge of content delivery, can in its turn sustain for serving the delivery request.

While the employment of multi-source transfer for content delivery has only recently emerged in commercial content delivery networks, such as Kontiki (Kontiki, Inc., 2011) and Velocix (Velocix, 2011), the technique is widely adopted in P2P systems for file sharing. Examples are Gnutella (Klingberg & Manfredi, 2002), BitTorrent (Izal, Urvoy-Keller, Biersack, Felber, Al Hamra, & Garcès-Erice, 2004) and Kazaa (Liang, Kuma, & Ross, 2005).

Free P2P file sharing systems do not use money-based trading mechanisms. On the contrary, P2P protocols are typically based on fair trading policies, in which a peer is incentivized to increase its service rate towards the peers that send back data to it (a tit for tat scheme) (Izal, Urvoy-Keller, Biersack, Felber, Al Hamra, & Garcès-Erice, 2004). Since no mechanisms to grant QoS are adopted, QoS-aware CDNs can not directly leverage such existing protocols.

The main approaches adopted for managing the content partitioning among replica servers involved in a multi-source content transfer can be static or dynamic (Gkantisidis, Ammar, & Zegura, 2003). Static approaches operate before the beginning of the content transfer, while dynamic ones operate during the content transfer. A very simple approach is based on the content partitioning into equal parts, each of which is retrieved from a different server (*static equal* approach). The main disadvantage of this approach is the lack of load-balancing among the downloads, which can cause high total transfer times due to low throughput of a server towards the receiver. This problem can be overcome adopting a load balancing technique which permits to assign content parts of different size to replica servers in a proportional way to their throughput (*static unequal* approach). The performance of this technique strongly depends on the quality of the throughput predictions of each replica server towards the receiver. Unfortunately, throughput prediction of servers involved in parallel transfers across the Internet is difficult.

In literature, some prediction algorithms for performing static unequal partitioning have been proposed. In (Rodriguez & Biersack, 2002) a history-based throughput estimation is presented. It adopts a database of previous throughputs of the replica servers towards a client, refreshed periodically with an automatic probing. A database maintains information for a group of clients connected through a proxy cache. In (Gkantisidis, Ammar, & Zegura, 2003), a throughput estimation based on the standard moving weighted average is proposed for a static unequal approach. In (Rodriguez & Biersack, 2002) a throughout prediction, based on the characteristics of the paths among the user and the replica servers and the server's load is also proposed.

Even when using accurate throughput estimation mechanisms during file transfer, throughput could be fluctuating. As a consequence, the SLAs can be guaranteed through a static unequal approach if the estimated throughput can be ensured over a minimum level during all the transfer time. This can be accomplished, for example, adopting reservation control mechanisms or re-executing the algorithm for content partitioning when network conditions change.

Reservation control mechanisms for network resources have been studied to introduce QoS levels in the Internet. A possible approach is the IETF Differentiated Services (Blake, Black, Carlson, Davies, Wang, & Weiss, 1998), a mechanism that delivers differentiated services based on the management of traffic classification. In this model, packets are marked according to the type of service they need. On the basis of these markings, routers and switches use various queuing strategies to tailor performance to requirements. This network-level solution is adopted in sophisticated enterprise networks but has not been widely deployed in the Internet.

Alternatively, mechanisms to prioritize flows to grant QoS levels at transport layer may be used. For example, multiple TCP connections and modified congestion avoidance mechanisms allow a flow to be more aggressive than a single TCP-based one (Crowcroft & Oechsli, 1998; Nabeshima, 2005).

Dynamic approaches adjust the size of the content part to retrieve from a replica server during the download process, so to request more data from servers that are currently performing better, and vice versa. The technique, proposed in (Gkantisidis, Ammar, & Zegura, 2003) and (Rodriguez & Biersack, 2002), is based on a centralized sender-initiated approach, in which the content is split into small equal parts. Initially, the client requests a part to each replica server. Every time the replica server finishes, the client asks for another part from that node, and this process continues until the whole content has been transferred. In spite of its adaptivity, the performance of this approach depends critically on the size of content parts: it has to be not too large, for granting a fine striping granularity, and also not too small, for limiting overheads due to many requests and many small parts of data to transfer.

In (Bhuvaneswaran, Katayama, & Takahashi, 2007), the dynamic co-allocation scheme with duplicate assignments is proposed. The ring-sorting algorithm adopted divides the content into a set of same-size parts which can be delivered by each replica server. Once a part is transferred by a replica server, another undelivered part will be assigned to this server, until all parts are completely transferred. However, this approach can lead to the waste of resources because multiple replica servers could repeatedly transfer the same part of the content.

Another dynamic approach, proposed in the context of Data Grid, is the recursive-adjustment co-allocation algorithm (Yang, Chi, & Fu, 2007). This approach adjusts continuously the workload on each replica server according to the throughput measured for previously assigned transfers, and anticipates the throughput for subsequent transfers, allowing to reduce the time wasted during transmission for waiting the slowest replica server.

Even if these techniques minimize the overall transfer time in given conditions, they do not estimate a priori the time needed for the overall content delivery and do not take into account the costs of resources usage.

In (Hsu, Chu, & Chou, 2009), server selection for parallel file transfer in data-intensive applications is performed on the basis of performance

and cost parameters. In particular, the common solutions for the Knapsack problem are adopted to select the servers with the highest performance-cost ratio, where performance is given by the average throughput of the server and cost is the price, per time unit, to download a file. If two servers have the same performance-cost ratio, the one with the lowest throughput fluctuation is preferred. Moreover, dynamic adjustment are adopted to avoid waste of economic costs in idle time due to dynamic behavior of replica servers throughput. The approach can be adopted to grant a maximum user-perceived latency but, on the other hand, it does not allow to choose replica servers on the basis of a maximum budget.

CONTENT DELIVERY IN A QOS-AWARE MULTI-CDN

The main focus of the chapter is the minimization of user-perceived latency while respecting the maximum budget that the delivering CDN can expend turning to other CDNs in a multi-CDN. The user-perceived latency is measured as *the total delay between a user's delivery request and receiving the content in its entirely*. The proposed solution is based on a multi-source content transfer approach for content updating, which exploits a static partitioning algorithm.

The multi-CDN infrastructure is characterized by multiple independent CDNs that handle large size contents owned by various content providers. In particular, we consider static contents, that is files characterized by low frequency of change, such as software produced by IT enterprises or audio and/or video files (streaming or not) owned by media companies. This type of content can be easily cached and the integrity among copies can be maintained using traditional caching techniques. A content provider stipulates a contract with a CDN, expressed through an SLA, that defines the expected QoS level, that is the maximum user-perceived latency, and the agreed price. The

Figure 1. Request routing in a QoS-aware multi-CDN

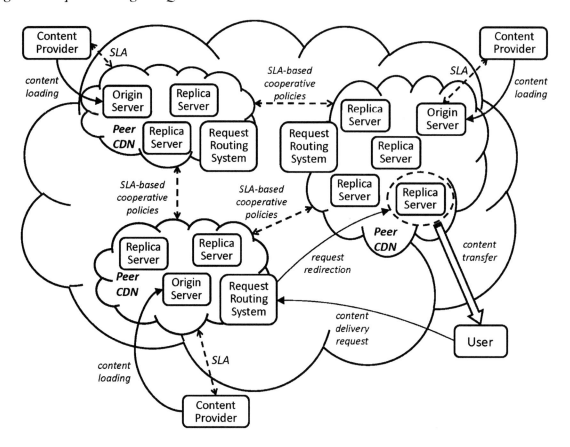

content provider loads the content on a CDN server called *origin server*. Clones of contents are stored on CDN servers called *replica servers*, distributed over the network (see figure 1).

Each CDN, participating in a multi-CDN, cooperates with other autonomous CDNs in order to meet the SLA negotiated with their own customers. A user's content request is received by the CDN owing the corresponding origin server, called *Primary CDN*, and is managed through a two-step mechanism that we call *routing and parallel updating algorithm*.

In the routing step, the "best" replica server, called *Aggregator*, is chosen to directly and transparently serve the request. We assume that the routing algorithm is performed by the request routing system (e.g. the popular DNS-based system) of the Primary CDN in cooperation with

request routing systems of the other CDNs. The routing phase aims to minimize the user-perceived response time and, at the same time, to avoid the overloading of CDN servers by selecting a replica server of any of the peer CDNs at the outer edge of the Internet near to the ISP's local point of presence (POP) accessed by the user.

If the Aggregator stores the requested content in its storage space (*content hit*), then it directly transfers the content to the user. On the contrary, if the Aggregator does not store the content (*content miss*), it starts the parallel updating step: replica servers, which store a copy of the same content, cooperate to get available the content to the user without decreasing the QoS level established between the content provider and the Primary CDN. Since we assume a business context for multi-CDNs, the updating mechanism is based on a pay-per-use multiple transfer approach. The selection of replica servers to involve in the parallel content updating and the assignment of content portions to transfer from each of them are performed through a partitioning heuristic, which aims to minimize the user-perceived latency while not exceeding a budget chosen by the Primary CDN.

During the parallel updating phase, the Aggregator simultaneously receives, stores and transfers the content to the user. We assume, in fact, that the parallel transfer from multiple replica servers of many small parts of the content is arranged in such a way to receive the content in a progressive and ordered manner. As a consequence, after starting the content updating, the Aggregator can simultaneous store the content and transfer it to the user. After the updating phase, moreover, the Aggregator will be able to directly serve the following requests for the same content and could be involved in the content updating phase of other CDN servers. The content updating request is sent by the Aggregator to the *Replica Registry*, a CDN component responsible for performing the partitioning algorithm and returning the result to the Aggregator. The Replica Registry keeps information on contents stored by the replica servers of a CDN (through notification mechanisms of content updates) and on service rates that they can grant, through the adoption of reservation control or network traffic differentiation mechanisms. When inner resources of a CDN are not enough to perform the content updating satisfying the agreed SLA with a content provider, the Replica Registry communicates with the Replica Registries of other CDNs in order to perform the partitioning algorithm on the set of replica servers available in the overall peering network. In order to avoid bottlenecks due to high updating traffic tied to a centralized implementation of the Replica Registry, we propose a distributed approach: each CDN is partitioned in a pool of clusters of replica servers (see Figure 2), obtained adopting, for example, the binning-based self-organizing

scheme proposed in (Ratnasamy, Handley, Karp, & Shenker, 2002). Each cluster of a CDN hosts a Replica Registry, called *Cluster Replica Registry* (CRR). Each replica server notifies content updates to the CRR of the cluster which it belongs to. Each CRR, moreover, maintains the updated list of CRRs of the same CDN and of the other peer CDNs.

The Aggregator sends the updating request to the CRR of its cluster. The CRR attempts to satisfy the content updating request performing the partitioning algorithm in three cases:

1. (*intra-cluster*) it adopts its information to check whether the content updating request can be satisfied exploiting the replica servers in the same cluster;
2. (*local inter-cluster*) when (1) fails, it contacts the CRRs of the other clusters of the same CDN to check whether the content updating request can be satisfied without involving other peering CDNs;
3. (*global inter-cluster*) when (2) fails, it contacts the CRRs of the other peer CDNs to gain information on content global replication and service rate of available replica servers and performs the partitioning algorithm in the overall multi-CDN.

If the algorithm fails even in the third case, then there will be an SLA violation with a possible loss of money for the Primary CDN.

During the execution of the parallel updating step, the CRR requires the reservation of the replica servers involved in the content updating in order to be able to grant the minimum stated performance against the requested monetary fee. When the partitioning algorithm ends with a positive result, the reservation on the selected replica servers is confirmed by the CRR and leads to the definition of an SLA among the Primary CDN and the peering ones involved in the content updating.

Before formalizing the routing and parallel updating algorithm, in the following, we define:

Figure 2. Content updating in a QoS-aware multi-CDN

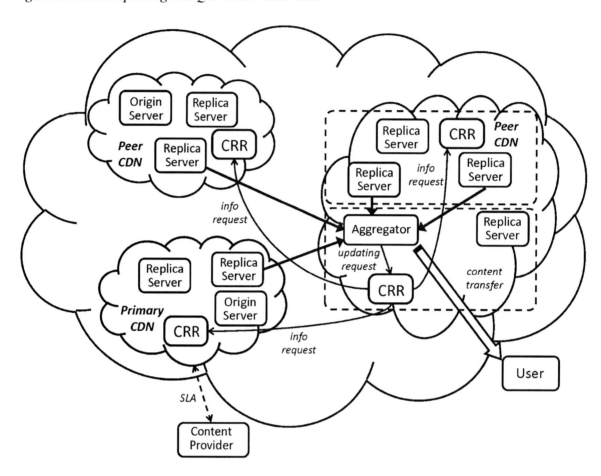

(1) the SLA (mainly QoS metrics and service price) for content delivery negotiated between a content provider and the CDN with the role of Primary CDN and (2) the SLAs negotiated between the Primary CDN and peer CDNs for content routing and updating.

SLA-Driven Content Delivery

Assume a multi-CDN composed of $P+1$ peer CDNs, denoted by CDN_i, $i:1,..,P+1$, cooperating to serve multiple content providers. CDN_i hosts a set of replica servers (RSs), denoted by RS_{ij}, $i:1,P+1$, $j:1,..S_i$.

A content provider negotiates with a CDN a *long-term SLA for content delivery* that defines the QoS metric in terms of the maximum user-

perceived latency and the delivery service price C_{del} tied to the amount of stored content, the amount of transferred content and to the contracted QoS (see Figure 3).

Assuming negligible the time for user's request, the maximum negotiated latency is proportional to the content size and to the minimum content delivery throughput, R_{min}, that represents the minimum number of bits transferred in a time unit. Denoted with O the size of the object to transfer, expressed in bytes, the maximum user-perceived latency T_{max} (in seconds) is:

$$T_{max} = \frac{O\,8}{R_{min}}$$

Figure 3. SLAs defined for a QoS-aware content delivery service in a multi-CDN

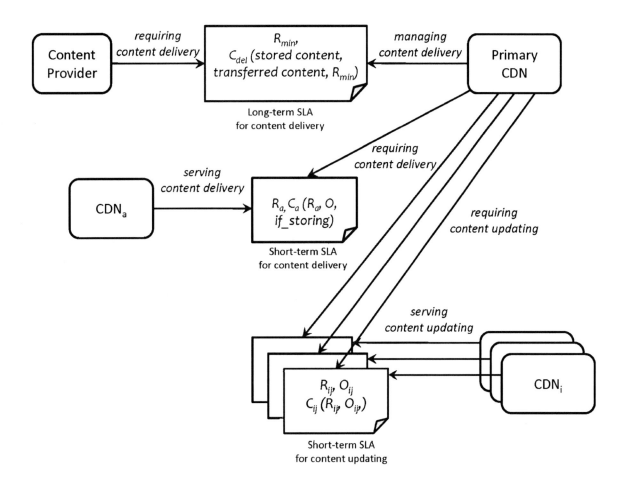

During content request handling, if the Primary CDN is not able to satisfy the long-term SLA for content delivery exploiting merely its internal capabilities, it can negotiate short-term SLAs with other peer CDNs. In particular, if the Aggregator, selected by the routing algorithm, does not belong to the Primary CDN but to a peer CDN, denoted by CDN_a, an SLA, called *short-term SLA for content delivery* between the Primary CDN and CDN_a is negotiated. This SLA uses, as a QoS metric, the minimum throughput R_a granted by the Aggregator towards the user and the delivery service price C_a, that is tied to: (1) the contracted QoS level, (2) the content size O and (3) the optional request to store the content for further delivery requests.

In case of content miss on the Aggregator, the content updating algorithm leads to the negotiation of an SLA, called *short-term SLA for content updating*, between the Primary CDN and each peer CDN involved in the parallel updating step. In particular, denoted by RS_{ij}, $i:1,..,U$, with $U<=P$, $j:1,..,U_i$, with $U_i<=S_i$, the RSs involved in the content transfer, the short-term SLA for content updating agreed between the Primary CDN and each CDN_i, $i:1,..,U$, defines the QoS metric in terms of the minimum throughput R_{ij} granted by each RS_{ij} of CDN_i, the content part O_{ij} assigned to RS_{ij} for the transfer process and the fee to pay for RS_{ij} exploitation, denoted by C_{ij}, $i:1,..,U$, $j:1,..,U_i$, that is tied to the corresponding parameters R_{ij} and O_{ij}.

Routing and Parallel Updating Algorithm

In this section, the two-step algorithm for serving a content delivery request is formalized with respect to the QoS-aware multi-CDN described before.

The algorithm is subject to two global constraints: (1) the minimum content delivery throughput R_{min} agreed between the Primary CDN and the content provider and (2) the maximum expense B_{max} that the Primary CDN establishes to incur for exploiting resources of peer CDNs for each content delivery request.

The expense B_{max} is decided individually by each CDN on the basis of internal business policies. It could be a dynamic parameter and, in particular, could depend on long-term SLAs for content delivery negotiated with content providers. Our work does not enter into details of economic theories, and for simplicity, considers a fixed budget b for one byte and an overall budget B_{max} linearly proportional to content size O:

$$B_{max} = O \, b$$

Content delivery expense, denoted by E_{del} is composed of two parts. The first one is tied to the routing phase, which can lead to the choice of an Aggregator not belonging to the Primary CDN. This component corresponds to C_a in the short-term SLA for content delivery. The second component is tied to the parallel updating phase, which can involve replica servers of various peer CDNs and is equal to the summation of costs for each exploited replica server, denoted by $C_{ij}, i:1,...,U, j:1,...,U_i$ in the short-term SLA for content updating.

$$E_{del} = C_a + \sum_{i=1}^{U}\sum_{j=1}^{U_i} C_{ij} \leq B_{max}$$

The routing algorithm regards the selection of the "best" RS for serving the request. It takes into account the QoS level desired by the content provider, expressed by means of the minimum content delivery throughput R_{min}, the throughput that can be granted towards the user by each replica server of the multi-CDN and usage cost of each replica. Moreover, we base our work on the following main assumptions: (1) the throughput of RSs can be granted above a minimum value and can be treated as nearly constant during the transmission phase; (2) concurrent transmission tasks from multiple RSs to the Aggregator do not affect each other from the point of view of minimum granted throughput; (3) transfer start-up overhead is negligible with respect to content transfer time.

Denote by $RA_{ij}, i:1,P+1, j:1,...,S_i$ the minimum throughput that can be granted by RS_{ij} towards the user, and by $CA_{ij}, i:1,P+1, j:1,...,S_i$ the cost for exploiting RS_{ij} as Aggregator. The routing algorithm selects the Aggregator as follows:

i. Find the set RA of RS_{ij} such that:
$$if \left(RA_{ij} >= R_{min} \right) \ and$$
$$\left(CA_{ij} < B_{max} \right) \rightarrow RS_{ij} \in RA \quad \forall i, \forall j$$

ii. Find the Aggregator in RA, denoted by $RS_{\overline{ij}}$, as the RS with the maximum ratio throughput-cost:
$$RS_{\overline{ij}} : \frac{R_{\overline{ij}}}{CA_{\overline{ij}}} >= \frac{R_{ij}}{CA_{ij}} \forall i, \forall j$$

If a content miss occurs, a request for content updating is sent by the Aggregator to the CRR. The updating algorithm exploits a pay-per-use based parallel transfer approach that aims to select a subset of overall RSs under the following goal: selected RSs have to perform a parallel transfer towards the Aggregator of the assigned content portions at an overall service rate equal to (or greater than) R_{min} in order to grant the maximum user-perceived latency T_{max} agreed between the content provider and the Primary CDN. We assume, in fact, that the content portions are small enough and transferred following a well-defined ordering to allow the Aggregator to concurrent receive, reorder and transfer the portions to the user.

Moreover, the content updating algorithm has to take into account the remaining budget for content updating, called *B*:

$$B = B_{\max} - CA_{\overline{ij}}$$

The pay-per-use based parallel transfer approach uses a content partitioning heuristic which efficiently solves the transfer time minimization problem under cost constraints. Such heuristic derives from the task mapping heuristic for computing resources proposed by the authors in (Ranaldo & Zimeo, 2006), based on the divisible load theory (Bharadwaj, Ghose, Mani, & Roberta, 1996).

The basic assumption of the divisible load theory is that the overall workload can be arbitrarily partitioned and assigned to a pool of resources with heterogeneous processing capabilities. Computation and communication times are modeled in a linear manner, without or with computation start-up latency, leading in many cases to optimal solutions obtained in analytic way. The optimality principle for time minimization states that all the resources must be exploited and that all have to end at the same time.

Further research was also conducted to obtain sub-optimal solutions using integer approximation techniques in a more realist scenario of workload that is divisible in a finite number of tasks that can be assigned to resources (Bharadwaj & Viswanadham, 2000). Some work, finally, was preliminary conducted to study as the constraint on the maximum budget and the modeling of resource cost linearly proportional to its usage affect the time minimization problem and the allocation of tasks to resources with different costs and capabilities (Sohn, Robertazzi, & Luryi, 1998; Charcranoon, Robertazzi, & Luryi, 2004).

The heuristic proposed in (Ranaldo & Zimeo, 2006) finds a sub-optimal solution to the time minimization problem of a master-slave workload taking into account: (1) the global constraints on maximum budget and execution deadline; (2) the assumption that all the resources start computation at the same time and (3) the discrete partitioning of overall workload. In a similar manner, in the context of content transfer, the proposed heuristic aims to assign an integer number of small parts of content to available RSs that are able to complete the content transfer as quickly as possible (within time T_{max}) and with an aggregate cost for their usage that is lower than budget *B*.

As already described in the previous section, the updating algorithm can require the execution of the heuristic in three cases. In the first case, the RSs of the Aggregator cluster are taken into account (intra-cluster case). If no solution can be found in this instance, the RSs of all the clusters of the Aggregator CDN are involved (local inter-cluster case). Finally, if even in this case no solution can be found, RSs of all peer CDNs are involved (global inter-cluster case).

Referring to the third case, in the following we denote by RS_i with $i:1,..,M$ the set of RSs belonging to the set of CDNs $\{CDN_p, with\ p:1,..,P+1\}$, storing the required content.

Let consider a large size content, that can be partitioned in a set of *N* small parts, called *chunks*, all of the same size *o* (expressed in bytes). Each chunk can be transferred in parallel with all the other ones and individually assigned to a RS.

Denote by n_i, with $i:1,..,M$, the number of chunks assigned to RS_i and by R_i, with $i:1,..,M$, the throughput available from RS_i towards the Aggregator. Moreover, assume the cost of RS usage be linearly proportional to number of chunks to transfer and denote by c_i, with $i:1,..,M$ the cost of RS_i for transferring a single chunk.

Under these assumptions, the transfer time minimization problem can be formalized as the following multi-objective function and multi-constrained problem:

Figure 4. Content parallel updating

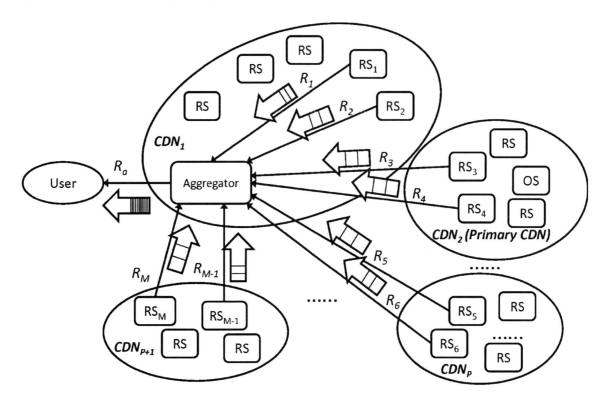

objective function :
$$\min_{i:1,..,M} \left\lceil \frac{n_i \cdot o \cdot 8}{R_i} \right\rceil \quad (1)$$

constrained by :

$$\sum_{i=1}^{M} n_i = N \quad (2)$$

$$E_{up} <= B \qquad \text{with } E_{up} = \sum_{i=1}^{M} n_i \cdot c_i \quad (3)$$

$$\frac{n_i \cdot o \cdot 8}{R_i} <= T_{\max} \quad i : 1,...,M \quad (4)$$

$$R_{par} <= R_a \qquad \text{with } R_{par} = \frac{O}{\max\limits_{i:1,..,M}\left(\dfrac{n_i \cdot o}{R_i}\right)} \quad (5)$$

$$n_i \in \mathrm{N}_0 \qquad i : 1,...,M \quad (6)$$

where (2) is the constraint on the actual transfer of the overall content O, (3) ensures that the expense for content updating, denoted by E_{up}, does not exceed budget B, (4) ensures that the maximum user-perceived latency is not overcome. Constraint

(4) can be equivalently expressed considering the maximum aggregate throughput R_{par} resulting by the parallel transfer flows from each RS_i, defined in (5):

$$R_{par} <= R_{min}$$

Constraint (5) regards the performance limit of the parallel content updating tied to throughput R_a granted by the Aggregator towards the end-user. It states that the aggregate throughput R_{par} must not exceed R_a, in order to avoid a resource employment (and typically economic expense) larger than the necessary one and the overload of the Aggregator in managing and buffering incoming data. Since a chunk, by definition, cannot be further divided, an additional constraint is (6), which states that n_i, which represents the number of chunks assigned to RS_i, must be a positive integer.

Because of constraints (3), (5) and (6), some RSs could not receive chunks to transfer that implies that the heuristic result for the parallel transfer does not necessarily involve all the available RSs.

The first step of the heuristic considers the optimality principle of the divisible load theory for transfer time minimization. To this aim, it assigns a non uniform amount of chunks to the available RSs such that they will complete the transmission at the same time, removing constraint (6).

So the objective function becomes:

$$\frac{n_i}{R_i} = \frac{n_j}{R_j} \quad i,j:1,..,M$$

The next step regards the check of constraints (2), (3) and (4). If they are satisfied it means that budget B is enough to not affect the optimal solution for transfer time minimization. Subsequently, check (5) is adopted to verify if the aggregate throughput R_{par} is larger than R_a. In this instance the re-allocation of transfer tasks in order to equal R_a is performed to decrease the expense and eventually the employment of all the RSs. Finally, in order to satisfy constraint (6), the integer approximation technique presented in (Ranaldo & Zimeo, 2009) is adopted to discretize the number of chunks n_i assigned to each RS_i.

If (2), (3) and (4) are not satisfied because of limited budget, the heuristic proceeds decreasing the number of chunks assigned to the most expensive RS and contemporarily increasing the ones assigned to the other RSs, with the objective to find the best solution without exceeding budget B. Under this adjustment, the RSs will not complete the transfer in about the same time, but the minimum possible time is still obtained by expending the overall budget.

The procedure starts from the solution without considering budget constraint (3) and that ensures the minimum transfer time for N chunks. Then, in an iterative way, the most expensive resource is used to attempt a re-assignment of chunks from

it to the other RSs, in a linearly proportional way to their capabilities and consuming all the available budget B ($E_{up}=B$). Considering, as an example, the first iteration and assuming R_M the current most expensive RS, the re-assignment of chunks is given by:

$$n'_M = n_M - \varepsilon$$
$$n'_i = n_i + \varepsilon_i \quad i:1,...,M-1$$
$$\varepsilon = \frac{\left(B - \sum_{i=1}^{M} n_i c_i\right) \cdot \sum_{i=1}^{M-1} R_i}{\sum_{i=1}^{M-1} c_i \cdot R_i - c_M \cdot \sum_{i=1}^{M-1} R_i}$$
$$\varepsilon_i = \frac{\varepsilon}{\sum_{j=1}^{M-1} R_j} R_i \quad i:1,...,M-1$$

If such re-assignment does not lead to a feasible solution, that happens when the two following conditions are not satisfied:

$$\varepsilon \geq 0$$
$$n_M - \varepsilon \geq 0$$

the most expensive RS, RS_M, is completely removed from the set of RSs and the procedure is repeated using the most expensive RS in the remaining pool. The procedure requires at most $M-1$ steps to find the solution, but can break during any iteration if the transfer time of one of the RSs overcomes the maximum latency T_{max}. In this case the procedure stops without a solution. After this iterative procedure, the result is further subject to integer approximation.

Routing and Updating Algorithm Analysis

We conducted the analysis of the proposed routing and parallel updating algorithm referring to a multi-CDN composed of three peer CDNs as shown in Figure 5.

Figure 5. Scenario adopted for routing and updating algorithm analysis

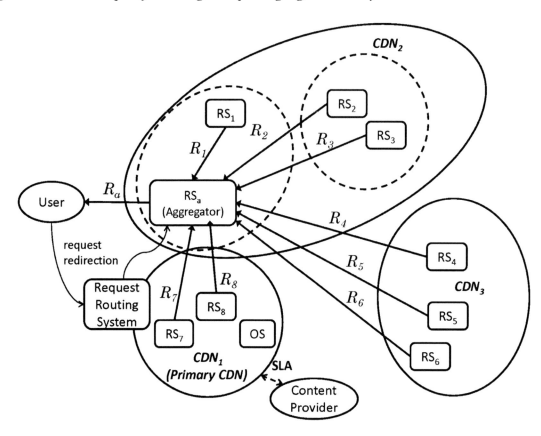

In this scenario, a user's content request is received by CDN_1, the peer CDN that manages the origin server and that takes the role of Primary CDN. Assume that the long-term SLA for content delivery negotiated between the Primary CDN and the content provider defines the following minimum throughput:

$$R_{min} = 6.4 \text{ Mbps}$$

Assume, moreover, that the request routing system of the Primary CDN redirects the request to the Replica Server RS_a (that will assume the role of Aggregator) belonging to the CDN_2, since it is able to grant the best ratio throughput-cost in serving the request. Let be R_a equals to 16 Mbps, a value that is consistent with respect to a typical Internet connection, at home or at work, which adopts a recent standard broadband technology, such as xDSL.

If a content miss happens on the Aggregator, the parallel transfer algorithm is used in order to grant the minimum throughput R_{min} agreed between the Primary CDN and the content provider and budget B that the Primary CDN can spend for the content updating. We consider a budget B linearly proportional to content size and a fixed budget b per byte.

We investigate the overall transfer time and the content partitioning among available RSs estimated by the transfer time minimization heuristic performed in the three cases of the updating algorithm, previously described. Considering the following parameters:

$$O = 488,28 \text{ MB}$$

o = 250 KB

b = 1.1x10⁻⁹ €

maximum user-perceived latency T_{max}, budget B and total number N of chunks are:

$$T_{\max} = (O\ 8)/R_{\min} = 640\ s$$

$$B = O\ b = 0.591\ €$$

$$N = O/o = 2000$$

Table 1 reports the performance and costs of each available RS, denoted by RS_i, with i: 1,..,8, that correspond respectively to the minimum guaranteed throughput R_i towards the Aggregator and the cost per chunk transfer c_i. RSs are distributed among the peer CDNs, in particular RS_1 belongs to the same cluster of the Aggregator RS_a in CDN_2, RS_2 and RS_3 belong to another cluster of CDN_2, RS_4, RS_5 and RS_6 belong to CDN_3, and, finally, RS_7 and RS_8 belong to CDN_1.

At the first step, the updating algorithm performs the transfer time minimization heuristic in the inter-cluster case, that is using RSs belonging to the same cluster of the Aggregator, that is R_1. The estimated transfer time is 4129.03 seconds with an expense of 0.4 €. Since the transfer time overcomes T_{max}, the updating algorithm adopts the heuristic in the local inter-cluster case, that is involving the RSs of the other clusters of CDN_2, that are RS_2 and RS_3. At this step, the estimated transfer time is 1267,33 seconds and the required expense is 0.484 €. Because of heterogeneous performances of RSs, the partitioning of chunks among them is non-uniform and, in particular, with integer approximation, it is given by:

$$n_1 = 614$$

$$n_2 = 669$$

$$n_3 = 717$$

Also in the local inter-cluster case the transfer time overcomes T_{max}. As a consequence the algo-

Table 1. Performance and costs of replica servers

Replica Server	R_i (Mbps)	c_i (10^{-4}€)
RS_1	0.992	2.0
RS_2	1.08	2.4
RS_3	1.16	2.8
RS_4	1.296	3.3
RS_5	1.376	3.6
RS_6	1.264	3.2
RS_7	1.184	2.9
RS_8	1.456	4.0

rithm is applied for the global inter-cluster case, in which the time minimization heuristic exploits the pool of all the available RSs belonging to the other peer CDNs, that are R_i with i:1,..,8. In this case, the minimum transfer time that is possible to obtain is 419.10 seconds with an expense of 0.619 €. Such budget allows to exploit all the available RSs under the optimality principle. The RSs, in fact, complete the transmission of the assigned chunks roughly at the same time.

Another boundary case that we analyse is the one adopting the minimum budget that allows to not violate time transfer constraint (4), that is 0.553 €. In this case the most expensive RSs, that are RS_5 and RS_8 are exploited not at all. Moreover, the limited budget does not allow to exploit at the best the other RSs. The heuristic, in fact, assigns a reduced number of chunks to RS_4, the most expensive RS among the remaining ones, and an increased number of chunks to the other RSs in a proportional way to their performance, in order to not overcome T_{max} but, at the same time, to obtain the lowest expense. The chunk partitioning among RSs in these two boundary cases is shown in Figure 6.

In the following, we analyse the influence of the available budget on the estimated transfer time and chunk partitioning among all the available RSs.

Figure 6. Chunk partitioning among RSs in two boundary cases adopting all the available RSs: (1) budget that allows to obtain the minimum transfer time (419.1 s), (2) minimum budget that allows to not overcome the maximum transfer time T_{max} = 640 s; N = 2000, O = 488.28 MB, o=250 KB.

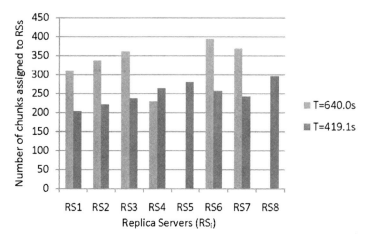

Figure 7 presents the distribution of chunks assigned to RSs varying the budget in the interval [0.553 €, 0.619 €].

In case of low budgets, the most expensive RSs, in particular RS_5 and RS_8, can not be exploited at the best to minimize the total transfer time, but it is necessary to decrease the number of chunks assigned to them and to increase the number of chunks assigned to cheaper ones. This adjustment causes an increasing transfer time as shown in Figure 8.

For budget B assumed in this analysis, that is 0.59 €, all the available RSs are exploited and the estimated transfer time is 486,05 seconds. Moreover, the number of chunks assigned to the most expensive RS (RS_8) is 23, a number much smaller than 296, that is the number of chunks assigned for minimizing the transfer time. In this case, the provisioned transfer time is about 30% greater than the minimum one, and the expended budget is about 44% less than the one that allows to obtain such minimum transfer time.

FUTURE RESEARCH DIRECTIONS

The proposed approach poses the basis for its integration in the cloud computing model (Armbrust, et al., 2010).

Cloud computing promises to significantly change the current business models adopted in IT industry by centralizing the infrastructures for service delivery in high performance, available and scalable nodes where the costs for software and hardware maintenance and management, energy consumption and disaster recovery can be statistically multiplexed among a large and variable number of customers, thus reducing the overall costs for unused resources owned by providers.

The availability of services at different abstraction levels, in Clouds, will make it possible both the rapid deployment of novel applications (at SaaS - Software as a Service - level) and platforms (at PaaS - Platform as a Service - level), and the creation of CDNs (at IaaS and PaaS levels) for efficient content delivery. This way, Cloud systems, on the one hand, will boost the development of novel network-based applications that will contribute to generate a huge amount of traffic in the Internet, and, on the other hand, it will become a

Figure 7. Chunk partitioning among RSs varying the budget; T_{max} = 640 s, N = 2000, O=488.28 MB, o=250 KB

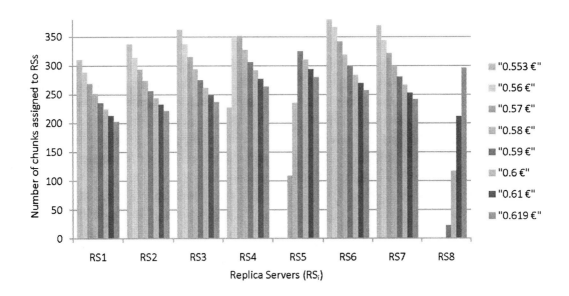

Figure 8. Estimated transfer time varying the budget; T_{max} = 640 s, N = 2000, O=488.28 MB, o=250 KB

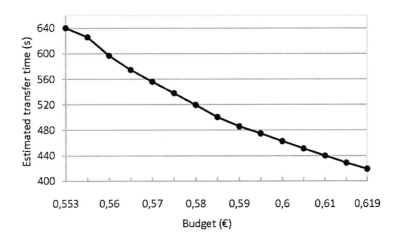

common infrastructure for enabling pay-per-use multi-CDNs that dynamically cooperate to efficiently deliver content to end-users, ensuring an adequate revenue for each CDN involved.

As consequence of this evolution, we expect that large IT organizations owning high-bandwidth networks will revise their business models in order to exploit their resources in a variety of applica-

tions, simply considering them as utility provided by Cloud-enabled infrastructures and consumed according to a pay-per-use model.

In the scenario depicted above, SLAs and efficient algorithms for content delivery assume an important role for the overall IT economy and promise to generate an even larger impact on the economy in general.

Therefore, in addition to the solution proposed in this chapter, we plan to investigate also more dynamic models to efficiently deliver contents by taking into account, on the one hand, the variability of network resource performance and availability, and, on the other hand, the differentiated needs of CDNs that, in turn, depend on the QoS levels agreed between the CDNs and content providers. To this end, we will consider each replica server characterized by differentiated updating services, with different QoS levels and costs, and we will adopt negotiation mechanisms to improve the flexibility of the overall delivery system.

CONCLUSION

The chapter proposed a multi-source content transfer, which exploits a partitioning algorithm based on the divisible load theory for minimizing the delivery time of content in a multi-CDN, while respecting the maximum budget that the delivering CDN can pay to other peer CDNs.

The reference scenario is characterized by multiple content providers and multiple CDNs that handle large files characterized by low frequency of change. In this scenario, a content provider stipulates a contract with a CDN, expressed through a long-term SLA, that defines the expected QoS level for content delivery and the agreed price. The QoS level is referred to the maximum user-perceived latency, measured as the total delay between a request for a content and receiving the object in its entirety.

The proposed architectural schema and algorithm try to satisfy the agreed SLAs by exploiting a partitioning technique to split the content in several chunks to transfer in parallel by exploiting replica servers of other CDNs. By assuming some working conditions, such as traffic estimation, reservation or differentiation, the algorithm is able to estimate the number of chunks to assign to each replica server with the aim of respecting the agreed SLAs, namely user-perceived content latency and monetary costs.

The proposed algorithm, applied to content updating in a QoS-aware multi-CDN, was analysed with respect to a feasible reference scenario in order to evaluate the influence of available budget on the chunk partitioning and on the provisioned transfer time. The results showed how this approach can contribute to increase efficiency of content delivery services taking into account the potential revenues for parties participating to the peering environment.

In the future, we intend to integrate the proposed algorithm in a CDN infrastructure in order to evaluate its viability and conduct experimental studies in real scenarios. We are investigating, in particular, CoralCDN (Freedman, Freudenthal, & Mazières, 2004), an open source CDN which currently adopts a single-transfer cooperative pull-based approach for content updating guided by QoS levels estimation among CDN nodes.

ACKNOWLEDGMENT

This chapter is partially supported by the COSA (Contract Oriented Service Architecture) project funded by MIUR - Italian Ministry of Education, University and Research.

REFERENCES

Amazon Web Services. (2010, November 9). *Amazon CloudFront service level agreement.* Retrieved from http://aws.amazon.com/cloudfront/sla

Amini, L., Shaikh, A., Schulzrinne, H., & Res, I. B. (2004). Effective peering for multi-provider content delivery services. *The 23rd Annual Joint Conference on the IEEE Computer and Communications Societies* (pp. 850-861).

Andrews, M., Shepherd, B., Srinivasan, A., & Winkler, P. (2002). Clustering and server selection using passive monitoring. *The Twenty-first Annual Joint Conference of the IEEE Computer and Communication Societies* (pp. 1717-1725).

Ardaiz, O., Freitag, F., & Navarro, L. (2001). Improving the service time of Web clients using server redirection. *ACM SIGMETRICS Performance Evaluation Review, 29*(2), 39–44. doi:10.1145/572317.572324

Armbrust, M., Fox, A., Griffith, R., Joseph, A. D., Katz, R., & Konwinski, A. (2010). A view of cloud computing. *Communications of the ACM, 53*(4), 50–58. doi:10.1145/1721654.1721672

Bharadwaj, V., Ghose, D., Mani, V., & Roberta, T. G. (1996). *Scheduling divisible loads in parallel and distributed systems*. Los Almitos, CA: Wiley-IEEE Computer Society Press.

Bharadwaj, V., & Viswanadham, N. (2000). Sub-optimal solutions using integer approximation techniques for scheduling divisible loads on distributed bus networks. *IEEE Transactions on Systems, Man, and Cybernetics. Part A, Systems and Humans, 30*(6), 680–691. doi:10.1109/3468.895891

Bhuvaneswaran, R., Katayama, Y., & Takahashi, N. (2007). A framework for an integrated co-allocator for data grid in multi-sender environment. *IEICE Transactions on Communications. E (Norwalk, Conn.), 90-B*(4), 742–749.

Biliris, A., Cranor, C., Douglis, F., & Rabinovich, M. (2002). CDN Brokering. *Computer Communications, 25*(4), 393–402. doi:10.1016/S0140-3664(01)00411-X

Blake, S., Black, D., Carlson, M., Davies, E., Wang, Z., & Weiss, W. (1998, December). *RFC 2475. An architecture for differentiatied services*. Retrieved from http://www.ietf.org/rfc/rfc2475.txt

Bouman, J., Trieneken, J., & van der Zwan, M. (1999). Specification of service level agreements, clarifying concepts on the basis of practical research. In Tilley, S., & Verner, J. (Eds.), *Software Technology and Engineering Practice '99* (pp. 169–180). IEEE Computer Society. doi:10.1109/STEP.1999.798790

Charcranoon, S., Robertazzi, T. G., & Luryi, S. (2004). Load sequencing for a parallel processing utility. *Journal of Parallel and Distributed Computing, 64*(1), 29–35. doi:10.1016/S0743-7315(03)00113-8

Crowcroft, J., & Oechsli, P. (1998). Differentiated end-to-end Internet services using a weighted proportional fair sharing TCP. *ACM SIGCOMM Computer Communication Review, 28*(3), 53–69. doi:10.1145/293927.293930

Day, M., Cain, B., Tomlinson, G., & Rzewski, P. (2003, February). *A model for content internetworking (CDI)*. Retrieved from http://tools.ietf.org/html/rfc3466

Dilley, J., Maggs, B., Parikh, J., Prokop, H., Sitaraman, R., & Weihl, B. (2002). Globally distributed content delivery. *IEEE Internet Computing, 6*(5), 50–58. doi:10.1109/MIC.2002.1036038

Foster, I., Kesselman, C., Nick, J., & Tuecke, S. (2002). *The physiology of the Grid: an open Grid services architecture for distributed systems integration*. Open Grid Service Infrastructure WG, Global Grid Forum.

Freedman, M. J., Freudenthal, E., & Mazières, D. (2004). *Democratizing content publication with Coral*. The 1st USENIX/ACM Symposium on Networked Systems Design and Implementation. USENIX Association.

Gkantisidis, C., Ammar, M., & Zegura, E. (2003). On the effect of large-scale deployment of parallel downloading. *The Third IEEE Workshop on Internet Applications, WIAPP 2003* (pp. 79-89).

Hofmann, M., & Beaumont, L. R. (2005). *Content networking: Architecture, protocols, and practice.* Morgan Kaufmann Publisher.

Hsu, C.-H., Chu, C.-W., & Chou, C.-H. (2009). Bandwidth sensitive co-allocation scheme for parallel downloading in Data Grid. *IEEE International Symposium on Parallel and Distributed Processing with Applications* (pp. 34-39).

Huang, C., & Addelzaher, T. (2005). Bounded-latency content distribution: feasibility and evaluation. *IEEE Transactions on Computers, 54*(11), 1422–1437. doi:10.1109/TC.2005.175

Izal, M., Urvoy-Keller, G., Biersack, E. W., Felber, P. A., Al Hamra, A., & Garcès-Erice, L. (2004). Dissecting BitTorrent: Five months in a torrent's lifetime. *Passive and Active Measurement Workshop, PAM 2004* (pp. 1-11). Springer.

Kangasharju, J., Roberts, J., & Ross, K. W. (2002). Object replication strategies in content distribution networks. *Computer Communications, 25*(4), 367–383. doi:10.1016/S0140-3664(01)00409-1

Klingberg, T., & Manfredi, R. (2002, June). *Gnutella 0.6.* Retrieved from http://rfc-gnutella. sourceforge.net/src/rfc-0_6-draft.html

Kontiki, Inc. (2011). *Enterprise content delivery network.* Retrieved from http://www.kontiki.com/ products/enterprise-content-delivery-network

Liang, J., Kuma, R., & Ross, K. W. (2005). The KaZaA overlay: A measurement study. *Computer Networks Journal (Special Issue on Overlays), 49*(6).

Malli, M., Barakat, C., & Dabbous, W. (2005). An efficient approach for content delivery in overlay networks. *The Second IEEE Consumer Communications and Networking Conference* (pp. 128-133).

Mirror Image Internet, Inc. (2011). *Content delivery network.* Retrieved from www.mirror-image. com/site/solutions/ContentDeliveryNetwork/ tabid/69/Default.aspx

Nabeshima, M. (2005). Performance evaluation of MulTCP in high-speed wide area networks. *IEICE Transactions on Communications. E88-B*(1), 392–396.

Pallis, G., & Vakali, A. (2006). Insight and perspectives for content delivery networks. *Communications of the ACM, 49*(1), 101–106. doi:10.1145/1107458.1107462

Pathan, M., & Buyya, R. (2008a). A taxonomy of CDNs. In Pathan, M., Buyya, R., & Vakali, A. (Eds.), *Content delivery networks* (pp. 33–77). Springer-Verlag. doi:10.1007/978-3-540-77887-5_2

Pathan, M., & Buyya, R. (2008b). Performance models for peering content delivery Networks. *The 16th IEEE International Conference on Networks, ICON 2008.*

Pathan, M., & Buyya, R. (2009). Architecture and performance models for QoS-driven effective peering of content delivery networks. *Multiagent and Grid Systems Journal, 5*(2), 165–195.

Ranaldo, N., & Zimeo, E. (2006). *An economy-driven mapping heuristic for hierarchical master-slave applications in grid systems.* The 20th IEEE International Conference on Parallel and Distributed Processing, IPDPS 2006.

Ranaldo, N., & Zimeo, E. (2009). Time and cost-driven scheduling of data parallel tasks in grid workflows. *Systems Journal, 3*(1), 104–120. doi:10.1109/JSYST.2008.2011299

Ratnasamy, S., Handley, M., Karp, R., & Shenker, S. (2002). Topologically-aware overlay construction and server selection. *INFOCOM 2002. The Twenty-first Annual Joint Conference of the IEEE Computer and Communication Societies* (pp. 1190-1199).

Rodriguez, P., & Biersack, E. W. (2002). Dynamic parallel access to replicated content in the Internet. *IEEE/ACM Transactions on Networking, 10*(4), 455–465. doi:10.1109/TNET.2002.801413

Sohn, J., Robertazzi, T. G., & Luryi, S. (1998). Optimizing computing costs using divisible load analysis. *IEEE Transactions on Parallel and Distributed Systems*, *9*(3), 225–234. doi:10.1109/71.674315

Velocix. (2011). *Advanced content distribution.* Retrieved from http://www.velocix.com/network_distribution.php

Xu, Z., Xianliang, H. M., Mengshu, H., & Chuan, Z. (2005). A speed-based adaptive dynamic parallel downloading technique. *ACM SIGOPS Operating Systems Review*, *39*(1), 63–69. doi:10.1145/1044552.1044559

Yang, C.-T., Chi, Y.-C., & Fu, C.-P. (2007). Redundant parallel file transfer with anticipative adjustment mechanism in Data Grids. *Journal of Information Technology and Applications*, *1*(4).

Young, J., & Faris, N. (2010, July 16). *Akamai delivers 2010 World Cup Internet coverage for two dozen broadcasters into 65 countries worldwide.* Retrieved from http://www.akamai.com/html/about/press/releases/2010/press_071610.html

Zhang, J., Lee, B.-S., Tang, X., & Yeo, C.-K. (2008). Impact of parallel download on job scheduling in data grid environment. *The 2008 Seventh International Conference on Grid and Cooperative Computing. GCC '08*, (pp. 102-109).

Zhihui, L., Yiping, Z., Shiyong, Z., & Jie, W. (2003). Study of main technology in rich media grid delivery. *International Conference on Computer Networks and Mobile Computing, IEEE ICCNMC '03* (pp. 488- 492). IEEE Computer Society Press.

ADDITIONAL READING

Armbrust, M., Fox, A., Griffith, R., Joseph, A. D., Katz, R., Konwinski, A., et al. (2009). *Above the clouds: A Berkeley view of cloud computing.* Technical Report No. UCB/EECS-2009-28, University of California, EECS Department, Berkeley.

Bharadwaj, V., Ghose, D., & Robertazzi, T. (2003). Divisible load theory: A new paradigm for load scheduling in distributed systems. *Cluster Computing*, *6*(1), 7–17. doi:10.1023/A:1020958815308

Broberg, J., Buyya, R., & Tari, Z. (2009). MetaCDN: Harnessing 'storage clouds' for high performance content delivery. *Journal of Network and Computer Applications*, *32*(5), 1012–1022. doi:10.1016/j.jnca.2009.03.004

Buyya, R., Pathan, A.-M. K., Broberg, J., & Tari, Z. (2006). A case for peering of content delivery networks. *IEEE Distributed Systems Online*, *7*(10).

Buyya, R., Yeo, C. S., & Venugopal, S. (2008). Market-oriented cloud computing: vision, hype, and reality for delivering IT services as computing utilities. *The 10th IEEE International Conference on High Performance Computing and Communications, HPCC '08* (pp. 5-13).

Chang, R.-S., Guo, M.-H., & Lin, H.-C. (2008). A multiple parallel download scheme with server throughput and client bandwidth considerations for data grids. *Future Generation Computer Systems*, *24*(8), 798–805. doi:10.1016/j.future.2008.04.006

Charcranoon, S., Robertazzi, T. G., & Luryi, S. (2004). Load sequencing for a parallel processing utility. *Journal of Parallel and Distributed Computing*, *64*(1). doi:10.1016/S0743-7315(03)00113-8

Chiu, C.-H., Lin, H.-T., & Yuan, S.-M. (2010). A content delivery system for storage service in cloud environment. *International Journal of Ad Hoc and Ubiquitous Computing*, *6*(4), 252–262. doi:10.1504/IJAHUC.2010.035536

Comuzzi, M., Kotsokalis, C., Spanoudakis, G., & Yahyapour, R. (2009). Establishing and monitoring SLAs in complex service based systems. *IEEE International Conference on Web Services, ICWS 2009*, (pp. 783-790).

Di Nitto, E., & Yahyapour, R. (Eds.). (2010). *Towards a service-based Internet*. The Third European Conference, ServiceWave 2010. Springer-Verlag.

Giallonardo, E., & Zimeo, E. (2007). More semantics in QoS matching. *IEEE International Conference on Service-Oriented Computing and Applications* (pp. 163-171).

Hsu, C.-H., Chen, T.-L., & Lee, K.-H. (2009). QoS based parallel file transfer for grid economics. *International Conference on Multimedia Information Networking and Security* (pp. 653-657).

Huang, C., & Abdelzaher, T. (2004). Towards content distribution networks with latency guarantees. *The Twelfth IEEE International Workshop on Quality of Service, IWQOS 2004* (pp. 181-192).

Marchal, L., Yang, Y., Casanova, H., & Robert, Y. (2005). A realistic network/application model for scheduling divisible loads on large-scale platforms. *The 19th International Parallel and Distributed Processing Symposium, IPDPS 2005*.

Menasce, D. (2002). Qos issues in Web services. *IEEE Internet Computing, 6*(6), 72–75. doi:10.1109/MIC.2002.1067740

Menasce, D., & Dubey, V. (2007). *Utility-based QoS brokering in service oriented architectures*. IEEE International Conference on Web Services, ICWS 2007.

Pathan, A. K. (2009). *Utility-oriented internetworking of content delivery networks*. PhD thesis, The University of Melbourne, Department of Computer Science and Software Engineering.

Pathan, M., Broberg, J., & Buyya, R. (2009). Maximizing utility for content delivery clouds. *The 10th International Conference on Web Information Systems Engineering* (pp. 13-28).

Pathan, M., & Buyya, R. (2009). *A utility model for peering of multi-provider content deliver services*. The 34th IEEE Conference on Local Computer Networks, LCN 2009.

Petri, I., Rana, O., & Silaghi, G. (2010). SLA as a complementary currency in peer-2-peer markets. *The 7th International Conference on Economics of Grids, Clouds, Systems, and Services* (pp. 141-152). Springer-Verlag.

Petri, I., Silaghi, G., & Rana, O. (2010). Trading service level agreements within a peer-to-peer market. *The 11th IEEE/ACM International Conference on Grid Computing* (pp. 242-251).

Rana, O., Warnier, M., Quillinan, T., & Brazier, F. (2008). Monitoring and reputation mechanisms for service level agreement. *The 5th International Workshop on Grid Economics and Business Models* (pp. 125-139). Springer-Verlag.

Ranaldo, N., & Zimeo, E. (2007). A time and cost-based matching strategy for data parallelizable tasks of grid workflows. *IEEE International Conference on e-Science and Grid Computing*.

Scellato, S., Mascolo, C., Musoles, M., & Crowcroft, J. (2011). Track globally, deliver locally: Improving content delivery networks by tracking geographic social cascades. *The 20th International Conference on World Wide Web* (pp. 457-466).

Wang, C.-M., Hsu, C.-C., Chen, H.-M., & Wu, J.-J. (2006). Efficient multi-source data transfer in data grids. *The Sixth IEEE International Symposium on Cluster Computing and the Grid, CCGRID 06* (pp. 421-424).

Wang, L., von Laszewski, G., Younge, A., He, X., Kunze, M., & Tao, J. (2010). Cloud-computing: A perspective study. *New Generation Computing, 28*(2), 137–146. doi:10.1007/s00354-008-0081-5

Wolfgang, T., Yahyapour, R., & Butler, J. (2008). Multi-level SLA management for service-oriented infrastructures. *The First European Conference, ServiceWave 2008* (pp. 324-335). Springer-Verlag.

KEY TERMS AND DEFINITIONS

Cloud Computing: A model based on virtualization, service oriented architecture and utility computing for allowing a company harnessing external resources on-demand through the Internet, in a pay-per-use and transparent manner. Cloud services are classified in **IaaS** (Infrastructure as a Service), hardware virtualization of a traditional computer, which includes resources such as CPU, RAM, storage and network devices; **PaaS** (Platform as a Service), platform virtualization to host applications; **SaaS** (Software as a Service), software applications delivering high level functions.

Content Provider: Source of contents, such as Web service providers, media companies and news broadcasters.

Multi-CDN: Virtual organization composed of several cooperating CDNs. Cooperation is enabled by SLA-based contracts.

Multi-Source Transfer (or Parallel Download): Content transfer that exploits multiple simultaneous connections among a client and a pool of servers that are in charge of transmitting different parts of the same content.

Origin Server: CDN server where the official release of a content is loaded by the content provider.

Pay-Per-Use: A business model in which a customer pays a provider for services it actually requires and only for the real usage time.

Replica Server: CDN server handling a clone of a content.

SLA: Stands for Service Level Agreement, a formal definition of a service contract between the customer and the service provider. It includes the definition of services, QoS levels the provider promises to meet while delivering a service, responsibilities of both the parties, charging and termination of the agreement. It may include penalties for both the parties in case guaranteed terms and/or actions are violated.

Chapter 8
Mechanisms for Parallel Data Transport

Jewel Okyere-Benya
Eindhoven University of Technology, the Netherlands & Politecnico di Torino, Italy

Georgios Exarchakos
Eindhoven University of Technology, The Netherlands

Vlado Menkovski
Eindhoven University of Technology, The Netherlands

Antonio Liotta
Eindhoven University of Technology, The Netherlands

Paolo Giaccone
Politecnico di Torino, Italy

ABSTRACT

Evolving paradigms of parallel transport mechanisms are necessary to satisfy the ever increasing need of high performing communication systems. Parallel transport mechanisms can be described as a technique to send several data simultaneously using several parallel channels. The authors' survey captures the entire building blocks in designing next generation parallel transport mechanisms by firstly analyzing the basic structure of a transport mechanism using a point to point scenario. They then proceed to segment parallel transport into four categories and describe some of the most sophisticated technologies such as Multipath under Point to Point, Multicast under Point to Multipoint, Parallel downloading under Multipoint to Point, and Peer to Peer streaming under Multipoint to Multipoint. The Survey enables the authors to stipulate that high performing parallel transport mechanisms can be achieved by integrating the most efficient technologies under these categories, while using the most efficient underlying Point to Point transport protocols.

DOI: 10.4018/978-1-4666-1794-0.ch008

INTRODUCTION

As Internet traffic increases, the use of sophisticated network and data transport technologies are required to meet the demands of today's Internet. These efforts have been boosted by the advent of Peer to Peer (P2P) networks. Even though P2P has the potential to address bandwidth problems faced by End Users, Content Providers, Internet Service Providers (ISP's), and Equipment Vendors, parameters such as Delay, QoS and packet loss still depend on the underlying technologies. Numerous data transport mechanisms, e.g. resource reservation protocols, can fairly solve the problem, but are unutilized or often too expensive to replace installed equipment. Parallel data transport holds the key to solving these problems and there has been tremendous amount of research in the field.

A huge percentage of the point to point communication in the Internet is made up of reliable transport mechanisms. Our initial study gives attention to literature in building simple unreliable point to point connections, and introduces features for building reliable point to point connections. We make an exhaustive overview of each feature especially Congestion management, and elaborate on new and bandwidth efficient techniques which uses network delay to manage congestion such as Low Extra Delay Background Transport (LEDBAT).

A single path or connection between two nodes is suboptimal compared to one with multiple paths or multiple connections. Our study of parallel transport begins here by analyzing several techniques to build multiple connections and multiple paths between Point to Point connections. Most TCP extensions enable setting up multiple connections. While multiple connections are good, discovering multiple paths between point to point connections and combining both over a single connection improves its fault resilience and bandwidth efficiency. Techniques such as Multi-homing, that can bind multiple IP addresses at each node, which

in turn provides a network interface redundancy, have also been discussed. Other techniques also captured include multilayer approaches such as Parallel TCP Transfer Helper (PATHEL) which can exploit interlayer benefits to strip the data flow among multiple TCP channels.

Computer applications which support group communication require parallel transport mechanisms that enable Point-Multipoint and Multipoint to Point communication. Under Point to Multi-point techniques, we will present some advance work on multicasting used in content delivery systems. This would include underlying architectures and mechanisms used for both IP multicast and Application Layer Multicast. A computer seeking to exploit the upload bandwidth of several other computers to improve its download capability falls into the Multi-point to Point parallel transport paradigm. Parallel downloading, as it is usually known, can significantly improve performance through a parallel access scheme, but this might come with some cost such as delays incurred by complex client server negotiations. Therefore a good parallel downloading system should consider these costs in its design.

Application layer services such as video streaming can be described as some of the currently most advance parallel transport mechanisms. Such streaming services are based or either structured or unstructured P2P overlay networks depending on the survivability of data files and the distributed nature of the network. P2P Video streaming provides the best platform for next generation Multi-point to Multi-point transport mechanisms because it supports technologies such as Adaptive streaming, Layered streaming and caching in P2P networks. To achieve the best performance, it is important to integrate these underlying schemes into one complete protocol as done in the "BitTorrent DNA" protocol. BitTorrent DNA is designed to deliver high performance for content delivery systems by providing (i) multiple video streams for multiple users with different bandwidth requirements, (ii)

Figure 1. Diagram of a simple transport mechanism without connection management

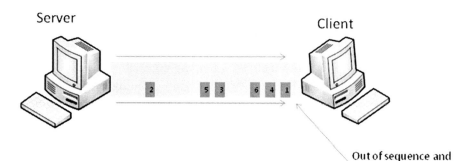

smarter peer selection and (iii) caching to reduce the amount of traffic that crosses the access point, thereby helping to alleviate blocking problems associated with Internet Service Providers (ISPs).

POINT TO POINT TRANSPORT MECHANISM: A SIMPLE APPROACH

A point-to-point transport mechanism is required to provide end-to-end communication between two applications on separate computers. This however must be done by ensuring that a host computer can sufficiently send information to another computer in an attempt to use the available network resources. Basic transport mechanism which establishes logical communication between two computers is therefore an important building block in the ever evolving Parallel transport paradigm.

To set up two applications to communicate, a simple model as shown in Figure 1 requires opening up ports on both the client and server side to transfer information needed by the client. This technique only requires the identification of destination port to which to forward information. This eliminates any persistent connection between sender and receiver, and renders it Connection-less. The connectionless nature of such point to point transport mechanisms, e.g. User datagram Protocol (UDP) implies that, there is no implicit

handshaking to guarantee important transport features such as (i) Reliability of data, (ii) Ordered delivery of packets, (iii) Prevention of data loss and (iv) Handling of duplicate packets. However Connectionless transport can multiplex information from different applications at the sender side and de-multiplex the information at the receiver side before sending it to the application layers.

Even though connectionless transport is only a best effort service, it has proved very useful in delay sensitive applications; especially video streaming where some network losses can be tolerated. UDP in such cases has been the underlying transport mechanism for other application layer protocols such as the Real Time Protocol (RTP) and the Domain Naming Server (DNS). Advanced transport mechanism which exploit the benefits of UDP such as UDT (UDP based Data Transport) was proposed by (Gu & Grossman, 2007) by adding reliability controls. The UDT mechanism is explained in the next subchapter.

The limitations of a simple point to point transport mechanism implies that better techniques, that would improve the fidelity of transmitted data and ensure the maximum usage of network resources through a reliable, synchronized and connection oriented approach, are required. The techniques usually employed include ways to manage data transfer such as flow control, congestion management, duplicate handling and error detection.

POINT TO POINT TRANSPORT MECHANISM WITH CONNECTION MANAGEMENT

A huge percentage of the point to point communication in the Internet is made up of reliable transport mechanisms. This overcomes the limitations of the simple point to point mechanism as described above, and ensures a high fidelity of transmitted information and ordered delivery of packets by using a persistent connection oriented approach. Connection oriented transport protocols as they are sometimes known, employ connection management techniques that enable data to flow between a synchronized transmitter and receiver. Some of the techniques include flow control, congestion control, duplicate handling and error handling. Connection oriented transport mechanisms are also very efficient in terms of multiplexing data from multiple processes at the transmitter and de-multiplexing such data at the receiver. Various forms of Reliable transport protocols exist. Popular among these are Transport Control protocol (TCP) and a more advance mechanism known as Stream Control Transport protocol (SCTP) as demonstrated in (Preethi Natarajan, Janardhan R. Iyengar, Paul D. Amer, & Randall Stewart, 2006). Our analysis on this topic would therefore focus on the core features of managing point to point connections, making an exhaustive overview of each, especially over Congestion management where new techniques using network delay have generated new set of protocols. Further discussion would introduce techniques to achieve reliability over an unreliable and connectionless transport layer and how multiple connections and parallelism are realized between two nodes.

In a connection oriented transport protocol, the sender sends information in datagram/segments encapsulated by a sender side port and IP address, and a destination port and IP address as illustrated in Figure 2. In TCP this is done after a Connection is setup by what is referred to as a three-way handshake between the sender and receiver. By this method, the source sends a SYNC packet to the receiver and the receiver sends a SYNC ACK packet back. Finally an ACK packet is sent back to the receiver to synchronize the connection to allow for a persistent two way data flow until a request to end the connection is received. This technique establishes a socket between the sender and receiver, and the number of sockets can be varied between two computers for parallelizing the connection between them. To ensure reliability of the information, the sender applies sequence numbers to the data packets which is used by the receiver to rearrange any packets which might be received out of order. Lost packets are retransmitted by the sender when notified by the receiver and duplicate packets would be discarded and not forwarded to the upper layers. Data can however be buffered and pipelined from transmitter to receiver to enable better bandwidth utilization and reduce ACK packets.

Flow control is used to limit the amount of losses by limiting the sender from inundating the receiver with information. A flow control algorithm is implemented to provide a speed-matching service (matching the send rate to the receivers drain rate). This algorithm gives the receiver the opportunity to advertize its available buffer space, enabling the sender to reduce the number of packets, thereby controlling the flow of data by matching the send and drain rates.

The major difference between Connection oriented transport protocols is the way Congestion is controlled. In TCP, congestion is controlled by an Additive Increase and Multiplicative Decrease (AIMD) algorithm, which regulates a parameter referred to as the congestion window. The size of the congestion window actually describes the transmission rate of the sender. This enables the congestion control algorithm to slowly increase the transmission rate until a packet loss. It however cuts the transmission rate dramatically to half its value when there is a loss event to prevent further losses. The multiplicative decrease prevents

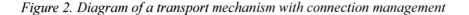

Figure 2. Diagram of a transport mechanism with connection management

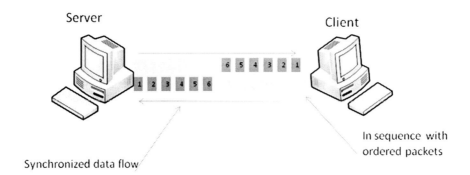

optimum usage of network resources, especially when a loss event occurs. This introduces some fairness issues when two competing TCP connection share the same bandwidth in cases where TCP are being parallelized. Because one node might be in the slow start phase while the other in the congestion avoidance phase (phase where rate grows considerably slowly to prevent loss). It is important to observe that TCP and SCTP both use the AIMD algorithm. However various forms of the AIMD protocol exist, an example is the wireless Control Protocol (WCP) presented by (Rangwala, Jindal, Jang, Psounis, & Govindan, 2008) which is adapted for wireless multi-hop mesh networks, and utilizes multiple node traffic information to control its sending rate. The main difference between TCP and SCTP is the ability of SCTP to support multi-streaming and multi-Homing transmissions. This proves very essential during the setup of parallel connection among nodes. Multi-streaming and Multi-homing is discussed further in the next subchapter.

Other congestion control techniques, controls network congestion by reducing the inter-packet gap which in turn adjusting their sending rate. This technique called SABUL (Oothongsap, Viniotis, & Vouk, 2008), is capable of improving the overall bandwidth and can be deployed with other protocols. SABUL makes use of a continuous network feedback of packet loss rate to estimate the inter-packet gap on the fly.

Current generation of Congestion control algorithm uses network delay instead of loss event to estimate whether to increase or reduce sending rate, this enable such algorithms to react better than standard TCP. The beauty of such algorithms is that they can work in the background of other protocols such as TCP and exploit the bandwidth not utilized by TCP. It also yields to TCP when necessary and appropriates to itself very small bandwidth in most cases. They are often referred to as less than best-effort-service since their transmission rate is often less than they can provide. The best example is LEDBAT (Rossi, Testa, Valenti, & Muscariello, 2010)- which has been chosen to work with TCP in the Bittorent protocol. Other examples of such protocols are TCP-NICE and TCP-LP discussed by (Welzl, 2010).

Reliability can be achieved in various ways. This includes implementing reliability controls over unreliable transport in both the transport layer and even the application layer. Transport layer techniques such as UDT is implemented over UDP to make it a reliable point to point transport mechanism. UDT uses UDP through socket interfaces provided by operating systems. Meanwhile, UDT is able to provide socket interfaces to applications. It uses a rate-based congestion control and a window based flow control to regulate the outgoing data traffic. UDT uses a modified AIMD algorithm where the additive parameter is decreasing by a given factor based on the network feedback, thereby reducing transmission rates. UDT was demonstrated by (John Bresnahan, Michael Link, Rajkumar Kettimuthu, & Ian Foster, 2009), as an efficient transport protocol for advanced parallel transport mechanism.

Application layer techniques to achieve reliability are often very common in video streaming application where some packet loss can be accepted, but the application is highly sensitive to network delay. RTP and RTCP are examples of application techniques which are applied to unreliable, connectionless and best effort transport, in a bid to make them more reliable and bandwidth efficient. This is done by applying error control methods such a Forward Error Correction, packet interleaving and error concealment to improve the errors as a result of packet losses.

Improvement to the congestion control algorithms used in reliable point to point transport mechanism has enabled an efficient use of network resources. Especially with the use of Delay based congestion control protocols as background transport mechanisms. This operates in a parallel nature with the main transport protocol to use the residual bandwidth and present some form of bandwidth aggregation necessary for exploiting network resources. This however is not optimum in terms of bandwidth usage even though the parallel nature of these protocols holds a lot more promise. The next subchapter discusses more advance forms of parallel techniques between point to point transport protocols which are more Bandwidth efficient.

POINT TO POINT TRANSPORT MECHANISM WITH PARALLEL PATHS

Introduction to Parallelism in Point to Point Networks

The concept of having multiple paths between point to point connections forms the founda-

tion of this chapter. It has been made evident by (Altman, Barman, Tuffin, & Vojnovic, 2006) and (Jinyu Zhang, Yongzhe Gui, Cheng Liu, & Xiaoming Li, 2009) that a single access path between two points in a network is suboptimal in terms of bitrates and resilience as compared to multiple paths between such points. Research on parallel data transmission to develop resilient transmission paths and improve bit-rate has motivated different approaches. Setting up multiple connections (often with TCP) between two points, as presented in (Hacker, Noble, & Athey, 2004) has been widely considered. An improvement to setting up multiple connections such as the use of aggregated paths between two points has greatly improved its performance. Other improvements include the use of dedicated paths and/or back up paths. Another very important technique is using multiple disjoint paths as in (J.R. Iyengar, P.D. Amer, & R. Stewart, 2006), which has proved to be very useful in terms of resilience. However, according to (Baldini, De Carli, & Risso, 2009), Multi layer approaches which exploit paths in other layers of the OSI reference model, are favorable multi-pathing techniques to be deployed in future networks for bulk data transfer. Various approaches have been considered and improvements to these techniques will be discussed in the next few paragraphs.

Point to Point with Multiple Connections

The most widely deployed transport protocol in today's Internet is the Transport control protocol (TCP). This is because of its many features which assist the reliable delivery of traffic. While TCP is not necessarily the most efficient transport protocol, its modifications has been very efficient in terms of consuming available network bandwidth. Parallelizing TCP or any other connection oriented transport protocol is however a very simple technique. Setting up multiple sockets between two hosts is sufficient to implement parallel link

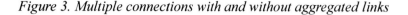

Figure 3. Multiple connections with and without aggregated links

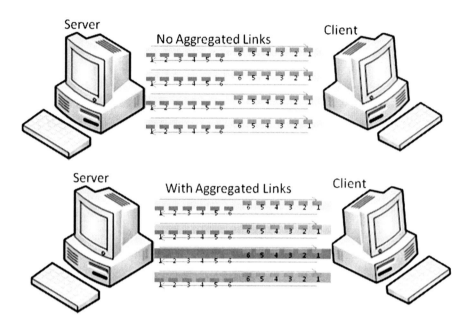

between the nodes. Figure 3 illustrates this process. For a given link with a Capacity "C", a number of connections "N" compete for the same bandwidth. Each link conforms to TCP Additive Increase and Multiplicative Decrease (AIMD) algorithm (Altman et al., 2006). When a network link is uncongested, either due to underutilization, non systemic or non-congestion packet loss, the combined set of parallel TCP streams will consume the unused bandwidth without appropriating bandwidth from existing single TCP streams (Hacker et al., 2004). This implies that individual connections between hosts can be of different aggregates or percentages of the link capacity. Fairness among these parallel streams can be achieved by the techniques as indicated in (Hacker et al., 2004). Aggregation is a very important area regarding parallel connections between two points in a network. While this is often the case in parallel networks, a more proactive way of achieve aggregation is to use more than one congestion control technique, where by one would yield to the other in when competing for bandwidth. Delay based protocols, e.g. LEDBAT (Stanislav Shalunov <shalunov@

bittorrent. com>, 2009) & (Rossi et al., 2010) is one such technique, which, when combined with other congestion control schemes, will perform a better link aggregation mechanism. This however is non intrusive and can exploit the available network resources. Other forms of delay based transport protocols which can achieve similar result are further discussed in (Welzl, 2010).

Point to Point with Multiple Paths

Multi-pathing is an effective way to achieve improved end to end throughput using disjoint paths to transfer data. This may include one or multiple nodes assisting the transfer of the file from one node to the other. As depicted in Figure 4, a path can be made of disjoint connections between several nodes from sender to receiver, whereby this path does not depend on the underlying routing network. These paths may be Overlay paths between two processes on different computers.

The discovery of which paths are optimum can be achieved by several means such as the use of a path probing algorithm similar to the path

Figure 4.Multiple paths with and without aggregated links

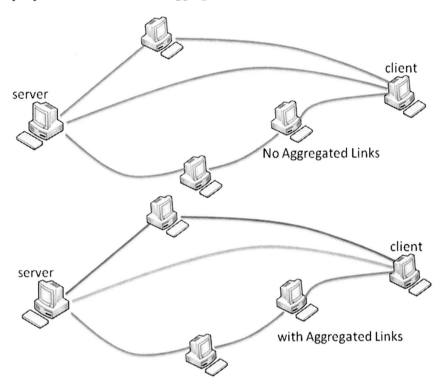

discovery protocol of IEEE 802.5. (Jinyu Zhang et al., 2009) proposed such a path probing algorithm which floods a probing packet across the network to find optimum paths between a sender and receiver. Nodes between the sender and receiver selectively accept and forward probing packets which it uses to set up connections with multiple nodes thereby creating multiple paths. The sender in this case strips the data to be sent into small packets and adaptively assign them to the best paths among the constructed overlay paths.

A new class of congestion control algorithms is capable of creating multi-paths between endpoints by using subflows or separate congestion windows between a node which has multiple addresses and other nodes in a network. An example of this algorithm was designed by the Internet Engineering Task force (IETF) and presented in (Mark Handley, Costin Raiciu, & Ford, 2010). While such algorithms may be good enough to create

multiple paths, it might fail in its attempt to utilize the uncongested paths. (Wischik, M. Handley, & C. Raiciu, 2009) through the use of mathematical fluid models have proposed a congestion control algorithm that does not only create multiple paths but also routes traffic through the best paths. This algorithm, which is also a design criterion for the IETF prototype, ensures that traffic flow does not flap abruptly among established paths in cases where a path may be perceived as being congested due to minor packet drops. It therefore performs efficient load balancing on these paths.

The Stream control Transport protocol (SCTP) has special features which can also be exploited to implement multipath data transport in the Internet. Multi-homing is one such feature which can bind multiple IP addresses at each node, enabling a network interface redundancy to improve resilience of the network (P. Natarajan, Baker, P.D. Amer, & Leighton, 2009). Concurrent Multipath Data Transfer, which can simultaneously setup multiple paths with network interface redundancy means that, a mobile user for instance, can connect to two separate wireless networks at the same time. This therefore leads to a very high network through put and fault tolerance. Algorithms to implement a Concurrent Multipath Data Transfer using multi-homing feature of the SCTP protocol are very well documented in (J.R. Iyengar et al., 2006). An implementation of this algorithm and the evaluation of its performance in terms of throughput and resilience, as well as some fairness issues were presented by (Dreibholz, Becke, Pulinthanath, & Rathgeb, 2010). While multi-homed devices can achieve better resilience and very high throughputs, however aggregating the bandwidth can enable optimum usage of network resources. In such a case, setting up multiple TCP sockets does not scale well when the link fluctuates or has different characteristics. Link aggregation can however be better achieved by a technique proposed by (Hsieh & Sivakumar, 2005) which uses a combination of mechanisms such as (i) decoupled congestion control and reliability, (ii) congestion window based stripping, (iii) dynamic reassignment, (iv) redundant striping to handle blackouts and (v) support for different congestion control scheme.

Combining Parallel Connections with Multipath

Mechanisms which can efficiently transfer very large files can be realized by the using a combination of multiple paths with parallel connections between any two nodes on this path. GridFTP is one such protocol which combines parallel data transfers methods to deliver a high performance, secure and reliable data transfer for high bandwidth in wide area networks. GridFTP provides a superset of features, including Grid security infrastructure, parallel data transfer, stripped data transfer, and automated negotiation of TCP buffers. GridFTP have been shown to deliver network speeds of between 27Gbits/sec and 30Gbits/sec.

It is therefore deployed over huge content delivery systems in well connected Grid environment where by only large file transfers are considered. This introduces the "Lots of Small Files Problem" in the case where smaller files are being sent, resulting in lower transfer rates. To solve this problem, pipelining of data is used to bind all the small files on the fly resulting in a large file transfer. Pipelining tries to minimize the amount of time between transfers and allows the client to have many outstanding unacknowledged transfer commands at once. Instead of being forced to wait for the "226 Transfer Successful" message; the client is free to send transfer commands at anytime. The concept of pipelining is well presented in (Bresnahan et al., 2007) and (John Bresnahan, Michael Link, Rajkumar Kettimuthu, Dan Fraser, & Ian Foster, 2008), with presentation and performance analysis.

To improve the throughput of the GridFTP protocol, the parallel data transfer mode must be optimized since it is a convex function of the number of parallel connections. Therefore tuning the number of parallel TCP connections is very important. GridFTP with Automatic Parallelism Tuning (GridFTP-APT) was proposed by (Ito, Ohsaki, & Imase, 2006), which searches for the optimal number of parallel TCP connections using the Golden Section Search (GSS) algorithm.

Other techniques which can improve the performance of the GridFTP protocol are Multi-Hop path splitting and Multi-pathing as proposed by (Khanna et al., 2008). Multi-hop path splitting is used to divide TCP connections into a set of shorter connections between intermediate points. This reduces the round trip time on each hop making it able to sense the throughput on each hope quickly. Multi-pathing is used to strip the data at the source and send it across multiple overlay paths. This increases the throughput since the data is transferred simultaneously using disjoint chunks of the file.

Multi Layer Approach

To enable parallel data transfer mechanisms to exploit the benefits of multiple layers (physical and logical), (Baldini et al., 2009) have proposed PATTHEL, a technique which is able to strip the data flow among multiple TCP channels. This solution is very simple and does not require invasive changes to the networking stack and can be implemented entirely in user space. It can also suit other scenarios such as splitting data transfer among multiple relays within a peer-to-peer overlay network. PATTHEL uses a scheduling algorithm which receives a sequence of application-generated data blocks and outputs a set of chunks, each one assigned to a data channel. The size of chunks and the scheduling policy determine the efficiency of the algorithm in using the available bandwidth. Such efficiency is maximized if all channels are fully loaded during the entire transfer. Generically most systems use multiple sockets to implement parallel data transfer using TCP, but TCP is not able to transparently use two different physical paths as a single logical channel. PATTHEL's main strengths are the capability to establish multiple communication channels transparently using TCP, its clever (and simple) scheduling algorithm for striping data over different channels, and its receiving module that limits the amount of memory copy operations in the receiver, thereby avoiding the need for an intermediate receiver buffer. Performance analysis according to (Baldini et al., 2009), indicates that PATTHEL can exploit multiple paths with a reasonable connection setup time, and approaches the theoretical connection setup time especially for large data transfers.

POINT TO MULTI-POINT PARALLEL TRANSPORT MECHANISM

Introduction to Multicast and Broadcast Transmission Mechanisms

Parallel data transmission is not restricted to the multiple connections or multiple paths between two nodes, but also multiple connections between a node and its neighbors in a network. In a computer network of more than two computers, the need to simultaneously communicate to multiple nodes has been an important area of research. Given a group of nodes in a network, a computer can communicate directly to a single node, as shown in Figure 5a also known as a Unicast data transfer. Unicast uses a simple point to point configuration to produce a single flow of information from one node to another. The connection between the two nodes however can have parallel paths. Another important feature of group communication is the ability to send information to all nodes in the network simultaneous. This is known as Broadcast and is depicted in Figure 5b. Given that Unicast and Broadcast are used for specific applications in the Internet, it is not the most efficient way to communicate to a select group among a bigger network. Unicast has the problem of setting up independent connections between a sender and each required node in order to transfer data, which ends up consuming the upload bandwidth of the sender. Broadcast on the other hand has serious network congestion and security issues if used to communicate to a given set of nodes in a network. Figure 5c shows Multicast which fits perfectly for communicating simultaneously with multiple select nodes while ensuring the bandwidth efficiency, reliability and security needed in a group communication. Multicast is the preferred mode of communication for multimedia application such as E-Learning where a single point source transmit data and the data is replicated at network nodes to an unlimited number of user nodes. Several

Figure 5. Diagram depicting unicast, broadcast, and multicast

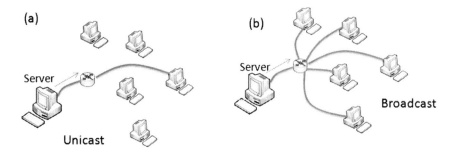

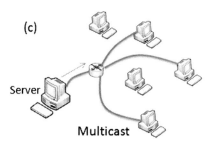

forms of multicast exist which provide reliable data transfer and are implemented in different parts of the OSI reference Layers. IP multicast is one of such techniques and implements a point to multi-point communication by identifying group members by their network identification. An example is Reliable Multicast transport protocol which is discussed in (Obraczka, 1998). Application layer multicast technologies on the other hand uses overlay networks for multicast purposes. Several examples exist such as Application Layer Multicast Infrastructure (AMLI) discussed in (Hosseini, Ahmed, Shirmohammadi, & Georganas, 2007). We however would restrict our discussion to a common design parameter, which is the topology on which a point to multipoint parallel data transport is realized. These topics, comprising of the Tree-based, Mesh, and Ring topologies shows how parallelism is achieved in group communication and are common to most multicast protocols. We would also make an ef-

fort to elaborate on their benefits and limitations, while we discuss some existing protocols under each topic.

Topologies: Tree Networks

Point to multipoint communication using tree topology is the most adopted way between a single node and several other nodes. In this case the sending node becomes the root node and the other nodes become leaves of the tree. The leaf nodes however serve as the parent nodes of other nodes in the tree according to increasing depth in the entire tree as indicated in Figure 6. The tree topology can be designed by several algorithms which enables a "single" path between a sender and each destination node in the group. Portions of a path may be reused to establish the path between the sender and other nodes. Of these algorithms, the recursive algorithm and the clustering algorithm are the most popular and are demonstrated in (El-

Figure 6. Tree network topology

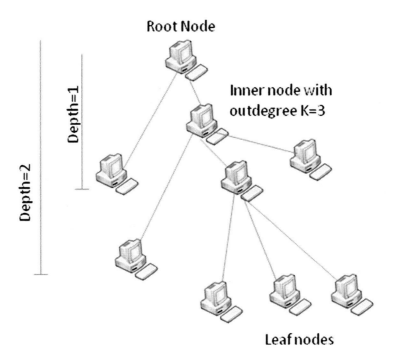

Sayed, Roca, & Mathy, 2003). In the recursive algorithm, a newcomer node first contacts the tree root, and selects the best node among the children of the root node with respect to some reference set of parameters. This procedure is repeated until an appropriate parent node is finally selected. The clustering algorithm on the other hand first creates a hierarchy of clusters, and then newcomer's recursively cross it to find the appropriate cluster (Popescu, Constantinescu, Erman, & Ilie, 2007).

The use of different algorithms results in different tree-based topologies. The Linear type topology, organizes its client into a chain with reference to the root server. The tree distribution type topology, with outdegree (k), organizes its clients into a tree with an outdegree k and an interior node in the tree serves k clients simultaneously. The Forest of parallel trees type topology uses an outdegree equal to the product (pk). In this case, a specific content is first split into p parts, each part is then distributed over an independent tree with outdegree (k) rooted at the

server, and finally the content is reconstructed at the receiver. The fundamental design components of these architectures are well articulated by (Hamra & Felber, 2005) and (Biersack, Rodriguez, & Felber, 2004). The advantage of using a tree-based topology is its applicability to typical content distribution networks. A content provider using a tree based multicast only sends the content to the root node for further distribution to multicast nodes.

Tree-based topologies are also the underling techniques used in most IP multicast protocols such as Reliable Multicast Transport Protocol (RMTP). However, larger amounts of data can be transported if tree-based architectures are used in Application Layer multicast. Application Layer multicast also has the drawback of larger amount of resources needed to provide the multicast communication service as well as the risk of inefficient use of available resources if compared to IP Multicast.

Topologies: Full Mesh Networks

Mesh-based point to multi-point communication is however usually applied to application layer Multicast. This implies that the network overlay nodes are organized in a perpetual mesh topology as indicated in Figure 7, where every node has knowledge of its neighbors. Multiple paths exist for communication between any two pair of nodes and every neighboring node cooperates to transfer data according to some predefined cooperation strategy. In Mesh based Application Layer multicast, joining members first form an overlay mesh, and then build a multicast tree on top of it. That is, alternative paths exist between any two nodes and therefore there is no need to reconstruct the path between two nodes in case of negative events, e.g. path crashes. Mesh based Application Layer Multicast offers some advantages in terms of routing stability as well as for QoS offerings. According to (Xing Jin, Wan-ching Wong, S. -h. Gary, & Chan Hoi-lun Ngan, 2008), because delivery trees are embedded in the overlay mesh, delivery efficiency depends on how well the overlay mesh is constructed. On the one hand, more overlay edges means more direct connections between hosts, and hence lower latency. On the other hand, fewer mesh edges means lower node stress. Therefore, in routing decision, selecting the overlay edges for low latency and node stress is important. For this reason, NARADA, a mesh based Application Layer Multicast protocol makes use of an algorithm for periodic mesh refinement to add or drop connections. This helps to incrementally improve the mesh, reduce the delay and improve the overall efficiency. Performance analysis of NADARA and other mesh based Application Layer Multicast presented by (Wang & H. Zhang, 2009) proves that NADARA is highly efficient but suitable for a multicast group of few nodes.

The main drawback of the mesh-based approach is related to difficulties in constructing loop-free forwarding paths among group members.

Figure 7. Mesh network topology

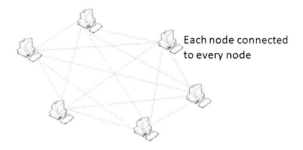

Other drawbacks are the increase of link stress and the complexity of algorithms needed for cooperation strategy, and for chunk selection (Popescu et al., 2007).

Architectures: Ring Networks

Search for architectures which are self organizing and operate in a distributed manner have resulted in point to multi-point communication using ring and multi-ring overlays. Ring overlay topologies are also very reliable, secure and able to survive in different network scenarios as compared to mesh and tree overlays. These distributed topologies also gives support to decentralized management of nodes. Rings are therefore able to deal with inherent flow and congestion control problems which are characteristic of Tree- and mesh-based topologies, especially when using acknowledgement (ACK) based error control for reliability. Rings are able to support an unlimited size of the multicast group, because each group member has constant number of neighbors in the overlay network as shown in Figure 8. Ring and multi-ring overlays also provide benefits in terms of inherent reliability and fault tolerance. Fault tolerance is possible because of the ring-based topology itself, which enables data packets to be easily looped back to the sender. Most versions of Ring and Multi-ring support situations where no ACKs or a low number of ACKs are needed to provide a successful communication. This is so because in

Figure 8. Ring and multi-ring network topologies

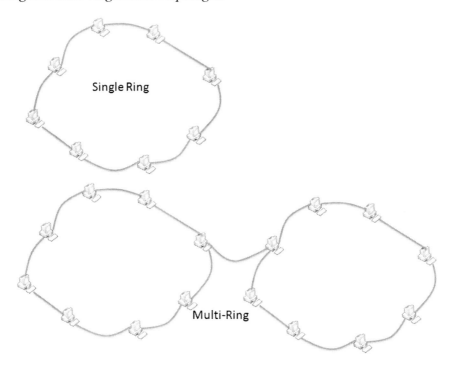

the case of a successful communication, the original packets are easily looped back to the sender.

Various forms of Ring based topologies such as Hierarchical-Rings, Hyper-Rings and Multi-Ring which are used in point to multi-point communication are discussed by (Jun Wang & William Yurcik, 2008). However these topologies are predominantly reserved for application layer Overlay multicast. A typical example "Virtual Ring" or "VRing" was proposed by (Sobeih, Yurcik, & Hou, 2004). VRing is a type of overlay network topology, capable of providing a spare ring for reliability reasons. This spare ring is utilized through a duplicate suppression mechanism that makes use of both the original ring and the spare ring for forwarding data packets.

The problems regarding Rings and Multi-Ring group communication is the long communication paths and larger delays and jitter. Ring architectures however suffer from some scalability issues, but this can be improved by building up hierarchical topologies. The Hierarchical topology

makes use of smaller Multi-Rings interconnected together to replace a large single ring.

MULTI-POINT TO POINT PARALLEL TRANSPORT MECHANISM

Introduction to Multipoint Parallel Data Retrieval

To dramatically improve the time used to complete the download of a single file in the Internet, the use of techniques to access the same file, or components of the same file from multiple points in the Internet has gained attention in the research community. The term "*paraloading*" and "*parallel Access*" are generally the most favorable terms used to describe such techniques. Mostly content is replicated at single or multiple servers which provide alternate sites (*Mirror Sites*) from which the content can be downloaded. This increases the availability of the content, coupled with a higher

Figure 9. Parallel downloading

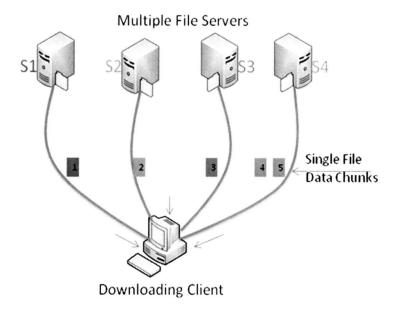

bandwidth for retrieving a single file which is made possible by the aggregated upload bandwidth of the parallel connections. An experimental study of parallel downloading schemes by (Philopoulos & Maheswaran, 2001), enumerates the advantages of these techniques as: *(a)* increased overall throughput to the client, *(b)* resilience to link and general route failures due to multiple connections, *and (c)* inherent load balancing associated with parallel loading because connections are spread over several servers, making it immune to individual server load fluctuations as well as traffic fluctuations. Our interest therefore is to understudy the techniques which enable us to establish these advantages. Indeed, while there are several ways to implement paraloading, research according to (Rodriguez & Biersack, 2002) indicates that, the core problem of paraloading is the selection of servers or mirror sites which optimizes the performance of a given parallel file retrieval system. We therefore proceed to discuss the foundational and more traditional techniques such as history based Parallel Access, Semi-Dynamic Parallel Access, Dynamic Parallel Access, following the hierarchy of the most advance with optimum

performance and move on to more futuristic approaches and recent research in the field. Figure 9 shows a simple paraloading system.

History Based Parallel Access

Prior information about servers, especially transmission rates from servers to clients can be exploited to set up multiple connections with the aim of implementing a parallel access network. History based Parallel Access uses this technique by recording each client-server transmission rate into a database and using it to set up the connection when required. (Rodriguez & Biersack, 2002) indicates that, a history based Parallel Access uses this information to decide *"a priori"* which part of a document should be delivered by each server. In a typical case, a client divides a single document into "M" multiple segments of varying sizes, each of which would be downloaded separately from a different mirror site. The variation in data segments is solely based on the expected transmission rate of each server. This enables downloading to finish at the same time for each server, whiles reducing the downloading time for a client. To ensure a server side transparent solution which can only be modified by the client, file blocks are downloaded from each individual server using the HTTP 1.1 byte range header feature. The problem of poor estimation of server transmission rate in a client database can strongly affect the performance of History based Parallel Access. This can be compensated by use of a shared database by a group of clients connect by a proxy cache, where by the database is updated whenever a client connects to any server. However, this does not entirely solve the problem of under-estimation or over-estimation of server transmission rates. A more dynamic approach is therefore required to exploit the exact transmission rate of each server to optimize its performance and reduce the downloading time per file.

Semi-Dynamic Parallel Access

Semi-dynamic paraloading, a term introduced by (Philopoulos & Maheswaran, 2001) is an improvement to history based paraloading method. This method can better exploit server side transmission rate. A receiver which intends to setup semi-dynamic paraloading would first have to send a request for the entire file size from one of the servers or mirror sites. It then segments the file to be requested into equal block sizes. The receiver then requests to download one block per each mirror site. (Pablo Rodriguez, Andreas Kirpal, & Ernst W. Biersack, 2000) indicates that requests to servers are done by an HTTP byte-range header. Once a server has completed sending the requested file block, the client will request a new (undelivered) block from the server. In case the number of blocks is less than the number of servers, a block which has been requested but not yet completed would be downloaded simultaneously by another server to potentially reduce the download time. The client reassembles all blocks into the original file after it has downloaded all the required blocks. To reduce the time needed to download a single file, persistent TCP connections

between the client and server is used to reduce overhead. Also block sizes should be chosen carefully to optimize the time required to download each block, and at the same time reduce the time required to setup requests. Block size selection therefore should consider the following points:

- That the number of blocks supersedes the number of mirror sites.
- That block sizes are small enough to ensure that the last block requested from each server is terminated at the same time.
- That each block is sufficiently large enough to ensure that the idle time between transmissions is smaller than the time used to download a block.

To reconcile the last two points, it is important to have the best block sizes usually in the order of several hundred Kbytes' which are considered optimal. Further enhancements proposed in (Philopoulos & Maheswaran, 2001) are essential to reducing the overall time per download, these are:

- Reducing the delay during startup by piggy-backing onto the data block a request for the file size and list of mirror sites.
- Pipelining requests to reduce idle times between requests.
- Dynamically adjusting the block sizes for the last blocks to reduce the idle times at that stage.

For very large files, better ways of exploiting the server side resources are needed. That is using a paraloading server which performs better than HTTP byte-range header, and employing a dynamic method to downscale the number of mirror sites restrict slow servers if they are seen as not adding any significant increase to the downloading process. A paraloading scheme capable of performing these functions is therefore presented below.

Dynamic Parallel Access

Some servers generally have very slow transmission rates for a given file with multiple mirror sites. While these servers may be important when the number of blocks is low towards the end of a download process, they can have an effect on the aggregated bandwidth if used during the initial part of the download process. Dynamic paraloading is an advanced form of the semi-dynamic downloading scheme which can support large file downloads. It introduces methods, to isolate slow severs when needed and to improve the paraloading process by using a propriety paraloading server which runs on top of the transport layer and not the HTTP byte-range header.

To initiate the download process, connections are made with all mirror sites which can be obtained by dynamically retrieving the server list from either a directory service or by making an extension to the DNS to provide such information. This is to eliminate the time used to probe individual severs for information about the file. Bigger block sizes are employed to reduce the number of requests and each block size is typically 1Kbyte. These sizes can however be varied. In order to maintain a high aggregated bandwidth with less overhead, the number of servers is reduced after the *downscaling testing* phase (monitoring initial sever rates when number of servers are more than four). Slow servers are then selected to remain idle. This is because, if the aggregated bandwidth after a slow server is eliminated is higher, equal or even lower than the initial aggregated bandwidth by a threshold percentage of 15% given by (Philopoulos & Maheswaran, 2001), the slow server is seen not to add any significant increase in bandwidth. Therefore eliminating it rather improves the performance of the paralleled servers. This procedure is iterated over the number of servers available and the next slow server is eliminated until a point where the aggregated bandwidth is less than the previous aggregate by a designated threshold percentage. The server downscaling

would however terminate if the number of servers is less than four. At this stage, server up-scaling testing initializes to prevent a significant decrease in aggregated bandwidth by adding additional servers when needed to improve the performance. Dynamic parallel Access therefore ensures that the combined transmission rate of all the active servers is close to that of the combined transmission rate if all servers transmit at the same speed of the fastest server. However straight forward negotiations between client and servers, induce some extra delay which prevents optimum usage of server resources. A more advance technique to enable dramatic downloading speedups by eliminating these complex negotiations is consequently needed.

Parallel Access Using Tornado Codes

The most advanced technique in accessing multiple servers or mirror sites in parallel is by using Tornado codes. This technique employs revolutionary ways to remove all complex client-server negotiation in a straight forward implementation, which naturally induce a lot of delay into the downloading time. While paraloading may significantly improve performance, (Miu & Shih, 1999) indicates that it comes with a cost; therefore a good paraloading system should consider the cost in its design. Downloading a large file from a heavily loaded server or through highly congested link can sometimes be very slow. (Byers, Luby, & Mitzenmacher, 2002) who employed Tornado codes, reveal a scalable approach which allow clients to access multiple servers even under stress conditions and improve the overall performance of the download process at the bottleneck. The straight forward approach as in dynamic parallel access can also have a substantial draw back in terms of complexity, scalability and their ability to handle heterogeneity among clients and servers. Tornado code is a sort of erasure code which when applied to a parallel downloading scheme, can enable a client to gather an encoded file in parallel from multiple servers, and with multiple connections between each server and the client. Tornado codes present a faster encoding and decoding, with the price of requiring a slightly higher number of packets which is needed to reconstruct the file. This also ensures a high resilience to packet loss during the downloading process.

MULTI-POINT TO MULTI-POINT

P2P Approach for Multi-point to Multi-point Transport Mechanism

Our study of parallel transport mechanism for large scale data transfers has included methods to improve a clients upload capabilities by the use of multicast techniques and ways to improve a clients download capabilities by use of parallel downloading techniques. To combine both capabilities for a highly efficient and scalable transport mechanism, a new parallel transport mechanism is needed. P2P provides such a platform with a distributed architecture and scalability which enables the system to partition upload task among peers and provide equal privileges in terms of download bandwidth among all peers. P2P systems are capable of providing a self organizing architecture, and can regulate peer node selection, redundant information storage, efficient search of data items, data availability and security. P2P networks build overlay networks on top of the physical network for data transmission. This makes them fault tolerant since they have the ability to augment their overlay network. Overlay networks are categorized into either structured or unstructured overlay networks.

Unstructured overlay networks are the category of P2P networks which build its overlay network nodes in a random and arbitrary fashion. A new peer node, which intends to join the overlay network, would first copy existing links of the overlay network from other peer nodes until it

builds its own links. In unstructured overlays, a node looking for a specific data item uses search techniques such as flooding, random walks and expanding-ring Time to Live (TTL) to query peer nodes for the needed content. Each node, upon receiving the query regardless of its complexity, can evaluate it and respond with the requested content if available. This method is however inefficient because content that has less popularity or are hardly replicated would require queries to be sent to a large fraction of the nodes. This ends up consuming a lot of bandwidth available to the network. Several improved search and replication schemes which can improve the scalability of unstructured networks have been studied and published by (Gkantsidis, Mihail, & Saberi, 2005) and (Thampi, 2010). Some of these search and replication schemes include techniques such as (i) preferential walk (ii) adaptive probabilistic search and (iii) search with weights. Unstructured P2P are the most commonly used P2P technologies, examples being Bittorent, Gnutella, Freenet and KazaA. Unstructured P2P protocols have been captured in surveys by (Eng Keong Lua, Crowcroft, Pias, Sharma, & Lim, 2005) and (Hyojin Park, Jinhong Yang, Juyoung Park, Shin Gak Kang, & Jun Kyun Choi, 2008).

Structured P2P on the other hand uses a consistent algorithm called Distributed Hash tables (DHT) to organize every node in the overlay network. The overlay creation is done by assigning keys to data items, which can be used to map a given key to a specific data item and therefore result in a highly efficient, scalable and reliable P2P network. Structured P2P however are unable to respond to complex queries and for this reason a copy or a pointer to each data item at the peer responsible for the key corresponding to that data item is necessary. This usually results in Load balancing issues among peer nodes since DHT abstraction may distribute objects randomly among peer nodes, which in turn would result in making one node assigned more data items or pointers than another node. Algorithms for load balancing in structured P2P exist which can improve the overall performance. (Surana, Godfrey, Lakshminarayanan, Karp, & Stoica, 2006) proposed a load balancing algorithm which can support rapid arrivals and departures of objects of varying load, This algorithm achieves load balancing for system utilizations as high as 90%. Examples of structured P2P include Chord, Pastry, Tapestry and Content Addressable Networks (CAN).

Since it is evident that both structured and unstructured P2P have peculiar limitations, which may span between, the distributed nature of the overlay, routing performance and ability to locate content, reliability, security and load balancing, designing P2P system which can mitigate these essential problems will improve the overall system performance. However the ideal parallel transport mechanism for the future which holds more promise for content delivery systems will require a system which integrates P2P to provide services to numerous clients such as video streaming and file sharing. P2P video streaming provides the best platform for next generation parallel transport mechanisms since it blend P2P with other techniques such as Network Coding, Video Coding and Caching to improve data quality and increase system performance. We therefore would analyze several P2P streaming technologies which have been proposed in current literature like Adaptive Streaming, Layered streaming, and Caching in P2P systems. Finally we would have a look at the all new "Bittorrent DNA" protocol for content distribution.

Adaptive Streaming

P2P video streaming applications can be designed to exploit the benefits of network coding and packet scheduling solutions. Adaptive streaming is a method to apply Network Stream processing techniques which improves its overall performance over P2P networks. Such techniques which include the use of redundant packet, network coding, packet scheduling, video coding or a

combination of these techniques has become the bedrock for next generation parallel transport mechanism.

Efficient packet scheduling algorithms which are able to determine packet arrival times and determine which packets should be forwarded at any given instant in order to maximize data quality is an essential building block in Adaptive streaming. According to (Jurca, Chakareski, Wagner, & Frossard, 2007), implementing completely distributed video-packet scheduling algorithms in individual peers is a complex task. Ideally, these algorithms run independently on each transmitting peer but unanimously decide the set of video packets to be sent, along with disjoint partitions allocated to each peer. The goal is to maximize the quality of the received data/video stream, while avoiding the wasting of network resources. Therefore a high performing packet scheduling algorithm is beneficial to adaptive streaming if a trade of between its complexity and the rate distortion efficiency is taken.

Video coding techniques, including the use of redundant packet information and error resilient and error concealment codes such as Forward error correction (FEC) and Multiple Description Codes (MDC) can be applied in Adaptive streaming under a P2P approach. MDC is able to encode a single stream into multiple sub-streams to suit peer nodes with different bandwidth requirements, while FEC generates redundant packets which enable peer nodes to reconstruct missing packets to reduce error propagation in the network. (Hongyun Yang, Ruiming Hu, Jun Chen, & Xuhui Chen, 2008) explains that whiles these techniques are very advantageous, MDC is unable to regenerate missing packets and FEC is also unable to satisfy peer nodes with different bandwidth requirement. Therefore a combination of the two or FEC with another multi-stream coding method is necessary to design a high performing Adaptive streaming P2P system.

Network Coding presents us with a very important technique for designing an Adaptive

Streaming system by enhancing network routing and providing a high reliability of traffic. Network coding can be applied perfectly to P2P networks because of its arbitrary overlay construction, and also because P2P nodes can perform complex operations such as decoding and encoding other than simply storing and forwarding messages. The main purpose of network coding is to enable nodes to generate output messages by encoding received messages. This makes all data packets equally important, and every encoded data packet is innovative to one receiver or the other in some way. This feature therefore encourages peer nodes to collaborate in sharing information. (Min Yang & Yuanyuan Yang, 2008) proposed a network coding technique for P2P file sharing called "PPFEED", this technique which can be applied to Video streaming, constructs overlay networks in the form of combination networks (i.e. a network with a Source node, relay node and receiver node) while applying network coding. This creates a scheme that can serve as a middleware for file sharing which is scalable, efficient, reliable and easy to implement. An even better system called "Chameleon" was proposed by (Anh Tuan Nguyen, Baochun Li, & Eliassen, 2010). Chameleon is an Adaptive Video streaming technique which uses network coding and integrates a video coding scheme called SVC (scalable video codec of the H.264/AVC). The benefits of this method is that, while Network coding simplifies the streaming protocol by better peer coordination and peer collaboration methods, SVC provides multiple video streams for peer nodes with different bandwidth requirements making Chameleon highly efficient and reliable.

Layered Streaming

Layered P2P is a generation of adaptive P2P streaming which is able to provide media content to satisfy the heterogeneity of client resource capabilities. Layered P2P encodes packets streams into multiple layers which can serve the network capabilities of a client. (Cui & Nahrstedt, 2003) proposed algorithms to implement layered P2P which is able to optimally utilize the outbound bandwidth of the sending peer with the smallest number of layers. Therefore the algorithm can regulate the maximum amount of layers a sending peer must have. The layer encoding can however be done by several media encoding methods such as video coding and arithmetic coding. (Rejaie & Ortega, 2003) proposed a receiver driven approach called PALS (P2P Adaptive Layered streaming), able to coordinate and provide an adaptation framework for streaming multiple layers of a file from multiple sending peers. The PALS framework therefore enables the receiver to cope with the variations and dynamics of the sending peers. The PALS framework is able to provide these capabilities to the receiver through methods such as smart peer selection, adaptive packet assignment and sender packet quality.

Advance research in Layered streaming has unearthed developments in a Hierarchical Network coding approach known as Layered Network Coding (LNC). By combining the hierarchy of layered source coding with random network coding, we are able to implement a Layered Streaming protocol. According to (Jingjing Si, Bojin Zhuang, Anni Cai, & Yinbo Cheng, 2009), who investigated LNC, at the playback deadline, if currently received data are not enough to recover the original data completely, LNC can recover the most important layers to maintain the smooth playback. Simulation results by (Jingjing Si et al., 2009) shows that LNC can recover the important layers with fewer received blocks than general network coding.

File Caching in P2P Streaming Systems

Caching is the temporal storage of a data file or files in a computer or server. The ability for P2P applications such as video streaming to provide caching can tremendously reduce the resource competition between peer nodes thereby improving the limited bandwidth available. Since P2P systems are part of the Internet, which include Internet service Providers (ISPs) and huge content Delivery servers which carry most load required by users, caching can be done either in proxy servers, client access points or even clients themselves to increase bandwidth, to improve availability of files and to reduce the traffic that traverse the wide area networks and ISPs.

According to (Xu, M. Zhang, Liu, Qin, & Ye, 2010), Proxy caching enables the gateway to intercept the P2P downloading requests which originates from its associated regional network and redirects them to the P2P cache server. Such interception can be either implemented by redirecting requests or using forged IP addresses of remote peers. The objective is to serve as many data requests locally as possible. The server will fetch data from remote peers only when the data cannot be found in its local cache. The old data will be evicted if the cache space is exhausted. In P2P live streaming, it is impossible to cache the whole data because it is unavailable until released and is partly unordered. For that reason special caching methods are required. (Xu et al., 2010) proposed the Sliding window (SLW) algorithm for P2P live streaming. The SLW algorithm is able to cache the hottest data items in the requesting window and distributes cached files among channels according to their popularity. The SLW algorithm explores both temporal and spatial locality of data requests and gets the best performance compared to most online caching policies. In wireless environments, caching of data files can also be done via the wireless access points. (Tan, Guo, & Chen, 2007) proposed a solution for wireless access point caching. This technique called Smart Caching in Access Points (SCAP), stores downstream traffic to buffers in the access point and applies an algorithm referred to as Rabin Fingerprinting to detect already cached data packets to prevent duplicating that packet. This procedure leads to conserving buffers in the access point while providing availability of data,

reducing the traffic that across the access point and improving the overall performance of the P2P streaming system.

Caching in peer nodes is another exciting area in P2P streaming technologies. GroCoca, a Group-based P2P Cooperative Caching, was proposed by (Chow, Leong, & Chan, 2007). GroCoca is built on a wireless peer environment with tightly coupled groups of nodes that possess similarities in terms of mobility pattern and data affinity. GroCoca uses a discovery algorithm to dynamically discover all coupled peer groups in the system. The algorithm also offers a cache signature scheme which provides hints for the peer nodes to make local decisions on whether to search another peers' cache for their desired data items or to perform a cooperative cache replacement in their coupled peer groups. The cache signature is compressed to reduce the power consumption on transmitting cache signatures between peer nodes. GroCoca provides a cooperative cache admission control and cooperative cache replacement scheme that can control data replicas and improve data accessibility in a coupled group respectively. Experimental results depict that GroCoca further improves system performance in comparison to standard cooperative caching schemes.

BitTorrent and BitTorrent DNA

BitTorrent is an unstructured P2P file sharing protocol designed to integrate seamlessly with the web and it identifies content by URL. BitTorrent supports concurrent multiple downloads, and peer nodes upload required files among each other. This makes it possible to share large files among a large number of downloaders in a very decentralize and distributed fashion unlike the traditional client server paradigm. According to (Cohen, 2010) the Bit Torrent protocol operates over TCP and performs efficiently without even setting any socket options. However, we can envision this system to change with development of more advanced transport protocols such as SCTP

(P. Natarajan et al., 2009) and LEDBAT (Rossi et al., 2010). BitTorrent in its simplest form contain entities such as (i) an ordinary web server, (ii) a static "metainfo" file, (iii) a BitTorrent tracker, (iv) a downloader and (v) an end user web browser. Some profound features of BitTorrent are the ability to provide symmetric information flow and the indexing scheme that is used to describe pieces of a file in the met info file starting at zero. To download a file, a peer node accesses the tracker and joins the torrent. The peer node then downloads a file which has been subdivided into blocks, while uploading to other peers what it has downloaded. This increases the upload bandwidth in the network and the peers contributing more are rewarded with more download bandwidth resulting in a Tit-for-Tat scenario.

BitTorrent DNA is a content delivery service and a function of the BitTorrent P2P protocol which supports video streaming in an optimal fashion. The core of this function is to reduce delay, increase bandwidth, and improve the user experience in content delivery systems while reducing throttling and blocking pressures on ISPs and content providers. BitTorrent DNA would require integrating the video streaming technologies discussed earlier such as adaptive streaming, layered streaming, and file caching to provide a very good content delivery service. BitTorrent DNA is proprietary and therefore the inner workings of the protocol have not been disclosed. However (Shalunov, 2008) of BitTorrent Incorporated gives a sneak-in view of what to expect. According to (Shalunov, 2008), BitTorrent DNA supports file caching, this implies that BitTorrent DNA implements either proxy caching, peer cooperation caching, or a combination of both to solve the ISP blocking problems and provide high data availability with reduced cost of downloading. BitTorrent DNA ability to support smarter peer selection probably stems from its use of Network Coding with multiple encoded streams or better still, a Multi Layer Network coding scheme as discussed earlier. This increases

peer coordination and collaboration which assist in discovering peer caches which supports every end-users bandwidth requirement. Furthermore the issue of "better congestion control" stems from the use of LEDBAT, the transport mechanism proposed by (Rossi et al., 2010). LEDBAT is a delay based Transport protocol that is very efficient in exploiting residual bandwidth when used with TCP. It is however TCP friendly and improves fairness per flow. Therefore to design the next generation parallel transport mechanism "of which BitTorrent DNA is obviously in the lead", a combination of the techniques discussed above such as Adaptive Streaming, Layered streaming and caching, coupled with highly efficient Transport Layer protocols is required.

DISCUSSION AND CONCLUSION

We have captured several techniques required to design a high performing parallel transport mechanism in this survey. Literature regarding the most basic Point to Point transport mechanisms has also been considered. This includes simple Point to Point connections without any form of connection management between sender and receiver, thereby resulting in a system where transmitted information is unreliable and has unordered packets. Reliable point to point transport mechanisms, e.g. TCP and SCTP which perform some sort of connection management such as flow control, congestion control and synchronized flow has also been covered. Most importantly, various congestion control techniques which enable optimum bandwidth usage were discussed. This includes delay based transport protocols such as LEDBAT which are very efficient in creating aggregated parallel connection between two nodes.

Parallel transport mechanisms was discussed under four different sections, i.e. Point to Point parallel transport, Point to Multi-point parallel transport, Multi-point to Point Parallel transport and Multi-point to Multi-point parallel transport.

Techniques such a Parallel Socket Connections, Multipath, Concurrent Multi-path, Multi-homing and Interlayer parallel transport such as PATHEL were presented under Point to Point parallel transport. Advanced IP Multicast and Application Layer Multicast architectures and techniques were presented for Point to Multi-point parallel transport, and Parallel Downloading was presented for Multipoint to Point parallel transport. The most advanced P2P streaming functions which are important building blocks for next generation parallel transport mechanisms were presented under Multi-point to Multi-point. Examples of these techniques are Adaptive streaming which provides efficient packet scheduling and error control methods, Layered streaming which provides scalable content for multiple users with different bandwidth requirement, and file Caching in P2P networks which reduce network traffic and increase the availability of data near the client.

We also presented BitTorrent DNA which is one of the most advanced content delivery protocols available. BitTorrent DNA combines streaming techniques such as Adaptive streaming, Layered streaming and file Caching which enables a Bit-Torrent DNA Client to perform parallelism in an optimal manner. It can be ascertained from this literature that, an optimal parallel transport mechanism must integrate not just P2P streaming techniques, but also the best performing Point to Point, Point to Multi-point and Multi-point to Point parallel transport mechanisms.

REFERENCES

Altman, E., Barman, D., Tuffin, B., & Vojnovic, M. (2006). Parallel TCP sockets: Simple model, throughput and validation. In *Proceedings INFOCOM 2006. 25th IEEE International Conference on Computer Communications* (pp. 1-12). doi:10.1109/INFOCOM.2006.104

Baldini, A., De Carli, L., & Risso, F. (2009). Increasing performances of TCP data transfers through multiple parallel connections. In *IEEE Symposium on Computers and Communications, ISCC 2009* (pp. 630-636). doi:10.1109/ISCC.2009.5202274

Biersack, E. W., Rodriguez, P., & Felber, P. (2004). Performance analysis of peer-to-peer networks for file distribution. *In Proceedings of the Fifth International Workshop on Quality of Future Internet Services (QOFIS'04)*. Retrieved from http://citeseerx.ist.psu.edu/viewdoc/summary?doi=10.1.1.58.9865

Bresnahan, J., Link, M., Kettimuthu, R., & Foster, I. (2009, December 22). *UDT as an alternative transport protocol for GridFTP*. Retrieved from http://citeseerx.ist.psu.edu/viewdoc/summary?doi=10.1.1.149.3153

Bresnahan, J., Link, M., Kettimuthu, R., Fraser, D., & Foster, I. (2008, April 3). *GridFTP pipelining*. Retrieved from http://citeseerx.ist.psu.edu/viewdoc/summary?doi=?doi=10.1.1.107.2284

Bresnahan, J., Link, M., Khanna, G., Imani, Z., Kettimuthu, R., & Foster, I. (2007). Globus GridFTP: What's new in 2007. In *Proceedings of the First International Conference on Networks for Grid Applications* (pp. 1-5). Lyon, France: ICST. Retrieved from http://portal.acm.org/citation.cfm?id=1386610.1386636

Byers, J. W., Luby, M., & Mitzenmacher, M. (2002). Accessing multiple mirror sites in parallel: Using tornado codes to speed up downloads. In *Proceedings INFOCOM'99, Eighteenth Annual Joint Conference of the IEEE Computer and Communications Societies* (Vol. 1, pp. 275–283).

Chow, C. Y., Leong, H. V., & Chan, A. T. (2007). GroCoca: Group-based peer-to-peer cooperative caching in mobile environment. *IEEE Journal on Selected Areas in Communications, 25*(1), 179–191. doi:10.1109/JSAC.2007.070118

Cohen, B. (2010). *The BitTorrent protocol specification*, version 11031.

Cui, Y., & Nahrstedt, K. (2003). Layered peer-to-peer streaming. In *Proceedings of the 13th International Workshop on Network and Operating Systems Support for Digital Audio and Video* (pp. 162-171). Monterey, CA: ACM. doi:10.1145/776322.776348

Dreibholz, T., Becke, M., Pulinthanath, J., & Rathgeb, E. P. (2010). Implementation and evaluation of concurrent multipath transfer for SCTP in the INET framework. In *Proceedings of the 3rd International ICST Conference on Simulation Tools and Techniques* (pp. 1-8). Torremolinos, Spain: ICST. Retrieved from http://portal.acm.org/citation.cfm?id=1808163

El-Sayed, A., Roca, V., & Mathy, L. (2003). A survey of proposals for an alternative group communication service. *IEEE Network, 17*(1), 46–51. doi:10.1109/MNET.2003.1174177

Gkantsidis, C., Mihail, M., & Saberi, A. (2005). Hybrid search schemes for unstructured peer-to-peer networks. In *Proceedings IEEE INFOCOM 2005, 24th Annual Joint Conference of the IEEE Computer and Communications Societies* (Vol. 3, pp. 1526-1537). doi:10.1109/INFCOM.2005.1498436

Gu, Y., & Grossman, R. L. (2007). UDT: UDP-based data transfer for high-speed wide area networks. *Computer Networks, 51*(7), 1777–1799. doi:10.1016/j.comnet.2006.11.009

Hacker, T., Noble, B., & Athey, B. (2004). Improving throughput and maintaining fairness using parallel TCP. In *INFOCOM 2004. Twenty-third Annual Joint Conference of the IEEE Computer and Communications Societies* (Vol. 4, pp. 2480-2489). doi:10.1109/INFCOM.2004.1354669

Hamra, A. A., & Felber, P. A. (2005). Design choices for content distribution in P2P networks. *SIGCOMM Computer Communication Review, 35*(5), 29–40. doi:10.1145/1096536.1096540

Handley, M., Raiciu, C., & Ford, A. (2010, August 25). *TCP extensions for multipath operation with multiple addresses*. Retrieved November 11, 2010, from http://tools.ietf.org/html/draft-ford-mptcp-multiaddressed-03

Hosseini, M., Ahmed, D. T., Shirmohammadi, S., & Georganas, N. D. (2007). A survey of application-layer multicast protocols. *IEEE Communication Surveys and Tutorials, 9*(3). Retrieved from http://citeseerx.ist.psu.edu/viewdoc/summary?doi=10.1.1.121.1896

Hsieh, H., & Sivakumar, R. (2005). A transport layer approach for achieving aggregate bandwidths on multi-homed mobile hosts. *Wireless Networks, 11*(1-2), 99–114. doi:10.1007/s11276-004-4749-6

Ito, T., Ohsaki, H., & Imase, M. (2006). *Gridftp-apt: Automatic parallelism tuning mechanism for data transfer protocol gridftp*. ccGrid, 0--454.

Iyengar, J., Amer, P., & Stewart, R. (2006). Concurrent multipath transfer using SCTP multihoming over independent end-to-end paths. *IEEE/ACM Transactions on Networking, 14*(5), 951–964. doi:10.1109/TNET.2006.882843

Jin, X., Wong, W.-C., Gary, S.-H., & Ngan, C. H.-L. (2008, April 2). *A survey and comparison of application-level multicast protocols*. Retrieved from http://citeseerx.ist.psu.edu/viewdoc/summary?doi=10.1.1.97.3413

Jurca, D., Chakareski, J., Wagner, J., & Frossard, P. (2007). Enabling adaptive video streaming in P2P systems. *Communications Magazine, 45*(6), 108–114. doi:10.1109/MCOM.2007.374427

Khanna, G., Catalyurek, U., Kurc, T., Sadayappan, P., Saltz, J., Kettimuthu, R., & Foster, I. (2008). Multi-hop path splitting and multi-pathing optimizations for data transfers over shared wide-area networks using gridFTP. In *Proceedings of the 17th International Symposium on High Performance Distributed Computing* (pp. 225-226). Boston, MA: ACM. doi:10.1145/1383422.1383457

Lua, E. K., Crowcroft, J., Pias, M., Sharma, R., & Lim, S. (2005). A survey and comparison of peer-to-peer overlay network schemes. *Communications Surveys & Tutorials, 7*(2), 72–93. doi:10.1109/COMST.2005.1610546

Miu, A., & Shih, E. (1999). *Performance analysis of a dynamic parallel downloading scheme from mirror sites throughout the internet. Term Paper.* LCS MIT.

Natarajan, P., Baker, F., Amer, P., & Leighton, J. (2009). SCTP: What, why, and how. *IEEE Internet Computing, 13*(5), 81–85. doi:10.1109/MIC.2009.114

Natarajan, P., Iyengar, J. R., Amer, P. D., & Stewart, R. (2006). SCTP: An innovative transport layer protocol for the web. In *Proceedings of the 15th International Conference on World Wide Web* (pp. 615-624). Edinburgh, UK: ACM. doi:10.1145/1135777.1135867

Nguyen, A. T., Li, B., & Eliassen, F. (2010). Adaptive peer-to-peer streaming with network coding. In *INFOCOM, 2010 Proceedings IEEE* (pp. 1–9). Chameleon. doi:10.1109/INFCOM.2010.5462032

Obraczka, K. (1998). Multicast transport protocols: A survey and taxonomy. *IEEE Communications Magazine, 36*, 94–102. doi:10.1109/35.649333

Oothongsap, P., Viniotis, Y., & Vouk, M. (2008). *Improvements of the SABUL congestion control algorithm.*

Park, H., Yang, J., Park, J., Kang, S. G., & Choi, J. K. (2008). A survey on peer-to-peer overlay network schemes. In *10th International Conference on Advanced Communication Technology, ICACT 2008* (Vol. 2, pp. 986-988). doi:10.1109/ICACT.2008.4493931

Philopoulos, S., & Maheswaran, M. (2001). Experimental study of parallel downloading schemes for internet mirror sites. In *Thirteenth IASTED International Conference on Parallel and Distributed Computing Systems, PDCS '01,* (pp. 44-48).

Popescu, A., Constantinescu, D., Erman, D., & Ilie, D. (2007). A survey of reliable multicast communication. In *3rd EuroNGI Conference on Next Generation Internet Networks,* (pp. 111-118). doi:10.1109/NGI.2007.371205

Rangwala, S., Jindal, A., Jang, K., Psounis, K., & Govindan, R. (2008). Understanding congestion control in multi-hop wireless mesh networks. In *Proceedings of the 14th ACM International Conference on Mobile Computing and Networking* (pp. 291-302). San Francisco, CA: ACM. doi:10.1145/1409944.1409978

Rejaie, R., & Ortega, A. (2003). PALS: Peer-to-peer adaptive layered streaming. In *Proceedings of the 13th International Workshop on Network and Operating Systems Support for Digital Audio and Video* (pp. 153-161). Monterey, CA: ACM. doi:10.1145/776322.776347

Rodriguez, P., & Biersack, E. W. (2002). Dynamic parallel access to replicated content in the internet. *IEEE/ACM Transactions on Networking, 10*(4), 455–465. doi:10.1109/TNET.2002.801413

Rodriguez, P., Kirpal, A., & Biersack, E. W. (2000). *Parallel-access for mirror sites in the internet.* Retrieved from http://citeseerx.ist.psu.edu/viewdoc/summary?doi=10.1.1.83.3395

Rossi, D., Testa, C., Valenti, S., & Muscariello, L. (2010). LEDBAT: The new BitTorrent congestion control protocol. In *2010 Proceedings of 19th International Conference on Computer Communications and Networks (ICCCN)*, (pp. 1-6). doi:10.1109/ICCCN.2010.5560080

Shalunov, S. (2008). *Users want P2P, we make it work*. In IETF P2P Infrastructure Workshop. (May 2008).

Shalunov, S. (2009, March 4). *Low extra delay background transport (LEDBAT)*. Retrieved October 14, 2010, from http://tools.ietf.org/html/draft-shalunov-ledbat-congestion-00

Si, J., Zhuang, B., Cai, A., & Cheng, Y. (2009). Layered network coding and hierarchical network coding for peer-to-peer streaming. In *Pacific-Asia Conference on Circuits, Communications and Systems, PACCS '09* (pp. 139-142). doi:10.1109/PACCS.2009.111

Sobeih, A., Yurcik, W., & Hou, J. C. (2004). VRing: A case for building application-layer multicast rings (rather than trees). In *Proceedings of the IEEE Computer Society's 12th Annual International Symposium on Modeling, Analysis, and Simulation of Computer and Telecommunications Systems, MASCOTS'04*, (pp. 437-446).

Surana, S., Godfrey, B., Lakshminarayanan, K., Karp, R., & Stoica, I. (2006). Load balancing in dynamic structured peer-to-peer systems. *Performance Evaluation, 63*(3), 217–240. doi:10.1016/j.peva.2005.01.003

Tan, E., Guo, L., & Chen, S. (2007). *SCAP: Smart caching in wireless access points to improve P2P streaming*. In ICDCS. Retrieved from http://citeseerx.ist.psu.edu/viewdoc/summary?doi=10.1.1.116.2072

Thampi, S. M. (2010). Survey of search and replication schemes in unstructured P2P networks. *Network Protocols and Algorithms, 2*(1), 93. doi:10.5296/npa.v2i1.263

Wang, J., & Yurcik, W. (2008, February 5). *A survey and comparison of multi-ring techniques for scalable battlespace group communications*. Retrieved from http://citeseerx.ist.psu.edu/viewdoc/summary?doi=10.1.1.60.7337

Wang, W., & Zhang, H. (2009). Study on application layer multicast technology based on P2P streaming media system. In *2009 International Symposium on Computer Network and Multimedia Technology* (pp. 1-4). doi:10.1109/CNMT.2009.5374604

Welzl, M. (2010, May 21). *A survey of lower-than-best effort transport protocols*. Retrieved October 14, 2010, from http://tools.ietf.org/html/draft-welzl-ledbat-survey-00

Wischik, D., Handley, M., & Raiciu, C. (2009). Control of multipath TCP and optimization of multipath routing in the Internet. *Proceedings of the 3ʳᵈ Conference on Network Control and Optimization*, 204–218.

Xu, K., Zhang, M., Liu, J., Qin, Z., & Ye, M. (2010). Proxy caching for peer-to-peer live streaming. *Computer Networks, 54*(7), 1229-1241. doi:10.1016/j.comnet.2009.11.013 Yang, H., Hu, R., Chen, J., & Chen, X. (2008). A review of resilient approaches to peer-to-peer overlay multicast for media streaming. In *4th International Conference on Wireless Communications, Networking and Mobile Computing, WiCOM '08* (pp. 1-4). doi:10.1109/WiCom.2008.802

Yang, M., & Yang, Y. (2008). Peer-to-peer file sharing based on network coding. In *The 28th International Conference on Distributed Computing Systems, ICDCS '08.* (pp. 168-175). doi:10.1109/ICDCS.2008.52

Zhang, J., Gui, Y., Liu, C., & Li, X. (2009). To improve throughput via multi-pathing and parallel TCP on each path. In *Fourth ChinaGrid Annual Conference, ChinaGrid '09* (pp. 16-21). doi:10.1109/ChinaGrid.2009.32

ADDITIONAL READING

Joseph, V., & Mulugu, S. (2011). *Deploying next generation multicast-enabled applications: Label switched multicast for MPLS VPNs, VPLS, and wholesale Ethernet* (p. 688). Morgan Kaufmann. Retrieved May 31, 2011, from http://www.amazon.com/Deploying-Next-Generation-Multicast-enabled-Applications/dp/0123849233

Koo, S. G. M. (2008). *Multimedia content distribution using peer-to-peer overlay networks: The design and analysis of the next generation peer-to-peer networks* (p. 88). VDM Verlag Dr. Müller. Retrieved May 31, 2011, from http://www.amazon.com/Multimedia-Content-Distribution-Overlay-Networks/dp/3639114833

Liotta, A., & Exarchakos, G. (2011). *Networks for pervasive services: Six ways to upgrade the internet (Lecture Notes in Electrical Engineering)* (p. 190). Springer. Retrieved May 31, 2011, from http://www.amazon.com/Networks-Pervasive-Services-Electrical-Engineering/dp/9400714726

Vu, Q. H., Lupu, M., & Ooi, B. C. (2009). *Peer-to-peer computing: Principles and applications* (p. 317). Berlin, Germany: Springer. Retrieved May 31, 2011, from http://www.amazon.com/Peer-Peer-Computing-Principles-Applications/dp/3642035132

KEY TERMS AND DEFINITIONS

Connection Oriented Transport: Connection oriented transport refer to protocols which employ connection management and acknowledgement between the Sender and receiver to enable data to flow in a synchronized fashion.

Connectionless Transport: Connectionless transport refer to protocols which does not employ any implicit acknowledgement or connection management between the sender and receiver, and therefore does not guarantee reliable data transfer or recovery of lost data

Link Aggregation: Link aggregation refers to the segmentation of a common end to end link into multiple links of different capacity in terms of bandwidth to enable the optimal usage of available network resources.

Load Balancing: Load balancing as used in Parallel Access techniques refers to the division of load (total Data to be accessed) evenly among multiple servers based on their capacities, making any individual server immune to server load fluctuations, thereby eliminating client download fluctuations.

Multicast: Multicast refers to the simultaneous communication between a single node and a multiple set of select nodes in a bigger network in order to ensure the efficient use of bandwidth, reliability and security as needed in a group communication.

Multi-Pathing: Multi-pathing refers to techniques used to effectively achieve improved end to end throughput using multiple disjoint paths to transfer data between two nodes. This may include one or multiple nodes assisting the transfer of the data or file.

Overlay Networks: Overlay network refers to a virtual network built on top of a physical network which are logically connected among each other even though they might be geographically separated or in different places

Parallel Access: Parallel access refers to techniques employed to access multiple files, or components of the same file from multiple points (e.g. Mirror sites) in the internet concurrently.

Chapter 9
Mobile Agent–Based Services for Real-Time Multimedia Content Delivery

Giancarlo Fortino
DEIS – University of Calabria, Italy

Wilma Russo
DEIS – University of Calabria, Italy

ABSTRACT

Technologies and applications that enable multi-party, multimedia communications are becoming more and more pervasive in every facet of daily lives: from distance learning to remote job training, from peer-to-peer conferencing to distributed virtual meetings. To effectively use the evolving Internet infrastructure as ubiquitously accessible platform for the delivery of multi-faceted multimedia services, not only are advances in multimedia communications required but also novel software infrastructures are to be designed to cope with network and end-system heterogeneity, improve management and control of multimedia distributed services, and deliver sustainable QoS levels to end users. In this chapter, the authors propose a holistic approach based on agent-oriented middleware integrating active services, mobile event-driven agents, and multimedia internetworking technology for the component-based prototyping, dynamic deployment, and management of Internet-based real-time multimedia services. The proposed approach is enabled by a distributed software infrastructure (named Mobile Agent Multimedia Space – MAMS) based on event-driven mobile agents and multimedia coordination spaces. In particular, a multimedia coordination space is a component-based architecture consisting of components (players, streamers, transcoders, dumper, forwarders, archivers, GUI adapters, multimedia timers) that provide basic real-time multimedia services. The event-driven mobile agents act as orchestrators of the multimedia space and are capable of migrating across the network to dynamically create and deploy complex media services. The effectiveness and potential of the proposed approach are described through a case study involving the on-demand deployment and management of an adaptive cooperative playback service.

DOI: 10.4018/978-1-4666-1794-0.ch009

INTRODUCTION

The global Internet is developed by using heterogeneous communication technologies (e.g., satellite, wireless, xDSL, and gigabit networks) in such a way to make it ubiquitously accessible on a world-wide scale by heterogeneous, even mobile end-systems (e.g. high-performance PC, low-cost lap-tops, 3G mobile phones, and handhelds). Heterogeneity and ubiquitous access allow the application service providers (ASP) to develop and timely deliver a wide gamma of diversified services and end-users to be rapidly notified and updated to connect to and utilize new available services.

In this context, it is challenging to dynamically build, deploy, and offer large-scale multimedia real-time services that are more and more exploited in application domains such as Education (e.g. distance learning), Business (e.g. remote meeting and continuous training) and, notably, Entertainment (e.g. video on-demand and virtual multimedia spaces).

Even though, from one perspective, "network" and "end-system" heterogeneity is the key enabling concept featuring ubiquitous service provision by content providers and service exploitation by users, on the other hand, such heterogeneity is the main barrier to the deployment of real-time multi-point multimedia infrastructures.

Network heterogeneity mainly concerns the bandwidth available between different unicast transmitter/receiver pairs or among multicast groups of interacting peers. In fact, while some hosts are connected by means of high-speed networks, others are attached through traditional LANs, ISDN and ADSL lines, slow speed dialup lines, or cellular networks of highly variable bandwidths. In addition the lack of efficient multipoint communication in the form of a widely available IP multicast infrastructure (McCanne, 1999) diminishes scalability and prevents an effective exploitation of multi-party real-time multimedia services.

End-systems heterogeneity concerns the multimedia computing capabilities, and, in particular, the different processing power and video/audio hardware configurations of the end-systems. In fact, while some end-systems are PCs equipped with powerful MPEG boards, others may be high-performance workstations with no specialized multimedia hardware or even handheld devices with constrained capabilities.

Both kinds of heterogeneity can be accommodated by exploiting the least common denominator solution, i.e., sustainable levels of Quality of Service, e.g., media flow rate (Busse, et al., 1996), video resolution, etc) are tuned to the lowest-performance host belonging to a multimedia session (e.g., conferencing, media broadcasts). However such a solution turns into a real problem as it is tuned to the lowest performance hosts so penalizing all the other hosts involved in a common multimedia session.

Network heterogeneity can be more fairly tackled by employing receiver-oriented end-to-end approaches, such as the Receiver-driven Layered Multicast (RLM) scheme (McCanne, 1999) for video transmission, which, even though easily deployable without enhancing the network system with additional functionality, provide a coarse-grained adaptation (e.g., on a media layer basis) and fulfill only a single dimension of heterogeneity (bandwidth) so not considering others (e.g., media format conversion).

Differently from end-to-end approaches, the approach centered on media gateways (Amir, et al., 1995) provides a more effective solution for masking of and finer-grained adaptation to network and end-systems heterogeneity.

Media gateways are multimedia agents placed at strategic points within the network system and basically perform format conversion (or transcoding), unicast/multicast tunneling, and rate limitation of real-time media streams. As the basic Internet service model has no native support for the dynamic deployment of agents such as media gateways, it is therefore crucial to build an effective application-level distributed infrastructure atop Internet which can support media gateways as well as other network services (e.g. application-level multicast) featuring real-time media. It is worth noting that IP multicast is not yet available at a world-wide scale so an effective support for application-level multicast would enable a wide range of multi-party multimedia services.

Although approaches that aim at reverse engineering the network system (such as Active Networks (Tennenhouse, et al., 1997)) have the potential to assure more dynamism and efficiency, nowadays, the application-level approach is the only viable one. Multimedia content distribution networks (CDNs) (Cranor, et al., 2001; Fortino, et al., 2007; Fortino & Palau, 2007; Verma, 2002) provide media services on the basis of overlay media networks developed by means of distributed platforms that are mainly centered on media streaming technology enabled by either Web technology (applet, servlet, web services) or Active Service technology (Amir, et al., 1998). The Web-based approach is the most attractive and spendable from a business perspective due to the easy world-wide accessibility of the Web, whereas active services are appealing as they exploit the active networking approach at application layer.

Apart from coping with network system issues, media service providers, have to face differentiated users' needs whose fulfilling requires the timely introduction of new kinds of services in order to be competitive in the current and future multimedia service market (Verma, 2002). In particular, the introduction of new media services, particularly those having real-time characteristics, require rapid prototyping and on-demand dynamic deployment and efficient management.

Beyond an even advanced web-based approach which is still too static and anchored to variants of the client/server model, a fully exploitation of the logical mobility paradigms (particularly the mobile agent paradigm) (Fuggetta, et al., 1998) have demonstrated to possess the potential to improve customizability and monitoring of dis-

tributed applications, which can be so visualized as aggregates of stationary and mobile building blocks. In addition, the capability of the active software components to select at run-time among a variety of coordination models (e.g., message passing, Tuples, Events) and interaction spaces (e.g., real-time data streaming, group coordination, etc.) according to the current conditions of the application service and network system can improve performance and optimize distributed resource usage.

In this paper we present an agent-oriented approach integrating a mobility-oriented active middleware with multimedia internetworking protocols and mechanisms (Crowcroft, et al., 1999) and supporting rapid prototyping, on-demand deployment and management of Internet-based multimedia services and applications.

The middleware software architecture and basic services are based on the ELDA (Event-driven Lightweight Distilled StateCharts Agents) framework (Fortino, et al., 2004; Fortino, et al., 2010a), an agent-oriented framework for highly dynamic distributed computing, currently based on the JADE platform (Fortino, et al., 2010b). The ELDA framework is centered on the mobile agent paradigm and on multiple coordination spaces that favor a multi-paradigm design approach to the construction of distributed applications. In particular, the ELDA agents are autonomous, event-driven lightweight agents that can travel across a network of Active Servers to accomplish assigned tasks. The agent interaction model is based on high-level events and seamlessly allows for multi-coordination through a set of dynamically installable coordination spaces that agents can locally and globally exploit in order to synchronize and communicate with each another.

To handle live and archived multimedia information, MultiMedia Mobile Agents (M^3As) have been defined. They incorporate and manage specific multimedia functionalities such as media retrieval, real-time media stream transcoding, recording, playing, control, tunneling, rate limiting. To establish multimedia sessions, instrument real-time interactions, and transmitting and filtering media streams, M³As exploit a multimedia coordination space (M²S), which is a programmable substrate based on the Internet multimedia protocol stack (Crowcroft, et al., 1999) and implemented atop the Java Media Framework (JMF, 2002).

The proposed approach to the dynamic deployment and management of media services is exemplified through a case study that concerns the on-demand installation and monitoring of a cooperative media streaming on-demand service (Fortino, et al., 2007).

The rest of this paper is organized as follows. The *"Background"* section introduces motivations and main architectural issues for dynamic multimedia service support and discusses related work. The *"The ELDA Agent Model"* section overviews the basic concepts of the ELDA model and the architecture of the JADE-based ELDA framework. In section *"The Mobile Agent Multimedia Space,"* the set of defined multimedia M³As and the component-based architecture of the multimedia space are described. The developed case study is detailed in section *"A Cooperative Media On-Demand Active Service."* Finally future research directions and conclusions are presented.

BACKGROUND

Development, deployment and management of distributed multimedia systems and applications whose key characteristics are interactivity, multimediality, dynamism, network distribution, high-performance, media synchronization, intensive data transmissions, are tasks intrinsically more complex in heterogeneous environments.

In the last years, intensive research efforts and notable results have been carried out in developing protocols, techniques and architectures for internetworking multimedia (Crowcroft, et al., 1999), and in defining software engineering

methodologies and programming frameworks able to fully support the multimedia software development lifecycle (Mühlhäuser & Gecsei, 1996), (Rowe, 2001).

The design phase of distributed multimedia systems (DMSs) is well supported by multimedia extensions of the Unified Modeling Language (UML) (UML, 2001), (Sauer & Engels, 1999) and by a host of formal models and languages ("Synchronization," 1996). Also the implementation phase is effectively assisted by multimedia-specific programming languages and frameworks (e.g., MASH Toolkit (MASH, 2000) and Java Media Framework (JMF, 2002)) that integrate multimedia internetworking and provide an easy-to-use API to build DMSs.

While design and implementation phases of DMSs are well sustained, techniques for their deployment, management and maintenance phases are still unsatisfactory.

As a matter of fact, media services installation and maintenance have to deal not only with application structure and functionality, but also with adaptive human-computer interaction (HCI) and static/dynamic aspects of the system such as distribution, stream control, resource management, multimedia repositories and/or databases, network facilities, and mobility.

Thus, to effectively deploy and manage distributed media services on the global Internet, the following technologies and paradigms featuring flexible architectures and customizable services can be exploited:

- *Active Networks.* The active network (AN) (Tennenhouse, et al., 1997) approach aims at replacing the Internet service model with a more flexible model in which the whole network is seen as a fully programmable computational environment. Within an active network, not only application-defined entities run on arbitrary nodes (or active nodes) in the network, but also individuals packets (or capsules) can be programmed to perform customized tasks as they propagate through the network.Video on Demand (VoD) and video streaming multicast services based on ANs have been ad-hoc prototyped as a "proof-of-concept" of the AN benefits in the multimedia domain. Noteworthy efforts are a VideoCast system featured by a user-oriented layered streaming (Ramanujan & Thurber, 1998) and a mobility-featured videoconference system (Baldi, et al., 1998). Although AN-based media services embody profitable characteristics of reconfigurability and customizability at run-time, they are not deployable on the current Internet infrastructure with no modifications of the infrastructure itself.

- *Active Services.* A viable and currently exploitable active networking approach is that of programmable service-oriented architectures based on Active Services (Amir, et al., 1998; Govindan, et al., 1998), built atop and consistently with the existing Internet service model, that allow plumbing and running code at strategic location within a network of active servers. The AS1 active service framework (Amir, et al., 1998), developed at the University of Berkeley, represents the most comprehensive framework for deployment of real-time media services over the Internet MBone. The AS1 architecture is decomposed into six core and interdependent components: service environment, service location, service management, service control, service attachment, and service composition. In particular, the service environment, which defines the multimedia programming model and interface, is based on the MASH toolkit (MASH, 2000). The main drawbacks of the AS1 framework are: (i) no web integration so limiting its usability from the user's perspective; (ii) lack of flexibility to install at run-time new services. Another example of active service framework is the HiFi

monitoring system (Al-Shaer, 2000) that is applied to the management of distributed multimedia systems. In order to monitor multimedia applications, HiFi uses agents, i.e., application-level monitoring programs, which filter and react to events coming from applications by performing controlling actions. Agents are hierarchically structured and categorized in local monitoring agents (LMA), which directly capture events from applications, and domain monitoring agents (DMA). However the system does not provide dynamic agent deployment and relocation.

- *Streaming Content Distribution Networks (SCDN).* SCDNs are special-purpose content distribution networks designed to improve the streaming-based delivery of multimedia content to end-users. Several research efforts have been to date devoted to develop SCDNs. The PoRtal Infrastructure for Streaming Media (or Prism) (Cranor, et al., 2001) is a research-oriented SCDN for distributing, storing, and delivering high-quality streaming media over IP networks. The Prism-based stored-TV (STV) service lets users select content based on the program name as well as the program time it was aired. Content stored inside the network is accessible throughout the whole Prism infrastructure. MarconiNet (Dutta & Schulzrinne, 2004) is a research-oriented architecture for IP-based radio and TV networks, built on standard Internet protocols including the Real-time Transport Protocol, RTSP, Service Announcement Protocol, and Session Description Protocol. It allows for the building of virtual radio networks—similar to traditional AM/FM radio—and TV networks. The research-oriented Video CDN (VCDN) architecture (Cahill & Sreenan, 2006) is a hybrid CDN/peer-to-peer network that exploits the dynamic nature of a P2P architecture while providing a CDN service atop this overlay network. This design choice is tailored to overcome the limitation of CDN extendibility and to minimize the amount of overall resources required to serve a given client request pattern. In VCDN, ISP servers can advertise their willingness to partake in the system by acting as peers. The commercial SinoCDN (Ni & Tsang, 2005) system is a dedicated streaming CDN that uses the Intelligent Streaming Gateway, the CDN Manager, and the Media Domain Name System components, which constitute a comprehensive solution to provide content routing, delivery, and distribution of multimedia content. The Intelligent Streaming Gateway is based on cooperative caching and application-level multicast mechanisms. Akamai (see http://www.akamai.com) is a worldwide commercial CDN provider that, after its fusion with Speedera, is currently the main CDN provider for video streaming delivered through a coordinated network of media proxies. The COMODIN system (Fortino, et al., 2007) is based on a content distribution network (CDN) (Fortino & Palau, 2007) and provides collaborative media playback services. Specifically, it enables Internet-based interactive media service for e-learning and e-entertainment, allowing an explicitly formed group of clients to view and cooperatively control a shared remote media playback.

- *Mobile Agents.* A mobile agent is a program able to autonomously migrate within a network of agent servers to fulfill a task assigned by a user or by an agent manager (Gray, et al., 2001). Software engineering research area has so far developed formalisms and methodologies for mobility-oriented and mobile agent-based systems and applications (Picco, et al., 2000). The integration of mobile agents with distrib-

uted multimedia systems can improve reconfigurability, dynamic media service deployment and management (Huber, 1997; Kwan & Karmouch, 1996). In this context, significant trials are: the AgentSys prototype (Falchuk & Karmouch, 1997a; Falchuk & Karmouch, 1997b) and a VoD system featured by MobileSpaces (Satoh, 2000). The former only provides an agent-based environment for access, interaction and retrieval of media information in which multimedia data can be carried by mobile agents. The latter is mainly an application of a Java-based framework designed upon a hierarchical model of mobile agents that provides media functionalities through the Java Media Framework (JMF, 2002).

Distinctly from the other proposals, the approach proposed in this paper integrates multimedia spaces and mobility within an active service framework which is able to adaptively support and manage user-centered and on-demand customizable media retrieval and streaming services. It is worth noting that the integration of mobility and multiple coordination spaces can offer more flexibility and even efficiency (Picco, et al., 2000; Fortino, et al., 2010a).

The ELDA Agent Model

The ELDA model is based on the concept of event-driven lightweight agent which is a single-threaded autonomous entity interacting through asynchronous events, executing upon reaction, and capable of migration. The behavior of ELDA agents is specified through the Distilled StateCharts (DSCs) (Fortino, et al., 2004; Fortino et al., 2002), a formalism derived from Statecharts (Harel, 1987; currently incorporated in UML 2.0) that have gained notable success in the software engineering community mainly due to its appealing graphical features and the means it offers for the modeling of complex software systems.

Figure 1. The FIPA-like ELDA agent behavior

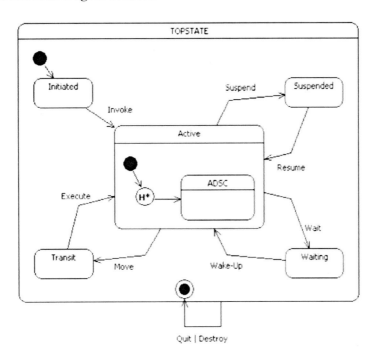

The ELDA agent behavior is defined according to an extended version of the FIPA agent lifecycle template (see Figure 1) (FIPA, 2002a) in which the ACTIVE state is always entered through a deep history pseudostate (H*) to restore the agent execution state after agent migration and, in general, after agent suspension. In particular, the ACTIVE state contains the active DSC (ADSC) composite state to which the default entrance of the H* points. The active agent behavior can be obtained by refining the ADSC.

The ELDA agent interactions are based on events that formalize both self-triggering events (internal events) and requests to (or notifications from) the local agent server (management, coordination and exception events). Events are further classified into OUT-events that are generated by the agent and always target the local agent server (where the agent is executing) and IN-events that are generated by the local agent server and delivered to target agents.

ELDA agents are programmed through the ELDAFramework that provides all the programming abstractions for the development of distributed software systems in terms of multi-agent systems based on the ELDA meta-model (Fortino, et al., 2010a). The reference architecture of the ELDAFramework is reported in Figure 2. The Active Server (AS) is the sandbox which provides a protected agent execution environment along with migration, coordination and host resource access services.

Each ELDA agent is provided with: (i) a composite object (STATE) which represents the DSC-based agent behavior; (ii) an event queue (EQ), which contains all the events delivered at the ELDA agent; (iii) an Event Processor which cyclically extracts an event from the EQ and passes it to STATE; (iv) the *generate(Event)* primitive to generate events.

Events are delivered to the top-level handler (TLH) of the AS which routes them toward the

Figure 2. The ELDA framework architecture

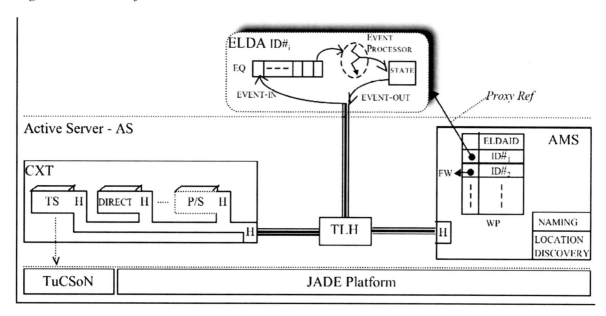

final handler. Event routing is performed according to the event type:

- Internal events have the ELDA agent itself as final handler;
- Management events are dispatched to the Agent Management System (AMS) component, which provides ELDAs with a white pages (WP) service and incorporates agent naming and location discovery services, e.g., based on forwarders (FW);
- Coordination events are dispatched to the handler of the Coordination Context (CXT) component that can support multiple coordination models (Cabri, et al., 2000; Fortino & Russo, 2005).

The CXT embeds specific event handlers, named coordination spaces that an agent can exploit to interact with other agents. Each coordination space is an on-demand installable component that implements a specific coordination model, e.g. Direct communication model, tuple space (TS) and publish/subscribe (P/S).

Currently the ELDAFramework is implemented in JADE (Fortino, et al., 2010b) (Bellifemine, et al., 2001) and supports agent lifecycle management and agent interaction based on the following coordination spaces: asynchronous messages, topic-based publish/subscribe and local tuple spaces. JADE directly provides the first two coordination spaces whereas the latter relies on TuCSoN (Omicini & Zambonelli, 1999).

THE MOBILE AGENT MULTIMEDIA SPACE

MAMS (Mobile Agent Multimedia Space) is a distributed software infrastructure based on ELDA agents and a multimedia coordination space. To support access to live and archived multimedia information and enable multimedia real-time interaction, the coordination context of the ELDA framework has been enhanced with a composable multimedia coordination space (M^2S). M^2S makes it available an extendible, component-based media service substratum that can be programmed by a set of multimedia mobile agents (M^3As) to

Table 1. Multimedia software components and related functionality

Multimedia Software Component	Functionality
Player (PLR)	Playing media streams and archived media content
Streamer (STR)	Streaming and controlling live media or archived media files to unicast and multicast addresses;
Transcoder (TRA)	Transcoding media streams to reduce and adapt their media information to limit the used bandwidth and accommodate different multimedia terminals;
Dumper (DMP)	Dumping and (possibly) storing RTP-based media streams in RTP-based media repositories or active media caches;
Archiver (ARC)	Managing access to media repositories;
Forwarder (FWR)	Tunneling media streams to forward media streams from multicast groups to unicast ones and vice versa.
GUI_Adapter (GUI)	Adapting media and control interactions with interfacing MAs and Graphical User Interface components.
Timer (TIM)	Timing events that target specific M^3As.

build complex distributed media services. This section describes the architecture of M^2S, the general characteristics of the basic media service components, and notably the specification of the interaction between M^3As and the M^2S media components at object and script level. More specific exemplification patterns are furnished for media streaming and streaming control functionalities that are proper of the streamer component and the streaming controller M^3As.

The Multimedia Coordination Space

The MultiMedia coordination Space (M^2S) is exploited by multimedia mobile agents (M^3As) to dynamically construct distributed multimedia services. The interaction between M^2S and M^3As is local and is realized through events.

In particular, events sent from M^3As to M^2S formalize requests for activating or managing specific MultiMedia Processes (M^2Ps), whereas events sent from M^2S to M^3As formalize request confirmations or specific events coming from M^2Ps.

Upon an activation request from an M^3A, M^2S spawns an M^2P that is then associated to the requesting M^3A. Such an association is also called owning relationship. An M^3A can own more than one M^2P.

M^2Ps are instances of single- or multi-threaded software components that perform multimedia internetworking, presentation and archiving tasks. Each multimedia software component belongs to a basic multimedia software component library (see Table 1) further specializable to accommodate new functionalities. Both M^2Ps and the interaction between M^2Ps and M^3As are described by high-level scripts that are interpreted at run-time for the activation of specific media processes and for the creation of the bindings that connect activated processes to their owning M^3As. The use of scripts greatly improves flexibility and allows for a completely dynamic enhancement and replacement of components.

In the following subsections, the component-based architecture of M^2S is first described, the event-based interface between M^2Ps and M^3As is then defined, and finally, the definition of the Streamer multimedia software component is discussed.

Component-Based Architecture

The M^2S structurally consists of the following components (Figure 3):

• The Manager component manages M^2Ps by performing the following tasks: (i) in-

Figure 3. The architectural schema of the M^2S: static and dynamic relationships between M^3As and M^2Ps

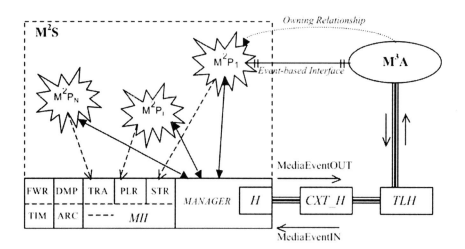

terpretation and filtering of incoming events (requests) and outcoming events (notifications); (ii) admission control and activation/deactivation of M^2Ps; (iii) monitoring of activated multimedia M^2Ps.

- The event handler, which is hooked to the handler of the coordination space (named CXT_H) and allows routing-in a media event (MediaEventIN) emitted by an M^3A and routing-out a media event (MediaEventOUT) generated by either the Manager or an M^2P and piped out by the Manager.
- The multimedia internetworking interface (MII) interfaces the multimedia software components described in Table 1 with the Manager.

A class diagram of the M^2S architecture is reported in Figure 4. The Manager class is associated to zero, one or more objects of type MediaProcess. The association is carried out by the Manager that contains an entry register with pairs <MediaProcessId, MediaProcess>. The basic interface of the Manager consists of:

- the *filterIN* method, which is invoked by the event Handler to deliver incoming media events (MediaEventIN) to the Manager;
- the *filterOUT* method, which allows to filter outcoming media events (MediaEventOUT) sent from M^2Ps;
- the *generate* method, which pipes events (MediaEventOUT) out to the event handler by invoking the *routeOUT* method of Handler.

MediaProcess is the abstract class from which further specializable multimedia components (concrete classes) can derive and is associated to the interfaces FilterIN and FilterOUT, which respectively define the *filterIN* and *filterOUT* methods that must be refined to specialize the handling of MediaEventIN and MediaEventOUT events of specific multimedia components.

The MediaProcessFactory class, which operates according to the Factory Method design pattern (Grand, 2002), makes it available the *createMediaProcess* method whose signature has three formal parameters: a reference to the Manager, the owning M^3A's identifier, and the M^2P descriptor (MediaProcessDescriptor) to be activated. This method interprets the descriptor and, if the admis-

Figure 4. UML class diagram of the component-based architecture of the M2S

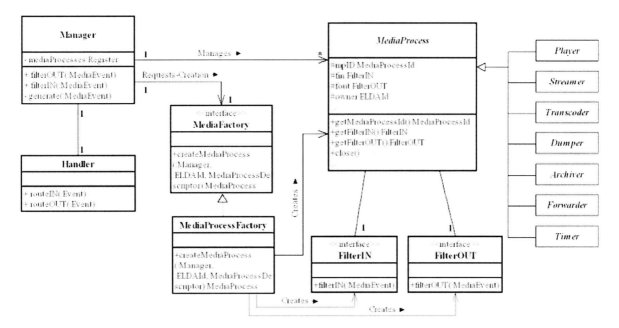

sion control checks are passed, creates and returns the corresponding media process (MediaProcess) with an identifier (MediaProcessId) assigned by the MediaProcessFactory. In addition, it creates the concrete media process-specific FilterIN and FilterOUT objects.

In Figure 5 it is reported the code of the *filterIN* method that elaborates the media process activation/deactivation requests, generates the related notifications, and delegates specific media process requests to the FilterIN object of the target MediaProcess.

Event-Based Interface Between M²P and M³A

The event-based interaction between M²Ps and M³As within the same agent server (AS) is described by a dialect of the Web Service Description Language (WSDL, 2007) named Media Service Description Language (MSDL).

A complete description of the MSDL service is composed of an abstract interface (or application-level service description) that is defined in terms of events exchanged in a service interaction and the concrete binding information and provides the bindings between the media events and the corresponding methods of the involved media process. The main components of the abstract interface are: the vocabulary, the events, and the interaction.

Like WSDL, MSDL employs external type systems to provide data type definitions for the information carried by events. Currently MSDL uses both types defined in XSD (XML Schema Definition) (XML, 2007) and types defined in external schemas.

MSDL defines event elements as compositions of parts, each of which is described by an XSD type or elements from a predefined vocabulary, and the serviceType and the service elements that combine events to define interactions. A serviceType is a set of services that are collectively supported by a media process. Each service represents an event exchange pattern that a media process supports that is basically described using media events labeled as input, output.

Figure 5. The basic filterIN method of the manager

```
public synchronized void filterIN(MediaEvent meventin){
  ELDAId eventSource = meventin.getSource(); // return the ELDAId of the M³A which generated meventin
  /* openMediaProcess */
  if (meventin instanceof OpenMediaProcess){// if it's a MediaProcess activation request
    try{
        /* try to create the MediaProcess described by the MediaProcessDescriptor object
           contained in the OpenMediaProcess event */
        MediaProcess mp = mediaProcessFactory.createMediaProcess(this, eventSource,
                            (OpenMediaProcess)meventin.getMediaProcessDescriptor());
        // register the created MediaProcess in the Register
        mediaProcesses.register(mp.getMediaProcessId(), eventSource, mp);
        // send the OpenedMediaProcess notification, containing the MediaProcessId, to the requesting M³A
        generate(new OpenedMediaProcess(eventSource, mp.getMediaProcessId());
    }catch(RefusedAdmissionException ex){generate(new RefusedAdmission(eventSource,
                                          mp.getMediaProcessId()));}
  }
  /*closeMediaProcess*/
  else if (inputMEevent instanceof CloseMediaProcess){// if it's a MediaProcess deactivation request
    // deregister the MediaProcess
    MediaProcess mp=mediaProcesses.deRegister((CloseMediaProcess)meventin.getMediaProcessId());
    mp.close(); // deactivate the MediaProcess
    // send the ClosedMediaProcess notification to the requesting M³A
    generate(new ClosedMediaProcess(eventSource));
  }
  else{// if it's a request targeting a MediaProcess
    // given the MediaProcessID, return the MediaProcess
    MediaProcess mp = mediaProcesses.getMediaProcess(inputMEevent.getMediaProcessId());
    // meventin is delagated to the FilterIN of the MediaProcess since the filtering logic is known only by the MediaProcess
    MediaEvent meventout= mp.getFilterIN().filterIN(inputMEevent);
    if (meventout!=null) generate(meventout);
  }
}
```

Figure 6 shows the MSDL script of the event-based interface to activate/deactivate a media process. In particular, MPDescriptor embodies both the type of media process to be activated and the SDP-like (Session Description Protocol) description (Handley & Jacobson, 1998) of the multimedia session to be created or joined.

In the basic script, MediaProcessManagement describes ActivateMediaProcess and Deactivate-MediaProcess services which are specified respectively by the input/output event pairs: (Open-MediaProcess, OpenedMediaProcess) and (CloseMediaProcess, ClosedMediaProcess).

MSDL binding elements associate an incoming media event (input event) to the method to be invoked which takes as formal parameters the event parts. Upon method invocation completion, the output event is generated. If the service input event is missing, the service output event is bounded to a specific method that is self-invoked by the media process.

At media process creation, a given script, interfacing the media process to be created and the requesting M³A, is parsed by the MediaProcess-Factory that constructs the FilterIN and FilterOUT objects and bind them to the created media process.

Since activation (OpenMediaProcess) and deactivation (CloseMediaProcess) of media processes are general services performed by the Manager, the script is translated at compile-time in the *filterIN* method of Manager (Figure 5).

The Streamer (STR) Component

The Streamer (STR) is the basic media streaming component which is specializable according to the task to be fulfilled (e.g., capturing and streaming live A/V flows, open and streaming archived media

Figure 6. The MSDL script for activation/deactivation of media processes

```
<event name="OpenMediaProcess">
  <part name="mediaProcessDescr" type="mpxsd:MPDescriptor"/>
  <part name="eventSource" type="eldaidxsd:ELDAId"/>
</event>
<event name="CloseMediaProcess">
  <part name="mediaProcessId" type="mpidxsd:MPId"/>
  <part name="eventSource" type="eldaidxsd:ELDAId"/>
</event>
<event name="OpenedMediaProcess">
  <part name="mediaProcessId" type="mpidxsd:MPId"/>
  <part name="eventTarget" type="eldaidxsd:ELDAId"/>
</event>
<event name="ClosedMediaProcess">
  <part name="eventTarget" type="eldaidxsd:ELDAId"/>
</event>

<serviceType name="MediaProcessManagement">         <component name = "MediaProcessX">
  <service name="ActivateMediaProcess">               <service name="ActivateMediaProcess">
    <input event="OpenMediaProcess"/>                            binding="openMediaProcess"
    <output event="OpenedMediaProcess"/>              </service>
  </service>                                          <service name="DeactivateMediaProcess">
  <service name="DeactivateMediaProcess">                        binding="closeMediaProcess"
    <input event="CloseMediaProcess"/>                </service>
    <output event="ClosedMediaProcess"/>            </component>
  </service>
</serviceType>
```

     ABSTRACT INTERFACE   *BINDING INFORMATION*

files). Figure 7 portrays the UML diagram of the hierarchy of the STR components.

The Streamer class, which derives from MediaProcess (Figure 4), provides the following self-explanatory basic interface: start, pause and stop. Streamer can be associated to more Media-Source and MediaAddress objects. The former represents a specific media source (e.g., video capture board, media file) whereas the latter represents the address/port pair (e.g., 224.2.100.100/10000) to which the streamed media source is to be transmitted. According to MediaAddress the streaming can be unicast or multicast. Streamer is specialized in MediaFileStreamer for media file streaming and LiveStreamer for live multimedia content streaming. The *seek* method of MediaFileStreamer allows seeking inside the media file. The boolean parameter of MediaFileStreamer, if true, enables the streamer component to send the ClipEndApproaching event through its FilterOUT object, signaling that the end of the media clip is being

approached, to its related sc-M^{3}A. RTPFileStreamer further specializes MediaFileStreamer for the streaming of RTP-based media files (Schulzrinne, 2003).

An MPDescriptor script of an RTPFileStreamer media process is reported in Figure 8. It contains the name of the media process component (MP-Component name) and the description of the media session (MediaSession) being created that includes details about media sources (MediaSource). The labels s (session name), i (media title), m (media name and transport address), c (connection information), b (bandwidth information) are SDP types which include their related values. Finally, the session attributes, control and sync, respectively enforce an aggregate control of the media streams and a tight synchronization between audio and video streams.

In Figure 9, the MSDL script specifying the interaction between the RTPFileStreamer process and the Streaming Controller M^{3}A (see next sec-

Figure 7. The hierarchy of streamer components

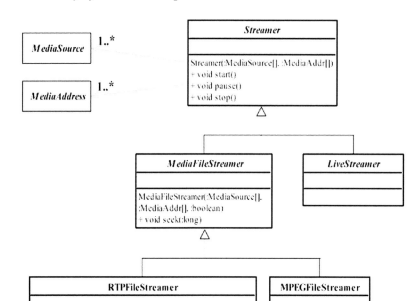

Figure 8. An XML-SDP descriptor script of the RTPFileStreamer media process

```
<MPDescriptor>
<MPComponent name="RTPFileStreamer"/>
<MediaSession s="Meeting1">
 <MediaSource i="AMeeting1"
              m="audio 10000 RTP/AVP 0"
              c="IN IP4 224.2.100.100/16"
              b="64 Kbps" />
 <MediaSource i="VMeeting1"
              m="video 20000 RTP/AVP 31"
              c="IN IP4 224.2.100.100/16"
              b="500 Kbps" />
 <Attribute control="aggregate" />
 <Attribute sync="tight" />
 ...
</MediaSession>
</MPDescriptor>
```

tion), which uses the RTPFileStreamer process, is reported.

In order to concretely exemplify the translation from the MSDL script to the *filterIN* method of the FilterIN interface (see Figure 4), which can be refined by the RTPFileStreamer itself, the code of the obtained *filterIN* method is portrayed in Figure 10.

Multimedia Mobile Agents

Multimedia mobile agents (M^3As) are ELDA agents that exploit the M^2S, equipped with local available or on-demand installable multimedia software components, for accomplishing multimedia tasks. The currently defined M^3As are:

Figure 9. The MSDL script of the interaction RTPFileStreamer/sc-M³A: (a) Abstract interface; (b) Binding information

```
<event name="StartStreaming">
 <part name="mediaProcessId" type="mpidxsd:MPId"/>
 <part name="eventSource" type="eldaidxsd:ELDAId"/>
</event>
<event name="PauseStreaming">
 <part name="mediaProcessId" type="mpidxsd:MPId"/>
 <part name="eventSource" type="eldaidxsd:ELDAId"/>
</event>
<event name="SeekStreaming">
 <part name="mediaProcessId" type="mpidxsd:MPId"/>
 <part name="eventSource" type="eldaidxsd:ELDAId"/>
 <part name="seekTimeUTC" type="xsd:long"/>
</event>
<event name="StopStreaming">
 <part name="mediaProcessId" type="mpidxsd:MPId"/>
 <part name="eventSource" type="eldaidxsd:ELDAId"/>
</event>
<event name="Played">
 <part name="currentTimeUTC" type="xsd:long"/>
 <part name="eventTarget" type="eldaidxsd:ELDAId"/>
</event>
<event name="Paused">
 <part name="currentTimeUTC" type="xsd:long"/>
 <part name="eventTarget" type="eldaidxsd:ELDAId"/>
</event>
<event name="Sought">
 <part name="currentTimeUTC" type="xsd:long"/>
 <part name="eventTarget" type="eldaidxsd:ELDAId"/>
</event>
event name="Stopped">
 <part name="currentTimeUTC" type="xsd:long"/>
 <part name="eventTarget" type="eldaidxsd:ELDAId"/>
</event>
event name="ClipEndApproaching">
 <part name="currentTimeUTC" type="xsd:long"/>
 <part name="eventTarget" type="eldaidxsd:ELDAId"/>
</event>
```

```
<serviceType name="RTPFileStreamerControl">
 <service name="StartStreamer">
  <input event="StartStreaming"/>
  <output event="Played"/>
 </service>
 <service name="PauseStreamer">
  <input event="PauseStreaming"/>
  <output event="Paused"/>
 </service>
 <service name="SeekStreamer">
  <input event="SeekStreaming"/>
  <output event="Sought"/>
 </service>
 <service name="StopStreamer">
  <input event="StopStreaming"/>
  <output event="Stopped"/>
 </service>
 <service name="ClipApproaching">
  <output event="ClipEndApproaching"/>
 </service>
</serviceType>
```
(a)

```
<component name = "RTPFileStreamer">
 <service name="StartStreamer">
        binding "start" </service>
 <service name="PauseStreamer">
        binding="pause" </service>
 <service name="SeekStreamer">
        binding="seek" </service>
 <service name="StopStreamer">
        binding="stop" </service>
 <service name="ClipApproaching">
        binding="clipEndApproaching"
 </service>
</component>
```
(b)

Figure 10. The filterIN method of the FilterIN interface

```
public MediaEvent filterIN(MediaEvent mevent){
 if (mevent instanceof StartStreaming){
  try{
   long time = mp.start();
   return new Played(mevent.getSource(), time);
  }catch(StreamerNotStartedException ex){return new Error(mevent.getSource(), ex);}
 }
 else if (mevent instanceof PauseStreaming){
  try{
   long time = mp.pause();
   return new Paused(mevent.getSource(), time);
  }catch(StreamerNotPausedException ex){return new Error(mevent.getSource(), ex);}
 }
 else if (mevent instanceof SeekStreaming){
  try{
   long time = mp.sought((SeekStreaming)mevent.getSeekTime());
   return new Sought(mevent.getSource(), time);
  }catch(StreamerNotSoughtException ex){return new Error(mevent.getSource(), ex);}
 }
 else if (mevent instanceof StopStreaming){
  try{
   long time = mp.stop();
   return new Stopped(mevent.getSource(), time);
  }catch(StreamerNotStoppedException ex){return new Error(mevent.getSource(), ex);}
 }
}
```

213

- *Media Streaming Controller (sc-M³A)*, which allows starting and controlling a media streaming process, based on an STR component, which can originate from either live cameras, archived media files, or both sources located on the hosting AS.

- *Media Searcher (ms-M³A)*, which is fed with a list of media resources (e.g., media files) to search for and moves from one AS to another to discover such resources. Upon a successful discovery, it can come back to the AS originating searcher or query their manager about further searching tasks.

- *Session Initiator (si-M³A)*, which uses a static or dynamic contact list in order to migrate across ASs of active users and invite such users to join or initiate a multimedia session. The functionality of the session initiator resembles that of SIP-based (Session Initiation Protocol) stationary agents (Schulzrinne, et al., 1999). On the client side, si-M³As interact with GUI components representing the software alter ego of users. si-M³As are driven by si-Inviters, which regulate their tasks according to a master/slave paradigm.

- *Media Gateway (gw-M³A)*, which operates on Transcoder (TRA) components in order to purposely activate filtering of media streams at crucial points within a network of AS. The installation of gw-M³A can be driven either by clients by means of a facilitator MA (called gw-Client) or by a distributed multimedia session aware manager MA called gw-Manager. gw-Client controls the media gateway agent using a client/server based interaction protocol. gw-Manager manages a set of media gateways using a master/slave based protocol.

- *Forwarder (fw-M³A)*, which allows the installation of Forwarder (FWR) components at strategic points within a network of ASs to enable tunneling of media streams and/or control messages from unicast to multi-

cast and from multicast to unicast addresses. fw-Manager and fw-Client are made available to control forwarders and their behavior is similar to that of gw-Manager and gw-Client.

- *Recorder (rc-M³A)*, which provides distributed recording of media streams at RTP (Schulzrinne, et al., 1996) or UDP level (Schulzrinne, 2003). rc-M³As use the Dumper (DMP) component to dump media streams from unicast and notably multicast addresses. Such media streams can derive from videoconferencing, distributed virtual meetings or media on-demand sessions. rc-M³A can be controlled either by rc-Client or rc-Manager MAs using RTSP-like commands (RECORD, PAUSE, STOP). In the context of multicast multimedia sessions, specialized rc-M³As can be organized in a distributed task force that, in a distributed way, records the same multimedia session for the purpose of enhancing "a posteriori" the registration since media packets can be lost. In fact, after the registration is terminated, the rc-M³As can on-demand or autonomously engage a peer-to-peer based restoration phase of the multimedia session by collecting as many media packets as possible.

- *Player (pl-M³A)*, which dynamically installs Player (PLA) components in the users' GUI. pl-M³A can be controlled by pl-Managers that can adapt the Player parameters (e.g., video size, sound quality, graphical component lay-out) according to user specific profiles.

- *QoS Controller (qc-M³A)*, which migrates to remote ASs in order to monitor the quality of service of selected multimedia processes. qc-M³As can interact with the defined multimedia components as they can be enabled to emit events referring to QoS parameters. For instance, the RTP-based Audio/Video Player component basically

Table 2. Associations between the basic set of M³As, the basic related components, their companions MAs and interaction paradigms

Multimedia MA	Multimedia Component	Companion MAs	
		Type	Interaction Paradigm
Streaming Controller sc-M³A	STR	sc-Client,	C/S
		sc-M³A	P2P
Media Searcher ms-M³A	ARC	ms-Manager	M/S
Session Initiator si-M³A	GUI	si-Inviter	M/S
Media Gateway gw-M³A	TRA	gw-Manager	M/S
		gw-Client	C/S
Forwarder fw-M³A	FWR	fw-Manager	M/S
		fw-Client	C/S
Recorder rc-M³A	DMP	rc-Client	C/S
		rc-Manager	M/S
		rc-M³A	P2P
Player pl-M³A	PLA	pl-Manager	C/S, M/S
QoS Controller qc-M³A	*all*	qc-Manager	M/S

raises the following QoS events: Jitter (which indicates the jitter intra-stream), Skew (which contains the a/v skew inter-stream), Losses (which provides the fraction of packet losses), Rate (which includes the media streaming bandwidth). Usually, the qc-Manager handles a set of qc-M³As by dislocating them in such a way to monitor the global QoS of an on-going media service.

The defined basic M³As can be extended by customizing and/or specializing the basic M³As' lifecycle that is formalized by a well-defined Distilled StateChart. M³As locally dialog with specific multimedia components and remotely interact with companion MAs according to master/slave (M/S), client/server (C/S) or peer-to-peer (P2P) paradigms. Table 2 lists the basic set of M³As, links them to their respective media process components and companion MAs, and reports the

interaction paradigms between M³As and their companion MAs.

In the following subsections, the sc-M³A and the ms- M³A will be described in details.

Media Streaming Controller (sc-M³A)

The basic sc-M³A is equipped with logics for activating, starting, pausing and stopping a media streaming process (Streamer). Specialized sc-M³As can be introduced to manage more specific media streaming processes (e.g., RTP-FileStreamer).

In particular, the basic media file streaming controller (mfsc-M³A) also embodies the seek operation which allows to move the playback time back and forth across a multimedia session. The DSC-based behavior of the mfsc-M³A is depicted in Figure 11 and is obtained by adding the bolded (visual and textual) elements to the DSC-based behavior of the basic sc-M³As.

Figure 11. The active behavior of the basic media file streaming controller mfsc-M³A

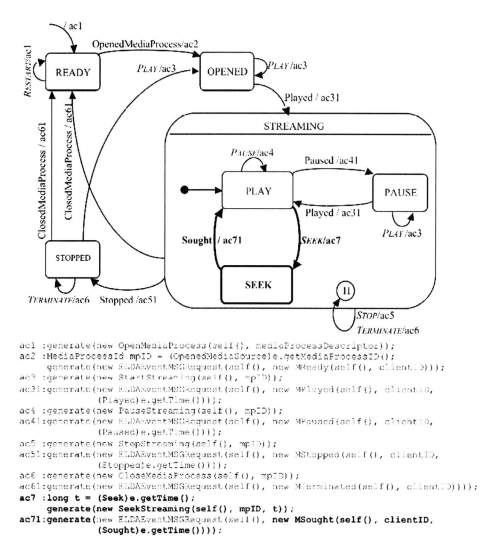

```
ac1  :generate(new OpenMediaProcess(self(), mediaProcessDescriptor));
ac2  :MediaProcessId mpID = (OpenedMediaSource)e.getMediaProcessID();
      generate(new ELDAEventMSGRequest(self(), new MReady(self(), clientID)));
ac3  :generate(new StartStreaming(self(), mpID));
ac31:generate(new ELDAEventMSGRequest(self(), new MPlayed(self(), clientID,
      (Played)e.getTime())));
ac4  :generate(new PauseStreaming(self(), mpID));
ac41:generate(new ELDAEventMSGRequest(self(), new MPaused(self(), clientID,
      (Paused)e.getTime())));
ac5  :generate(new StopStreaming(self(), mpID));
ac51:generate(new ELDAEventMSGRequest(self(), new MStopped(self(), clientID,
      (Stopped)e.getTime())));
ac6  :generate(new CloseMediaProcess(self(), mpID));
ac61:generate(new ELDAEventMSGRequest(self(), new MTerminated(self(), clientID)));
ac7  :long t = (Seek)e.getTime();
      generate(new SeekStreaming(self(), mpID, t));
ac71:generate(new ELDAEventMSGRequest(self(), new MSought(self(), clientID,
      (Sought)e.getTime())));
```

mfsc-M³A enters its sub-active behavior by issuing a request for activating a streaming process whose description is specified by a given media process descriptor (see Figure 8). After receiving the OpenedMediaSource event, mfsc-M³A becomes ready for streaming. From now on, mfsc-M³A can be controlled by RTSP-like (Real Time Streaming Protocol) (Schulzrinne, et al., 1998) commands (Play, Pause, Seek, Stop, Terminate, Restart) sent from its remote companion mobile agent (called sc-Client) dynamically got installed on the user application that is controlling the

media streaming session. The event-based interaction between mfsc-M³A and the media file streaming process is detailed in the *"The Streamer (STR) component"* section. The interaction between mfsc-M³A and sc-Client, which is of Client/Server type, imposes that mfsc-M³A reflects back to sc-Client the media process notifications (MReady, MPlayed, MPaused, MSought, MStopped, MTerminated) in order to update the client's control session state.

A further specialization of the mfsc-M³A embodies the management of the streaming of a

Figure 12. An extended active behavior of mfsc-M³A

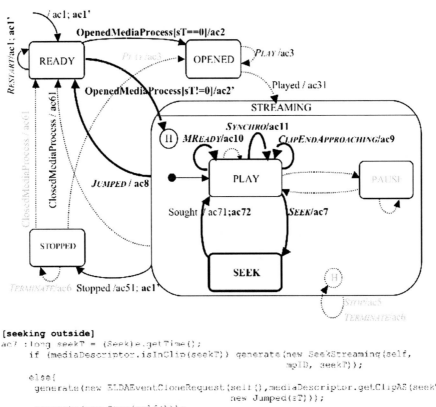

```
[seeking outside]
ac7 :long seekT = (Seek)e.getTime();
      if (mediaDescriptor.isInClip(seekT)) generate(new SeekStreaming(self,
                                           mpID, seekT));
      else{
        generate(new ELDAEventCloneRequest(self(),mediaDescriptor.getClipAS(seekT),
                                           new Jumped(sT)));
        generate(new Stop(self()));
      }
ac8 :generate(new OpenMediaProcess(mediaDescriptor));
      sT = (Jumped)e.getTime();
ac1':int sT=0;
ac2':MediaProcessId mpID = (OpenedMediaSource)e.getMediaProcessID();
      generate(new SeekStreaming(self(), mpID, seekT));
ac72:sT=(Sought)e.getTime();
[playing outside]
ac9 :generate(new ELDAEventMSGRequest(self(),mediaDescriptor.getSuccessiveClipAS(),
                   new Jumped(0)));
ac2 :MediaProcessId mpID = (OpenedMediaSource)e.getMediaProcessID();
      generate(new ELDAEventMSGRequest(self(), new MReady(self(), parent())));
ac10:ELDAId clone = (MReady)e.getSource();
      generate(new ELDAEventMSGRequest(self(),new StopSynchroTimer(self(),clone,mpID)));
ac11:generate(new ELDAEventMSGRequest(self(), new Play(self(), clone)));
      generate(new Stop(self()));
```

media file that is split in media clips dislocated onto more media repositories. Such specialization is reported in Figure 12, which only shows the added transitions as well as the actions enhancements.

When the end of a clip is approaching (ClipEndApproaching), mfsc-M³A clones itself on the multimedia active server (AS) where the next clip is archived. The cloning request (CloneRe-quest), which is managed by the Agent Management System (AMS), contains the Jumped self-event that drives the clone to create the media process. After the media process creation, the clone notifies (MReady) the original that it is waiting for playing in the Opened state. Upon MReady reception, the original sets a timing service (StopSynchroTimer) that notifies through

Synchro the original itself when it is time to start the clone (Play) and stop itself. The StopSynchro-Timer timing service engages a synchronization phase that allows minimizing the temporal gap between the original's playing stop and the clone's playing start.

Moreover, a cloning can also occur when a Seek event causes the positioning of the virtual playing head to fall inside a remote clip (Jump). In this case there is no need to tightly synchronize the clones since a seek operation always consists of a pause and a successive play. In fact, the clone spontaneously starts playing by re-entering the Seek state through the shallow history connector (H). For sake of readability, the handling of exceptional cases in which other Seek, Pause, Stop or Terminate occur just after a cloning is not reported in Figure 12.

It is worth noting that, the redirection mechanism is implicit in both cases and not explicit as in RTSP. In fact, in the seeking outside case, sc-Client is updated by MSought, containing the identifier of the clone mfsc-M³A, whereas, in the playing outside case, the sc-Client gets aware upon receiving MPlayed, which also includes the cloned mfsc-M³A's id.

Moreover, the interaction between mfsc-M³A and sc-Client is of client/server type whereas that between the two mfsc-M³As, the original and the clone, is peer-to-peer.

Media Searcher (ms-M³A)

Media searchers are fed with a list of media resources (e.g., media files) to search for and moves from one AS to another to discover such resources. Upon a successful discovery, they can come back to the searchers' originating AS or query their manager about future missions.

In figure 13 the basic ms-M³A's DSC and the related UML event sequence diagram, which shows the interactions among ms-M³A, the ms-M³A's manager (ms-Manager), and the Archiver component (ARC), are reported.

An ms-M³A is created by its ms-Manager on the first AS from which to start searching for the media resource described by MediaResourceDescr. ms-M³A first obtains the activation of a MediaArchiver media process and then submits a query to it. If the answer (QueryResultDescr) is positive, ms-M³A sends the result about the discovered media resource to ms-Manager and waits for instructions. Conversely, if the answer is negative, ms-M³A moves to the next AS by following an itinerary. If the itinerary is covered and no discovery results are obtained, ms-M³A notifies ms-Manager with the MatchNotFound event.

The interaction between ms-M³A and ms-Manager is of master/slave type.

A COOPERATIVE MEDIA ON-DEMAND ACTIVE SERVICE

The most valuable current trend of the Internet-based services is that they will be addressing specific user needs by employing a smart user-centered approach. Such an approach specialized in the multimedia application domain, which is now the main concern of Content Distribution Networks (Verma, 2002), aims at delivering to requesting users customized and ad-hoc media services.

By exploiting MAMS, we have instrumented a multimedia active platform (M²AP) that is able to deliver user-oriented adaptive real-time multimedia services. M²AP currently provides a user-centered, dynamically installable cooperative media streaming on-demand service, even though new services can be easily deployed and furnished. A cooperative media on-demand service (Fortino, et al., 2007) allows a group of users to request and jointly control the streaming of an archived multimedia file.

Figure 13. (a) The basic ms-M3A's active behavior; (b) The ms-M3A's sequence diagram

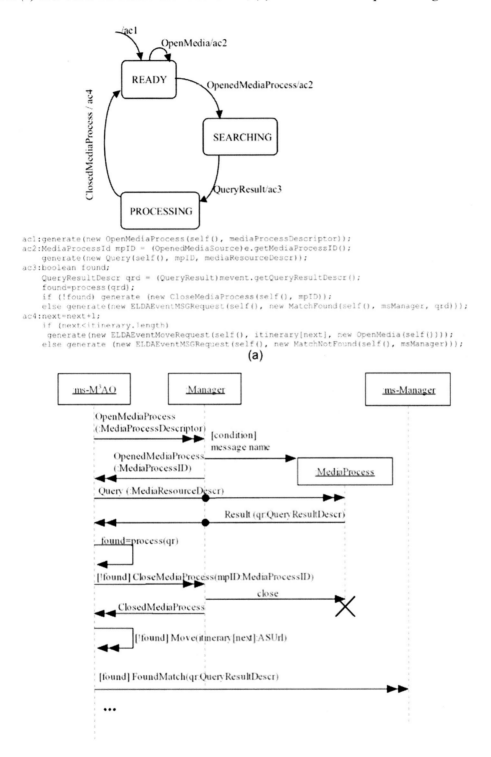

```
ac1:generate(new OpenMediaProcess(self(), mediaProcessDescriptor));
ac2:MediaProcessId mpID = (OpenedMediaSource)e.getMediaProcessID();
    generate(new Query(self(), mpID, mediaResourceDescr));
ac3:boolean found;
    QueryResultDescr qrd = (QueryResult)mevent.getQueryResultDescr();
    found=process(qrd);
    if (!found) generate (new CloseMediaProcess(self(), mpID));
    else generate(new ELDAEventMSGRequest(self(), new MatchFound(self(), msManager, qrd)));
ac4:next=next+1;
    if (next<itinerary.length)
     generate(new ELDAEventMoveRequest(self(), itinerary[next], new OpenMedia(self())));
    else generate (new ELDAEventMSGRequest(self(), new MatchNotFound(self(), msManager)));
```

(a)

The Deployment Infrastructure: acti-ASP and Basic Services

M²AP media services are provided to users by an active Application Service Provider (acti-ASP) that owns and manages an active domain (acti-ASP Domain) composed of a networked set of high-level active macronodes:

- *Web-based Active Service Access Point* (WASAP). It provides the entry point to access the active service domain and request media services. WASAP is composed of the following components:
  - *Java-enabled Web Server* (JWS), which provides the basic service start-up mechanism to the M2AP users that utilize a JavaPlug-in enabled Browser (JPB) to connect, visualize and select the available services.
  - *Class and Script Repository Manager* (CSRM), which manages a repository containing application classes, MSDL and XML-SDP scripts which can be on-demand downloaded through JWS.
  - *Active Server* (AS), which furnishes the computation environment for agents and media service components.
- *Active Multimedia Server* (AMS). It supports specific multimedia internetworking activity of multimedia components and multimedia agents by means of media repositories and/or multimedia databases, and active caching. It basically consists of an AS and a dynamic multimedia archive (DMA), which contains media file and their content description and can support temporary caching of media objects.

Since WASAPs usually are located near user hosts according to the "action at the edge" philosophy of peer-to-peer based CDN (Verma, 2002), not only media services are dynamically offered by WASAPs but also WASAPs can be purposely integrated with AMS peculiar functionalities by moving media resources into WASAPs so reducing service latency (e.g., latency for controlling the streaming of a "very" remote media file). When a user contacts a WASAP through its JPB and decides to access a media service, he/she implicitly joins the acti-ASP Domain, i.e., his/her host (or acti-Client) dynamically becomes an active node of the acti-ASP Domain. Such node called Dynamic Active Node (DAC) is supported by a certified Active Service Applet (ASA), downloaded and got installed as a consequence of the media service access, which an Active Server is bounded to. The security policies of ASA can be programmed according to users' profile using digital certificates. Usually ASA retains full access to the host resources but the file system access, which is to be explicitly granted by the user.

Testbed and Case Study Description

Figure 14 shows M²AP mapped onto our experimental testbed, where media services can be actually deployed and furnished.

In order to access and exploit the cooperative media on-demand service (also called COPS – COoperative Playback Service), a user (e.g., Media Client #1) connects to the closest WASAP through its JPB and requests a COPS. A COPS-specific DAC is so activated at client side that further provides the user with a Swing-based GUI through which it is possible perform the following tasks:

- Searching for a specific multimedia object to be streamed;
- Inviting active companions (i.e., clients already connected to the acti-ASP domain) for cooperatively watching a multimedia session (e.g., a movie, a tele-teaching session, etc.);
- Set-up a media session;

Figure 14. Deployment testbed for adaptive media services

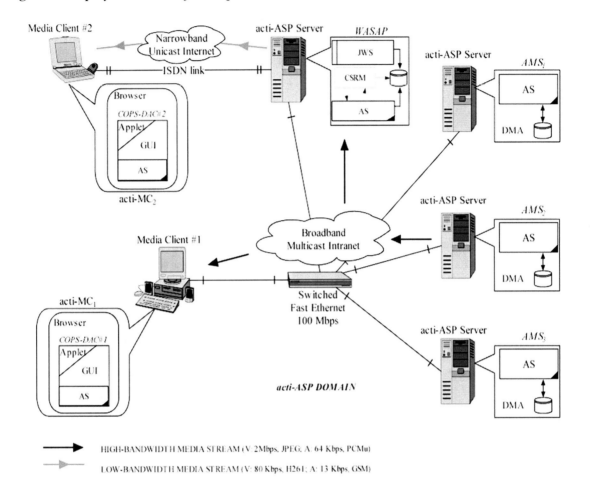

• Presenting and controlling, cooperatively if any companion is available, the activated media session.

Such tasks are dynamically supported by the acti-ASP at client (DAC) and server sides (WASAP and AMS) by using a specific set of M^3As and related multimedia components activated and managed at run-time (see section "*Multimedia Mobile Agents*").

In the following, we describe a cooperative playback service scenario realized over the active testbed (Figure 14) which allows to concretely highlight the flexibility of the proposed approach.

The active Media Client #1 (or acti-MC_1) first requests the streaming of an audio/video media file which is located on AMS_2 and then invites the active Media Client #2 (or acti-MC_2) to join the set up playback session. Since acti-MC_1 is directly attached to the multicast broadband intranet of the acti-ASP Domain, it requests that the media file is streamed at its full quality. acti-MC_2 is conversely attached to the acti-ASP Domain through a narrowband unicast Internet based on a 128 Kbps ISDN link. To actually join the media session, the total rate of the audio/video media streams should be kept below 128 Kbps and the streams themselves should be tunneled from the multicast network to the unicast one. Thus, the developed M^2AP

dynamically configures a pair of media gateway and forwarder agents on WASAP that captures, transcodes and forwards onto the unicast link the media streams available on the multicast network so overcoming the aforementioned network constraints. The parameters of the audio/video media streams transcoded and forwarded on the unicast link are reported in Figure 14.

In addition, since the media session is cooperative, both the VCR-like control commands sent from acti-MC_2 for streaming control and the collaboration messages sent to acti-MC_1 are forwarded from unicast addresses to multicast ones by two message forwarder agents. Translation from multicast to unicast is also needed for the control and collaboration messages sent from acti-MC_1. This task is performed by the same pair of message forwarder agents.

Analyzing Interactions Among Active Components

The prototyped cooperative media on-demand active service involves the following tasks:

1. Media searching, which is performed by an ms-M^3A driven by an ms-Manager installed in the COPS-DAC_1;
2. Invitation of companion users, which is performed by a si-M^3A that recovers the list of the active media clients to be invited on WASAP.
3. RTP-based media file streaming set-up, which is activated by an mfsc-M^3A located in AMS_2 and actually performed by an RTPFileStreamer component. Media streams are presented by the COPS-DAC GUI featured by a pl-M^3A.
4. Media transcoding and forwarding, which are started and controlled by a composition of media gateway and forwarder agents called gfw-M^3A and hosted by WASAP.
5. Cooperative control and messaging, which are realized respectively by cooperative sc-

Clients and collaborative message-oriented mobile agents (colab-MA) placed in the COPS-DACs.
6. Service global QoS monitoring, which is regulated by a qc-Monitor agent, belonging to WASAP, which governs qc-M^3As installed in COPS-DAC_1, COPS-DAC_2, WASAP, and AMS_2.

Figure 15 portrays an enhanced UML collaboration diagram showing the interactions among the static and mobile software components, which constitute the offered media service, at active macronode level (i.e., in the large). The interactions that occur inside the high level active macronode (i.e., in the small) are discussed in section "*The Mobile Agent Multimedia Space*." The diagram highlights the interactions afterwards the acti-MC_1 activates COPS-DAC_1, i.e., its GUI-supported cooperative active environment.

As one can note, there exists a 1-to-1 mapping between these components and those reported in Figure 14. In the following, each sequence of labels is orderly associated to the specific tasks of the above numbered list:

- «*1.x searching.*" ms-M^3A first moves (1, 1.1) to WASAP to retrieve the updated list of available AMSs, then starts searching by moving to AMS_1 (1.2, 1.3), AMS_2 (1.4, 1.5) and AMS_3 (1.6, 1.7). If the multimedia object is found, i.e., it matches the media descriptor provided by the user, ms-M^3A comes back with the locator of the AMS and the media object description (or with multiple AMS locators if the multimedia object spans across more AMSs).
- «*2.x invitation*». si-M^3A is launched onto WASAP to obtain a list of active users (2, 2.1) and then moves (2.2, 2.3) to the top-list acti-MC (acti-MC_2). If acti-MC_2 agrees to join the session, a COD-based interaction (2.4, 2.5), promoted by si-M^3A, activates COPS-DAC_2 so that acti-MC_2 is able

Figure 15. A UML collaboration diagram of the high-level active macronodes

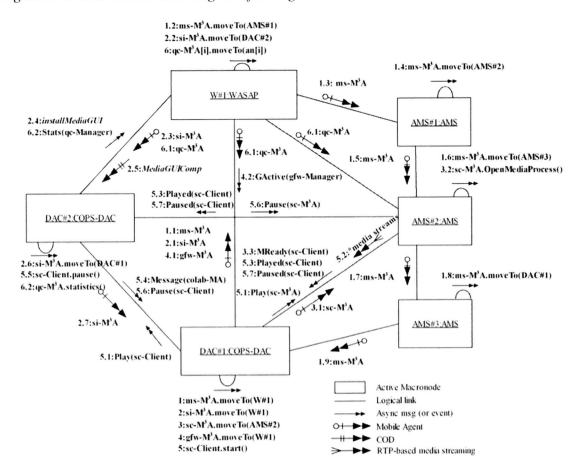

to receive and play the multicast session media streams. si-M³A comes back (2.6, 2.7) to DAC₁ carrying the acti-MC₂ identity (or the identity list of those clients that have accepted the invitation).

- *«3.x streaming set-up»*. The mfsc-M³A moves (3, 3.1) to AMS₂ where is located the multimedia object (or its first clip), docks into the AS, activates (3.2) the media file streaming process and sends the MReady event (3.3) to its sc-Client.

- *«4.x transcoding and forwarding»*. fgw-M³A is sent (4, 4.1) into WASAP to tunnel the multicast media session from the multicast network to the unicast one, and to transcode the audio/video media streams.

After activating and composing a forwarder and a media gateway media processes, fgw-M³A sends (4.2) the GActive event to its gfw-Manager.

- *«5.x cooperative control and messaging."* sc-Client of DAC₁ can now start mfsc-M³A by issuing the Play event (5, 5.1) so that media streaming (5.2) can start. Afterwards, sc-Client of DAC₁ and sc-Client of DAC₂ can cooperatively control (5.5, 5.6) mfsc-M³A and interact with each other through messages (5.4).

- *«6.x QoS monitoring»*. The cooperative playback session manager located on WASAP (qc-Manager) spawns four qc-M³A (6, 6.1). One qc-M³A monitors the media gateway process on WASAP, whereas the others move to DAC_1, DAC_2, and AMS_2 for monitoring the player and the streamer processes. They filter the QoS events received by the media processes and send (6.1, 6.2) statistics reports to qc-Manager.

FUTURE RESEARCH DIRECTIONS

Future and emerging trends are related to the definition and deployment of ambient real-time multimedia services for multimedia social-networking applications (Aarts, 2004). Such applications will be based on PDA/smartphones and people wearing body area networks to sense human vital parameters and the surrounding environment where people are situated. In particular, the foreseen applications will allow users not only to share static multimedia objects as in social networks applications like Facebook, but also to exchange media streams for multi-party audio/video interactions or for peer-to-peer media streaming on-demand. To develop such applications, new design methods and distributed multimedia platforms should be defined. The approach presented in this paper could be extended with physical mobility to obtain M^3S (Mobile MultiMedia Space) that allows for dynamic creation and deployment of real-time multimedia services atop mobile devices in pervasive computing scenarios. M^3S will therefore enable ad-hoc multimedia-based social interaction through multimedia portable devices and wearable sensors. M^3S can also interface the Internet Protocol Multimedia Subsystem (IMS) recently defined for mobile communication services in multimedia ubiquitous computing environments (Cueva, et al., 2006).

CONCLUSION

Delivering multimedia real-time services to users according to their peculiar needs is a topical issue which emerging Content Distribution Networks should timely tackle and efficiently resolve in order to obtain competitive advantages in application domains such as academic and company Education, and notably Entertainment.

This paper has proposed and exemplified an approach, which blends multiple coordination spaces and lightweight agents with multimedia internetworking protocols and mechanisms, for prototyping, dynamic deployment and management of adaptive real-time multimedia services.

The proposed approach is enabled by the ELDAFramework, our high-level Java-based framework, currently implemented atop the JADE platform, which provides agent-oriented programming of highly dynamic distributed applications. The ELDAFramework is based on the ELDA agent model that is centered on (i) the concept of single-threaded event-driven agent whose behavior is formalized using the Distilled StateCharts formalism and (ii) a multi-coordination context dynamically made up of composable global and local interaction spaces able to support diversified coordination models. In particular, the mobile multimedia agents (M^3As) act as activators and managers of high-performance and off-the-shelf components, based on the Internet multimedia protocol stack, which are aggregated in a composable multimedia space (M^2S) that only provide basic, even advanced, media services. More complex multimedia services can be dynamically created by programming M^2S. Such a task is carried out by an application-specific set of M^3As that coordinate with each another and/or are coordinated by client and manager mobile agents.

Media services can dynamically be deployed and on-demand activated over a multimedia active platform (M^2AP) centered on the concept of the active application service provider domain (acti-ASP Domain) which is a dynamic grid of the following active macronodes: Web-featured active service access points (or WASAP servers), active multimedia servers (AMSs), and dynamic active client (DAC). Notably users, which connect to an active domain for requesting a media service, implicitly join the active domain itself by providing support to incoming agents.

In order to concretely show the real capability of the platform to provide adaptive media services, we developed a case study concerning with an adaptive cooperative playback service which allows a group of users, heterogeneous both in bandwidth and in the end-system, to request and cooperatively watch and control the streaming of a remote media file by collaborating with each other.

The deployed media service is much more flexible than the one obtainable by using more traditional, even adaptive, approaches to multicast-based media streaming on-demand (Almeroth & Ammar, 1998; Busse, et al., 1996; Fortino & Nigro, 1998, Fortino & Nigro, 2000a; Fortino & Nigro, 2000a; Fortino & Nigro, 2003) which have the following limitations:

- *Computing power and bandwidth.* The streaming rate is set and adapted according to the lowest common denominator principle. This limits higher performance media clients if the performance of the media client originating the playback session is very low as the QoS media session parameters are set upon the session originator. Such limitation further worsens if the high performance client is the session originator, since the lower performance clients are unable to join the session.
- *Multicast issues.* A media client that is not connected to an IP-multicast broadband network cannot access the multicast media session. To enable such a client to join the session, ad-hoc and off-line changes, such as the installation of mrouted programs (Crowcroft, et al., 1999), should be applied to the networking infrastructure or the ex-

ploitation of multicast routers should be widely available.

Moreover, our experience also highlights that software engineering methodologies supporting mobile and multimedia agent-based software development are highly required. In fact, standard software modeling techniques such as UML should be enhanced to properly support code mobility, non-conventional coordination models, and multimedia internetworking abstractions.

Additional work is currently being devoted to:

- Evaluating the performance of the developed media service and comparing the results with those obtainable using an ad-hoc, more traditional multicast media service platform in order to quantify high flexibility versus efficiency of the media service;
- Enhancing the developed set of basic multimedia agents and media process components with streaming encryption and secret key management (Fortino, et al., 2003), and robust streaming (Fortino, et al., 2011; Calafate, et al., 2012).

REFERENCES

W3C. (n.d.). *eXtensible markup language, specifications.* Retrieved June 15, 2007, from http://www.w3.org/XML/Schema

W3C. (n.d.). *Web services description language, specifications.* Retrieved June 15, 2007, from http://www.w3c.org/TR/wsdl.html

Aarts, E. (2004). Ambient intelligence: A multimedia perspective. *IEEE MultiMedia, 11*(1), 12–19. doi:10.1109/MMUL.2004.1261101

Al-Shaer, E. (2000). Active management framework for distributed multimedia systems. *Journal of Network and Systems Management, 8*(1), 49–72. doi:10.1023/A:1009415025046

Almeroth, K. C., & Ammar, M. H. (1998). The Interactive Multimedia Jukebox (IMJ): A new paradigm for the on-demand delivery of audio/video. *Proceedings of the 7th International World Wide Web Conference (WWW7)*, (pp. 431-441).

Amir, E., McCanne, S., & Katz, R. (1998). An active service framework and its application to real-time multimedia transcoding. *Proceedings of ACM SIGCOMM'98*, (pp. 178-189).

Amir, E., McCanne, S., & Zhang, H. (1995). An application-level video gateway. *Proceedings of ACM Multimedia'95*, (pp. 255-265).

Baldi, M., Picco, G. P., & Risso, F. (1998). Designing a videoconference system for active networks. *Journal of Personal Technologies, 2*, 75–84. doi:10.1007/BF01324937

Bellifemine, F., Poggi, A., & Rimassa, G. (2001). Developing multi agent systems with a FIPA-compliant agent framework. *Software, Practice & Experience, 31*, 103–128. doi:10.1002/1097-024X(200102)31:2<103::AID-SPE358>3.0.CO;2-O

Busse, I., Deffner, B., & Schulzrinne, H. (1996). Dynamic QoS control of multimedia applications based on RTP. *Computer Communications, 19*(1), 49–58. doi:10.1016/0140-3664(95)01038-6

Cabri, G., Leonardi, L., & Zambonelli, F. (2000). Mobile-agent coordination models for internet applications. *IEEE Computer, 33*(2), 82–89. doi:10.1109/2.820044

Cahill, A. J., & Sreenan, C. J. (2006). An efficient resource management system for a streaming media distribution network. *International Journal of Interactive Technology and Smart Education, 3*(1), 31–44. doi:10.1108/17415650680000051

Calafate, C. T., Fortino, G., Fritsch, S., Monteiro, J., Cano, J. C., & Manzoni, P. (2012). An efficient and robust content delivery solution for IEEE 802.11p vehicular environments. *Journal of Network and Computer Applications, 35*(2), 753–762. doi:10.1016/j.jnca.2011.11.008

Cranor, C. D., Green, M., Kalmanek, C., Shur, D., Sibal, S., Sreenan, C. J., & Van der Merwe, J. E. (2001). Enhanced streaming services in a content distribution network. *IEEE Internet Computing, 5*(4), 66–75. doi:10.1109/4236.939452

Crowcroft, J., Handley, M., & Wakeman, I. (1999). *Internetworking multimedia*. San Francisco, CA: Morgan Kaufmann Publisher.

Cuevas, A., Moreno, J. I., Vidales, P., & Einsiedler, H. (2006). The IMS service platform: A solution for next-generation network operators to be more than bit pipes. *IEEE Communications, 44*(8), 75–81. doi:10.1109/MCOM.2006.1678113

Dutta, A., & Schulzrinne, H. (2004). Marconi-NET: Overlay mobile content architecture. *IEEE Communications, 42*(2), 64–75. doi:10.1109/MCOM.2003.1267102

Falchuk, B., & Karmouch, A. (1997). A mobile agent prototype for autonomous multimedia information access, interaction, and retrieval. *Proceedings of Multimedia Modeling, 97*, 33–48.

Falchuk, B., & Karmouch, A. (1997). AgentSys: A mobile agent system for digital media access and interaction on an Internet. *Proceedings of Globecom, 97*, 1876–1880.

FIPA. (2002). *Agent management support for mobility specification.* (DC00087C, 2002/05/10). Retrieved October 1, 2010, from http://www.fipa.org

Fortino, G., Calafate, C., & Manzoni, P. (2011). Robust broadcasting of media content in urban environments. In Fortino, G., & Palau, C. E. (Eds.), *Next generation content networks*. Hershey, PA: IGI Global.

Fortino, G., Frattolillo, F., Russo, W., & Zimeo, E. (2002). Mobile active objects for highly dynamic distributed computing. *Proceedings of IEEE 16th International Parallel and Distributed Processing Symposium,* (pp. 211-217). IEEE Computer Society.

Fortino, G., Garro, A., Mascillaro, S., & Russo, W. (2010). Using event-driven lightweight DSC-based agents for MAS modeling. *International Journal on Agent Oriented Software Engineering, 4*(2).

Fortino, G., & Nigro, L. (1998). QoS centred Java and actor based framework for real/virtual teleconferences. *Proceedings of SCS EuroMedia,* (pp. 4-6).

Fortino, G., & Nigro, L. (2000a). ViCRO: An interactive and cooperative videorecording on-demand system over MBone. *Informatica (Slovenia), 24*(1).

Fortino, G., & Nigro, L. (2000b). A cooperative playback system for on-demand multimedia sessions over Internet. *Proceedings of IEEE Multimedia and Expo (ICME 2000),* (pp. 41-44).

Fortino, G., & Nigro, L. (2003). Collaborative learning on-demand on the internet MBone. In Ghaoui, C. (Ed.), *Usability evaluation of online learning programs*. Hershey, PA: Idea Publishing Group. doi:10.4018/978-1-59140-105-6.ch003

Fortino, G., & Palau, C. E. (2007). An open streaming content distribution network. In Tatnall, A. (Ed.), *Encyclopaedia of portal technology and applications* (pp. 677–683). Hershey, PA: Idea Publishing Group. doi:10.4018/978-1-59140-989-2.ch112

Fortino, G., Rango, F., & Russo, W. (2010). Statecharts-based JADE agents and tools for engineering multi-agent systems. In R. Setchi, I. Jordanov, R. J. Howlett, & L. C. Jain (Eds.), *Knowledge-Based and Intelligent Information and Engineering Systems, 14th International Conference (KES 2010), LNAI 6276* (pp. 240-250). Berlin, Germany: Springer Verlag.

Fortino, G., & Russo, W. (2005). Multi-coordination of mobile agents: A model and a component-based architecture. *Proceedings of ACM Symposium on Applied Computing (SAC'05),* (pp. 443-450).

Fortino, G., Russo, W., Mastroianni, C., Palau, C. E., & Esteve, M. (2007). CDN-supported collaborative media streaming control. *IEEE MultiMedia, 14*(2), 60–71. doi:10.1109/MMUL.2007.29

Fortino, G., Russo, W., & Zimeo, E. (2003). Enhancing cooperative playback systems with efficient encrypted multimedia streaming. *Proceedings of IEEE International Conference on Multimedia and Expo (ICME'03),* (pp. 657-660).

Fortino, G., Russo, W., & Zimeo, E. (2004). A statecharts-based software development process for mobile agents. *Information and Software Technology, 46*(13), 907–921. doi:10.1016/j.infsof.2004.04.005

Fuggetta, A., Picco, G. P., & Vigna, G. (1998). Understanding code mobility. *IEEE Transactions on Software Engineering, 24*(5), 342–361. doi:10.1109/32.685258

Georganas, N. D., Steinmetz, R., & Nakagawa, T. (Eds.). (1996). Synchronization issues in multimedia communications. *Journal of Selected Areas in Communications, 14*(1).

Govindan, R., Alaettinoglu, C., & Estrin, D. (1998). *Extensible distributed services*. Tech Report 98-669, Computer Science Department, University of Southern California, Jan. 1998.

Grand, M. (2002). *Patterns in Java* (*Vol. 1*). Indianapolis, IN: Wiley Publishing Inc.

Gray, R., Kotz, D., Cybenko, G., & Rus, D. (2001). Mobile agents: Motivations and state of the art systems. In J. Bradshaw (Ed.), *Handbook of agent technology*. AAAI/MIT Press.

Handley, M., & Jacobson, V. (1998). *Session description protocol*. IETF RFC 2327.

Harel, D. (1987). Statecharts: A visual formalism for complex systems. *Science of Computer Programming*, *8*, 231–274. doi:10.1016/0167-6423(87)90035-9

Huber, O. J. (1997). Multimedia services based on agents. *Proceedings of IBC Intelligent Agents Conference*.

Kwan, W., & Karmouch, A. (1996). Multimedia agents in a distributed broadband environment. *Proceedings of International Conference on Communications (ICC'96)*, (pp. 1123-1127).

McCanne, S. (1999). Scalable multimedia communication using IP multicast and lightweight sessions. *IEEE Internet Computing*, *3*(2), 33–45. doi:10.1109/4236.761652

Mühlhäuser, M., & Gecsei, J. (1996). Services, frameworks, and paradigms for distributed multimedia applications. *IEEE MultiMedia*, *3*(3), 48–61. doi:10.1109/MMUL.1996.556539

Ni, J., & Tsang, D. H. K. (2005). Large-scale cooperative caching and application-level multicast in multimedia content delivery networks. *IEEE Communications*, *43*(5), 98–105. doi:10.1109/MCOM.2005.1453429

Omicini, A., & Zambonelli, F. (1999). Tuple centres for the coordination of internet agents. *Proceedings of ACM Symposium on Applied Computing (SAC'99)*, (pp. 183-190).

Picco, G. P., Murphy, A. L., & Roman, G.-C. (2000). Software engineering for mobility: A roadmap. In Finkelstein, A. (Ed.), *The future of software engineering* (pp. 241–258). New York, NY: ACM Press.

Ramanujan, R. S., & Thurber, K. J. (1998). An active network based design of a QoS adaptive video multicast service. *Proceedings of International Conference on Information Systems, Analysis and Synthesis (ISAS'98)*, (pp. 643–650).

Rowe, L. A. (2001). Streaming media middleware is more than streaming media. *Proceedings of the 2001 International Workshop on Multimedia Middleware (M3W)*.

Satoh, I. (2000). A hierarchical model of mobile agents and its multimedia applications. *Proceedings of the IEEE International Workshop on Multimedia Network Systems (MMNS'2000)*, (pp. 103-108).

Sauer, S., & Engels, G. (1999). OMMMA: An object-oriented approach for modeling multimedia information systems. *Proceedings of the 5th International Work. on Multimedia Information Systems (MIS)*, (pp. 64-71).

Schulzrinne, H., et al. (2010). *RTP tools* (v. 1.18). Retrieved January 1, 2005, from http://www.cs.columbia.edu/IRT/software/rtptools/

Schulzrinne, H., Casner, S., Frederick, R., & Jacobson, V. (1996). *RTP: A transport protocol for real-time applications*. IETF RFC 1889.

Schulzrinne, H., Rao, A., & Lanphier, R. (1998). *Real time streaming protocol (RTSP)*. IETF RFC 2326.

Schulzrinne, H., Schooler, E., & Rosemberg, J. (1999). *SIP: Session initiation protocol*. IETF RFC 2543.

Source Forge. (n.d.). *MASH toolkit.* Openmash. org, University of Berkeley (CA), USA, Retrieved April 15, 2008, from http://sourceforge.net/projects/openmash/

Sun Microsystems Inc. (n.d.). *Java media framework.* Retrieved November 15, 2009, from http://java.sun.com/products/java-media/jmf/index. html

Tennenhouse, D. L., Smith, J. M., Sincoskie, W. D., Wetherall, D. J., & Minden, G. J. (1997). A survey of active networks research. *IEEE Communications Magazine, 35,* 80–86. doi:10.1109/35.568214

The Unified Modeling Language. OMG specification (N. Formal/01-09-67), v. 1.4. (2001).

Verma, D. C. (2002). *Content distribution networks: An engineering approach.* Indianapolis, IN: John Wiley & Sons. doi:10.1002/047122457X

KEY TERMS AND DEFINITIONS

Cooperative Playback Systems: Cooperative playback systems (CPS) are distributed multimedia systems that allow an explicitly formed group of clients to view and cooperatively control a shared remote media playback.

Distilled StateCharts: The Distilled StateCharts (DSCs) is a state machine formalism derived from Statecharts that allows modeling the behavior of single-threaded, event-driven mobile agents. Its appealing graphical features ease the modeling of complex agent-based software systems.

ELDA Model: The ELDA model is based on the concept of event-driven lightweight agent which is a single-threaded autonomous entity interacting through asynchronous events, executing upon reaction, and capable of migration. The behavior of ELDA agents is specified through the Distilled StateCharts whereas interaction are formalized through events referring multiple coordination infrastructures (message-based, tuple-oriented, event-based, etc.)

JADE: The Java Agent DEvelopment Framework (JADE) is a Java-based software framework for multi-agent systems. The JADE platform allows the management and coordination of multiple FIPA-compliant agents through the use of the standard FIPA-ACL communication language.

Mobile Multimedia Agents: Multimedia mobile agents (M^3As) are ELDA agents that exploit the M^2S, equipped with local available or on-demand installable multimedia software components, for accomplishing multimedia tasks. The currently defined M^3As are: Streaming Controller, Media Searcher, Session Initiator, Media Gateway, Forwarder, Recorder, Player, QoS Controller.

Multimedia Internetworking: Multimedia internetworking refers to network infrastructures, protocols, models, applications and techniques that are available for supporting the development, deploying and execution of multimedia distributed applications on the Internet.

Multimedia Space: The multimedia space (M^2S) is an extendible, component-based media service substratum that can be programmed by a set of multimedia mobile agents to build complex distributed media services.

Chapter 10
Remote Delivery of Video Services over Video Links

Jesús M. Barbero
OEI/EUI, Technical University of Madrid, Spain

ABSTRACT

The spreading of new systems of broadcasting and distribution of multimedia content has had as a consequence a larger need for aggregation of data and metadata to traditionally based contents of video and audio supply. Broadcasting chains of this type of channels have become overwhelmed by the quantity of resources, infrastructures, and development needed for these channels to provide information. In order to avoid this kind of shortcoming, several recommendations and standards have been created to exchange metadata between production and distribution of taped programs. The problem lies in live programs; producers sometimes offer data to channels, but most often, channels are not able to face required developments. The key to this problem is cost reduction. In this work, a study is conducted on added services which producers may provide to the media about content; a system is found by which additional communication expenses are not made, and a model of information transfer is offered which allows low cost developments to supply new media platforms.

INTRODUCTION

The model change which Digital Terrestrial Television (DTT) is causing, IP-based television in all its forms or simply diffusion on Internet is provoking on one hand, that traditional broadcast companies look for new markets with new technologies and on the other hand, other companies have started to broadcast material by these new means with only having rights and not necessarily licenses, as in the case of broadcasting.

The proliferation of chains and transmission channels have consequently put into motion, as a consequence, the abandoning of productions, and

DOI: 10.4018/978-1-4666-1794-0.ch010

concentration on transmission itself while at the same time, companies specialized in production have emerged which generate cheaper content and which can be commercialized on different supports.

Audiovisual contents which are generated are sent to different clients by two clearly differentiated types of transmission:

- Delivery in real time (live programs). The video material is coded in MPEG2 Transport Stream for its transfer to the destination by a data link. On the other end of the link it is connected to a decoder to decode the data stream on base band.
- Delivery in a file or tape (recorded or taped). By this means of delivery, the edited file is sent by disk or tape to transmitting stations.

Production companies have the data; they are experts in each of the subjects they produce. For data and metadata interchange of taped programs, different standards and recommendations exist, the problem arises in data exchange for live programs in which channels have to adapt their applications or create new ones to be able to give service to viewers.

In this work, the need to create a standard of data service on distribution networks of live programs will be presented based on the following principles:

- The producer of the event generates data, because he best knows the content of the broadcasting.
- Data on XML documents for a better adaptation to existing technologies. This data exchange facilitates creation of new applications.
- Data delivery on the same video networks, so that data go tightly connected to the signal itself with the consequent saving in communications.

In this chapter, technological aspects related to the work presented are reviewed. The main objective is to show an analysis of services which can be offered from producers to broadcaster, and to present solutions to these services. We finished with the models which differ from the general model in order to adapt special services and the solutions are discussed in more depth, and we include conclusions as well as mention of future work to be developed.

BACKGROUND (PRODUCTION ISSUES)

In this section we will review some aspects in the professional video production.

Data Exchange

What are metadata? Metadata provide information about data content. Literally, metadata are data further than data, and characterize the content by a group of attributes. These attributes may not only describe content in the form of raw data, meaning, and/or key concepts, content is also characterized in terms of author, quality, production time, format, etc. Also, added information during delivery service (such as receipt information) or information about permits for use of content must be correctly described by metadata. In short, metadata (referring to multimedia/audiovisual content) contain information about all related aspects to the entire chain of content provision.

The fact that audiovisual content has associated metadata offers many advantages. One of the main ones is to be able to make searches for content in a very intense way. Due to the great quantity of information metadata contain, very complex and varied searches may be carried out: by author, description, permits, etc. Another advantage is the ease of content exchange or distribution, since metadata are associated with content, distribution or exchange information is

Figure 1. Subtitling workflow

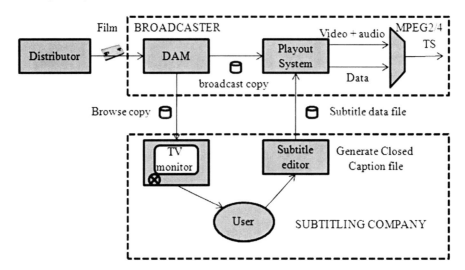

incorporated. Content classification is made easier for storage, for example, perhaps a certain kind of content should be stored in a concrete format so as not to lose quality, while other types of content may be less important. Upon broadcasting, if one does not have rights, this will avoid violation of broadcasting rights.

On several occasions, there has been an effort to standardize the storage process of audiovisual data: for example, code ISAN (ISO, 2004) and code VISAN (ISO, 2002); technical reports collected by the EBU (European Broadcasting Union) in its projects: TV-Anytime (Evain, 2000), ESCORT (EBU, 2007) or P/META (EBU, 2005); the BBC data model SMEF (BBC Technology, 2003); Dublin-Core (DublinCore, 2003), etc. Many of these proposals have been worked on in parallel and a common representation has still not been reached of this knowledge. On the other hand, each organization has its internal needs of storing certain types of information, needing an effective and efficient data model according to its specific needs.

Subtitling

Subtitling is used extensively by television channels to attract public with hearing impairment, viewers who want to learn a language or simply to be able to understand dialog of an event with original sound (e.g. opera).

At present, distributors send tapes or discs with series content. This content is usually video material and two audios: original sound and natural. Original sound is that corresponding to dialog in the language of the film while natural is the rest of the sounds different from dialog, this way dubbing companies change the original sound with that of each country. When channels receive material from the distributors, they send a copy of video with low quality to companies specializing in subtitling. These formats integrate the broadcasting system in such a way that audio and video are synchronized with subtitle information, as can be seen in Figure 1.

As can be observed in Figure 2, copies of the film are distributed in each country to companies who have the rights; these companies send a copy to subtitling companies sending a file so that the broadcasting system of the channels incorporates

Figure 2. Content distribution

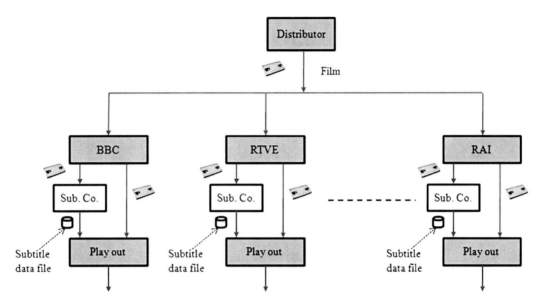

this information for diffusion. Two types of subtitles are defined as such:

- Dialog subtitling. This is done so that viewers can see the dialog in the language of the country where the original sound is heard. In the
- Emission, the text forms part of the image and cannot be changed, commands may be sent to change typography.
- Subtitling for the deaf (closed caption). In contrast to the above, the text does not form part of the image and is shown on the same receptor as the viewer desires. It is closely linked to data transmission in the same video signal.

The arrival of the MPEG compression format has allowed greater possibilities and larger bandwidths to transmit data than analog transmission, this transmission being limited by bandwidth of the vertical deletion lines.

The subtitling regulation **(ETSI, 1997)** specifies how regions, colours, formats etc are to be transmitted in the different transmission forms:

DVB-T, DVB-S, DVB-C and DVB-H (terrestrial, satellite, cable and mobile). An exhaustive review of all these can be found in **(Reimers, 2006)**.

Distribution Format Exchange Profile (DFXP)

Currently, EBU has adopted the Timed Text (TT) Authoring Format 1.0 – Distribution Format Exchange Profile (DFXP) **(W3C, 2010)** and has created a working group for use the standard DFXP for exchange subtitling information in XML.

The timed text authoring format is a content type that represents timed text media for the purpose of interchange among authoring systems. Timed text is textual information that is associated with timing information, it serves as a bidirectional interchange format among a heterogeneous collection of authoring systems, and as a unidirectional interchange format to a heterogeneous collection of distribution formats after transcoding or compilation to the target distribution formats as required, and where one particular distribution format is DFXP. Authoring users produces, exchange data, transcode information to different

Figure 3. DFXP workflow

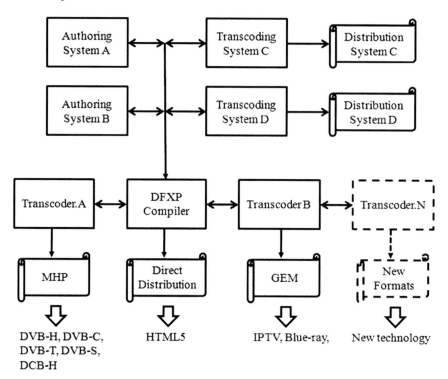

formats and compile to DXFP for distribution to DXFP clients or transcoding to other formats as see in Figure 3.

In the figure it can be see how there are several authority systems (two in the figure) working in collaborative systems. Data can be trascode do other formats (System C or System D), at the same time, data can be compiled as DFXP document for direct distribution or transcoding to other formats as Multimedia Home Platform (MHP), Global Executable MHP (GEM) for IPVT chains or future formats.

A DFXP document contains a header and a body. Header specifies document level metadata, styling definitions and layout definitions; body specifies text content intermixed with references to style and layout information and inline timing information. In Box 1 there is an example with DFXP structure, where the head contains the metadata, styling, layout definitions and the body.

The body part performs as a container for a sequence of textual content units represented as logical divisions (see Box 2).

A simple example of content is shown in Box 3.

Where a subtitle "How are you?" is presented in the image between seconds 5" and 7" when the picture file associated with the subtitle are played. The standard provides more fields in order to indicate other characteristics about the subtitle (position, color, font, etc.).

The text to be displayed is within a "P" element in the DFXP metamodel. A "P" element represents a logical paragraph, serving as a transition between block level and inline level formatting semantics and it has his corresponding identification attribute. This attribute will be used to link original subtitle format and text to the corresponding translated text. There are also two important attributes: begin and duration. The XML structure of a "P" element is shown in Figure 4.

Box 1.

```
<tt xml:lang="" xmlns="http://www.w3.org/2006/10/ttaf1">
  <head>
     <metadata/>
     <styling/>
     <layout/>
  </head>
  <body/>
</tt>
```

Box 2.

```
<body
  begin = <timeExpression>
  dur = <timeExpression>
  end = <timeExpression>
  region = IDREF
  style = IDREFS
  timeContainer = (par|seq)
  xml:id = ID
  xml:lang = string
  xml:space = (default|preserve)
  {any attribute in TT Metadata namespace}
  {any attribute in TT Style namespace}
  {any attribute not in default or any TT namespace}>
  Content: Metadata.class*, Animation.class*, div*
</body>
```

Box 3.

```
<body region="subtitleArea">
  <div>
    <p xml:id="subt1" begin="5s" end="7s">
     How are you?
    </p></div>
</body>
```

Begin and duration attributes are time expressions that can be a clock time or an offset. The span of time a subtitle is about to be displayed is included in the original file as offset time expressions, setting the begin value to an estimate time and the duration attribute to the corresponding offset (usually, only few seconds more).

Live Programs

As mentioned above, producers usually make programs for different chains, not only stored programs but also live programs. Clear examples are international sports events, where from a source station images are sent to different chains or broadcasting companies as is shown in Figure 5. Chains lower the signal (normally satellite) to place content in the emission system for its packeting and emission playout. Each of the channels has to adapt the signal arriving to the broadcasting format for which it has acquired the rights to that event.

Figure 4. XML structure of a "P" element

A Playout control room can be show in Figure 6 where all audiovisual material is put on air in the appropriate order.

Titling and Graphics

In signal production, usually an international signal is generated with titles in English to provide all channels with a general and uniform heading service. This advantage in production becomes an inconvenience: one is the impossibility of generating differentiated titles because they would collide with those from the original signal when being superimposed on the same image. Filing of the image in the general chain file is another inconvenience since images are already dirty; the value of the image is reduced because the type of production and its possibilities are limited.

To solve the image titling problem, it is usually looked at from different points of view.

1. Signal Production: Whoever produces the signal usually sends two different satellite signals: clean signal and titled signal in international language, each of the chains is free to choose one signal or the other. This alternative has the disadvantage of a cost increase from the renting of another channel for signal distribution.
2. Event Broadcasting: In each country, owners of diffusion rights of an event, packet the video signal for transmission with their programmes. The form of packeting differs

Figure 5. Contribution and program broadcasting

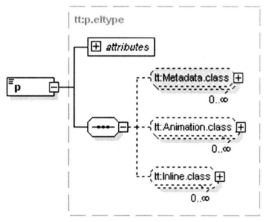

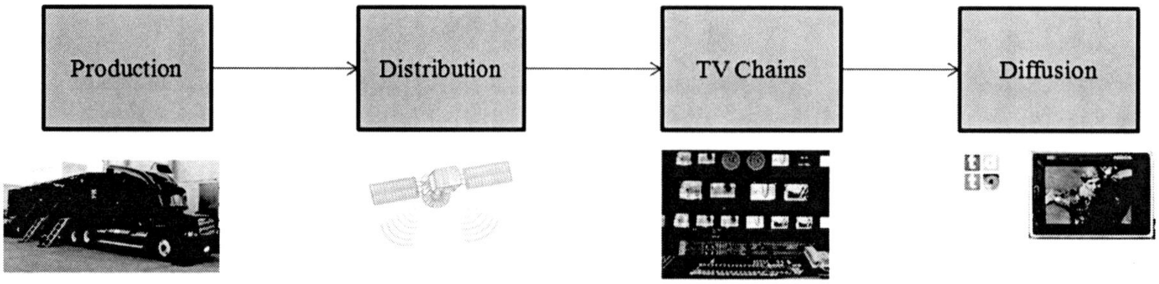

Figure 6. Playout control room (courtesy of Antena 3 de Televisión)

from the importance which is given to an event so that specific content can be created in each country. This way a range of possibilities exists from coverage with their own cameras in the stadium which are mixed with the general production, to the simple rebound of the contribution signal to diffusion without adding anything intermediary. Each of these possibilities has its advantages and disadvantages with its increases in associated costs and in general headings are usually poorer than international broadcasting.

3.   Titling Production: Graphics are made in stations by templates; these templates have a fixed content and another variable. Fixed information refers to common elements which are in the same type of title, which are usually one or sequences of TGA's with the key information necessary so that the mixer can incrust the title into the video. The variable part can be an image (static or dynamic) or a text with the classical characteristics of text as far as font, size, etc.

The work process for titling of an event goes from enumeration all the templates types to be used, the creation of common elements of the titles, and the creation of spaces where the variable data of the models will be placed, characteristics and types of content (e.g. text, images, etc.).

Before the event begins, titles are prepared according to templates and stored on pages or sites to be called from the control terminal where the signal is generated. During the event broadcasting, data is updated and new titles are generated in a dynamic way on pages for emission.

New Ways of Broadcasting

For analog broadcasting, this adaptation is trivial and has been in use for a long period of time, the problem occurs when it is necessary to adapt content to each of the different technologies. If adaptation is only image and sound, it is still simple, but the characteristics which each of the systems provides are not taken advantage of. In the case of digital television, information will need

Figure 7. Multiplexing of a program on a transport

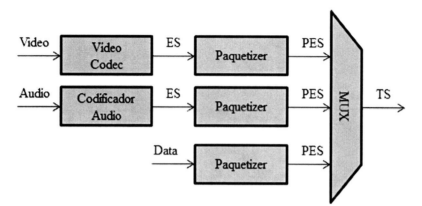

to be provided to feed programs in MHP (Multimedia Home Platform), in the case of the web, the program will need additional data to exploit the advantages which it allows, and similarly for cable, mobiles or future technologies.

To fill these gaps, chains create departments to feed content to these new broadcasting formats and/or adapt their computer systems to select data they need from the production sources themselves. Production sources do not always provide this data and if they do, they are in varying formats, using different communication channels for each event. Channels have to adapt their equipment and communications in each program or event which need this type of data in such a way that they must continuously develop interfaces for content adaptation. These adaptation jobs are carried out by each of the channels, investing in jobs with limited or no return.

MPEG 2 Transport Stream

Despite the different encoding formats that have appeared on the market, the most accepted video transmission format for the contribution, distribution and broadcasting of professional quality video signals remains the standard MPEG2(ISO/IEC, 2000).

In this standard two types of formats are specified, i.e. the transport stream and the program stream. The first is used for transmission because of its greater robustness concerning noises in the channel and the second is used for production in environments with low error rates.

The various errors that may occur during transmission of the transport stream are corrected at reception so as to minimize the effects that may occur in the image. Multiple jobs and methods have been developed for this purpose.

A program consists of several types of data (video, audio, data) which are encapsulated into Elementary Streams (ES) and multiplexed into a data stream. Each of these elementary streams is packaged into Packetized Elementary Stream (PES). In order to keep synchronization between the audio and video data, time stamps are inserted for a correct decoding and displaying of images and sound.

Figure 7 shows the multiplexing of a video signal, audio signal and other data associated with a program stream. In each program stream multiple video, audio or data channels may be associated. The speed of the elementary stream may vary depending on the quality required for the images. To contribute to a central location, the speed can vary from 8 to 50 Mbps. The nature of the images and the transmission purposes will determine the selected quality. To broadcast the signal 2.5 to 7 Mbps is generally used.

Figure 8. N programs multiplexed on a transport stream

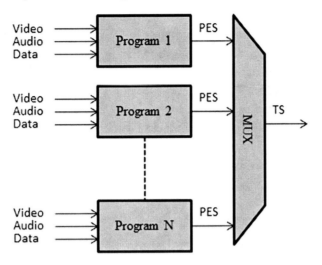

For monitoring distribution channels, either DVB or VoIP, the channels can be compressed to higher rates (e.g. of 4 to 8 Mbps) and several programs can be multiplexed as a single transport stream as shown in Figure 8.

In either case, previous data is accessible from the transport stream which is, thus, generated at the source with the application of inverse operations from the transport stream.

File Transfer

In order to link video between two points, data links are often used unidirectionally to transmit the charge transport stream. The corresponding demultiplexer is installed at the reception.

To transfer over unidirectional links, there are various file transfer protocols based on retransmission patterns of the same file. The Reliable Multicast Transport (RMT) IETF Working Group deals with standardizing reliable multicast one to many transport protocols.

In (Neumann, 2005), a study discusses three types of transfer protocols that can be used in unidirectional networks. The Asynchronous Layered Coding (ALC) (M. Luby, 2002) does not require any feedback from the receivers and the data are encoded using FEC codes. Repetitions of the symbols shipment guarantee the integrity of the file at the expense of effective bandwidth loss.

The Nack Oriented Reliable Multicast (NORM) (B. Adamson, 2004) retransmits only the damaged parts from one of the receptors that send signals of Negative Acknowledgments (NACK) over damaged blocks.

The File Delivery over Unidirectional Transport (FLUTE) (T. Paila, 2004), based on ALC protocol, with the extension to be used in any type of transmission channel (unidirectional or not), offers metadata which complete the image signal itself (e.g. name file, codec, etc.).

MAIN FOCUS OF THE CHAPTER (ANALYSIS)

The spreading of new systems of broadcasting and distribution of multimedia content has had as a consequence a larger need for aggregation of data and metadata to traditionally based contents of video and audio supply. Broadcasters have to add value as data or interactive services to the classic programmes. Broadcasting chains of this type of channels have become overwhelmed by the quantity of resources, infrastructures and development needed for these channels to provide information; channels often lack knowledge about subjects they broadcast because production is performed externally. Knowledge of the material is passing to production companies who in fact fully know the topics of the programs.

When an event will be transmitted, producer companies usually send data or specify the data format with the communication link and parameters to use during the event. Broadcasting companies have to adapt and/or develop their IT and communication infrastructure in order to receive the data associated to the program itself. Data have to be transformed, filtered, processed and adapted for each technology. These processes increase the production cost for the events, and this events usually occurs during a short period of time (normally hours).

The creation of data and additional content to the program signal require a close coordination between producers and broadcasters, modification of channel systems, adaptation of the media and application vigilance during emission. These jobs increase production cost and are not normally undertaken in live retransmissions. Necessary conditions for these services to be offered to viewers pass from:

• Decrease cost of content production
• Decrease cost of system development
• Establish communications systems
• Ensure dissemination of this content during the event.

In order to avoid this kind of shortcomings, several recommendations and standards have been created to exchange metadata between production and distribution of stored programs. The problem lies in live programs, which in many of them, data is a very important part for understanding the event to be broadcasted. Producers sometimes offer data to channels but most often, channels are not able to face developments which are required,

due to above all, uncertainty of the return in their investment. The solution to this problem includes reduction of implementation costs for development of services on these new platforms.

For this type of work, creation of a team composed of producers, chains, communication companies, viewer associations, etc. would be needed to define the needs of each.

Environment

In order to achieve the above mentioned objectives, the purpose of this work is based on three models: data, application and communications.

A. Data: Coordination between production and broadcasting can be avoided if data to be transferred among different agents is standardized; in such a way that each knows the format in which data will arrive at any time. This standardization could be done under any technology; the one suggested in this work is the use of XML documents for this transfer, so that creation of a metamodel would be necessary to include all possible services which can be offered among all parties. The choice of XML documents would be of great assistance when using the application.

B. Application: To avoid system modification for each event, the application would have the capacity to receive the metamodel which is created for data exchange and also proposes the following characteristics:
  ◦ Data filtering, for cases in which channels do not want to receive the shower of data some kinds of events may generate.
  ◦ Processing and management of alarms, to determine which of the received data is more interesting and to use alarms which alert different types of events.
  ◦ Distribution to different broadcasting media, so that received and processed

data can be shown on web, DVB-h, mobiles, etc.

C.   Communications: The communications channel between the different parties should be conducted with the same medium, so that communications adaptation will not be necessary for any type of event.

Services

To be able to affront the data model which can serve producers as well as distribution chains, analysis of the type of services which can or usually are offered by producers is necessary.

A.   Assistance to commentators: In certain events, commentators have screens with data at their desks which assist them during retransmission. These screens are usually video monitors in which data the organizers deem appropriate appear in a cyclical way. Also, they are usually terminals connected to a data network with a program which shows these data. Commentators must physically be in the stadium to be able to receive these data.

B.   Graphics and titling: The program signal usually comes with heading in international language. To allow chains to be able to insert their own heading, a clean feed is distributed, so that TV channels can insert their own titles with graphics and language they are interested in (if they have the rights to do so).

C.   Subtitling: For taped programs, as was seen in the above chapter, there is much redundant information, areas and processes when doing subtitling work. The model proposed for this application is classification, as in audio, of original and natural subtitles.

D.   File: One of the discussions which are usually repetitive over time in TV channels revolves around the philosophy of the file to be implemented in each company. One of the aspects of these discussions is the filing of material with or without graphics, titled images are usually considered to be "dirty" but they contain information about test data, clean images are perfect for filing because of their ease of reuse, when the image is titled it is more complicated to remake another heading because there may be problems with composition among titles.

E.   Advertising: This is the main return on the investment made in purchase of retransmission rights of events. Many of these events have strict regulations on spaces in which publicity can be broadcasted; this publicity may range from lengthy spaces to small headings inserted in the image. TV channels must decide in real time the moment they can insert their advertisement publicity as the event develops. To provide this service, delivery of a signal would be necessary to indicate the possibility of showing advertisements, their length and type of advertisement that can be included.

F.   Education: In our society, e-learning is being used more and more by people who want to acquire different types of knowledge. Events of a minority nature have regulations which many times are unknown to viewers who are not used to these shows. A visualization of the rules as far as how a game is played can enrich content and provide comprehension. This delivery of rules can be made in a structured way, to be shown on a web page during internet emission or on screen when each of the rules is applied, when the user chooses.

Programs

In this section, the convenience or not of each of the above services will be analyzed. It will be necessary to see the type of programs which are usually shown live and associate them to the different services.

A.   Sports: These are of the programs in which data are very important for the commentators as well as for graphic generation.

B.   Live Music: Retransmission of music concerts is becoming more frequent, classical as well as modern. In the specific case of opera, most people do not understand the meaning of the songs or the plot. Subtitling song lyrics can assist a great deal in understanding opera.

C.   Elections: They are of the most important events in politics. Data are generated by each organism. In Spain there are at least 23 elections every four years: European, national, Senate, 17 regional and local elections. Chains have video links with each electoral seat where results are read; chains can receive homogeneous information in the same video signal.

General Model

As has been put forward in previous chapters, the data delivery model between production companies and dissemination chains is made on the same video signal and is extensible to diffusion between users by DVB in its modes of satellite, terrestrial, mobiles or cable.

A.   File transmission: For delivery of XML documents, the transmission model which is used must be taken into account:

   ◦   Contribution. For delivery of information from a production centre to a receiving centre, it is a one on one communication. It is the typical case of delivery of generated data in a stadium to the International Broadcaster Centre (IBC) in Olympic Games. Because it is a one-few type of delivery, transmission will be by means of NORM (B. Adamson, 2004), since it has a good response for few receiving stations.

   ◦   Distribution. For information delivery from one centre to many receivers. It is the type of one to many transmissions. A clear example might be delivery of the final Wimbledon tennis match in which there are large quantities of receiving stations that need information. For this case, the use of FLUTE (T. Paila, 2004) is proposed, with a return line by Internet, so that chains which do not receive information can ask for retransmission of data.

   ◦   Broadcasting. In order to send files from a broadcasting chain to viewers, in this case the number of receivers increases considerably and poor radio electrical installations may influence poor reception of the files, so that re-delivery petitions which are demanded on return lines may collapse transmission. The best adapted protocol is FLUTE without return line.

B.   Distribution and content filtering: In production as well as reception, depending on the type of event, filtering or distribution of content may be necessary. Application of XML technologies simplifies these tasks since using XSLT documents they can be done in a simple way. XSLT is a language which transforms XML documents into other documents whether they are XML or other formats, see Figure 9.

Depending on the type of service, this conversion can be made at the source or at the destination. For the specific case of the Olympic Games and data distribution in each channel in the IBC, this transformation is made at the signal distribution to each channel. For the case of a channel that wishes to send content to different distribution media, this filter can be made at each channel, sending data to each broadcasting channel.

Figure 9. Generic process for XML by XSLT

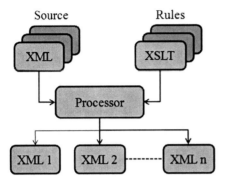

XSLT has the necessary functions to be able to manage complex transformation requirements and provide great flexibility to the system since exit data, as well as their configuration can be modified in a simple way only by changing the XSLT document, with the need to recompile the program since the document is read in execution time.

C.   *Communications:* The medium proposed in this work is the use of the same video channel where image and sound is received for transfer of these data. This proposal is based above all on synchronization of data with image and audio, being the same physical medium, data will pass through on the same way, so that synchronization will occur naturally. If it were sent otherwise, synchronization would be necessary by insertion of common time codes. This solution would require the slowing of material which arrives before, if data arrive before, the slowing is simple, the problem occurs when video arrives before because this causes serious inconveniences for emission. The MPEG2 TS, is used not only to carry compressed images in MPEG2 but also for other types of formats such as MPEG4 or JPEG2000 *(S. Narasimhan, 2009)*, this is being studied by the European Broadcaster Union (EBU) for its use in professional distribution links.

Titling

Titling is an example of service. For remote form heading, production data generation and extraction will be needed; its delivery and production in the remote position (J. Martínez Barbero, 2009).

A.   Data extraction: There are two types of installations, master and slave. As can be seen in Figure 10 corresponding to the master, the mixer consists of 1 to n entrances with its corresponding signal entrances (10 ..In) and an exit of Gpi's (On). The system consists of spy software in charge of watching operations which are conducted in the title station, the data will be: the label model next to text, pages which are prepared for broadcasting next to the page which is at the titling exit.

In the figure, the classical installation of the mixer of a production control can be observed. The video entrances enter to the mixer to choose one source or another in the exit channel. Titling is completed on other independent equipment which acts as an entry source and when one wants to insert a heading, this signal is mixed with the exit at each moment. The GPI signal associated with titling must be taken into account; this signal is activated when the heading is shown in the exit.

The blue part of Figure 7 is the added components to the installation. The system consists of spy software in charge of watching operations which are made in the titling station, the data will be: the heading model next to its text, pages which are prepared for emission next to the page which is at the titling exit. On the other hand, detection will be needed every time the title to emission is clicked on by the GPI's detector, each time this signal is set to one, the trigger detector sends an impulse to indicate the mixer going on air. The different data are multiplexed on the exit transport stream together with the video without heading and international audio for its distribution to different televisions.

Figure 10. Titling and mixing connections

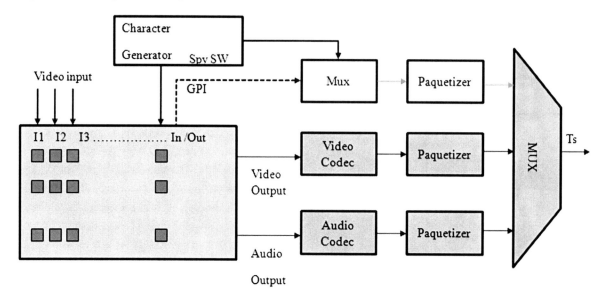

In the broadcasters' installations, the signal must be multiplexed to extract different signals and data. The installation will be an opposite replica of the base station. By the remote control of the titler, the same commands of heading generation and presentation are made as at the origin. The GPI signal is regenerated again to order the mixer to put the title on air each time that a heading is clicked on in the mixer at the origin.

B.   Distribution and content conversion: Files to be transmitted will have an XML structure, for better adaptation of different results to the titling device, a stream of data will be obtained from union of the different files which will be absorbed on the video stream.

At the destination station, the system must process the content which arrives together with the image, for delivery of commands to titling stations. Two types of translation will be necessary: adaptation of messages to language, possibly including personalization of publicity and adaptation of commands to the titling machine, since the destination broadcaster may have equipment with a different protocol to that producing the signal.

Before retransmission of each event, a distribution of the texts will be necessary that are presumably going to be used so that in each television translations can be made of each item and generating XSLT's for language and for destination equipment commands.

As shown in Figure 11, the XML entrance generates a continuous stream of data by XML files. To give the system more modularity, it is divided into two processes, translation to the country's language and the corresponding translation to equipment commands. For each type of message which arrives from event production, there is an associated XSLT which contains message translations. Once conversion of language is completed, conversion is carried out of specific commands for the type of equipment required; there will also be an XSLT for each type of command which will be run.

The problem: In sporting event transmissions of international significance, broadcasting in each country is carried out by the owner of the rights for that particular country. The output signal (program signal) in the original production center normally contains the graphic elements presented

Figure 11. Language and equipment translation steps

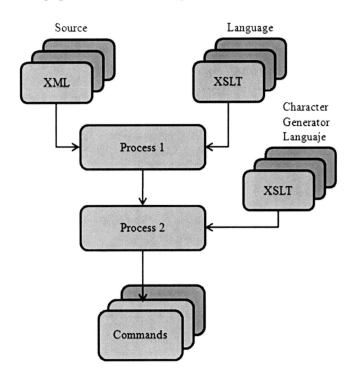

in the language considered the most international: English.

The problem created by this "dirty" signal in the different broadcasters is double: On one hand, title adaptation produces the superposition of different graphics on a same image. On the other hand, those titles will remain in the channel's historical files.

If we send the data into the MPEG2 stream we solve both problems.

C.   Production side: There will be two types of installations: Master and Slave installations. As Master figure shows in Figure7, the mixer consists of 1 to n inputs (10...In) and a GPI's (On) output (General Purpose Interface).

The system consists of spy software in charge of watching over the operations performed in the titling station. The type of data generated will consist of: The model of title together with its text,

the pages being prepared for their broadcast and the page located at the character generator output.

On the other hand it will be necessary to detect every time the character generator for broadcast is "punctured" by means of the GPI's detector. Each time this signal is set to 1, the triggering detector sends an impulse to indicate the mixer has been set to air. The various data are multiplexed over the output transport stream, together with the video without titling and the international audio, for its distribution to the different televisions. The transport stream is uplinked to the satellite for its distribution as in Figure 12 to the different broadcasters.

Within the broadcasters' facilities, the signal must be multiplexed to obtain the different signals and data. By means of the character generator's remote control, they are being executed the same generation and title-display commands as in the origin. As we can see in Figure 13, the GPI signal regenerates again to command the mixer to punc-

Figure 12. Delivery of video, audio, and data in a transport stream over satellite link

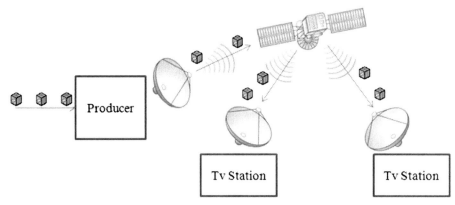

Figure 13. Data flow between production and TV channels for remote titling

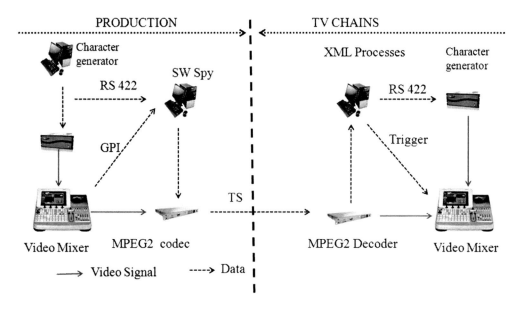

ture the character generator, every time that, in its origin, a title is punctured in the mixer.

Subtitling

Live events: Two types of tasks are presented: preproduction and playout. In preproduction, a distribution of files is carried out with identification of each heading while in emission only the identifier absorbed in the video signal is sent (Barbero & Pérez, 2009).

- Preproduction: Files are distributed to chains, which carry out translation of each of the subtitles in the languages desired, information as far as entry time for each subtitle is only one reference, never a real data, since it is a live program, this data can vary. The DFXP file contains all necessary information; with the exception that fields begin and end is purely tentative being a live program, if time of duration

Figure 14. File distribution workflow

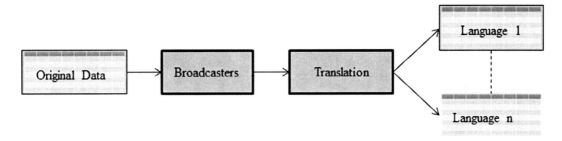

Box 4.

```
<body region="subtitleArea">
  <div>
    <p xml:id="subt1" begin="25s" end="27s" duration="2.0s" Hello Figaro
      </p></div>
<p xml:id="subtitle2" begin="30s" end="32s" duration="2.0s">
      Are you alone?
    </p>
</body>
The translated file is shown in Box 5.
Box 5.
<body region="subtitleArea">
  <div>
        <p xml:id="subt1" begin="25s" end="27s" duration="2.0s"
          Hola Fígaro
      </p></div>
<p xml:id="subtitle2" begin="30s" end="32s" duration="2.0s">
      ¿Estás solo?
    </p>
</body>
```

exposition is more real. The workflow can see in Figure 14.

An example of the distribution file is shown in Box 4.

• Playout: During emission the text identifier is sent which is to be shown in the PES packet of data in the MPEG2 TS ass it can see in Figure 15. Each packet can be sent

many times by FLUTE protocol to avoid transmission errors. Delay in audio or video is usually quite troublesome in such a way that de-synchronization between audio-video is produced, this margin is usually 200mS, in the case of headings, this delay is not as strict and almost a second can be waited without the viewer noticing, so that the identifier can be sent many times using this protocol.

Figure 15. Identification transmission

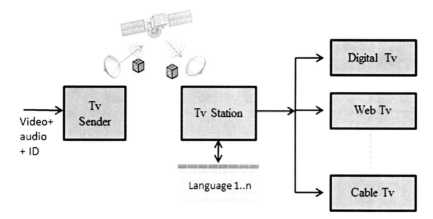

Box 5.

```
<body region="subtitleArea">
  <div>
        <p xml:id="subt1" begin="28s" end="30s" duration="2.0s"
           Hola Fígaro
    </p></div>
<p xml:id="subtitle2" begin="32s" end="34s" duration="2.0s">
        ¿Estás solo?
    </p>
</body>
```

When an identifier reaches the television channel, a simple search is conducted of the identifier in the translated file, selecting information to incorporate it as a subtitle in the broadcasting.

On a parallel, a DFXP file is generated with the synchronized information of audio, video and data and its later filing for possible future broadcasting.

An example of XML which is sent in broadcasting will be

```
<div>
        <p xml:id="subt1"
    </p></div>
```

Showing the text "Estás solo?" for another two seconds.

The file being stored for file will have real data synchronized with the time code of the video (see Box 5).

Rest of Services

To assist commentators, each of the channels can prepare its own XSLT to receive information they consider to be most appropriate.

Before saving file material, the filter can be made in the same buildings of the TV chains; selecting data they want to store and which each company believes useful for later broadcasting or viewing.

Filtering of entry data flow can be made the same way for its distribution to other media so they feed each of the installed platforms without need to create specific content for each of them, in the same way education can be carried out with possible levels of aid.

CONCLUSION AND FUTURE RESEARCH DIRECTIONS

In this work an effort has been made to lower development costs of broadcasting companies in audiovisual content, based on delivery of data and metadata associated with live programs by video lines which are necessary for program broadcasting. This lowering of cost not only benefits broadcasting companies but also users who can benefit from the advantages they will have by being able to access data and assistance that the producer of the program has. On the other hand, the advantages have been shown of the possibility that the video itself carries incorporated data, advantages in synchronization, filing, program reuse etc.

There is a long road to development, there are still more services needed, documentary automatic systems from the metadata which are carried by video, alerting systems, automatic production systems which select video lines from data which are sent along them and to be redefined by user and artistic, etc.

REFERENCES

Adamson, B., Bormann, C., Handley, M., & Macker, J. (2004). *Negative-acknowledgment (NACK)-oriented reliable multicast (NORM) protocol.*

Barbero, J. M., & Pérez, M. B. (2009). *Multi-language opera subtitling exchange between production and broadcaster companies.* 7th International Conference Information Research and Applications. Madrid, Spain: iTECH.

BBC Technology. (2003). *Standard media exchange framework -- SMEF data model version 1.10. (Technical report).*

DublinCore. (2003). *Dublin Core metadata element set, version 1.1: Reference description.*

EBU. (2005). *P/Meta metadata exchange scheme v1.1. Technical report.* Tech. European Broadcasting Union.

EBU. (2007). *Escort: EBU system of classification of RTV programmes.*

ETSI. (1997). *Digital video broadcasting (DVB): Subtitling systems.* European Telecommunications Standards Institute.

Evain, J. (2000). *TV-Anytime metadata: A preliminary specification on schedule.* EBU Tchnical Review No.284.

ISO. (2002). *International standard audiovisual number (ISAN)- Part 1: Audiovisual work identifier. ISO 15706-1.*

ISO. (2004). *Guidelines on V-ISAN. ISO 15706.*

ISO/IEC. (2000). *13818-1 Information technology — Generic coding of moving pictures and associated audio information: Systems.*

Luby, M., Watson, M., & Vicisano, L. (2002). *Asynchronous layered coding (ALC) protocol instantiation, request for comments 3450.*

Martínez Barbero, J., Santos Menendez, E., & Gutierrez Rodriguez, A. (2009). *Automatic titling for international sporting events.* Conference UPGRADE-CN '09 High Performance Distributed Computing HPDC, Garching, Germany, June 09 - 09, 2009. ACM.

Narasimhan, S. (2009). *Working draft 1.0 – Transport of ISO/IEC 15444-1/AMD4 video over ITU-T Rec H.222.0 | ISO/IEC 13818-1.* Londres.

Neumann, C. R. (2005). Large scale content distribution protocols. *SIGCOMM Computer Communicaiton Review, 35*(5).

Paila, T. (2004). *FLUTE - File delivery over unidirectional transport.*

Reimers, U. (2006). DVB-The Family of International Standards for Digital Video Broadcasting. *Proceedings of the IEEE, 94*(1), 173–182. doi:10.1109/JPROC.2005.861004

W3C. (2010). *Timed text markup language (TTML) 1.0 – Distribution format exchange profile (DFXP).*

Chapter 11
Estimating the Completeness of Range Queries over Structured P2P Databases:
Fundamentals, Theory, and Effective Applications to Distributed Information Systems

Alfredo Cuzzocrea
ICAR-CNR, Italy & University of Calabria, Italy

Marcel Karnstedt
DERI, NUI Galway, Ireland

Manfred Hauswirth
DERI, NUI Galway, Ireland

Kai-Uwe Sattler
Ilmenau University of Technology, Germany

Roman Schmidt
Ecole Polytechnique Federale de Lausanne, Switzerland

ABSTRACT

Range queries are a very powerful tool in a wide range of data management systems and are vital to a multitude of applications. The hierarchy of structured overlay systems can be utilized in order to provide efficient techniques for processing them, resulting in the support of applications and techniques based on range queries in large-scale distributed information systems. On the other hand, due to the rapid development of the Web, applications based on the P2P paradigm gain more and more interest, having such systems started to evolve towards adopting standard database functionalities in terms of complex query processing support. This goes far beyond simple key lookups, as provided by standard distributed hashtables (DHTs) systems, which makes estimating the completeness of query answers a crucial chal-

DOI: 10.4018/978-1-4666-1794-0.ch011

lenge. Unfortunately, due to the limited knowledge and the usually best-effort characteristics, deciding about the completeness of query results, e.g., getting an idea when a query is finished or what amount of results is still missing, is very challenging. There is not only an urgent need to provide this information to the user issuing queries, but also for implementing sophisticated and efficient processing techniques based on them. In this chapter, the authors propose a method for solving this task. They discuss the applicability and quality of the estimations, present an implementation and evaluation for the P-Grid system, and show how to adapt the technique to other overlays. The authors also discuss the semantics of completeness for complex queries in P2P database systems and propose methods based on the notion of routing graphs for estimating the number of expected query answers. Finally, they discuss probabilistic guarantees for the estimated values and evaluate the proposed methods through an implemented system.

INTRODUCTION

Many new applications on the Web are based on the idea of collecting and combining large public data sets and services. In such public data management applications, the information, its structure and its semantics in many cases are the result of the collaborative effort of the participants. Examples of such applications are social networks, e.g., friend-of-a-friend networks, distributed recommender systems, distributed directory and index services, and sharing of sensor data. These applications typically require the indexing and management of data distributed over a large number of independent data stores, which is a typical scenario targeted by overlay networks.

P2P systems and particularly structured overlays based on distributed hashtables (DHTs) are recognized as a promising infrastructure for large-scale distributed data management. The main reasons are their effectiveness and scalability as well as the predictable behavior. After the first generation supporting only basic key lookups, recent research efforts address also the problem of efficiently querying range predicates (Bharambe, A., Agrawal, M., Seshan, S. (2004); Datta, A., Hauswirth, M., Schmidt, R., John, R., Aberer, K. (2005)). Typically, these approaches exploit the structure of the overlay (e.g., a tree structure) by implementing some kind of multicast protocol. In this context, a main challenge is to estimate the progress of query processing, i.e., to answer the question which fraction of the total query result is already received. The difficulties are due to the purely decentralized nature of the structured overlay, the lack of global knowledge (no peer knows how many peers are responsible for the queried key range), the dynamics of the network (peers may leave the network during processing a query), as well as the often used best-effort strategy for query routing and answering. Indeed, P2P data management is inherently open world: While processing a query, peers can fail, leave or join the network, or simply send no or a delayed answer (Gribble, S.D., Halevy, A.Y., Ives, Z.G., Rodrig, M., Suciu, D. (2001)). Though this can be mitigated by replication and delay-tolerant query techniques, there is no guarantee that all answers which potentially exist can be returned. On the other hand, DHTs, the most efficient family of overlay networks, so far have only been applicable to a certain degree in these scenarios, as support for managing and querying structured data in DHTs still is limited.

Estimating the completeness of a query result is not only a helpful information for the user issuing the query, but it is also needed for processing complex queries. For instance, query operators like aggregation or ranking-based queries (e.g., skyline queries (Börzsönyi, S., Kossmann, D., Stocker, K. (2001); Karnstedt, M.,Müller, J., Sattler, K. (2007))) require to know when all input data is arrived in order to calculate the aggregate value or to sort the input. Thus, we argue that estimating the completeness of query answers is a key aspect of reliable query processing in P2P databases.

In this chapter, we propose a solution to problems above. The general idea underlying our vision is that an approximated, but prompt estimation is often satisfying for the user. The objective of our work is to estimate the completeness of range queries as a fundamental operator for more complex query operators and to give guarantees on the quality of this estimation. The idea is to map the completeness on data level to a completeness on peer level, thus, estimating a number of replies expected for each query. This, of course, is still very challenging in the investigated systems. We achieve this by estimating the number of query answers without explicitly analyzing the actual content of each answer. Note that we are not trying to guarantee completeness, neither we want to improve the functionality of the underlying DHT. Instead we only get what is available at query time ("in situ querying") but are able to assess the completeness of this result. Furthermore, we aim at an incremental and online refinement of the estimation.

We have implemented the proposed approach in our UniStore system (Karnstedt, M., Sattler, K., Richtarsky, M., Müller, J., Hauswirth, M., Schmidt, R., John, R. (2007)), which is based on the P-Grid overlay (Aberer, K. (2001)). But we show also how the main idea can be applied to other DHTs, too. UniStore supports complex structured database-like queries and thus, strongly benefits from a method for estimating query completeness. For instance, aggregation queries and skyline queries internally rely on range queries. Results of such queries can be processed after a satisfyingly significant portion of the result data (e.g., 90%) is received, rather than demanding for complete result sets. Due to the usually parallelized processing of range queries in DHT overlays, the decision whether a result set is complete or satisfyingly large can only be made using a

sophisticated method for completeness estimation as proposed in this work. This will not save bandwidth or processing power, as later replies are still transmitted, but eliminates the need for static waiting states and enables speedy processing of subsequent operators of complex queries.

Overall, the main contribution of our work is the development of lightweight techniques for providing reliable information about the result completeness of complex database-like queries in a dynamic and unreliable P2P environment. This leverages modern Web applications without the need for precomputed data summaries or detailed global information.

The remainder of this chapter is structured as follows. Section 2 introduces definitions of range queries over structured P2P databases and their implementation on P-Grid – the Section also gives an insight on the main (range) query completeness concept. Section 3 formally provides principles and definition of completeness estimation, by also discussing some critical aspects coming from practical observations deriving from preliminary experiments. In Section 4, we review related work that is relevant for our research. In Section 5, we present in detail the novel method for estimating the completeness of range queries over structured P2P databases we propose, which represents the effective main contribution of our research. Section 6 shows how completeness estimation can be successfully exploited in order to effectively and efficiently process range queries over structured P2P databases. Section 7 contains closed theoretical formulas for providing probabilistic guarantees over completeness estimates retrieved by our proposed method. In Section 8, we provide a comprehensive experimental evaluation and assessment that clearly shows the benefits due to our proposed completeness estimation method, under the variation of several experimental parameters and perspectives. Finally, we conclude the chapter by highlighting conclusions and future work of our research in Section 9.

BACKGROUND

Problem Statement: Range Queries over Structured P2P Databases, and the (Range) Query Completeness Concept

Range queries were proposed in the past for several structured overlays (Datta, A., Hauswirth, M., Schmidt, R., John, R., Aberer, K. (2005)), (Bharambe, A., Agrawal, M., Seshan, S. (2004)), (Aspnes, J., Shah, G. (2003); Aspnes, J., Kirsch, J., Krishnamurthy, A. (2004)), (Ramabhadran, S., Ratnasamy, S., Hellerstein, J.M., Shenker, S. (2004); Liau, C.Y., Ng, W.S., Shu, Y., Tan, K.L., Bressan, S. (2004)), (Gupta, A., Agrawal, D., Abbadi, A.E. (2003); Sahin, O.D., Gupta, A., Agrawal, D., Abbadi, A.E. (2004)). Like UniStore, (Daniel, B., Hurley, P., Pletka, R., Waldvogel, M. (2004)) proposes methods for range queries and advanced query types on DHT overlays. But, this work lacks discussion about estimating query completeness. We base our work on the approach presented in (Datta, A., Hauswirth, M., Schmidt, R., John, R., Aberer, K. (2005)) using P-Grid (Aberer, K. (2001)) as structured overlay network. P-Grid organizes nodes in a binary trie structure, which is a standard indexing structure from databases to support among others range queries. A key benefit of tries is that they cluster semantically close data items, which is a critical pre-condition for efficient processing of range queries. Traditional DHTs such as Chord or Pastry use uniform hashing functions to map application keys to their identifier space. While this achieves good storage load-balancing and efficient discovery of exact keys, it is in conflict with preserving the semantic proximity as it destroys existing relations among the application-specific keys. Keys which are semantically close at the application level are heavily fragmented in a DHT. We will now briefly present the P-Grid overlay and its range query algorithm. More details can be found in (Datta, A., Hauswirth, M., Schmidt, R., John, R., Aberer, K. (2005)).

The P-Grid Overlay

In P-Grid peers refer to a common underlying binary trie structure to organize their routing tables. Data keys are computed using an order-preserving hash function to generate keys. Without constraining general applicability binary keys are used in P-Grid. Each peer constructs its routing table such that it holds peers with exponentially increasing distance in the key space from its own position. This technique basically builds a small-world graph (Kleinberg, J. (1999)) which enables search in $O(\log N)$ steps. Each peer $p \in P$ is associated with a leaf of the binary trie, i.e., a key space partition which corresponds to a binary string $\pi(p) \in \Pi$ called the peer's *path*. For search, the peer stores for each prefix $\pi(p, l)$ of $\pi(p)$ of length l a set of references $\rho(p, l)$ to peers q with property $\overline{\pi(p, l)} = \pi(q, l)$, where $\overline{\pi}$ is the binary string π with the last bit inverted. This means that at each level of the trie the peer has references to some other peers that do not pertain to the peer's sub-trie at that level which enables the implementation of prefix routing.

Each peer stores a set of data items $\delta(p)$. For $d \in \delta(p)\ key(d)$ has $\pi(p)$ as prefix but it is not excluded that temporarily also other data items are stored at a peer, that is, the set $\delta(p, \pi(p))$ of data items whose key matches $\pi(p)$ can be a proper subset of $\delta(p)$. Moreover, for fault-tolerance, query load-balancing, and hot-spot handling, multiple peers are associated with the same key-space partition (structural replication), and peers additionally also maintain multiple references $\sigma(p)$ to peers with the same path (data replication).

Figure 1 shows a simple example of a P-Grid tree consisting of 6 peers responsible for 4 partitions, e.g., peer F's path is 00 leading to two entries in its routing table: peer E with path 11 at the first level and peer B with path 01 at the second level.

Figure 1. P-Grid overlay network

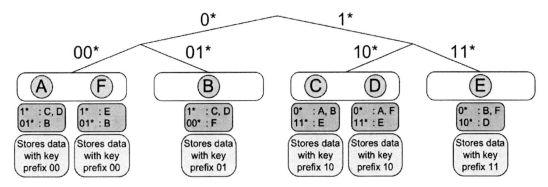

Further, peer F is responsible for all data with key prefix 00. A search initiated at peer F for key 100 would first be forwarded to peer E because it is the only entry in F's routing table at level 1*. As peer E is responsible for 11 and not for the key 100, peer E further forwards the query to peer D, which can finally answer the query.

Range Queries

Range queries in P-Grid are first forwarded to an arbitrary peer responsible for any of the key space partitions within the range, and then the query is forwarded to the other partitions in the interval using this peer's routing table. The process is recursive, and since the query is split in multiple queries, which appear to trickle down to all the key-space partitions in the range, it is called the *shower algorithm*. The intuition of the algorithm is shown graphically in Figure 2.

In the course of forwarding, it is possible that the query is forwarded to a peer responsible for keys outside the range. However, it is guaranteed that this peer will forward the range query back to a key-space partition within the range. Moreover, the P-Grid routing ensures that no key space partition will get duplicates of the range queries. Algorithm 1 gives the pseudo code for the shower algorithm.

(Datta, A., Hauswirth, M., Schmidt, R., John, R., Aberer, K. (2005)) also proposes a more in-

tuitive algorithm, which could further be applied to any other structured overlay. The basic idea is to first find the lower (or upper) bound of a range query and then sequentially forward the query along neighbors till the upper (or lower) bound is reached. The simplicity of using only one message has the disadvantages that (i) losing the query message results in the immediate termination of the range query as no further peer is reached and no further data will be returned; (ii) forwarding one message sequentially along neighbors can result in a very long query response time depending on the size of the queried range and the number of peers involved. We will therefore focus on the shower algorithm as its performance is considerable better in terms of response time whereas requiring only a slightly larger number of messages.

Query Completeness

Though it is guaranteed by the shower algorithm that all peers receive exactly one range query message, it is currently not possible for the initiating peer to estimate the number of peers concerned by a range query, i.e., estimating the number of response messages it has to expect. For keyword based queries, a peer receives only one query response by one peer in a structured overlay network as only one peer (or any of its replicas) is responsible for the given keyword. A peer is

Figure 2. Range query illustration

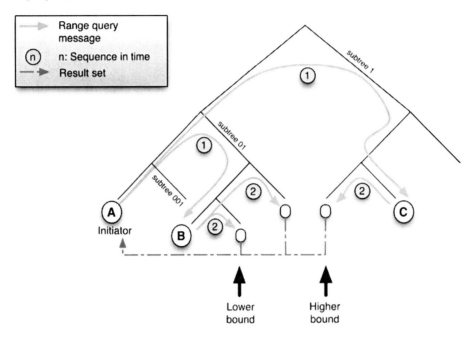

Algorithm 1. shower(R,$l_{current}$, p)

1: **if** $\pi(p) \subseteq R$ **then**

2:     return$(d \in \delta(p)|key(d) \in R)$;

3: **end if**

4: determine l_l such that $\pi(min(R),l_l) = \overline{\pi(p,l_l)}$;

5: determine l_h such that $\pi(max(R),l_h) = \overline{\pi(p,l_h)}$;

6: $l_{min} = max(l_{current}, min(l_l,l_h))$;

7: $l_{max} = max(l_l,l_h)$;

8: **if** $l_{current} < l_{max}$ **then**

9:     **for** $l = l_{min}$ to l_{max} **do**

10:         r = randomly selected element from $\rho(p,l)$;

11:         shower(R, l+1, r);

12:     **end for**

13: **end if**

therefore able to determine when a query finished and when it received all matching items to either inform a user, start post-processing or initiate subsequent queries. This is currently not possible for range queries in structured overlay networks as the number of response messages depends on the number of peers in the target range, which is usually not know for a peer. We will present in the following section our approach to estimate this number based on the local information available in a peer's routing table and corrected by intermediate peers forwarding range queries or peers responding to range queries. We thereby assume a load-balanced system where each peer holds approximately the same amount of data. Load-balancing in DHTs has been studied intensively as it is one of the main principles of DHTs and (Aberer, K., Datta, A., Hauswirth, M., Schmidt, R. (2005)) presents its realization for P-Grid and evaluation on a real-world test-bed. Hence estimating the number of responding peers is equivalent to estimating the number of query hits expected to be retrieved by a range query.

Completeness Estimation: Principles and Definitions

Estimating the completeness of queries should intuitively be bound to the data level: the user is interested in what fraction of all expected result hits he already received. This also holds for subsequent processing steps following the execution of range queries. As briefly mentioned in the last section, predicting completeness on data level is almost impossible without enormous costs. Fortunately, in a load-balanced overlay system this completeness can be mapped to completeness on reply level, because each reply should deliver approximately the same number of results. This is especially true for range queries, because no filtering steps are applied – if a peer is responsible for a part of the range, it will return all of its local data items. Moreover, we will show that we are able to guarantee to identify the last query reply when receiving it. Thus, a completeness of 100% on reply level corresponds to a guaranteed completeness of 100% on data level. So, for subsequent operations that rely on complete range query replies estimation on reply level is absolutely satisfying. In order to show its applicability for other situations, in Section 8 we show that completeness on data level and reply level almost match. Note that, due to the characteristics of sophisticated overlays, the majority of queries will be answered completely.

The notion of completeness has been discussed in the literature mainly in the context of data quality, e.g., in (Motro, A. (1986); Naumann, F., Freytag, J.C., Leser, U. (2004)) where completeness is typically understood as the ratio of answer set size to the total amount of known data. However, this definition does not apply in our context as it requires the knowledge of the total amount of data in the system and relies on the closed world assumption. To come to a meaningful definition which is applicable in our context we have to distinguish between data availability and completeness of query answering. We introduce the following refined definitions.

Data availability denotes the classical notion of completeness, i.e., what amount of data w.r.t. the real world is stored in a system. Availability can be seen (more or less) as a static aspect if we assume that good replication techniques are used to deal with churn (peer failures or peers joining/leaving) (Bhagwan, R., Moore, D., Savage, S., Voelker, G.M. (2002)).

Completeness of query answers, in contrast, denotes the ratio of the amount of data of the answer A to a query Q and the amount of answers $\overline{A}$ we would get if all peers participating at query time t would respond: $C(Q)[t] = \dfrac{|A(Q)[t]|}{|\overline{A(Q)[t]}|}$. Note, that this also holds true for any sub-query of Q, i.e., for each intermediate operator the completeness of its result can be estimated.

Our notion of completeness deals with the dynamic aspects inherent in P2P systems and addresses the problem of churn during query processing. Note, that replication helps to solve the problem of "guaranteeing" that data is available over time but may not help if peers which are expected to process portions of a certain query fail or leave during processing (Bhagwan, R., Moore, D., Savage, S., Voelker, G.M. (2002)). Figure 3 shows this problem in a real-world situation from a Planet-Lab experiment: it shows the fraction of received results and expected results versus time for three queries each initiated 15 times.

Depending on the complexity of the query, the average result size is significantly below the expected size. This is normal in such systems, but cannot be recognized nor handled accordingly without an accurate completeness estimation.

For estimating completeness of query answers in P2P systems we can basically distinguish two main approaches: estimating (1) on *data level* and (2) on *peer level*. The data level approach is based on data summaries representing the distribution of data of all or only a subset of peers. Using this information, the received answers can be compared to the expected answers to estimate the ratio be-

Figure 3. Result quality in Planet-Lab

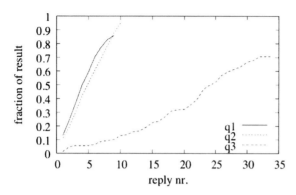

tween these two sets. In contrast, the peer level approach does not count the received data items in the answer but the responding peers. Based on this and on information about the structure of the DHT, the numbers of the responding peers and the expected number of responding peers are compared. The underlying assumption is that data is balanced among the peers and that a linear correlation between the number of failed peers and the resulting miss of data from the expected answers exists. This assumption holds in DHTs providing load balancing features such as P-Grid (Aberer, K., Hauswirth, M., Punceva, M., Schmidt, R. (2002)). For peer level estimation the above definition of completeness has to be modified accordingly: $C(Q)[t] = \dfrac{|P(Q)[t]|}{|\overline{P}(Q)[t]|}$ where P and $\overline{P}$ denote the set of all peers responding to query Q and the set of expected peers responding to Q resp.

In this chapter, we focus on this peer level approach for the following reason: because there is no need to maintain summary information about data beside the routing information which is needed anyway, the peer level approach is much cheaper and better suited for large-scale and dynamic networks.

In the following, we will introduce our basic approach and the principles it is based on. An empirical evaluation and thoughts on determining

a quality of the estimation are presented in the subsequent sections.

Analysis of Related Work

Existing works on completeness estimation exists both in relational and distributed database systems, e.g., (Motro, A. (1986)), where the concept of partial completeness in relational databases by means of *completeness constraints* is first formalized. The notion of completeness in terms of the relations that are true in the real world and the actual relations available in the database is presented in (Levy, A.Y. (1996)) relating the problem of query answering from incomplete databases to that of independence of queries from updates. (Brevik, J., Nurmi, D., Wolski, R. (2004)) and (Massoulié, L., Merrer, E.L., Kermarrec, A.M., Ganesh, A. (2006)) discuss the effect of peer availability on data availability is discussed and propose a peer prediction mechanism based on statistical and random walk methods following the approaches used in managed servers. Completeness is considered as a specific facet of information quality in (Naumann, F., Freytag, J.C., Leser, U. (2004)). Most of these works apply completeness estimation from a different point of view than we do. The aimed application scenario is usually located in the area of information integration and focuses on data quality. We focus on completeness as the fraction of received results and expected results.

A recent system dealing with the problem of completeness estimation in structured overlays is Seaweed (Narayanan, D., Donnelly, A., Mortier, R., Rowstron, A. (2006)), which facilitates to estimate query completeness directly on data level. For this, Seaweed uses data summaries representing the data distribution of neighboring peers, which are regularly updated using a heartbeat mechanism. In contrast to Seaweed our approach targets different application scenarios and is based on different assumptions: We assume a wider variety of different query types and query processing strategies, exceeding the idea of broadcast and spanning trees. Our method for completeness estimation is designed specifically to be generic in order to support other modern processing strategies, such as similarity and skyline search. The idea behind Seaweed is to provide delay-aware querying, which means data summaries and availability models of currently unavailable nodes are used in order to predict query completeness and response times. A heartbeat mechanism provided by the underlying DHT MSPastry (Castro, M., Costa, M., Rowstron, A.I.T. (2004)) is utilized for maintaining the statistical information and modeling certain cost in terms of bandwidth, especially during stable periods. In contrast to this, we use the DHT to handle unavailable and new nodes, usually by managing replicated data objects and corresponding routing techniques, which incurs network message overhead only when required to maintain the system. We primarily use completeness estimation to measure the currently received portion of a query result in the context of slow peers. Unavailable peer data is handled in a best-effort manner, where completeness estimation helps to rate the significance of partial results. The idea of regularly maintained data summaries is a very interesting possibility to extend our approach, because it allows for estimating query completeness directly on data level. In this work, however, we only rely on an estimation on peer level to get an understanding of the basic properties of the approach which can be improved later on. Further, we evaluate the appropriateness of assuming a correlation to query completeness on data level in a load-balancing overlay network.

Concerning P2P query processing, the most related work is PIER (Huebsch, R., Hellerstein, J.M., Lanham, N., Thau Loo, B., Shenker, S., Stoica, I. (2003)). The authors propose a similar database-like style of query processing as we do (see Section 6). However, until now, PIER provides no mechanisms for estimating query completeness, but the authors mention this as future work. Query operators such as equi-selection, range selection and hash joins, and their implementation, using

modified Chord search algorithms are presented in (Triantafillou, P., Pitoura, T. (2004)). A couple of distributed triple stores, e.g., (Cai, M., Frank, M. (2004)), are based on a similar data model, preferably used to manage and query RDF data. Despite that they provide sophisticated query processing capabilities as well, query processing is based on a rather different approach and completeness estimation is not supported. Our own approach, the UniStore system (Karnstedt, M., Sattler, K., Richtarsky, M., Müller, J., Hauswirth, M., Schmidt, R., John, R. (2007)), is also a DHT-based triple store using self-describing schemas. It supports a structured query language with several advanced query operators such as similarity selection, joins, and skyline queries. In (Karnstedt, M., Sattler, K., Schmidt, R. (2007)) we have presented an initial approach for completeness estimation in UniStore. However, this approach was restricted to range queries only and can be seen as a prerequisite for the work presented here.

A NOVEL METHOD FOR ESTIMATING THE COMPLETENESS OF RANGE QUERIES OVER STRUCTURED P2P DATABASES

We focus on the mentioned shower algorithm implemented in P-Grid. In Section 5.3 we discuss the possibilities for other systems to provide completeness estimation for range queries and the applicability of our approach to them.

A peer initiating a range query starts this query by providing the interval bounds of the desired range. Afterwards, each intermediate peer responsible for routing the query, forwards it to one or more sub-trees, depending on its own path, the paths of peers from its routing table, and the paths of the queried range. Thus, the crucial point is to estimate the number of peers responsible for a certain key range. But, due to load-balancing aspects, this is quite difficult. The idea is to use all available path information in order to build an

Figure 4. Estimating the P-Grid trie

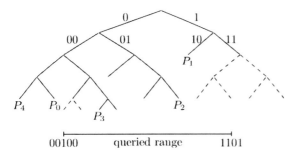

estimated P-Grid trie. Based on this tree, we can determine a minimal number of replies expected.

In the following we will explain, how we can determine the minimal number of replies from an estimated P-Grid trie. Let

$$b_1 b_2 b_3 \ldots b_x$$

denote the x bits that form the binary key of such a peer. From this path, we can deduce the existence of at least x other peers: Let $\bar{b}_i$ denote the inverted bit b_i. For each path

1: $\bar{b}_1$
2: $b_1 \bar{b}_2$
3: $b_1 b_2 \bar{b}_3$
...
x: $b_1 b_2 \ldots b_{x-1} \bar{b}_x$

there must exist *at least one* responsible peer. Knowing about several paths from peers in a range, the initiator can deduce a minimal number of peers in that range. In order to achieve this, the initiator builds a tree from those paths and reflects to the minimal number of peers.

Figure 4 illustrates this. The figure shows an example P-Grid tree. Assume a query for the range 00100 - 1101 was initiated. Further, the initiator P_0 knows about four peers, where the paths from P_1, P_2 and P_3 are in the range. As every peer has at least one reference to another peer for each of the positions of its path, P_0 must at least know about

four peers, each located in a different sub-tree. The part of the tree the initiator can deduce from its local routing information is shown in solid lines. The dashed lines indicate that part of the tree not known to the initiator, which results in a small error in this first estimate. The minimal number of peers in the range estimated in this situation is 8, the correct value is 10.

Estimation Refinement

The first estimation performed by the query initiating peer is solely based on the routing information available at that peer. The local routing table stores at least one reference per level. In other words, we know about at least one peer of each sub-tree a range query is sent to. For fault-tolerance and load-balancing reasons structured overlays usually keep multiple references at each level to remain operational during peer churn or to select the least loaded peer for query load-balancing. Therefore, the information a query initiating peer has about the structure and peers in a sub-tree increases with the number of references per level.

But, the information gathered like this is still not complete and the estimation might still be too small as some peers remain "invisible" from the local point of view. Therefore, initiating peers piggy-back with each query sent to a sub-tree the estimate of peers considered in a sub-tree. For example in Figure 4, the range query sent from peer P_0 to peer P_3 also contains the estimate that three peers build the sub-tree 001*. As P_0 only knows that P_3 has path 00110, it knows that there must be a peer 00111 and at least one peer for 0010, though P_0 does not know that the sub-tree 0010* actually consists of two peers. P_3 is aware of this fact, because P_3's routing table must contain at least one of the peers from sub-tree 0010*, and can return the correct number of peers in sub-tree 001* with its query reply to peer P_0. P_0 can then correct the estimate of query replies expected for the initiated range query. Peers receiving a range query with correct information do not have to "correct" the initial estimate.

The required message overhead for our completeness estimation is therefore minimal as no additional messages have to be sent and only small information are piggy-backed with sent query and query reply messages. In case a range query hits a peer outside the target range with an incorrect estimate, the receiving peer can either react by replying with a short acknowledgment message correcting the initial estimate, or it forwards the incorrect estimate to target peers in the range and the correction will be returned in the query reply messages. In the first case, the query initiator can sooner correct the estimated completeness at the cost of a small extra message, whereas in the second case the correction is done at a later time with the reception of query results without additional messages.

Applying the method as described above, we will never over-estimate the number of expected replies. Moreover, when a query is finished, we will always recognize this for sure. This is possible because the paths of the replying peers are analyzed. Thus, receiving these replies, we always know for sure the actual size of the corresponding sub-tree.

Further Improvements

There was much research spent on designing overlay systems as much stable and reliable as possible. Thus, we can even cache estimated trees once they are built. These cached trees can later be used for subsequent queries. The trees should then be adapted to changes in the overlay structure registered –which may, of course, occur, but are expected to be rather rare. In this way, we achieve a quite accurate and satisfyingly exact completeness estimation, which is automatically maintained with each query initiated.

The task of achieving complete query results is due to the used overlay system, in this case the P-Grid overlay. Nevertheless, incomplete results may occur in rather unstable and unreliable large-scaled systems. This also effects the completeness estimation, as, for instance, we will experience a difference in the *static* completeness concerning all data that should be available, and the *dynamic* completeness based on the results actually received. This should be involved into completeness considerations. A nice aspect of the method proposed here is that it allows for estimating the size of results missing in this case.

Usability in Other Overlay Systems

Our approach is based on a parallel resolution of range queries in a binary trie similar to a prefix hash tree, whereby in the case of P-Grid the depth of each sub-tree can be estimated by the known nodes of this sub-tree stored in the local routing table. To the best of our knowledge no other system can already provide completeness estimation for range queries. In this section, we briefly discuss the possibilities for other systems to estimate the number of query replies and the usability of our approach for them.

The approach for range queries in SkipGraphs (Aspnes, J., Shah, G. (2003); Aspnes, J., Kirsch, J., Krishnamurthy, A. (2004)) is the most similar one to the one of P-Grid as peers also maintain routing information at multiple levels. Our proposed method can also be used by SkipGraphs to estimate the number of peers in other sub-trees. The only problem is the number of peers remaining in the bucket layer below the lowest interconnected skip-list level. But, as load-balancing is in place, this number should be similar to the number of buckets the current node is in.

Approaches like (Ramabhadran, S., Ratnasamy, S., Hellerstein, J.M., Shenker, S. (2004)) and (Liau, C.Y., Ng, W.S., Shu, Y., Tan, K.L., Bressan, S. (2004)) are based on a prefix hash tree where peers remain at each level of the tree, unlike in P-Grid where peers only remain at the leaf level. The routing in this tree starts at the root level and trickles down the tree from nodes to their children until all nodes in the target range are reached. As we assume that nodes do not know the exact number of their children, it is not possible for them to estimate how many nodes will return results for a range query. If this number can be estimated, the technique presented in this paper can also be adapted for completeness estimation in systems based on prefix hash trees.

Finally, approaches forwarding a range query sequentially along neighbors cannot estimate the final number of nodes involved in a range query. This holds for CAN-based systems presented in (Gupta, A., Agrawal, D., Abbadi, A.E. (2003); Sahin, O.D., Gupta, A., Agrawal, D., Abbadi, A.E. (2004)) and the Chord-ring based system Mercury (Bharambe, A., Agrawal, M., Seshan, S. (2004)).

Completeness Estimation from the User's Perspective

In the last sections, we motivated the need for an exact completeness estimation and proposed a technique for achieving this on the physical layer. Now we will discuss how the introduced method is applied internally and how completeness information are presented to the user, used for subsequent processing steps, respectively.

By applying the method as introduced, we can always determine a minimal value for the number of replies expected. With each reply received, we just compute the ratio

$$\frac{\text{received replies}}{\text{expected replies}}$$

By this, we are always able to provide a satisfyingly exact estimation and identify the final reply for sure. With the first replies this completeness value may be over-estimated, because we expect less replies than finally received. But, as Section 8 will show, the number of corrections needed for determining an exact estimate is rather low. Moreover, the final completion of a query can

always be determined by 100%. Preferably we should also provide a corresponding probability or intervals of (un-)certainty for all intermediate replies.

One idea is to provide an expected average number rather than the minimal number of replies. This can be achieved by using information about the average depth of a P-Grid trie, which could be taken from empirical studies. The minimal number of replies could be used as a lower bound in this case, and an estimated maximal number (again, based on empirical studies) as an upper bound. Like this, we can easily provide a completeness estimate plus an interval of certainty. Of course, the value estimated for the maximal number of replies will rise suddenly when a query reply from an unexpectedly deep sub-tree is received. It is a fact that the quality of estimation is the worse, the more unknown sub-trees we have *and* the higher they are located in the tree, i.e., the shorter the known paths are. This can be even improved if we base the completeness estimations on cached estimation trees. These trees, built with queries already finished, usually reflect a relatively good view of the routing trie. Even if we have no clue about the actual size of the tree, we could still use, if available, an estimated number of peers joining the system in order to determine upper bounds for the number of expected replies and thus, provide goodness intervals.

Another conceivable approach is to compute a kind of error approximation. For instance, we could use the estimated maximal tree depth in order to compute an additional quality estimation. One suggestion for such a factor of uncertainty ε_l is:

$$\varepsilon_l = 1 - \frac{|B_l|}{|B_l| + \sum_{b \in B_l} 2^{b_{max} - |b|}}.$$

B_l is the set of all paths known to the initiator overlapping the queried range, $\overline{B_l}$ represents the minimal set of paths b predicted to be still missing in the range – in other words, the number of sub-trees we know overlapping the range but we still miss any information from. b_{max} stands for the assumed maximal path length/tree depth $(\forall b \in B_l \cup \overline{B}_l : b_{max} \geq | b |)$. Assuming $b_{max} = 5$ in the small example from Section 5 we would predict a factor of uncertainty

$$\varepsilon = 1 - \frac{3}{3 + (2 + 1 + 4 + 2 + 8)} = 0.85.$$

On the first look, this seems to be an unjustified high value – but, at this point, we only know of three peers among at least eight in the range, which is only 37.5%.

As one example for applications that will benefit from the proposed method for completeness estimation we refer to UniStore (Karnstedt, M., Sattler, K., Richtarsky, M., Müller, J., Hauswirth, M., Schmidt, R., John, R. (2007)). UniStore is a light-weight system for universally storing and managing structured data in a distributed manner based on a structured overlay. Range queries are only a part of the variety of query processing techniques supported by UniStore. There is a need to provide exact completeness estimation for all of these types. An example for processing techniques relying on range queries and an exact completeness estimation are skyline queries (Börzsönyi, S., Kossmann, D., Stocker, K. (2001); Karnstedt, M.,Müller, J., Sattler, K. (2007)). One step during the processing of these queries is to initiate range queries for each of the queried attributes – and continuing with subsequent processing steps after all (or a satisfyingly large fraction) range query replies are received. Other supported operators that rely on range queries are aggregates. For instance, the average of an attribute is determined by initializing a range query for the attribute. This is possible because the values are inserted into the storage system by applying a hashing function on the attribute name concatenated with its value. Note that P-Grid uses a prefix-preserving hashing approach, so all items for one attribute are stored in a continuous range.

Basic Query Processing

We implemented our approach for estimating query completeness in the UniStore system (Karnstedt, M., Sattler, K., Richtarsky, M., Müller, J., Hauswirth, M., Schmidt, R., John, R. (2007)). This section summarizes the fundamentals of query processing in this system required to understand the subsequent sections. We used the implementation in UniStore as a proof-of-concept, but would like to point out that our approach is generally applicable to DHT-based query systems.

The philosophy of UniStore is similar to that of PIER (Huebsch, R., Hellerstein, J.M., Lanham, N., Thau Loo, B., Shenker, S., Stoica, I. (2003)). Both systems aim at supporting structured queries on structured data from multiple users, managed in a structured overlay (i.e., a DHT overlay). Queries are transformed into according query plans and processed relying only on routing functionality provided by the DHT. In contrast to PIER, UniStore targets very heterogeneous environments, typical for the Web. UniStore uses a triple-based storage model, where each triple (o, a, v) includes a (system-generated) object ID o (OID for short), an attribute name a (schema level) and a value v for this attribute (instance level). The benefits of this storage model are its flexibility and it is self-descriptive and easily extensible. All triples are indexed multiple times in the DHT to support various functionalities: For instance, we build an index on the OIDs to support efficient tuple reconstruction, an index on the concatenation of a and v for prefix and range-queries over attributes, a *qgram* index to support string similarity, etc. UniStore also supports special operators which are helpful in heterogeneous environments such as similarity queries, ranking queries, skyline queries, etc.

UniStore's query language supports the triple model very similar to RDF query languages. For

Table 1. Used operators

Operator	Description
ξ_A	extracts all tuples with attribute A
ω_B	materializes attribute B for each input tuple, if exists (join on OID)
$\bowtie_{A=B}$	equal join on $A = B$ ($\sim$: similarity join)
α	aggregation operator
op^{RQ}	physical operator op based on contacting all responsible peers using a range query (DOR)
op^{ParOID}	physical operator op based on parallel direct lookups for input OIDs (FNR)

processing queries, the query engine chooses among different processing strategies by applying different access paths (different indexes build on top of the DHT). Multiple instances of a query plan (called sub-plans) are shipped where relevant data is expected to be (using the DHT's hash functions). At these peers the plans are processed, physical operators are successively replaced by (partial) result data and the plan is forwarded again. Finally, a reply (which can be empty) is sent to the query initiator for every finished sub-plan (i.e., the last plan operator has been processed). Thus, in order to estimate completeness on peer level, we have to determine the number of plans generated during the processing of one query.

We use a graph-based notation for representing query plans, where each node represents a plan operator symbolized by a Greek letter. We will use the following abbreviations and symbols: DOR (Dynamic Overlay Routing), FNR (Fixed Number Routing), R (estimated number of final replies), $\Re$ (actual number of final replies), r (number of currently received replies), and L (maximal routing level of a routing graph). Table 1 lists the operators used in the following sections.

Query plans and operators used in this work are chosen in order to illustrate the proposed approach as much intuitive as possible, and to capture the three different general processing

strategies proposed in related works: sequential (peers to finish an operator are contacted in sequence), intra-operator parallel (all peers needed to finish one operator are contacted in parallel), and inter-operator parallel (allows for processing branches in parallel, e.g., both input sides of a join).

Query processing in P2P networks depends on the underlying topographic structure and the routing principles of the concrete system. For equality queries, the query originator only has to expect no or one reply from the peer holding matching data. For more complex query types, e.g., range queries and similarity queries, the query initiator is usually unaware of the number of peers involved in resolving its query and will receive an *a priori* unknown number of query replies. It is therefore not possible to determine when the result set is final.

Routing Methods

We observed that the different processing strategies can be classified by only two relevant routing methods. The crucial difference is whether a peer starting a routing knows about how many peers will be contacted (i.e., the out-degree of the corresponding routing point is known a priori) or not. Following, we distinguish:

1. Dynamic Overlay Routing (DOR). The out-degree is not known a priori. Usually, this is done by addressing a certain key space and let the overlay decide how to forward the separate plans to all peers in this key space. In most cases, this means that the routing of plans is independent of already determined data. We apply this concept by issuing range queries in order to extract or materialize certain attributes. The number of peers in a queried range is not known, though the range itself is.

2. Fixed Number Routing (FNR). This class of routing methods covers all processing strategies where the peer starting a routing knows the number of generated sub-plans. In most cases, the routing of plans is dependent of intermediate input data. As an example, imagine a nested-loop like processing of a join using an appropriate attribute-value index.

In the following, we will base our explanations on these two classes of routing methods, because the processing strategies implemented in our system perfectly match them. Special cases, like a mixture of both approaches (e.g., issuing a fixed number of range queries depending on the input data) or simplified routing methods (e.g., if the number of peers contacted in one processing step is already known at query planning time) integrate easily in the proposed framework. For example, an operator processed sequentially corresponds to an FNR with a fixed out-degree of 1 at each routing point.

Query Evaluation by Routing Graphs

The idea is to build a *routing graph* that represents the peers and connections a query travels during processing. Each node in the graph, a *routing point*, represents one peer involved in query processing. Actually, the graph is a tree. The number of leafs in the tree is $\Re$, the number of replies we

need to estimate. Each operator is processed on one *routing level*, which corresponds to the according level in the routing graph. A peer may represent multiple vertices of a routing graph because it may be contacted several times for processing different parts of q. As a consequence, the query routing graph is a topology overlaid on the topology of the overlay (ring, tree, etc.). The graph also differs from its query plan q as the processing of one operator may span multiple routing points and at one routing point multiple operators may be processed. The latter is true when multiple operators can be processed locally on one peer without routing.

Imagine the query plan in Figure 5. ξ_A^{RQ} extracts all data items for attribute A using a range query to contact all peers responsible for a part of A. Thus, first routing method is DOR. ω_B^{ParOID} and ω_C^{RQ} materialize attributes B and C as additional information for each input data item. For any reasons, e.g., cost-based decisions, ω_B^{ParOID} uses direct lookups for candidate items' IDs and ω_C^{RQ} is range-based again.

This means, second routing method is FNR, third is DOR. If the query would contain a select filter on A or B, this would be processed at the peers contacted for extracting/materializing A/B. Thus, the routing graph would look the same.

At time t the following knowledge is available at the query initiator: the ranges r_A and r_C of attributes A and C, subsets K_A and K_C of all paths from peers responsible for a part of r_A and r_C, a subset D_1 of all peers on level 1 with their fanout d, $|D_1| = |K_A|$. Naturally, we assume $t \, t_0$, where t_0 is the time of the first reply. Before t_0, completeness is always 0. From r_A and K_A we can estimate a minimal number p_1 of peers on level 1, as shown previously. Thus, the following holds:

$$p_2 = \sum_{d \in D_1} d + (p_1 - |D_1|) \quad .$$

Figure 5. Example query

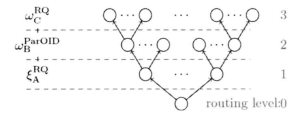

This corresponds to the minimal number of replies to be expected, because we assume an out-degree of 1 for each peer on level 1 we do have no exact knowledge of. In analogy to p_1, we estimate d_2 (the fanout of each routing point on level 2) from r_C and K_C. Finally, the number of expected replies at time t is

$$R = p_3 = d_2 \, p_2 \, .$$

Here you can see why assuming static query planning eases completeness estimation and improves its quality: we can assume the fanout of d_2 for each peer from level 2, even for those we did not receive information from until now.

In general, the number of leafs can be described by a recursive formula:

$$p_0 = 1, \quad p_l = \sum_{k=1}^{p_{l-1}} d_{(l-1),k} \quad (l = 1, \mathrm{K}, L), \quad \Re = p_L$$

where p_l is the number of vertices at level l, and $d_{l,k}$ is the fanout of the kth vertex at level l.

Based on the notion of routing graphs, the basic idea of estimating query completeness works as shown in Algorithm 2. This procedure is called every time a new reply arrives at the initiator. After updating necessary information in the estimated overlay structure and the routing graph *RG* (one for each initiated query), the fraction of received results r and estimated final replies R is returned. Thus, a currently estimated completeness (on peer level) is determined in an online fashion.

In contrast to, for instance, Seaweed, we do not estimate this completeness directly on data level. Note that also aggregation queries return multiple replies, as the computed aggregation values are refined in an online fashion.

Routing Trace

But why is it adequate to differ only between two routing methods, when there is such a wide variety of possible processing strategies and indexes to be used? The point is the amount of information we can extract from a single reply received. Into each reply, we integrate information about the way the sub-plan took when traveling through the network during processing. As a consequence, this *routing trace* allows to identify the one path from the query initiator to a leaf of the routing graph that corresponds to this reply. Intuitively, for estimating the number of replies a query results in, the quality of this estimation depends on the kind of information about each routing point we can extract. For instance, if we know the out-degree d of a routing point before starting that routing, we can include this information in each of the d resulting routing traces – and thus, we know this information at the query initiating side as soon as the first of the corresponding sub-plans is replied.

Overhead

The proposed method comes along with a very low overhead. In terms of messages, there is no overhead at all, because any information needed is included into query plan messages and reply messages. The bandwidth consumption resulting from applying completeness estimation is almost negligible. Query plans contain only small additional information, which is the routing trace and a sketch of the overlay structure as it is known at the query initiator. The size of the routing trace depends on the size of the routing graph (more exact, on the maximal routing level L). Each entry of the routing trace has a constant size. The

Algorithm 2. Basic algorithm: new-reply()

1: update-overlay();

2: update-RG();

3: $r = r + 1$;

4: $R = 1$;

5: **for all** routings $\rho \in RG \rightarrow$ get-levels() **do**

6: $\quad R = R + \rho \rightarrow$ estimate(R);

7: **end for**

8: **return** $\frac{r}{R}$;

---

overlay structure grows with the number of peers participating in the system. In UniStore, we have $|p|$B for each path p known to the current peer. Thus, the bandwidth overhead for each (sub-)plan generated at routing point rp is in bits:

$$B_{rp} = \sum_{\text{known paths } p} |p| + B_m \in O(N),$$

where B_m refers to the size of the *Milestone Message* (MiMe – see Section 7) sent from this routing point. Note that information of size B_m is always added to a query plan, regardless if MiMes are sent separately or not. Thus, bandwidth consumption for one query neglecting MiMes is

$$\sum_{rp \in RG} d(rp) \cdot B_{rp} \in O(N \cdot N^{L-1}) = O(N^L).$$

To make the completeness estimation work, we only have to keep small information for each routing level. Further, we have to detect replicated replies, which can occur in replicating overlays, and rely on the DHT to provide estimation techniques for every DOR method used.

Probabilistic Guarantees over Estimates of Range Queries over Structured P2P Databases

Completeness estimation as introduced up to this point is a nice tool, but it only gains really significance and importance if we provide guarantees, more generally, meaningful quality measures. This section deals with this important aspect. First, we have to consider which kind of measurements are conceivable and meaningful in order to weight the accuracy of the query completeness predicted. We distinguish between three different kinds of guarantees:

1. A general guarantee for the accuracy that says: "If completeness is predicted as $c\%$, this is true with a probability of $x\%$".

2. A guaranteed boundary: "If completeness is predicted as $c\%$, this is above/below the actual completeness with a probability of $x\%$".

3. A confidence interval: "If completeness is predicted as $c\%$, the actual completeness is between *(c-y)%* and *(c+z)%* (with a probability of $x\%$)".

Which guarantee should be preferred will depend on the specific application. We always predict an expected number of replies which is guaranteed to be below the actual number of replies. This results in a predicted completeness $\frac{r}{R}$, which is guaranteed to be above the actual query completeness. This and the fact that, if completeness is predicted to be 100%, the actual completeness is 100% can be proved straightforward. The idea is to apply an induction over the number of routing levels in the routing graph. We omit the full details here. Note that this guarantee holds for peer and data level, because if all potential replies are received all result data is received as well.

Providing a completeness which is always above the actual one is more than many systems can provide. But, of course, we are interested in a general accuracy and in a guaranteed lower bound. We investigate three different estimation techniques: estimate *(i)* a *minimal* number of replies, as introduced before, *(ii)* an *average* number of replies, and *(iii)* a *maximal* number of replies.

Unfortunately, the unpredictable nature of the underlying systems prevents from providing exact guarantees for the latter two methods. After briefly introducing them, we will discuss how to provide probabilistic guarantees instead.

Both approaches are based on the already received information about the routing graph. The idea is best illustrated using the small example graph in Figure 6. The middle routing point from level 1 is known, but not its out-degree in the FNR level. From the other two subtrees, we already received 4 replies. By this, we know that there will be 2 more replies for sure (we know the out-degrees of both routing points) plus at least 1 from the "missing" subtree. Thus, with the minimal method we estimate 7 replies. As its name suggests, the average method calculates the average of out-degrees on the routing level in question, which is 3. Thus, 9 replies are estimated. Similar, the maximal method uses the maximum of out-degrees and estimates 10 replies. This methodology is applied for each routing point with an unknown out-degree. DOR estimations are based on a predicted structure of the overlay. As UniStore uses P-Grid, a corresponding tree structure is maintained at every peer. Here, average and maximal path lengths from that tree are used in order to predict the shape of the actual P-Grid tree. The actual number of replies may still be higher than predicted with the maximal method. In early states we also tried a method based on maximal values learned during time and from different setups. We soon observed that this method is always far below the maximal method introduced above – and as we will show in Section 8 this one itself is below the actual completeness

in most cases and times. Thus, we focus on the three methods introduced so far.

Next, we can relax the conditions needed in order to achieve a completeness estimation guaranteed by 100%. In fact, we already reach this point as soon as all needed information about the routing graph is achieved. For a better understanding, we introduce the notion of *minimal routing graphs*. For DOR, we need to know about the queried range (known when planning the query) and the exact number of peers in that range. This is achieved if one of all identical sub-queries is completely answered, all the same from which part of the routing graph. This can also be true if no subtree is completely known at all, depending on the paths of replying peers. If all paths of a range are known, the exact number of responsible peers is known. In the FNR case, much more information is needed in order to achieve an exact completeness. The out-degree of each routing point must be known. Thus, at least one result from each routing point on level $L - 1$ must be received. This results in complete knowledge of the routing graph below level L.

Figures 7 and 8 illustrate this. All routing points and connections drawn solid are needed at minimum in order to achieve the 100% guarantee. We picture two out of many possibilities. In the first one the required information is located "as much left-oriented as possible", the second one is random.

The notion of minimal routing graphs helps to understand the possible errors we make during completeness estimation. If any of the solid parts in Figures 7 and 8 is missing, we include such an error. The depth of the routing graph is known as long as we expect homogeneous subtrees, because at least one reply is already received. Thus, the only errors we can make are to estimate a wrong number of peers in a range when applying DOR, and estimating a wrong out-degree of a routing point when applying FNR. In order to provide a probabilistic guarantee, we have to weight these

Figure 6. FNR example for min, max, and average

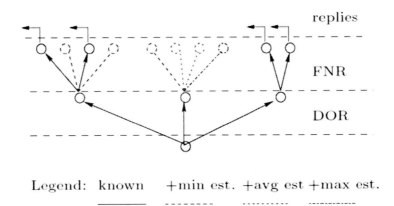

Figure 7. Minimal routing trees for complete DOR

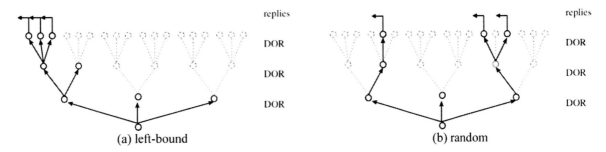

errors for each point in time where we estimate the query completeness c as $0 < c < 100$.

On each routing level, we assume the out-degrees of routing points, the path lengths of nodes in the overlay tree respectively, to follow a specific distribution model. In principle, any distribution model can be applied, even histograms for describing arbitrary distributions can be used. Problematic is the complexity of the following calculations. (Theobald, M., Weikum, G., Schenkel, R. (2004)) gives suggestions and instructions for some of the most popular models. We refer to the Poisson distribution for out-degrees and path lengths, because it fits the actual distributions particularly good and calculations based on this model are very easy and efficient to implement.

In order to provide a lower bound of query completeness, below we describe a formula for determining the probability that the estimated

completeness is below the actual. We expect all occurring random variables to be independent from each other. Let N_l denote the random variable that estimates the number of routing points on routing level l, and n_l the actual number. Looking only on the maximal routing level, the probability $P(N_L = n_L)$ under the condition that n_{L-1} routing points exist on level

$L-1$ is

$$P(N_L = n_L \mid N_{L-1} = n_{L-1}) =$$

$$\sum_{S_{L-1}} \prod_{i=1}^{n_{L-1}} P(D_i = d_i),$$

where S_{L-1} is the set of all combinations $\{d_1, ..., d_{nL-1}\}$ such that $d_1 + ... + d_{nL-1} = n_L$. D_i describes the out-degree of an arbitrary routing point on level $L-1$. This formula computes the convolution of

Figure 8. Minimal routing trees for complete FNR

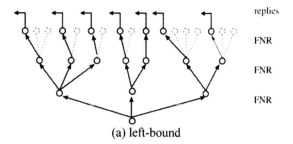
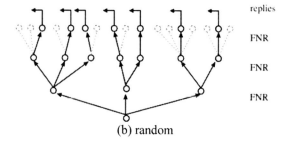

(a) left-bound   (b) random

the n_{L-1} random variables. As mentioned above, using Poisson distributions

$$P(D_i = d) = \frac{\lambda_i^d}{d!} e^{-\lambda_i}$$

we can easily calculate this convolution using

$$P(D = d) = \frac{\left(\sum_i \lambda_i\right)^d}{d!} e^{-\left(\sum_i \lambda_i\right)}$$

Known out-degrees are simply excluded from this summation. This works directly for distributions describing the observed out-degrees on FNR routing levels. A distribution describing the path lengths in the overlay must be mapped to a distribution of out-degrees accordingly. Currently, we do this using a repository of trees observed over time, but are investigating other approaches. Using the cumulative distribution, the guarantee is determined by

$$P(\text{est. compl.} \leq \text{actual compl.}) = P(\Re \leq R) = P(D \leq R).$$

Including lower levels results in a recursive formula. Let K_l refer to the set of out-degrees already known on level l, k_l to the sum of all out-degrees in K_l. Then,

$$P(N_L \leq n_L) =$$
$$\sum_{n_{L-1}=k_{L-1}}^{u_{L-1}} P(N_L \leq n_L \mid N_{L-1} = n_{L-1}) \cdot P(N_{L-1} = n_{L-1}).$$

if we use $u_{L-1} := k_{L-1} + n_L - k_L - (k_{L-1} - |K_L|)$ for the maximal number of nodes that is possible on level $L-1$ (respecting known out-degrees and the estimated number of nodes on level L). This gets

$$P(N_L \leq n_L) = \sum_{n_{L-1}=k_{L-1}}^{u_{L-1}} P(N_L \leq n_L \mid N_{L-1} = n_{L-1}) \cdot$$
$$\sum_{n_{L-2}=k_{L-2}}^{u_{L-2}} P(N_{L-1} = n_{L-1} \mid N_{L-2} = n_{L-2}) \cdot \ldots \cdot$$
$$\sum_{n_1=k_l}^{u_1} P(N_2 = n_2 \mid N_1 = n_1) \cdot P(N_1 = n_1).$$

If levels of the routing graph are completely known, corresponding probabilities resolve to either 1.0 or 0.0 and these parts could be extracted from the calculation. This is what we did with level 0 in the above formula. If individual parts of one level are unknown, this requires computing the convolution in the according routing level. With Poisson distributions and the information gathered for completeness estimation this probabilistic guarantee can be calculated with ease. An according line $P = P(\Re \leq R)$ is added between line 7 and 8 in Algorithm 2, and the determined probability P is returned together with the estimated completeness. In early query states, the significance of the calculations will be very poor. With proceeding time this improves quickly. Evaluating different distribution models and the significance of applying them is part of our ongoing work.

As an optimization technique, we introduce *Milestone Messages* (MiMes). The idea is to send information from each routing point in a separate message directly back to the initiator while forwarded sub-plans are still processed in the network. They only include information that is available in the routing trace of a reply as well. But, due to slow or failing peers, they help to improve the accuracy of the estimation in early states. MiMes are sent irregularly when a certain part of the query plan is processed. They are not essential for applying the proposed completeness estimation, but increase estimation quality represented by better probabilistic guarantees. The number of generated MiMes increases with the number of peers involved in processing a single plan. Thus, it increases with the number of peers in the system. The bandwidth overhead can be regarded as a constant factor. Due to space restrictions, we omit further details here.

EXPERIMENTAL EVALUATION AND ASSESSMENT

In order to carefully probe the effectiveness and the efficiency of our completeness estimation method, we devised a comprehensive campaign of experiments oriented to stress the proposed method under the variation of several experimental parameters and perspectives. This results in two distinct class of experiments, namely *basic experiments* and *advanced experiments*. Basic experiments are devoted to test the general performance of our completeness estimation method, whereas advanced experiments deal with complex aspects of the method. In the following, we focus on both classes of experiments, and provide useful discussion on retrieved results, respectively.

Basic Experiments and Analysis

The focus of the basic experimental evaluation is to show the applicability, exactness and quality of the proposed completeness estimation. These aspects are not directly depending on the size of the network, but rather on the size of the constructed overlay trie. This, in turn, also but not exclusively depends on the network size. We created a local and reliable but real environment consisting of 61 nodes. These nodes were physically distributed over 20 machines, each running up to 4 instances listening on different ports. As the environment was stable, we were able to use a low replication factor, lowering the number of replicas responsible for one path in the P-Grid trie. This resulted in a wider and deeper tree. Thus, the results are also significant for larger scaled networks, where usually a higher replication factor is used. We used two environments, the first with a replication factor of 2, the second with a factor of 1. In unreliable systems, this factor will be set to 5 or higher compensating frequent joins and leaves of peers. Our evaluation focuses on the completeness estimation of range queries and we assume that P-Grid guarantees the availability of at least one peer per partition even in very dynamic or unreliable setups like PlanetLab.

We inserted 48 data items from each of the peers, resulting in a total of 2928 data items. The used string data taken from IMDB (http://www.imdb.com/) represents information about movie titles and shows a skewed heavy-tail key distribution (power-law like). The average number of leafs, maximal path length and the average path length were 32, 8 and 5 for a replication factor of 1. For a factor of 2, the values were 19, 6 and 4.5, respectively. The resulting P-Grid trie was not balanced. Almost 40% of the leafs were located under key prefix 0 and the tree was deeper and wider under key prefix 1.

In order to evaluate the influence of the number of references for one level of the local routing table we built three environments, using a maximal number of references of 1, 3 and 5. A query mix of three different range queries, involving different parts of the trie and therefore resulting in a different number of replies, was run. Query q1 asks for all index entries with prefix 10 (range 100...0-101...1), q2 for all with prefix 11 and q3 uses an empty prefix, thus querying the whole trie. Each query was initiated 10 times, each time on a randomly chosen node. In the following, we present and discuss the results of the described experiments.

The first figure shows the correspondence between completeness on data level and on peer level. Figure 9 shows the percentage of the final result received with respect to the number of replies received. We exemplary chose one of the described network environments (replication factor 2, maximal references 5) – in the other settings results look similar. The plot shows that, especially for the two queries resulting in fewer answers, the development of the result size is almost linear. For the query involving the whole P-Grid trie the last query replies contain larger fractions of the result than earlier replies. Even if P-Grid implements a sophisticated load-balancing, there might exist keys to which a particular high number of data items is mapped to. P-Grid's load-balancing technique splits high frequented key space partitions more fine-granular than others, but does not "split" single keys. Thus, some peers are still responsible for a higher number of items than others. Due to the locally used storage system, the answer time correlates to the amount of data to be processed locally. Therefore, replies from these peers arrive with later replies, resulting in a higher increase of the result size with the final answers. A perfect mapping would be indicated by a straight line. The figure shows that the mapping from completeness on data level to the completeness on reply level is satisfyingly realistic in load-balanced overlay systems.

Figure 10 shows the number of replies we estimated using the proposed technique with each

reply received. Additionally, the straight line represents the actual completeness on reply level. The figure clearly shows that our method always estimates the number of replies correctly at the end. Moreover, it gets evident that only a small number of first replies is needed in order to determine a correct value in the end. As expected, the higher the number of references for each level of the routing table, the more exact the initial estimation and the less corrections are needed. The figure also shows that in this case the size of the temporary errors is smaller than with lower references per level. The differences in the number of replies for identical queries are due to the need for starting networks with different parameters from scratch every time. By this, and the application of a random-walk strategy in order to build the P-Grid trie, this results in (only slightly) different overlay trees.

The smaller the part of the trie involved into range query processing the less information is needed in order to achieve exact estimations. For the first two queries, even the settings using a replication factor of 1 and/or a maximal number of references per level of 3 and 1 are quite satisfying. As sub-trees are queried more probably than the whole tree, this shows that the proposed method provides quick and exact estimations even with low information. This also indicates the effectiveness for larger scaled and unreliable systems where, in turn, more information shall be contained in the local routing tables.

Summarizing, we can state that for each of the considered cases we only need a fraction of replies in order to achieve an exact completeness estimation. As the method goes along with very low additional effort, this proves its powerfulness for trie structured overlays in general.

The last figures show the relative completeness $\frac{\text{estimated}\#\text{replies}}{\text{final}\#\text{replies}}$ estimated with each reply. Thus, it illustrates the ratio of error correction. Moreover, this time the queries were run on two

Figure 9. Completeness on data level

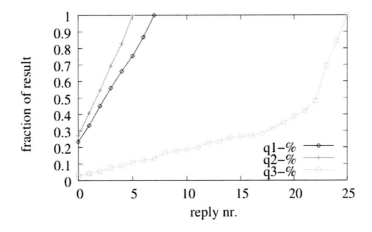

different networks for each setting, each of them run for a different time before starting queries. Results from the hence four runs were averaged. Thus, effects of slightly different overlay tries are eliminated. Figure 11 shows that the ratio of correction is always almost equal for each of the used environments. Following, independent from the query actually initiated, completeness estimation is comparably good and corrections provide equally good improvements with respect to the size of the final result. The figures also show that the initial estimate is good for all tests, but it is better if more references are stored at each routing table level. As expected, an error correction can be recognized only for the first query replies and converges to 0 for later replies. Another important observation is that the estimation for the queries with less replies are very exact with little information and that the corresponding plots approach each other with rising numbers of references.

All in all the proposed method for completeness estimation is absolutely satisfying. The initial estimation, based on no further knowledge than the local one, is quite good for any type of query and environment. Even if this first estimate is erroneous, only a small amount of replies is needed in order to determine an exact estimate.

In the presented experiments, we omitted any dynamics, which is of course a natural ingredient of P2P systems. But, providing complete results under churn is a task the overlay is responsible for, not the system layered on top of it, like UniStore. If the overlay guarantees complete results, which modern overlay systems achieve by applying adequate replication algorithms, the proposed approach will work correct, as shown above. Moreover, in recent time the super-peer approach, relying on a fraction of all peers which are rather reliable and robust, gains boosted attention. Referring to this, the static network used in our tests corresponds to such robust super-peers. The only point where minor errors may occur is if a peer crashes right after receiving and acknowledging a query, but before replying to it, which is rather unlikely.

Advanced Experiments and Analysis

In the advanced experimental evaluation, we evaluated the proposed approach running an extended set of experiments on a local environment running up to 74 independent instances. Further, we repeated these tests on Planet-Lab (Chun, B., Culler, D., Roscoe, T., Bavier, A., Peterson, L., Wawrzoniak, M., Bowman, M. (2003)), a worldwide consortium created especially for running large-scale distributed experiments. Planet-Lab is specifically dynamic and unreliable. At the time of

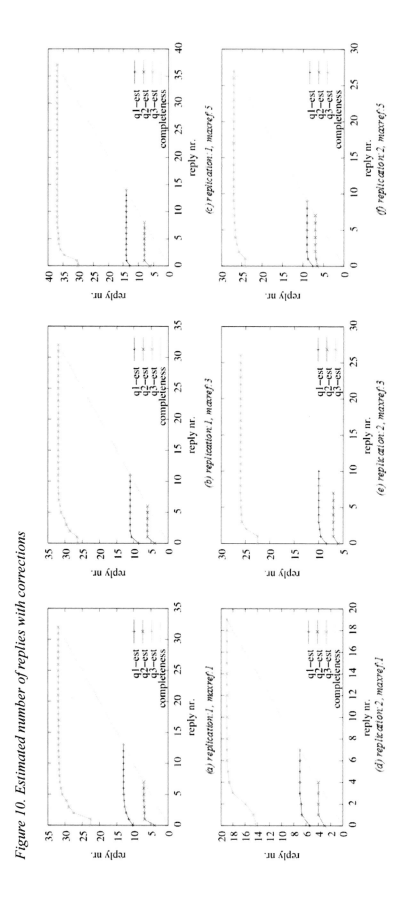

Figure 10. Estimated number of replies with corrections

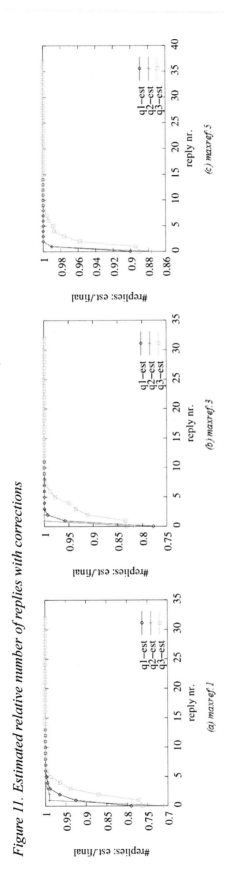

Figure 11. Estimated relative number of replies with corrections

our experiments, we could allocate only very few resources, so that we could only run a couple of our queries in a meaningful sense. In each run we built a P-Grid network with standard parameters from scratch. We based our experiments on a mixture of triple data from DBPedia (http://dbepdia.org), geographical data in relational format from Mondial (http://www.dbis.informatik.uni-goettingen.de/Mondial/), and a small set of ontology data. This data is taken from a realistic scenario combining geographical data from both sets. After a certain waiting time for establishing a suitable overlay trie, we initiated the queries described below. Applying UniStore's vertical data scheme and building two different indexes, this resulted in a total of about 16,000 index entries. The set of all generated keys shows a skewed heavy-tail distribution (power-law like). We ran the tests on networks of size 25, 50 and 74. In Planet-Lab we were able to include about 400 nodes in each run.

The used query mix was chosen in order to be representative for both routing methods introduced and to span from simple to rather complex queries. We divided them into classes of queries, which we refer using $q1$, $q2$, ..., qA, qB etc. Figure 12 shows the general shapes of 5 of these classes. They were issued using different access paths. In addition, we ran two complex queries q_A and q_B involving ontology data and combining it with data from DBPedia and Mondial. qg_1, qg_2 and qg_3 represent queries containing only FNR routings.

The aim of the evaluation is to show that the proposed method works correctly. Further, we will highlight the benefits of using MiMes for achieving a higher accuracy in early query states and compare the three different estimation techniques min, max and avg. From all experiments, we selected the results that are particularly suited for this. In all of the following figures we plot the number of received replies on the x axis. Thus, actual completeness for each query is the straight line from (0,0) to $(\Re, \Re)$. We omit this line in order to improve readability. Rather, we plot

Figure 12. Shape of evaluation queries

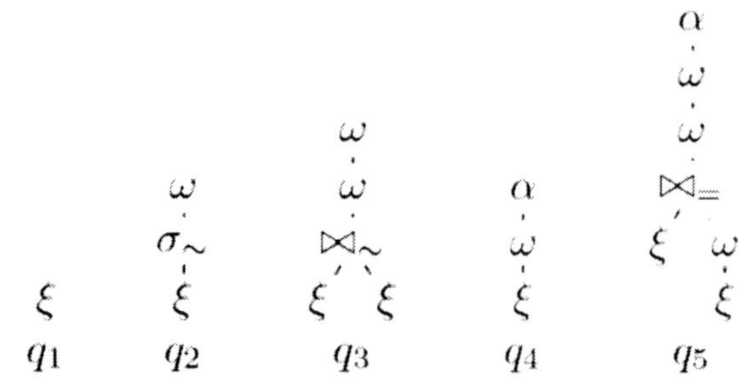

completeness on data level (denoted by *dl*) to additionally show the correlation between both.

We begin with evaluating the accuracy of completeness estimation separately for the supported routing methods. As already shown in the basic experimental evaluation, we expect DOR routings to be estimated very accurate. A more challenging task is to satisfyingly estimate FNR routings, because more information from the routing graph is needed for that. Figure 13 shows representative results by plotting the minimal CE calculated with each received reply. As expected, DOR routings (13(a)) are estimated very accurately with first replies. This is due to the fact that sufficient information about the overlay structure can be collected by one sub-plan traveling through the network. Depending on the number of FNR parts, estimation gets inaccurate in early query states. If only FNR is applied (13(b)), there is a clear gap between estimated and actual query completeness. This gap can also be observed with less FNR parts, e.g., when integrating sequential operators (13(c)). All three figures show that completeness on data level is satisfyingly good approximated by peer level, albeit the drift between both increases with rising query complexity.

Next, we want to investigate the impact of the introduced average and maximal estimation methods. As DOR routings seem to be a by far lower challenge than FNR routings, we focus on queries containing at least one FNR routing. Figure 14 shows corresponding results for selected queries. In 14(a)-14(c) we show that there can be significant differences between all three

techniques. As expected, the minimal number estimation is always above the actual completeness, whereas the maximal one is mostly located below. To our pleasure, completeness on data level is mostly very well approximated by both, minimal and average completeness. The maximal method is rather pessimistic, resulting in a predicted completeness far below the actual one – but this also means, it provides what it was invented for: a guaranteed lower bound. The observed probabilistic guarantee approaches 90% for the maximal estimation rather quickly, whereas the average one usually balances between 50%-80%. As expected, the proposed guarantee is around 2%-5% for the minimal estimation technique.

All the results presented up to here were gathered using MiMe support. We believe in the small overhead worth for achieving a higher quality of estimation. This is approved by the results shown in Figure 15. We chose to picture a query with high degree of parallelism, because MiMes become particularly advantageous in this case. The differences between 15(a) and 15(b) reveal that without heartbeats corrections to the estimated value are bigger and occur more often. The overhead paid for this increases linearly with the number of received replies (15(c)).

Finally, we show that scalability in terms of network size is really no issue for the achieved accuracy. In Figure 16 we picture the completeness plots for three selected queries. All three estimation techniques behave analog to the local setup. As seen before, completeness on peer level is estimated very exactly. This matches the data level very well in most cases, but obviously not in all situations. An irritating point is that our maximal completeness estimation reaches a value higher than 1.0, which should not happen by implementation. This can only be due to high inconsistencies in the overlay structure, caused by the painfully slow nature of Planet-Lab. Currently, we are investigating this issue in detail.

Summarizing, we were able to show the accuracy of the proposed method for estimating query completeness. By introducing three different techniques, we are also able to determine guaranteed lower and upper bounds. The resulting curves show either a straight line or a lightning-like shape, getting the more escalating the higher the degree of parallelism (and data-dependence) gets. The curves produced by Seaweed show a Z-shape instead. This is due to the fact that Seaweed aims at providing delay-aware querying while focusing on aggregate queries. Downtime of unavailable peers is predicted and results are gathered when this time passes. In contrast, UniStore follows a best-effort approach, which is also reflected in the dynamic and online character of its completeness estimation.

CONCLUSION AND FUTURE WORK

In this chapter we faced the problem of completeness estimation in structured overlay systems, where knowledge is usually bounded locally. We motivated the need of an exact estimation for both, user and internal requirements. We have defined completeness in the context of structured P2P systems and motivated its need for both user and system requirements. Beside the limited knowledge, the problem of completeness estimation is quite challenging due to the natural aim of the investigated systems to parallelize a query as much as possible. This gets especially obvious for efficient approaches of range query processing.

For completeness estimation, we distinguished two basic classes of routing methods underlying the query processing strategies. Based on this, we have described the estimation of completeness by observing the progress of query execution at peer (routing) level. Furthermore, we have discussed the accuracy of the estimations in terms of probabilistic guarantees and introduced milestone messages for tracking the query progress.

The proposed method solves this task for several system architectures, while being low-effort but though exact. Thus, it represents an efficient and powerful technique for modern

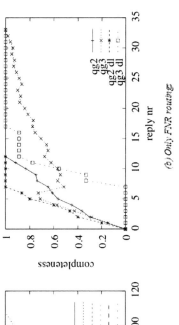

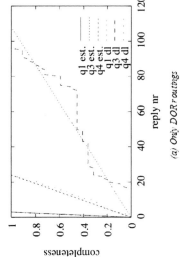

Figure 13. Accuracy for separated routing methods

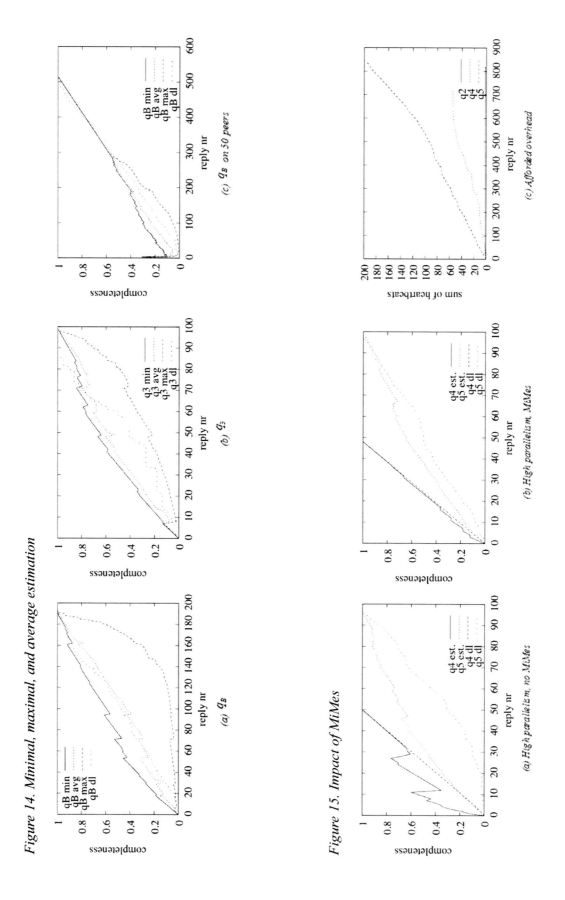

Figure 14. *Minimal, maximal, and average estimation*

Figure 15. *Impact of MiMes*

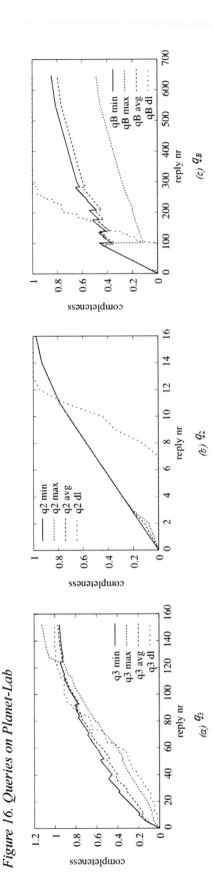

Figure 16. Queries on Planet-Lab

distributed data- and information systems. We have implemented the overall approach as part of our P-Grid-based UniStore system where it is exploited both for giving feedback to the user as well as for supporting blocking operators such as aggregations or skyline operators efficiently. The results of our large-scale experimental evaluation show the suitability of the approach as well as the validity of the estimations.

Main aspects of our ongoing work are the integration of the approach into a sophisticated completeness estimation supported by complex systems like UniStore and the investigation of further algorithmic improvements as well as an extended analytical and empirical evaluation.

ACKNOWLEDGMENT

The work presented in this chapter was (partly) carried out in the frameworks of the EU project TripCom (FP6-IST-4-027324-STP), the Líon project supported by the Science Foundation Ireland under Grant No. SFI/02/CE1/I131 as well as under Grant No. SFI/08/CE/I1380 (Lion-2) and under Grant No. 08/SRC/I1407 (Clique: Graph \& Network Analysis Cluster), and the EPFL Center for Global Computing and supported by the Swiss National Funding Agency OFES as part of the European project NEPOMUK No FP6-027705.

REFERENCES

Aberer, K. (2001). P-grid: A self-organizing access structure for p2p information systems. In *CoopIS'01*, (pp. 179–194).

Aberer, K., Datta, A., Hauswirth, M., & Schmidt, R. (2005). Indexing data-oriented overlay networks. In *VLDB'05*, (pp. 685–696).

Aberer, K., Hauswirth, M., Punceva, M., & Schmidt, R. (2002). Improving data access in P2P systems. *IEEE Internet Computing*, 6.

Aspnes, J., Kirsch, J., & Krishnamurthy, A. (2004). Load balancing and locality in range-queriable data structures. In *ACM PODC*, (pp. 115–124).

Aspnes, J., & Shah, G. (2003). Skip graphs. In *ACM-SIAM Symposium on Discrete Algorithms*, (pp. 384–393).

Bhagwan, R., Moore, D., Savage, S., & Voelker, G. M. (2002). Replication strategies for highly available peer-to-peer storage. In *Future Directions in Distributed Computing*, (pp. 153–158).

Bharambe, A., Agrawal, M., & Seshan, S. (2004). Mercury: Supporting scalable multi-attribute range queries. *SIGCOMM Computer Communication Review, 34*, 353–366. doi:10.1145/1030194.1015507

Börzsönyi, S., Kossmann, D., & Stocker, K. (2001). The skyline operator. In *ICDE'01*, (pp. 421–432).

Brevik, J., Nurmi, D., & Wolski, R. (2004). Automatic methods for predicting machine availability in desktop grid and peer-to-peer systems. In *International Symposium on Cluster Computing and the Grid*, (pp. 190–199).

Cai, M., & Frank, M. (2004). RDFPeers: A scalable distributed RDF repository based on a structured peer-to-peer network. In *WWW'04*, (pp. 650–657).

Castro, M., Costa, M., & Rowstron, A. I. T. (2004). Performance and dependability of structured peer-to-peer overlays. In *DSN'04*, (pp. 9–18).

Chun, B., Culler, D., Roscoe, T., Bavier, A., Peterson, L., Wawrzoniak, M., & Bowman, M. (2003). PlanetLab: An overlay testbed for broad-coverage services. *ACM SIGCOMM Computer Communication Review, 33*, 3–12. doi:10.1145/956993.956995

Daniel, B., Hurley, P., Pletka, R., & Waldvogel, M. (2004). Bringing efficient advanced queries to distributed hash tables. In *Local Computer Networks (LCN'04)*, (pp. 6–14).

Datta, A., Hauswirth, M., Schmidt, R., John, R., & Aberer, K. (2005). Range queries in trie-structured overlays. In *P2P'05*, (pp. 57–66).

Gribble, S. D., Halevy, A. Y., Ives, Z. G., Rodrig, M., & Suciu, D. (2001). What can database do for peer-to-peer? In *WebDB 2001*, (pp. 31–36).

Gupta, A., Agrawal, D., & Abbadi, A. E. (2003). *Approximate range selection queries in peer-to-peer systems.* In CIDR'03.

Huebsch, R., Hellerstein, J. M., Lanham, N., Thau Loo, B., Shenker, S., & Stoica, I. (2003). Querying the Internet with PIER. In *VLDB'03*, (pp. 321–332).

Karnstedt, M., Müller, J., & Sattler, K. (2007). Cost-aware skyline queries in structured overlays. In *ICDE Workshop on Ranking in Databases (DBRank'07)*, (pp. 285–288).

Karnstedt, M., Sattler, K., Richtarsky, M., Müller, J., Hauswirth, M., Schmidt, R., & John, R. (2007). Querying a DHT-based universal storage. In *ICDE'07, Demonstrations Program* (pp. 1503–1504). UniStore.

Karnstedt, M., Sattler, K., & Schmidt, R. (2007). Completeness estimation of range queries in structured overlays. In *P2P'07*, (pp. 71–78).

Kleinberg, J. (1999). *The small-world phenomenon: An algorithmic perspective.* Technical Report 99-1776, Cornell Computer Science.

Levy, A. Y. (1996). Obtaining complete answers from incomplete databases. In *VLDB'96*, (pp. 402–412).

Liau, C. Y., Ng, W. S., Shu, Y., Tan, K. L., & Bressan, S. (2004). Efficient range queries and fast lookup services for scalable p2p networks. In *DBISP2P'04*, (pp. 93–106).

Massoulié, L., Merrer, E. L., Kermarrec, A. M., & Ganesh, A. (2006). *Peer counting and sampling in overlay networks: Random walk methods* (pp. 123–132). ACM PODC.

Motro, A. (1986). Completeness information and its application to query processing. In *VLDB '86*, (pp. 170–178).

Narayanan, D., Donnelly, A., Mortier, R., & Rowstron, A. (2006). Delay aware querying with seaweed. In *VLDB '06*, (pp. 727–738).

Naumann, F., Freytag, J. C., & Leser, U. (2004). Completeness of integrated information sources. *Information Systems, 29*, 583–615. doi:10.1016/j. is.2003.12.005

Ramabhadran, S., Ratnasamy, S., Hellerstein, J. M., & Shenker, S. (2004). Brief announcement: Prefix hash tree. In *ACM PODC*, (p. 368).

Sahin, O. D., Gupta, A., Agrawal, D., & Abbadi, A. E. (2004). A peer-to-peer framework for caching range queries. In *ICDE '04*, (p. 165).

Theobald, M., Weikum, G., & Schenkel, R. (2004). Top-k query evaluation with probabilistic guarantees. In *VLDB '04*, (pp. 648–659).

Triantafillou, P., & Pitoura, T. (2004). Towards a unifying framework for complex query processing over structured peer-to-peer data networks. In *DBISP2P '04, Workshop at SIGMOD '04*, (pp. 169–183).

Compilation of References

Aarts, E. (2004). Ambient intelligence: A multimedia perspective. *IEEE MultiMedia, 11*(1), 12–19. doi:10.1109/MMUL.2004.1261101

Aberer, K. (2001). P-grid: A self-organizing access structure for p2p information systems. In *CoopIS'01*, (pp. 179–194).

Aberer, K., Datta, A., Hauswirth, M., & Schmidt, R. (2005). Indexing data-oriented overlay networks. In *VLDB'05*, (pp. 685–696).

Aberer, K., Hauswirth, M., Punceva, M., & Schmidt, R. (2002). Improving data access in P2P systems. *IEEE Internet Computing, 6*.

Adamson, B., Bormann, C., Handley, M., & Macker, J. (2004). *Negative-acknowledgment (NACK)-oriented reliable multicast (NORM) protocol.*

Agilent. (2006). *IPTV QoE: Understanding and interpreting MDI values.* Retrieved January 11, 2006, from http://www.agilent.com

Agrawal, D., Giles, J., & Verma, D. (2001). On the use of content distribution networks. *Proceedings International Symposium on Performance Evaluation of Computer and Telecommunication Systems*, (pp.221-229). Orlando, FL.

Ahmed, T. (2005). Adaptive packet video streaming over IP networks: A cross-layer approach. *IEEE Journal on Selected Areas in Communications, 23*(2), 385–401. doi:10.1109/JSAC.2004.839425

AirSpan. (2011). Retrieved May 21, 2011, from http://www.airspan.com

Akamai. (2011). *Website.* Retrieved May 11, 2011, from: http://www.akamai.com.

Akimbo. (2010). Retrieved from http://www.akimbo.ca/

Alaya, I., Solnon, C., & Ghdira, K. (2007). Ant colony optimization for multi-objective optimization problems. In *Proceedings of IEEE International Conference on Tools with Artificial Intelligence*, (pp. 450–457).

Almeroth, K. C., & Ammar, M. H. (1998). The interactive multimedia jukebox (IMJ): A new paradigm for the on-demand delivery of audio/video. *Proceedings the 7th Int. World Wide Web Conference (WWW7)*, 431-441.

Al-Shaer, E. (2000). Active management framework for distributed multimedia systems. *Journal of Network and Systems Management, 8*(1), 49–72. doi:10.1023/A:1009415025046

Altman, E., Barman, D., Tuffin, B., & Vojnovic, M. (2006). Parallel TCP sockets: Simple model, throughput and validation. In *Proceedings INFOCOM 2006. 25th IEEE International Conference on Computer Communications* (pp. 1-12). doi:10.1109/INFOCOM.2006.104

Amazon Web Services. (2010, November 9). *Amazon CloudFront service level agreement.* Retrieved from http://aws.amazon.com/cloudfront/sla

Amini, L., Shaikh, A., & Schulzrinne, H. (2003). Modeling redirection in geographically diverse server sets. *Proceedings 12th International Conference on World Wide Web (WWW'03)*, (pp. 472-481).

Amini, L., Shaikh, A., Schulzrinne, H., & Res, I. B. (2004). Effective peering for multi-provider content delivery services. *The 23rd Annual Joint Conference on the IEEE Computer and Communications Societies* (pp. 850-861).

Amini, L., Shaikh, A., Schulzrinne, H., Res, I. B. M., & Hawthorne, N. Y. (2004). Effective peering for multi-provider content delivery services. *Proceedings - IEEE INFOCOM, 04*, 850–861.

Amir, E., McCanne, S., & Katz, R. (1998). An active service framework and its application to real-time multimedia transcoding. *Proceedings ACM SIGCOMM, 98*, 178–189. doi:10.1145/285243.285281

Amir, E., McCanne, S., & Zhang, H. (1995). An application-level video gateway. *Proceedings ACM Multimedia, 95*, 255–265.

Anandasivam, A., & Premm, M. (2009). Bid price control and dynamic pricing in clouds. *Proceedings 17th European Conference on Information Systems (ECIS'09)*.

Andrews, M., Shepherd, B., Srinivasan, A., & Winkler, P. (2002). Clustering and server selection using passive monitoring. *The Twenty-first Annual Joint Conference of the IEEE Computer and Communication Societies* (pp. 1717-1725).

Androutsellis-Theotokis, S., & Spinellis, D. (2004). A survey of peer-to-peer content distribution technologies. *ACM Computing Surveys, 36*(4), 335–371. doi:10.1145/1041680.1041681

Ardaiz, F. F., Ardaiz, O., Freitag, F., & Navarro, L. (2001). Improving the service time of Web clients using server redirection. *ACM SIGMETRICS Performance Evaluation Review, 29*(2), 39–44. doi:10.1145/572317.572324

Arlitt, M., & Jin, T. (2000). A workload characterization study of the 1998 World Cup Web site. *IEEE Network, 14*(3), 30–37. doi:10.1109/65.844498

Armbrust, M., Fox, A., Griffith, R., Joseph, A. D., Katz, R., & Konwinski, A. (2010). A view of cloud computing. *Communications of the ACM, 53*(4), 50–58. doi:10.1145/1721654.1721672

Aspnes, J., & Shah, G. (2003). Skip graphs. In *ACM-SIAM Symposium on Discrete Algorithms*, (pp. 384–393).

Aspnes, J., Kirsch, J., & Krishnamurthy, A. (2004). Load balancing and locality in range-queriable data structures. In *ACM PODC*, (pp. 115–124).

Avanes, A., & Freytag, J. (2008). Adaptive workflow scheduling under resource allocation constraints and network dynamics. In *Proceedings of VLDB Endowment, 1*(2), 1631–1637.

Bakiras, S., & Loukopoulos, T. (2005). Combining replica placement and caching techniques in content distribution networks. *Computer Communications, 28*(9), 1062–1073. doi:10.1016/j.comcom.2005.01.012

Baldi, M., Picco, G. P., & Risso, F. (1998). Designing a videoconference system for active networks. *Journal of Personal Technologies, 2*, 75–84. doi:10.1007/BF01324937

Baldini, A., De Carli, L., & Risso, F. (2009). Increasing performances of TCP data transfers through multiple parallel connections. In *IEEE Symposium on Computers and Communications, ISCC 2009* (pp. 630-636). doi:10.1109/ISCC.2009.5202274

Barbero, J. M., & Pérez, M. B. (2009). *Multilanguage opera subtitling exchange between production and broadcaster companies*. 7th International Conference Information Research and Applications. Madrid, Spain: iTECH.

Barbir, A., Cain, B., Nair, R., & Spatscheck, O. (2003). Known content network (CN) request-routing mechanisms. *Internet Engineering Task Force RFC 3568*.

Barford, P., & Crovella, M. (1999). A performance evaluation of hyper text transfer protocols. *ACM SIGMETRICS Performance Evaluation Review, 27*(1), 188–197. doi:10.1145/301464.301560

Bawa, M., Deshpande, H., & Garcia-Molina, H. (2003). Transience of peers & streaming media. *SIGCOMM Computer Communication Review, 33*(1), 107–112. doi:10.1145/774763.774780

BBC Technology. (2003). *Standard media exchange framework -- SMEF data model version 1.10. (Technical report)*.

Bektas, T., Oguz, O., & Ouveysi, I. (2008). Designing cost-effective content distribution networks. *Computers & Operations Research, 34*(8), 2436–2449. doi:10.1016/j.cor.2005.09.013

Bellifemine, F., Poggi, A., & Rimassa, G. (2001). JADE: A FIPA2000 compliant agent development environment. In *Proceedings of the Fifth International Conference on Autonomous Agents*, (pp. 216–217). ACM Press.

Bellifemine, F., Poggi, A., & Rimassa, G. (2001). Developing multi agent systems with a FIPA-compliant agent framework. *Software, Practice & Experience, 31*, 103–128. doi:10.1002/1097-024X(200102)31:2<103::AID-SPE358>3.0.CO;2-O

Berners-Lee, T., Hendler, J., & Lassila, O. (2001). The Semantic Web. *Scientific American, 284*, 34–43. doi:10.1038/scientificamerican0501-34

Bhagwan, R., Moore, D., Savage, S., & Voelker, G. M. (2002). Replication strategies for highly available peer-to-peer storage. In *Future Directions in Distributed Computing*, (pp. 153–158).

Bharadwaj, V., Ghose, D., Mani, V., & Roberta, T. G. (1996). *Scheduling divisible loads in parallel and distributed systems*. Los Almitos, CA: Wiley-IEEE Computer Society Press.

Bharadwaj, V., & Viswanadham, N. (2000). Sub-optimal solutions using integer approximation techniques for scheduling divisible loads on distributed bus networks. *IEEE Transactions on Systems, Man, and Cybernetics. Part A, Systems and Humans, 30*(6), 680–691. doi:10.1109/3468.895891

Bharambe, A., Agrawal, M., & Seshan, S. (2004). Mercury: Supporting scalable multi-attribute range queries. *SIGCOMM Computer Communication Review, 34*, 353–366. doi:10.1145/1030194.1015507

Bhattacharjee, B. (2010). *NICE*. Retrieved from http://www.cs.umd.edu/projects/nice/

Bhuvaneswaran, R., Katayama, Y., & Takahashi, N. (2007). A framework for an integrated co-allocator for data grid in multi-sender environment. *IEICE Transactions on Communications. E (Norwalk, Conn.), 90-B*(4), 742–749.

Biersack, E. W., Rodriguez, P., & Felber, P. (2004). Performance analysis of peer-to-peer networks for file distribution. *In Proceedings of the Fifth International Workshop on Quality of Future Internet Services (QOFIS'04)*. Retrieved from http://citeseerx.ist.psu.edu/viewdoc/summary?doi=10.1.1.58.9865

Biliris, A., Cranor, C., Douglis, F., Rabinovich, M., Sibal, S., Spatscheck, O., & Sturm, W. (2002). CDN brokering. *Computer Communications, 25*(4), 393–402. doi:10.1016/S0140-3664(01)00411-X

BitTorrent Specification. (2010). Retrieved from http://wiki.theory.org/bittorrentspecification

BitTorrent. (2010). Retrieved from http://www.bittorrent.com

Blake, S., Black, D., Carlson, M., Davies, E., Wang, Z., & Weiss, W. (1998). *An architecture for differentiated service*. Request for Comments 2475, IETF. Retrieved June 10, 2011, from http://www.ietf.org/rfc/rfc2475.txt

Bonastre, O. (2009). Quality models for IPTV content distribution. In O. Bonastre (Ed.), *10th Conference on Telecommunications*, (pp.100-101). Zagreb, Croatia: IEEE Press.

Börzsönyi, S., Kossmann, D., & Stocker, K. (2001). The skyline operator. In *ICDE'01*, (pp. 421–432).

Bouman, J., Trieneken, J., & van der Zwan, M. (1999). Specification of service level agreements, clarifying concepts on the basis of practical research. In Tilley, S., & Verner, J. (Eds.), *Software Technology and Engineering Practice '99* (pp. 169–180). IEEE Computer Society. doi:10.1109/STEP.1999.798790

Braden, R., Clark, D., & Shenker, S. (1994). *Integrated services in the internet architecture: An overview*. Request for Comments 1633, IETF. Retrieved June 10, 2011, from http://www.ietf.org/rfc/rfc1633.txt

Braet, O., & Ballon, P. (2008). Cooperation models for mobile television in Europe. *Telematics and Informatics, 25*(3), 216–236. doi:10.1016/j.tele.2007.03.003

Bresnahan, J., Link, M., Kettimuthu, R., & Foster, I. (2009, December 22). *UDT as an alternative transport protocol for GridFTP*. Retrieved from http://citeseerx.ist.psu.edu/viewdoc/summary?doi=10.1.1.149.3153

Bresnahan, J., Link, M., Kettimuthu, R., Fraser, D., & Foster, I. (2008, April 3). *GridFTP pipelining*. Retrieved from http://citeseerx.ist.psu.edu/viewdoc/summary?doi=?doi=10.1.1.107.2284

Bresnahan, J., Link, M., Khanna, G., Imani, Z., Ketti-muthu, R., & Foster, I. (2007). Globus GridFTP: What's new in 2007. In *Proceedings of the First International Conference on Networks for Grid Applications* (pp. 1-5). Lyon, France: ICST. Retrieved from http://portal.acm.org/citation.cfm?id=1386610.1386636

Brevik, J., Nurmi, D., & Wolski, R. (2004). Automatic methods for predicting machine availability in desktop grid and peer-to-peer systems. In *International Symposium on Cluster Computing and the Grid*, (pp. 190–199).

Broberg, J., Buyya, R., & Tari, Z. (2009). MetaCDN: Harnessing 'storage clouds' for high performance content delivery. *Journal of Network and Computer Applications*, *32*(5), 1012–1022. doi:10.1016/j.jnca.2009.03.004

Bubak, M., Gubala, T., Kapalka, M., Malawski, M., & Rycerz, K. (2005). Workflow composer and service registry for grid applications. *Future Generation Computer Systems*, *21*(1), 79–86. doi:10.1016/j.future.2004.09.021

Busse, I., Deffner, B., & Schulzrinne, H. (1996). Dynamic QoS control of multimedia applications based on RTP. *Computer Communications*, *19*(1), 49–58. doi:10.1016/0140-3664(95)01038-6

Buyya, R., Pathan, M., & Vakali (Eds.), A. (2008). *Content delivery networks* (Vol. 9). Springer, Germany.

Buyya, R., Pathan, M., Broberg, J., & Tari, Z. (2006). A case for peering of content delivery networks. *IEEE Distributed Systems Online*, *7*(10), 3. doi:10.1109/MDSO.2006.57

Buyya, R., Yeo, C. S., Venugopal, S., Broberg, J., & Brandic, I. (2009). Cloud computing and emerging IT platforms: Vision, hype, and reality for delivering computing as the 5th utility. *Future Generation Computer Systems*, *25*(6), 599–616. doi:10.1016/j.future.2008.12.001

Byers, J. W., Luby, M., & Mitzenmacher, M. (2002). Accessing multiple mirror sites in parallel: Using tornado codes to speed up downloads. In *Proceedings INFOCOM'99, Eighteenth Annual Joint Conference of the IEEE Computer and Communications Societies* (Vol. 1, pp. 275–283).

Cabri, G., Leonardi, L., & Zambonelli, F. (2000). Mobile-agent coordination models for internet applications. *IEEE Computer*, *33*(2), 82–89. doi:10.1109/2.820044

Cahill, A. J., & Sreenan, C. J. (2006). An efficient resource management system for a streaming media distribution network. *International Journal Interactive Technology and Smart Education*, *3*(1), 31–44. doi:10.1108/17415650680000051

Cai, M., & Frank, M. (2004). RDFPeers: A scalable distributed RDF repository based on a structured peer-to-peer network. In *WWW'04*, (pp. 650–657).

Calo, S., Verma, D., Agrawal, D., & Giles, J. (2002). On the effectiveness of content distribution networks. *Proceedings International Symposium on Performance Evaluation of Computer and Telecommunication Systems*, (pp. 331-338). San Diego, CA.

Cameron, C. W., Low, S. H., & Wei, D. X. (2002). High-density model for server allocation and placement. *Proceedings ACM SIGMETRICS*, *02*, 152–159. doi:10.1145/511399.511354

Canali, C., Rabinovich, M., & Xiao, Z. (2004). Utility computing for Internet applications. In Tang, X., Xu, J., & Chanson, S. T. (Eds.), *Web content delivery* (pp. 131–151). Springer.

Caragea, D., & Syeda-Mahmood, T. (2004). Semantic API matching for automatic service composition. In *WWW Alt. '04: Proceedings of the 13th international World Wide Web Conference on Alternate Track Papers & Posters*, (pp. 436–437). New York, NY, USA.

Cardellini, V., Colajanni, M., & Yu, P. S. (2000). Geographic load balancing for scalable distributed Web systems. *Proceedings International Symposium on Modeling, Analysis and Simulation of Computer and Telecommunication Systems (MASCOTS'00)*.

Cardellini, V., Casalicchio, E., Colajanni, M., & Yu, P. S. (2002). The state of the art in locally distributed Web-server systems. *ACM Computing Surveys*, *34*(2), 263–311. doi:10.1145/508352.508355

Cardellini, V., Colajanni, M., & Yu, P. S. (2003). Request redirection algorithms for distributed web systems. *IEEE Transactions on Parallel and Distributed Systems*, *14*(4), 355–368. doi:10.1109/TPDS.2003.1195408

Case, J., Mundy, R., Partain, D., & Stewart, B. (2002). *Introduction and applicability statements for internet-standard management framework. RFC 3410.* Informational.

Castro, M., Costa, M., & Rowstron, A. I. T. (2004). Performance and dependability of structured peer-to-peer overlays. In *DSN'04*, (pp. 9–18).

Castro, M., Druschel, P., Kermarrec, A. M., Nandi, A., Rowstron, A., & Singh, A. (2003). High-bandwidth content distribution in a cooperative environment. In *IEEE IPTPS'03.* Splitstream. doi:10.1007/978-3-540-45172-3_27

Caviglione, L., & Cervellera, C. (2011). Design, optimization and performance evaluation of a content distribution overlay for streaming. *Computer Communications, 34*(12), 1497–1509. doi:10.1016/j.comcom.2010.04.047

Cha, M., Choudhury, G., Yates, J., Shaikh, A., & Moon, S. (2006). Resilient backbone network design for IPTV services. *Proceedings of International Workshop on IPTV Services over World Wide Web,* Edinburgh, UK.

Cha, M., Rodriguez, P., Moon, S., & Crowcroft, J. (2008). On next-generation telco-managed P2PTV architectures. In *Proceedings of International Workshop on Peer-To-Peer Systems* (IPTPS), Toronto, Canada.

Charcranoon, S., Robertazzi, T. G., & Luryi, S. (2004). Load sequencing for a parallel processing utility. *Journal of Parallel and Distributed Computing, 64*(1), 29–35. doi:10.1016/S0743-7315(03)00113-8

Chawathe, Y. D. (2000). *Scattercast: An architecture for internet broadcast distribution as an infrastructure service.* PhD thesis.

Chen, Y., Katz, R. H., & Kubiatowicz, J. (2002). Dynamic replica placement for scalable content delivery. *Lecture Notes in Computer Science, Peer-to-Peer Systems: Revised Papers of 1st International Workshop on Peer-to-Peer Systems (IPTPS'02), 2429,* (pp. 306–318).

Cheng, B., Stein, L., Jin, H., Liao, X., & Zhang, Z. (2008). Gridcast: Improving peer sharing for p2p VOD. *ACM Transactions on Multimedia Computing and Communication Applications, 4*(4), 1–31. doi:10.1145/1412196.1412199

Chen, Y., Qiu, L., Chen, W., Nguyen, L., & Katz, R. H. (2003). Efficient and adaptive Web replication using content clustering. *IEEE Journal on Selected Areas in Communications, 21*(6), 979–994. doi:10.1109/JSAC.2003.814608

Chow, C. Y., Leong, H. V., & Chan, A. T. (2007). GroCoca: Group-based peer-to-peer cooperative caching in mobile environment. *IEEE Journal on Selected Areas in Communications, 25*(1), 179–191. doi:10.1109/JSAC.2007.070118

Christin, N., & Chuang, J. (2004). On the cost of participating in a peer-to-peer network. *Lecture Notes in Computer Science, Peer-to-Peer Systems III: Revised paper of 4th International Workshop on Peer-to-Peer Systems (IPTPS'04), 3279,* (pp. 22-32).

Christin, N., & Chuang, J. (2005). A cost-based analysis of overlay routing geometries. *Proceedings IEEE INFOCOM'05, 4,* (pp. 2566-2577).

Christin, N., Chuang, J., & Grossklags, J. (2008). Economics-informed design of CDNs. In Buyya, R., Pathan, A.-M. K., & Vakali, A. (Eds.), *Content delivery networks* (pp. 183–210). Germany: Springer-Verlag. doi:10.1007/978-3-540-77887-5_7

Chu, Y. H., Ganjam, A., Ng, T. S., Rao, S. G., Sripanidkulchai, K., Zhan, J., & Zhang, H. (2004). *Early experience with an internet broadcast system based on overlay multicast.* In USENIX Annual Technical Conference.

Chu, Y. H., Rao, S. G., & Zhang, H. (2000). A case for end system multicast. In *SIGMETRICS '00: Proceedings of the 2000 ACM SIGMETRICS International Conference on Measurement and Modeling of Computer Systems,* (pp. 1–12). New York, NY: ACM.

Chun, B., Culler, D., Roscoe, T., Bavier, A., Peterson, L., Wawrzoniak, M., & Bowman, M. (2003). PlanetLab: An overlay testbed for broad-coverage services. *ACM SIGCOMM Computer Communication Review, 33,* 3–12. doi:10.1145/956993.956995

Clarke, I., Sandberg, O., Wiley, B., & Hong, T. (2001). Freenet: A distributed anonymous information storage and retrieval system. In H. Federrath (Ed.), *Proceedings of Designing Privacy Enhancing Technologies: International Workshop on Design Issues in Anonymity and Unobservability,* (pp. 46-66). Berkeley, CA.

Cohen, B. (2010). *The BitTorrent protocol specification*, version 11031.

Cohen, R. (2008). Content delivery cloud (CDC). *ElasticVapor: Life in the Cloud.*

Conti, M., Gregori, E., & Panzieri, F. (2001). QoS-based architectures for geographically replicated Web servers. *Cluster Computing*, *4*(2), 109–120. doi:10.1023/A:1011412830658

CoolFish. (2011). Retrieved from http://www.cool-fish.org

Cranor, C. D., Green, M., Kalmanek, C., Shur, D., Sibal, S., Van der Merwe, J. E., & Sreenan, C. J. (2001). Enhanced streaming services in a content distribution network. *IEEE Internet Computing*, *5*(4), 66–75. doi:10.1109/4236.939452

Crowcroft, J., Handley, M., & Wakeman, I. (1999). *Internetworking multimedia*. San Francisco, CA: Morgan Kaufmann Publisher.

Crowcroft, J., & Oechsli, P. (1998). Differentiated end-to-end Internet services using a weighted proportional fair sharing TCP. *ACM SIGCOMM Computer Communication Review*, *28*(3), 53–69. doi:10.1145/293927.293930

Cuevas, A., Moreno, J. I., Vidales, P., & Einsiedler, H. (2006). The IMS service platform: A solution for next-generation network operators to be more than bit pipes. *IEEE Communications*, *44*(8), 75–81. doi:10.1109/MCOM.2006.1678113

Cui, Y., & Nahrstedt, K. (2003). Layered peer-to-peer streaming. In *Proceedings of the 13th International Workshop on Network and Operating Systems Support for Digital Audio and Video* (pp. 162-171). Monterey, CA: ACM. doi:10.1145/776322.776348

Cui, Y., Li, B., & Nahrstedt, K. (2004). Ostream: Asynchronous streaming multicast in application-layer overlay networks. *IEEE Journal on Selected Areas in Communications*, *22*(1), 91–106. doi:10.1109/JSAC.2003.818799

Daniel, B., Hurley, P., Pletka, R., & Waldvogel, M. (2004). Bringing efficient advanced queries to distributed hash tables. In *Local Computer Networks (LCN'04)*, (pp. 6–14).

Datta, A., Hauswirth, M., Schmidt, R., John, R., & Aberer, K. (2005). Range queries in trie-structured overlays. In *P2P'05*, (pp. 57–66).

Davis, A. G., Bayart, D., & Hands, D. S. (2006). Quality assurance for IPTV. *IEEE International Symposium on Broadband Multimedia Systems and Broadcasting* (BMSB '09), (pp. 1-7). Bilbao, Spain.

Day, M., Cain, B., Tomlinson, G., & Rzewski, P. (2003). A model for content internetworking (CDI). *Internet Engineering Task Force RFC 3466.*

Day, M., Cain, B., Tomlinson, G., & Rzewski, P. (2003, February). *A model for content internetworking (CDI).* Retrieved from http://tools.ietf.org/html/rfc3466

De Laat, C., & Blom, J. (2000). User-level performance monitoring program. *In Proceedings of TERENA Network Conference 2000,* Lisbon, Portugal.

De Laat, C., Radius, E., & Wallace, S. (2003). The rationale of the current optical networking initiatives. *3rd Biennial International Grid Applications-Driven Testbed Event. Future Generation Computer Systems*, *19*(6), 999–1008. doi:10.1016/S0167-739X(03)00077-3

Deelman, E., Gannon, D., Shields, M., & Taylor, I. (2009). Workflows and e-Science: An overview of workflow system features and capabilities. *Future Generation Computer Systems*, *25*(5), 528–540. doi:10.1016/j.future.2008.06.012

Deshpande, H., Bawa, M., & Garcia-Molina, H. (2001). *Streaming live media over a peer-to-peer network.* Technical Report 2001-30, Stanford InfoLab.

Di Stefano, A., & Santoro, C. (2008). An economic model for resource management in a Grid-based content distribution network. *Future Generation Computer Systems*, *24*(3), 202–212. doi:10.1016/j.future.2007.07.014

Digital Fountain. (2010). *DF Raptor R11 encoder/decoder 2.2.1 software development kit.*

Dilley, J., Maggs, B., Parikh, J., Prokop, H., Sitaraman, R., & Weihl, B. (2002). Globally distributed content delivery. *IEEE Internet Computing*, *6*(5), 50–58. doi:10.1109/MIC.2002.1036038

DMTF. (2011). *Common information model* (CIM). Retrieved from http://www.dmtf.org/ standards/cim/

Do, T. T. (2004). P2vod: Providing fault tolerant video-on-demand streaming in peer-to-peer environment. In *IEEE International Conference on Communications 2004*, (pp. 1467–1472).

Doyle, R. P., Chase, J. S., Gadde, S., & Vahdat, A. M. (2002). The trickle-down effect: web caching and server request distribution. *Computer Communications, 25*(4), 345–356. doi:10.1016/S0140-3664(01)00406-6

Dreibholz, T., Becke, M., Pulinthanath, J., & Rathgeb, E. P. (2010). Implementation and evaluation of concurrent multipath transfer for SCTP in the INET framework. In *Proceedings of the 3rd International ICST Conference on Simulation Tools and Techniques* (pp. 1-8). Torremolinos, Spain: ICST. Retrieved from http://portal.acm.org/citation.cfm?id=1808163

DublinCore. (2003). *Dublin Core metadata element set, version 1.1: Reference description.*

Dumitru, C., Koning, R., & de Laat, C. (2010). *ClearStream: End-to-end ultra fast transmission over a wide area 40Gbit/s Lambda.* Demo Supercomputing 2010.

Dutta, A., Das, S., Chen, W., McAuley, A., Schulzrinne, H. A., & Altintas, O. (2002). MarconiNet supporting streaming media over localized wireless multicast. *Proceedings of the 2nd International Workshop on Mobile Commerce*, (pp. 61-69). Atlanta, GA

Dutta, A., & Schulzrinne, H. (2004). MarconiNET: Overlay mobile content architecture. *IEEE Communications, 42*(2), 64–75. doi:10.1109/MCOM.2003.1267102

EBU. (2005). *P/Meta metadata exchange scheme v1.1. Technical report. Tech.* European Broadcasting Union.

EBU. (2007). *Escort: EBU system of classification of RTV programmes.*

El-Sayed, A., Roca, V., & Mathy, L. (2003). A survey of proposals for an alternative group communication service. *IEEE Network, 17*(1), 46–51. doi:10.1109/MNET.2003.1174177

Elson, J., & Howell, J. (2008). Handling flash crowds from your garage. *Proceedings USENIX 2008 Annual Technical Conference (USENIX'08)*, (pp. 171-184).

Erçetin, O., & Tassiulas, L. (2003). *Request routing in content distribution networks.* (Technical Report). Retrieved from http://digital.sabanciuniv.edu/elitfulltext/3011800000049.pdf

Etoh, M. (2005). Advances in wireless video delivery. *Proceedings of the IEEE, 93*(1), 111–122. doi:10.1109/JPROC.2004.839605

ETSI. (1997). *Digital video broadcasting (DVB): Subtitling systems.* European Telecommunications Standards Institute.

European Commission. (2007). *Future Internet of creative media: Workshop report.* Brussels 26-27/11/2007, organized by "Networked Media Systems Unit" DG INFSO, EC.

Evain, J. (2000). *TV-Anytime metadata: A preliminary specification on schedule.* EBU Tchnical Review No.284.

eXtensible Markup Language. (n.d.). *Specifications.* Retrieved June 15, 2007, from http://www.w3.org/XML/Schema

Falchuk, B., & Karmouch, A. (1997). A mobile agent prototype for autonomous multimedia information access, interaction, and retrieval. *Proceedings of Multimedia Modeling, 97*, 33–48.

Falchuk, B., & Karmouch, A. (1997). AgentSys: A mobile agent system for digital media access and interaction on an internet. *Proceedings of Globecom, 97*, 1876–1880.

Fang, Q., Peng, X., Liu, Q., & Hu, Y. (2009). *A global QOS optimizing Web services selection algorithm based on moaco for dynamic web service composition* (pp. 37–42). International Forum on Information Technology and Applications.

Farrel, A., & Bryskin, I. (2006). *GMPLS: Architecture and applications* (1st ed.). Morgan Kaufmann.

Fei, Z. (2001). A novel approach to managing consistency in content distribution networks. *Proceedings of the 6th International Workshop on Web Caching and Content Distribution*, (pp.77-86), Boston, MA.

Fenius. (2011). Retrieved June 17, 2011, from http://code.google.com/p/fenius/

FFMPEG. (2008). *FFMPEG multimedia system*. Retrieved March 1, 2008, from http://ffmpeg.sourceforge.net/index.php

Fiore, M., Casetti, C., & Chiasserini, C. (2005). On-demand content delivery in vehicular wireless networks. *Proceedings of the 8th ACM international Symposium on Modeling, Analysis and Simulation of Wireless and Mobile Systems*, Montréal, Canada, October 10-13, (pp. 87-94). New York, NY: ACM.

FIPA. (2002). *Agent management support for mobility specification*, (DC00087C, 2002/05/10). Retrieved October 1, 2010, from http://www.fipa.org

FIPA. (2011). *The Foundation for Intelligent Physical Agents*. Retrieved from www.fipa.org

Floyd, S., & Paxson, V. (2001). Difficulties in simulating the Internet. *IEEE/ACM Transactions on Networking*, 9(4), 392–403. doi:10.1109/90.944338

FLUTE implementation. (2010). Retrieved May 2, 2010, from http://mad.cs.tut.fi/

Fortino, G., Garro, A., Mascillaro, S., Russo, W., & Vaccaro, M. (2009). Distributed architectures for surrogate clustering in CDNs: A simulation-based analysis. *UPGRADE-CN'09, Proceedings 18th IEEE International Symposium on High Performance Distributed Computing (HPDC'09) Workshops*, (pp. 3-10).

Fortino, G., Rango, F., & Russo, W. (2010). Statecharts-based JADE agents and tools for engineering multi-agent systems. In R. Setchi, I. Jordanov, R. J. Howlett, & L. C. Jain (Eds.), *14th International Conference Knowledge-Based and Intelligent Information and Engineering Systems, (KES 2010), LNAI 6276* (pp. 240-250). Berlin, Germany: Springer Verlag.

Fortino, G., Russo, W., & Zimeo, E. (2003). Enhancing cooperative playback systems with efficient encrypted multimedia streaming. *Proceedings of IEEE International Conference on Multimedia and Expo (ICME'03)*, (pp. 657-660).

Fortino, G. (2007). CDN-supported Collaborative Media Streaming Control. *IEEE MultiMedia*, 14(2), 60–71. doi:10.1109/MMUL.2007.29

Fortino, G., Calafate, C., & Manzoni, P. (2011). Robust broadcasting of media content in urban environments. In Fortino, G., & Palau, C. E. (Eds.), *Next generation content networks*. Hershey, PA: IGI Global.

Fortino, G., Garro, A., Mascillaro, S., & Russo, W. (2010). Using event-driven lightweight DSC-based agents for MAS modeling. *International Journal on Agent Oriented Software Engineering*, 4(2).

Fortino, G., Mastroianni, C., & Russo, W. (2005). Cooperative control of multicast-based streaming on-demand systems. *Future Generation Computer Systems*, 21(5), 823–839. doi:10.1016/j.future.2004.08.002

Fortino, G., Mastroianni, C., & Russo, W. (2009). A hierarchical control protocol for group-oriented playbacks supported by content distribution networks. *Journal of Network and Computer Applications*, 32(1), 135–157. doi:10.1016/j.jnca.2008.04.001

Fortino, G., & Palau, C. E. (2007). An open streaming content distribution network. In Tatnall, A. (Ed.), *Encyclopaedia of portal technology and applications* (pp. 677–683). Hershey, PA: Idea Publishing Group. doi:10.4018/978-1-59140-989-2.ch112

Fortino, G., & Russo, W. (2008). Using P2P, GRID and agent technologies for the development of content distribution networks. *Future Generation Computer Systems*, 24(3), 180–190. doi:10.1016/j.future.2007.06.007

Fortino, G., Russo, W., Mastroianni, C., Palau, C. E., & Esteve, M. (2007). CDN-supported collaborative media streaming control. *IEEE Multimedia Magazine*, 14(2), 60–71. doi:10.1109/MMUL.2007.29

Fortino, G., Russo, W., & Zimeo, E. (2004). A statecharts-based software development process for mobile agents. *Information and Software Technology*, 46(13), 907–921. doi:10.1016/j.infsof.2004.04.005

Foster, I., Kesselman, C., Nick, J., & Tuecke, S. (2002). *The physiology of the Grid: an open Grid services architecture for distributed systems integration*. Open Grid Service Infrastructure WG, Global Grid Forum.

Francis, P. (2010). *YOID*. Retrieved from http://www.isi.edu/div7/yoid/

Freedman, M. (2010). Experiences with CoralCDN: A five-year operational view. *Proceedings 7th USENIX Symposium on Network Design and Implementation (NSDI '10).*

Freedman, M. J., Freudenthal, E., & Mazieres, D. (2004). Democratizing content publication with Coral. *Proceedings 1st USENIX/ACM Symposium on Networked Systems Design and Implementation (NSDI'04)*, (pp. 239-252).

Fröjdh, P., Horn, U., Kampmann, M., Nohlgren, A., & Westerlund, M. (2006). Adaptive streaming within the 3GPP packet-switched streaming service. *IEEE Network Magazine*, *20*(2), 34–40. doi:10.1109/MNET.2006.1607894

Fuggetta, A., Picco, G. P., & Vigna, G. (1998). Understanding code mobility. *IEEE Transactions on Software Engineering*, *24*(5), 342–361. doi:10.1109/32.685258

Gadde, S., Chase, J., & Rabinovich, M. (2000). Web caching and content distribution: A view from the interior. *Proceedings of the 5th International Workshop on Web Caching and Content Distribution*, (pp.1-12), Lisbon, Portugal.

Gayek, P., Nesbitt, R., Pearthree, H., Shaikh, A., & Snitzer, B. (2004). A Web content serving utility. *IBM Systems Journal*, *43*(1), 43–63. doi:10.1147/sj.431.0043

Geng, X., Gopal, R. D., Ramesh, R., & Whinston, A. B. (2003). Scaling Web services with capacity provision networks. *IEEE Computer*, *36*(11), 64–72. doi:10.1109/MC.2003.1244537

Georganas, N. D., Steinmetz, R., & Nakagawa, T. (Eds.). (1996). Synchronization issues in multimedia communications. *Journal of Selected Areas in Communications*, *14*(1).

Giannoulis, A., Fiore, M., & Knightly, E. W. (2008). Supporting vehicular mobility in urban multi-hop wireless networks. *In Proceedings of the 6th International Conference on Mobile Systems, Applications, and Services*, Breckenridge, CO, USA, June 17-20, (pp. 54-66). New York, NY: ACM.

Gkantisidis, C., Ammar, M., & Zegura, E. (2003). On the effect of large-scale deployment of parallel downloading. *The Third IEEE Workshop on Internet Applications, WIAPP 2003* (pp. 79-89).

Gkantsidis, C., Mihail, M., & Saberi, A. (2005). Hybrid search schemes for unstructured peer-to-peer networks. In *Proceedings IEEE INFOCOM 2005, 24th Annual Joint Conference of the IEEE Computer and Communications Societies* (Vol. 3, pp. 1526-1537). doi:10.1109/INFCOM.2005.1498436

Google Analytics. (2010). Retrieved from http://www.google.com/analytics

Google TV. (2010). Retrieved from http://www.google.com/tv/

Gottfrid, D. (2007). Self-service, prorated super computing fun! *The New York Times.*

Govindan, R., Alaettinoglu, C., & Estrin, D. (1998). *Extensible distributed services.* Tech Report 98-669, Computer Science Department, University of Southern California, Jan. 1998.

Graf, T., Maxwell, G., van Mook, R., van Oosterhout, M., Schroeder, P. B., Spaans, J., & Larroy, P. (2010). *Linux advanced routing & traffic control.* Retrieved April 15, 2010 from http://lartc.org/

Grand, M. (2002). *Patterns in Java (Vol. 1).* Indianapolis, IN: Wiley Publishing Inc.

Grasa, E., Figuerola, S., Recio, J., Lopez, A., Palol, M., & Ribes, L. (2006). Video transcoding in a Grid network with user controlled LightPaths. *Future Generation Computer Systems*, *22*(8), 920–928. doi:10.1016/j.future.2006.03.003

Gray, R., Kotz, D., Cybenko, G., & Rus, D. (2001). Mobile agents: Motivations and state of the art system. In Bradshaw, J. (Ed.), *Handbook of agent technology. AAAI/MIT Press, 2001.*

Gribble, S. D., Halevy, A. Y., Ives, Z. G., Rodrig, M., & Suciu, D. (2001). What can database do for peer-to-peer? In *WebDB 2001*, (pp. 31–36).

Gridnets. (2006). Retrieved June 17, 2011 from https://oscars.es.net/OSCARS/docs/papers/gridnets.pdf

Grossman, R., Gu, Y., Hanley, D., Sabala, M., Mambretti, J., & Szalay, A. (2006). Data mining middleware for wide-area high-performance networks. *Future Generation Computer Systems*, *22*(8), 940–948. doi:10.1016/j.future.2006.03.024

Guo, Y., Suh, K., Kurose, J., & Towsley, D. (2003). P2cast: Peer-to-peer patching scheme for VOD service. In *WWW '03* (pp. 301–309). New York, NY: ACM. doi:10.1145/775152.775195

Gupta, A., Agrawal, D., & Abbadi, A. E. (2003). *Approximate range selection queries in peer-to-peer systems.* In CIDR'03.

Gu, Y., & Grossman, R. L. (2007). UDT: UDP-based data transfer for high-speed wide area networks. *Computer Networks*, *51*(7), 1777–1799. doi:10.1016/j.comnet.2006.11.009

Hacker, T., Noble, B., & Athey, B. (2004). Improving throughput and maintaining fairness using parallel TCP. In *INFOCOM 2004. Twenty-third Annual Joint Conference of the IEEE Computer and Communications Societies* (Vol. 4, pp. 2480-2489). doi:10.1109/INFCOM.2004.1354669

Ham, J., Dijkstra, F., Travostino, F., Andree, H., & de Laat, C. (2005). *Using RDF to describe networks.* Future Generation Computer Systems, Feature topic iGrid.

Ham, J., Dijkstra, F., Grosso, P., Pol, P., Toonk, A., & de Laat, C. (2008). A distributed topology information system for optical networks based on the semantic web. *Optical Switching and Networking*, *5*(2–3), 85–93.

Hamra, A. A., & Felber, P. A. (2005). Design choices for content distribution in P2P networks. *SIGCOMM Computer Communication Review*, *35*(5), 29–40. doi:10.1145/1096536.1096540

Handley, M., & Jacobson, V. (1998). Session description protocol. *IETF RFC 2327.*

Handley, M., Raiciu, C., & Ford, A. (2010, August 25). *TCP extensions for multipath operation with multiple addresses.* Retrieved November 11, 2010, from http://tools.ietf.org/html/draft-ford-mptcp-multiaddressed-03

Harada, F., Ushio, T., & Nakamoto, Y. (2007). Adaptive resource allocation control for fair QoS management. *IEEE Transactions on Computers*, *1*(56), 344–357. doi:10.1109/TC.2007.39

Harel, D. (1987). Statecharts: A visual formalism for complex systems. *Science of Computer Programming*, *8*, 231–274. doi:10.1016/0167-6423(87)90035-9

Härri, J., Filali, F., & Bonnet, C. (2007). Mobility models for vehicular ad hoc networks: A survey and taxonomy. *Research Report RR-06-168*, Institut Eurecom, March.

Hefeeda, M., Habib, A., Botev, B., Xu, D., & Bhargava, B. (2003). Promise: Peer-to-peer media streaming using collectcast. In *MULTIMEDIA '03* (pp. 45–54). New York, NY: ACM.

Hei, X., et al. (2006). Insight into PPLive: Measurement study of a large scale P2P IPTV system. *Proceedings of WWW Conference*, Edinburgh, UK.

Hjelm, J. (2008). *Why IPTV? Interactivity, Technologies and Services.* J. Wiley & Sons, Inc.

Hofmann, M., & Beaumont, L. R. (2005). *Content networking: Architecture, protocols, and practice.* Morgan Kaufmann Publisher.

Holub, P., Matyska, L., Liska, M., Hejtmanek, L., Denemark, J., & Rebok, T. (2006). High-definition multimedia for multiparty low-latency interactive communication. *Future Generation Computer Systems*, *22*(8), 856–861. doi:10.1016/j.future.2006.03.014

Hosanagar, K., Chuang, J., Krishnan, R., & Smith, M. D. (2008). Service adoption and pricing of content delivery network (CDN) services. *Management Science*, *54*(9), 1579–1593. doi:10.1287/mnsc.1080.0875

Hosseini, M., Ahmed, D. T., Shirmohammadi, S., & Georganas, N. D. (2007). A survey of application-layer multicast protocols. *IEEE Communication Surveys and Tutorials*, *9*(3). Retrieved from http://citeseerx.ist.psu.edu/viewdoc/summary?doi=10.1.1.121.1896

Hsieh, H., & Sivakumar, R. (2005). A transport layer approach for achieving aggregate bandwidths on multi-homed mobile hosts. *Wireless Networks*, *11*(1-2), 99–114. doi:10.1007/s11276-004-4749-6

Hsu, C.-H., Chu, C.-W., & Chou, C.-H. (2009). Bandwidth sensitive co-allocation scheme for parallel downloading in Data Grid. *IEEE International Symposium on Parallel and Distributed Processing with Applications* (pp. 34-39).

Hua, K., Tran, D., & Sheu, S. (2003). Zigzag: An efficient peer-to-peer scheme for media streaming. In *INFOCOM 2003*. IEEE.

Huang, C., & Addelzaher, T. (2005). Bounded-latency content distribution: feasibility and evaluation. *IEEE Transactions on Computers, 54*(11), 1422–1437. doi:10.1109/TC.2005.175

Huang, Y., Fu, T. Z. J., Chiu, D.-M., Lui, J. C. S., & Huang, C. (2008). Challenges, design and analysis of a large-scale p2p-VOD system. *ACM SIGCOMM Computer Communication Review, 38*(4), 375–388. doi:10.1145/1402946.1403001

Huber, O. J. (1997). Multimedia services based on agents. *Proceedings of IBC Intelligent Agents Conference.*

Huebsch, R., Hellerstein, J. M., Lanham, N., Thau Loo, B., Shenker, S., & Stoica, I. (2003). Querying the Internet with PIER. In *VLDB'03,* (pp. 321–332).

Hulu. (2010). Retrieved from http://www.hulu.com

IETF. (2011). *Netconf working group.* Retrieved June 17, 2011, from http://www.ops.ietf.org/netconf/

International Telecommunications Union. (ITU) (March 2000). *Generic functional architecture for transport networks. Recommendation ITU-T G.805.* Retrieved June 17, 2011 from http://www.itu.int/rec/T-REC-G.805/

ISO. (2002). *International standard audiovisual number (ISAN)- Part 1: Audiovisual work identifier. ISO 15706-1.*

ISO. (2004). *Guidelines on V-ISAN. ISO 15706.*

ISO/IEC. (2000). *13818-1 Information technology — Generic coding of moving pictures and associated audio information: Systems.*

Ito, T., Ohsaki, H., & Imase, M. (2006). *Gridftp-apt: Automatic parallelism tuning mechanism for data transfer protocol gridftp.* ccGrid, 0--454.

ITU. (2009), *Mechanisms for service discovery and selection for IPTV*, retrieved October 9, 2009, from: http://www.itu.int/md/T09-SG16-090626-TD-WP2-0168/en

Iyengar, J., Amer, P., & Stewart, R. (2006). Concurrent multipath transfer using SCTP multihoming over independent end-to-end paths. *IEEE/ACM Transactions on Networking, 14*(5), 951–964. doi:10.1109/TNET.2006.882843

Izal, M., Urvoy-Keller, G., Biersack, E. W., Felber, P. A., Al Hamra, A., & Garcès-Erice, L. (2004). Dissecting BitTorrent: Five months in a torrent's lifetime. *Passive and Active Measurement Workshop, PAM 2004* (pp. 1-11). Springer.

Jain, R. (2005). I want my IPTV. *IEEE MultiMedia, 12*(3), 95–96. doi:10.1109/MMUL.2005.47

Jannotti, J., Gifford, D. K., Johnson, K. L., Kaashoek, M. F., & O'Toole, J. F., Jr. (2000). Overcast: Reliable multicasting with an overlay network. In *OSDI'00: Proceedings of the 4th conference on Symposium on Operating System Design & Implementation*, Berkeley, CA, USA, USENIX Association.

Jenkac, H., Stockhammer, T., & Xu, W. (2006). Asynchronous and reliable on-demand media broadcast. *IEEE Network Magazine, Special Issue on Multimedia over Wireless Broadband Networks, 20*(2), 14-20.

Jiang, W., Zhang-Shen, R., Rexford, J., & Chiang, M. (2008). Cooperative content distribution and traffic engineering. *Proceedings Workshop on the Economics of Networks, Systems, and Computation (NetEcon'08),* (pp. 7-12).

Jiang, X., Dong, Y., Xu, D., & Bhargava, B. (2003). Gnustream: A p2p media streaming system prototype. In *ICME '03: Proceedings of the 2003 International Conference on Multimedia and Expo,* (pp. 325–328). Washington, DC: IEEE Computer Society.

Jin, X., Wong, W.-C., Gary, S.-H., & Ngan, C. H.-L. (2008, April 2). *A survey and comparison of application-level multicast protocols.* Retrieved from http://citeseerx.ist.psu.edu/viewdoc/summary?doi=10.1.1.97.3413

Johnson, K. L., Carr, J. F., Day, M. S., & Kaashoek, M. F. (2000). The measured performance of content distribution networks. *Proceedings of the 5th International Workshop on Web Caching and Content Distribution,* (pp.1-12), Lisbon, Portugal.

Jo, J., Hong, W., Lee, S., Kim, D., Kim, J., & Byeon, O. (2006). Interactive 3D HD video transport for e-science collaboration over UCLP-enabled GLORIAD lightpath. *Future Generation Computer Systems, 22*(8), 884–891. doi:10.1016/j.future.2006.03.006

Jurca, D., Chakareski, J., Wagner, J., & Frossard, P. (2007). Enabling adaptive video streaming in P2P systems. *Communications Magazine*, *45*(6), 108–114. doi:10.1109/MCOM.2007.374427

Juve, G., & Deelman, E. (2008). Resource provisioning options for large-scale scientific workflows. In *Proceedings of ESCIENCE '08: The 2008 Fourth IEEE International Conference on eScience*, (pp 608–613). Washington, DC: IEEE Computer Society.

Kangasharju, J., Roberts, J., & Ross, K. W. (2002). Object replication strategies in content distribution networks. *Computer Communications*, *25*(4), 367–383. doi:10.1016/S0140-3664(01)00409-1

Kangasharju, J., Ross, K. W., & Roberts, J. W. (2001). Performance evaluation of redirection schemes in content distribution networks. *Computer Communications*, *24*(2), 207–214. doi:10.1016/S0140-3664(00)00316-9

Karaul, M., Korilis, Y. A., & Orda, A. (2000). A market-based architecture for management of geographically dispersed, replicated Web servers. *Decision Support Systems*, *28*(1-2), 191–204. doi:10.1016/S0167-9236(99)00068-8

Karbhari, P., Rabinovich, M., Xiao, Z., & Douglis, F. (2002). ACDN: A content delivery network for applications. *Proceedings of the 2002 ACM SIGMOD International Conference on Management of Data*, (p. 619). Madison, WI.

Karnstedt, M., Müller, J., & Sattler, K. (2007). Cost-aware skyline queries in structured overlays. In *ICDE Workshop on Ranking in Databases (DBRank '07)*, (pp. 285–288).

Karnstedt, M., Sattler, K., & Schmidt, R. (2007). Completeness estimation of range queries in structured overlays. In *P2P '07*, (pp. 71–78).

Karnstedt, M., Sattler, K., Richtarsky, M., Müller, J., Hauswirth, M., Schmidt, R., & John, R. (2007). Querying a DHT-based universal storage. In *ICDE '07, Demonstrations Program* (pp. 1503–1504). UniStore.

Kay, A. (1984). Computer software. *Scientific American*, *251*(3), 53–59. doi:10.1038/scientificamerican0984-52

Kerpez, K. (2006). IPTV service assurance. *IEEE Communications Magazine*, *44*(9), 166–172. doi:10.1109/MCOM.2006.1705994

Khanna, G., Catalyurek, U., Kurc, T., Sadayappan, P., Saltz, J., Kettimuthu, R., & Foster, I. (2008). Multi-hop path splitting and multi-pathing optimizations for data transfers over shared wide-area networks using gridFTP. In *Proceedings of the 17th International Symposium on High Performance Distributed Computing* (pp. 225-226). Boston, MA: ACM. doi:10.1145/1383422.1383457

Khan, S. U., & Ahmad, I. (2008). Comparison and analysis of ten static heuristics-based Internet data replication techniques. *Journal of Parallel and Distributed Computing*, *68*(2), 113–136. doi:10.1016/j.jpdc.2007.06.009

Kleinberg, J. (1999). *The small-world phenomenon: An algorithmic perspective*. Technical Report 99-1776, Cornell Computer Science.

Kleinrock, L., & Gail, R. (1996). *Queueing systems: Problems and solutions*. New York, NY: John Wiley & Sons.

Klingberg, T., & Manfredi, R. (2002, June). *Gnutella 0.6*. Retrieved from http://rfc-gnutella.sourceforge.net/src/rfc-0_6-draft.html

Klusch, M., Fries, B., & Sycara, K. (2006). Automated semantic web service discovery with OWLS-MX. In *AAMAS '06: Proceedings of the Fifth International Joint Conference on Autonomous Agents and Multiagent Systems*, (pp. 915–922). New York, NY, USA.

Kontiki, Inc. (2011). *Enterprise content delivery network*. Retrieved from http://www.kontiki.com/products/enterprise-content-delivery-network

Kostic, D., Rodriguez, A., Albrecht, J., & Vahdat, A. (2003). Bullet: High bandwidth data dissemination using an overlay mesh. *SIGOPS Operation Systems Review*, *37*(5), 282–297.

Kothari, R., & Ganz, A. (2005). Archies: An end-to-end architecture for adaptive live MPEG-4 video streaming over wireless networks. *Proceedings of IEEE International Conference on Wireless and Mobile Computing, Networking and Communications*, (pp. 181-188). Amherst, MA: IEEE Press.

Krishnamurthy, B., Wills, C., & Zhang, Y. (2001). On the use and performance of content delivery networks. *Proceedings of the 1st ACM SIGCOMM Workshop on Internet Measurement*, (pp.169-182), New York, NY

Kusmierek, E., Czyrnek, M., Mazurek, C., & Stroinski, M. (2007). iTVP: Large-scale content distribution for live and on-demand video services. *Proceedings SPIE '07.*

Kwan, W., & Karmouch, A. (1996). Multimedia agents in a distributed broadband environment. *Proceedings of International Conference on Communications (ICC '96),* (pp. 1123-1127).

Kwon, M., & Fahmy, S. (2005). Synergy: An overlay internetworking architecture. *Proceedings 14th International Conference on Computer Communications and Networks (ICCCN '05),* (pp. 401-406).

Lacan, J., Roca, V., Peltotalo, J., & Peltotalo, S. 2009. Reed Solomon error correction scheme. *IETF RMT Working Group, RFC 5510* ("Standards Track/Proposed Standard"), April.

Larribeau, B. (2006). *2006 IPTV standards survey report — Summary, streaming media whitepapers.* Internet Streaming Media Alliance. Retrieved May 30, 2006, from http://www.isma.tv

Lázaro, O., et al. (2007). MULTINET: Enabler for next generation pervasive wireless services. *Proceedings 16th IST Mobile and Wireless Communications Summit,* Budapest, Hungary.

Lecue, F., & Mehandjiev, N. (2009). Towards scalability of quality driven semantic web service composition. In *Proceedings of IEEE International Conference on Web Services,* (pp. 469–476).

Lee, Y.-J., Min, O.-G., & Kim, H.-Y. (2005). Performance evaluation technique of the RTSP based streaming server. *Proceedings of the 4th Annual ACIS International Conference on Computer and Information Science* (pp. 414-417). Washington, DC.

Leighton, T. (2009). *Akamai and cloud computing: A perspective from the edge of the cloud* (No. White Paper). Akamai Technologies, Inc. Retrieved from http://www.akamai.com/cloud

Levy, A. Y. (1996). Obtaining complete answers from incomplete databases. In *VLDB '96,* (pp. 402–412).

Li, Y., & Xu, Z. (2003). An ant colony optimization heuristic for solving maximum independent set problems. In *Proceedings of International Conference on Computational Intelligence and Multimedia Applications.*

Li, Y., Chen, M., Wen, T., & Sun, L. (2008). Quality driven web services composition based on an extended layered graph. In *Proceedings of International Conference on Computer Science and Software Engineering,* (pp. 53– 156).

Liang, J., Kuma, R., & Ross, K. W. (2005). The KaZaA overlay: A measurement study. *Computer Networks Journal (Special Issue on Overlays), 49*(6).

Liau, C. Y., Ng, W. S., Shu, Y., Tan, K. L., & Bressan, S. (2004). Efficient range queries and fast lookup services for scalable p2p networks. In *DBISP2P '04,* (pp. 93–106).

Li, B., Golin, M., Italiano, F., Deng, X., & Sohrabi, K. (1999). On the optimal placement of web proxies on the internet. *Proceedings - IEEE INFOCOM,* 1282–1290.

Liben-Nowell, D., Balakrishnan, H., & Karger, D. (2002). Analysis of the evolution of peer-to-peer systems. *Proceedings of the 21st Annual Symposium on Principles of Distributed Computing,* (pp.233-242), Monterey, CA.

Limelight Networks. (2011). retrieved May 11, 2011, from http://www.limelightnetworks.com

Liston, R., & Zegura, E. (2001). Using a proxy to measure client-side web performance. *Proceedings International Web Content Caching and Distribution Workshop (WCW '01).*

Liu, Z., Wu, C., Li, B., & Zhao, S. (2009). *Distilling superior peers in large-scale P2P streaming systems.* In IEEE INFOCOM 2009. Nicolosi, A. (2003). *P2pcast: A peer-to-peer multicast scheme for streaming data.* In 1st IRIS Student Workshop (ISW03).

Li, Y., Markopoulou, A., Apostolopoulos, J., & Bambos, N. (2008). Content-aware playout and packet scheduling for video streaming over wireless links. *IEEE Transactions on Multimedia, 10*(5), 885–895. doi:10.1109/TMM.2008.922860

Lloret, J., Garcia, M., Bri, D., & Diaz, J. R. (2009). Study and performance of a group-based content delivery network. *Journal of Network and Computer Applications, 32*(5), 991–999. doi:10.1016/j.jnca.2009.03.008

Loulloudes, N., Pallis, G., & Dikaiakos, M. D. (2008). Information dissemination in mobile CDNs. In Buyya, R., Pathan, A.-M. K., & Vakali, A. (Eds.), *Content delivery networks* (pp. 343–366). Germany: Springer-Verlag. doi:10.1007/978-3-540-77887-5_14

Lua, E. K., Crowcroft, J., Pias, M., Sharma, R., & Lim, S. (2005). A survey and comparison of peer-to-peer overlay network schemes. *Communications Surveys & Tutorials*, 7(2), 72–93. doi:10.1109/COMST.2005.1610546

Luby, M. & Vicisano, L. (2004). Compact forward error correction (FEC) schemes. *RFC 3695*, February.

Luby, M., Gemmell, J., Vicisano, L., Rizzo, L., & Crowcroft, J. (2002). Asynchronous layered coding (ALC) protocol instantiation. *IETF RFC 3450*, December.

Luby, M., Watson, M., & Vicisano, L. (2002). *Asynchronous layered coding (ALC) protocol instantiation, request for comments 3450.*

Luby, M., Gasiba, T., Stockhammer, T., & Watson, M. (2007). Reliable multimedia download delivery in cellular broadcast networks. *IEEE Transactions on Broadcasting*, 53(1), 235–246. doi:10.1109/TBC.2007.891703

Maassen, J., Verstoep, K., Bal, H. E., Grosso, P., & de Laat, C. (2009). Assessing the impact of future reconfigurable optical networks on application performance. In Proceedings of *the 2009 IEEE International Symposium on Parallel & Distributed Processing*, (pp. 1-8).

MacAskill, D. (2007). *Scalability: Set Amazon's servers on fire, not yours.* O'Reilly Emerging Technology Conference (ETech'07).

Malli, M., Barakat, C., & Dabbous, W. (2005). An efficient approach for content delivery in overlay networks. *The Second IEEE Consumer Communications and Networking Conference* (pp. 128-133).

Mao, Z. M., Cranor, C. D., Douglis, F., Rabinovich, M., Spatscheck, O., & Wang, J. (2002). A precise and efficient evaluation of the proximity between Web clients and their local DNS servers. *Proceedings USENIX 2002 Annual Technical Conference (USENIX'02)*, (pp. 229-242).

Mao, Z., Cranor, C., Douglis, F., & Rabinovich, M. (2002). A precise and efficient evaluation of the proximity of web clients and their local DNS servers. *Proceedings USENIX 2002 Annual Technical Conference* (USENIX'02), (pp.229-242), Monterey, CA

Martínez Barbero, J., Santos Menendez, E., & Gutierrez Rodriguez, A. (2009). *Automatic titling for international sporting events.* Conference UPGRADE-CN '09 High Performance Distributed Computing HPDC, Garching, Germany, June 09 - 09, 2009. ACM.

Martinez, F. J., Cano, J.-C., Calafate, C. T., & Manzoni, P. (2009). A performance evaluation of warning message dissemination in 802.11p based VANETs. In *Proceedings of the 34th IEEE Conference on Local Computer Networks*, Zürich, Switzerland, October 20-23, (pp. 221-224). IEEE Computer Society.

Masa, M., & Parravicini, E. (2003). Impact of request routing algorithms on the delivery performance of content delivery networks. *Proceedings 22nd IEEE International Performance Computing and Communications Conference*, (pp.5-12), Phoenix, AZ

Mas, I. (2007). IMS-TV: An IMS-based architecture for interactive, personalized IPTV. *IEEE Communications Magazine*, 46(11), 156–163. doi:10.1109/MCOM.2008.4689259

Massonet, P., Deville, Y., & Neve, C. (2002). From AOSE methodology to agent implementation. In *Proceedings of the First International Joint Conference on Autonomous Agents and Multi Agent Systems*, (pp. 27–34). ACM Press.

Massoulié, L., Merrer, E. L., Kermarrec, A. M., & Ganesh, A. (2006). *Peer counting and sampling in overlay networks: Random walk methods* (pp. 123–132). ACM PODC.

McCanne, S. (1999). Scalable multimedia communication using IP multicast and lightweight sessions. *IEEE Internet Computing*, 3(2), 33–45. doi:10.1109/4236.761652

Mendonça, N. C., Silva, J. A. F., & Anido, R. O. (2008). Client-side selection of replicated web services: An empirical assessment. *Journal of Systems and Software*, 81(8), 1346–1363. doi:10.1016/j.jss.2007.11.002

Michlmayr, A., Rosenberg, F., Leitner, P., & Dustdar, S. (2009). Service provenance in QoS-aware web service runtimes. In *Proceedings of IEEE International Conference on Web Services*, (pp. 115–122).

Miller, R. (2008). *Microsoft building own CDN network.* Data Center Knowledge.

Mirror Image Internet, Inc. (2011). *Content delivery network.* Retrieved from www.mirror-image.com/site/solutions/ContentDeliveryNetwork/tabid/69/Default.aspx

Miu, A., & Shih, E. (1999). *Performance analysis of a dynamic parallel downloading scheme from mirror sites throughout the internet. Term Paper.* LCS MIT.

Molina, B., Palau Salvador, C. E., Esteve Domingo, M., Alonso Peña, I., & Ruiz Extremera, V. (2006). On content delivery network implementation. *Computer Communications, 29*(12), 2396–2412. doi:10.1016/j.comcom.2006.02.016

Molina, B., Palau, C., Esteve, M., Alonso, I., & Ruiz, V. (2006). On content delivery network implementation. *Computer Communications, 29*(12), 396–412.

Molina, B., Pileggi, F., Esteve, M., & Palau, C. (2009). A negotiation framework for content distribution in mobile transient networks. *Journal of Network and Computer Applications, 32*(5), 1000–1011. doi:10.1016/j.jnca.2009.03.007

Montpetit, M. J., Klym, N., & Dain, E. (2009). The future of mobile TV: When mobile TV meets social networking. In Cereijo-Roibas, A. (Ed.), *Mobile TV: Customizing content and experience* (pp. 305–326). Springer. doi:10.1007/978-1-84882-701-1_21

Moreau, L., Freire, J., Futrelle, J., & Robert, E. Mcgrath, Myers, J., & Paulson, P. (2008). The open provenance model: An overview. *Provenance and Annotation of Data and Processes,* (pp. 323–326). Berlin, Germany: Springer-Verlag.

Motro, A. (1986). Completeness information and its application to query processing. In *VLDB '86,* (pp. 170–178).

Mühlhäuser, M., & Gecsei, J. (1996). Services, frameworks, and paradigms for distributed multimedia applications. *IEEE MultiMedia, 3*(3), 48–61. doi:10.1109/MMUL.1996.556539

Nabeshima, M. (2005). Performance evaluation of MulTCP in high-speed wide area networks. *IEICE Transactions on Communications. E (Norwalk, Conn.), 88-B*(1), 392–396.

Nan, K., Ma, Y., Zhang, H., & Chen, G. (2006). Transfer, processing and distribution of cosmic ray data from Tibet. *Future Generation Computer Systems, 22*(8), 852–855. doi:10.1016/j.future.2006.03.015

Narasimhan, S. (2009). *Working draft 1.0 – Transport of ISO/IEC 15444-1/AMD4 video over ITU-T Rec H.222.0 | ISO/IEC 13818-1.* Londres.

Narayanan, D., Donnelly, A., Mortier, R., & Rowstron, A. (2006). Delay aware querying with seaweed. In *VLDB '06,* (pp. 727–738).

Natarajan, P., Iyengar, J. R., Amer, P. D., & Stewart, R. (2006). SCTP: An innovative transport layer protocol for the web. In *Proceedings of the 15th International Conference on World Wide Web* (pp. 615-624). Edinburgh, UK: ACM. doi:10.1145/1135777.1135867

Natarajan, P., Baker, F., Amer, P., & Leighton, J. (2009). SCTP: What, why, and how. *IEEE Internet Computing, 13*(5), 81–85. doi:10.1109/MIC.2009.114

Naumann, F., Freytag, J. C., & Leser, U. (2004). Completeness of integrated information sources. *Information Systems, 29*, 583–615. doi:10.1016/j.is.2003.12.005

NETLI. (2011). Retrieved May 11, 2011, from http://www.akamai.com/html/about/press/releases/2007/press_020507.html

Neumann, C. R. (2005). Large scale content distribution protocols. *SIGCOMM Computer Communicaiton Review, 35*(5).

Nguyen, T. V., Chou, C. T., & Boustead, P. (2003). Provisioning content distribution networks over shared infrastructure. *Proceedings 11th IEEE International Conference on Networks (ICON '03),* (pp. 119-124).

Nguyen, A. T., Li, B., & Eliassen, F. (2010). Adaptive peer-to-peer streaming with network coding. In *INFOCOM, 2010 Proceedings IEEE* (pp. 1–9). Chameleon. doi:10.1109/INFCOM.2010.5462032

Nichols, K., Blake, S., Baker, F., & Black, D. (1998). *Definition of the differentiated services field (DS Field) in the IPv4 and IPv6 headers*. Request for Comments 2474. Retrieved June 17, 2011, from http://www.ietf.org/rfc/rfc2474.txt

Ni, J., & Tsang, D. H. K. (2005). Large-scale cooperative caching and application-level multicast in multimedia content delivery networks. *IEEE Communications, 43*(5), 98–105. doi:10.1109/MCOM.2005.1453429

Nsi-Wg. (2011). Retrieved June 17, 2011, from http://forge.ogf.org/sf/projects/nsi-wg/

Obraczka, K. (1998). Multicast transport protocols: A survey and taxonomy. *IEEE Communications Magazine, 36*, 94–102. doi:10.1109/35.649333

OGF. (2011). *Open Grid Forum homepage*. Retrieved June 17, 2011, from www.ogf.org

OMG Specification. (2001). *The unified modeling language*, (N. Formal/01-09-67), v. 1.4, 2001.

Omicini, A., & Zambonelli, F. (1999). Tuple centres for the coordination of internet agents. *Proceedings of ACM Symposium on Applied Computing (SAC'99)*, (pp. 183-190).

Oothongsap, P., Viniotis, Y., & Vouk, M. (2008). *Improvements of the SABUL congestion control algorithm*.

OpenDrac. (2011). *The open dynamic resource allocation controller*. Retrieved June 17, 2011, http://www.opendrac.org

Openmash.org. (n.d.). *MASH toolkit*. University of Berkeley (CA), USA, Retrieved April 15, 2008, from http://sourceforge.net/projects/openmash/

Padmanabhan, V. N., & Sripanidkulchai, K. (2002). The case for cooperative networking. In *IPTPS '01: Revised Papers from the First International Workshop on Peer-to-Peer Systems*, (pp. 178–190). London, UK: Springer-Verlag.

Padmanabhan, V. N., Wang, H. J., Chou, P. A., & Sripanidkulchai, K. (2002). Distributing streaming media content using cooperative networking. In *NOSSDAV '02: Proceedings of the 12th International Workshop on Network and Operating Systems Support for Digital Audio and Video*, (pp. 177–186). New York, NY: ACM.

Paila, T. (2004). *FLUTE - File delivery over unidirectional transport*.

Paila, T., Luby, M., Lehtonen, R., Roca, V., & Walsh, R. (2005). FLUTE – File delivery over unidirectional transport. *IETF RFC 3926*, October.

Pai, V. S., Aron, M., Banga, G., Svendsen, M., Druschel, P., Zwaenepoel, W., & Nahum, E. (1998). Locality-aware request distribution in cluster-based network servers. *ACM SIGPLAN Notices, 33*(11), 205–216. doi:10.1145/291006.291048

Pallis, G., & Vakali, A. (2006). Insight and perspectives for content delivery networks. *Communications of the ACM, 49*(1), 101–106. doi:10.1145/1107458.1107462

Park, H., Yang, J., Park, J., Kang, S. G., & Choi, J. K. (2008). A survey on peer-to-peer overlay network schemes. In *10th International Conference on Advanced Communication Technology, ICACT 2008* (Vol. 2, pp. 986-988). doi:10.1109/ICACT.2008.4493931

Park, K., Pai, V. S., Peterson, L., & Wang, Z. (2004). CoDNS: Improving DNS performance and reliability via cooperative lookups. *Proceedings of the 6th Symposium on Operating Systems Design and Implementation* (OSDI '04), (p. 14). San Francisco, CA

Pathan, M. (2010). *Content delivery networks (CDNs) research directory*.

Pathan, M., & Buyya, R. (2007). Economy-based content replication for peering content delivery networks. *TCSC Doctoral Symposium, Proceedings 7th IEEE International Symposium on Cluster Computing and the Grid (CCGrid'07)*, (pp. 887-892).

Pathan, M., & Buyya, R. (2008b). Performance models for peering content delivery Networks. *The 16th IEEE International Conference on Networks, ICON 2008*.

Pathan, M., Broberg, J., & Buyya, R. (2009). Maximizing utility for content delivery clouds. *Lecture Notes in Computer Science, Proceedings 10th International Conference on Web Information Systems Engineering (WISE'09), 5802*, (pp. 13-28).

Pathan, M., Broberg, J., & Buyya, R. (2008). Inter-networking of CDNs. In Buyya, R., Pathan, A.-M. K., & Vakali, A. (Eds.), *Content delivery networks* (pp. 389–413). Germany: Springer-Verlag. doi:10.1007/978-3-540-77887-5_16

Pathan, M., & Buyya, R. (2008a). A taxonomy of CDNs. In Pathan, M., Buyya, R., & Vakali, A. (Eds.), *Content delivery networks* (pp. 33–77). Springer-Verlag. doi:10.1007/978-3-540-77887-5_2

Pathan, M., & Buyya, R. (2009a). Architecture and performance models for QoS-driven effective peering of content delivery networks. *Multiagent and Grid Systems*, *5*(2), 165–195.

Pathan, M., & Buyya, R. (2009b). Resource discovery and request-redirection for dynamic load sharing in multi-provider peering content delivery networks. *Journal of Network and Computer Applications*, *32*(5), 976–990. doi:10.1016/j.jnca.2009.03.003

Peltotalo, S., Peltotalo, J., & Roca, V. (2004). *Simple XOR, Reed-Solomon, and parity check matrix-based FEC schemes*. IETF RMT Working Group, draft-peltotalo-rmt-bb-fec-supp-xor-pcm-rs-00.txt (Work in Progress), June.

Peng, G. (2003). *CDN: Content distribution network*. Technical Report TR-125, Experimental Computer Systems Lab, Department of Computer Science, State University of New York, Stony Brook, NY.

Philopoulos, S., & Maheswaran, M. (2001). Experimental study of parallel downloading schemes for internet mirror sites. In *Thirteenth IASTED International Conference on Parallel and Distributed Computing Systems, PDCS '01*, (pp. 44-48).

Picco, G. P., Murphy, A. L., & Roman, G.-C. (2000). Software engineering for mobility: A roadmap. In Finkelstein, A. (Ed.), *The future of software engineering* (pp. 241–258). New York, NY: ACM Press.

Pierre, G., & van Steen, M. (2001). Globule: A platform for self-replicating Web documents. *Lecture Notes in Computer Science, Proceedings 6th International Conference on Protocols for Multimedia Systems (PROMS'01)*, *2213*, (pp. 1-11).

Pierre, G., & van Steen, M. (2006). Globule: A collaborative content delivery network. *IEEE Communications Magazine*, *44*(8), 127–133. doi:10.1109/MCOM.2006.1678120

PlanetLab. (2011). Retrieved May 11, 2011, from http://www.planet-lab.org/

Popescu, A., Constantinescu, D., Erman, D., & Ilie, D. (2007). A survey of reliable multicast communication. In *3rd EuroNGI Conference on Next Generation Internet Networks*, (pp. 111-118). doi:10.1109/NGI.2007.371205

PPLive. (2010). Retrieved from http://www.pplive.com

PPStream. (2010). Retrieved from http://www.ppstream.com

Presti, F. L., Bartolini, N., & Petrioli, C. (2005). Dynamic replica placement and user request redirection in content delivery networks. *Proceedings International Conference on Communications (ICC'05)*, (pp. 1495-1501).

Pueschel, T., Anandasivam, A., Buschek, S., & Neumann, D. (2009). Making money with clouds: Revenue optimization through automated policy decisions. *Proceedings 17th European Conference on Information Systems (ECIS'09)*.

Qiu, L., Padmanabhan, V. N., & Voelker, G. M. (2001). On the placement of web server replicas. *Proceedings - IEEE INFOCOM*, 1587–1596.

Qualcomm. (2009). *WiMAX vs 3G whitepaper*. Retrieved January 11, 2009, from http://www.qualcomm.com

Qureshi, A., Weber, R., Balakrishnan, H., Guttag, J., & Maggs, B. (2009). Cutting the electric bill for Internet-scale systems. *Proceedings ACM SIGCOMM'09*.

Rabinovich, M., Xiao, Z., & Aggarwal, A. (2003). Computing on the edge: A platform for replicating internet applications. *Proceedings 8th International Workshop on Web Content Caching and Distribution (WCW'03)*.

Rahul, H., Kasbekar, M., Sitaraman, R., & Berger, A. (2006). Towards realizing the performance and availability benefits of a global overlay network *Proceedings 7th International Conference on Passive and Active Network Measurement (PAM'06)*.

Raicu, I., Zhao, Y., Dumitrescu, C., Foster, I., & Wilde, M. (2007). Falkon: A fast and light-weight task execution framework. In *SC '07: Proceedings of the 2007 ACM/ IEEE Conference on Supercomputing*, (pp. 1–12). New York: ACM.

Rajbhandari, S., Contes, A. F., Rana, O., Deora, V., & Wootten, I. (2006). Trust assessment using provenance in service oriented applications. In *Proceedings of International Conference on Enterprise Distributed Object Computing Workshops*.

Ramabhadran, S., Ratnasamy, S., Hellerstein, J. M., & Shenker, S. (2004). Brief announcement: Prefix hash tree. In *ACM PODC*, (p. 368).

Ramanujan, R. S., & Thurber, K. J. (1998). An active network based design of a QoS adaptive video multicast service. *Proceedings of International Conference on Information Systems, Analysis and Synthesis (ISAS'98),* (pp. 643–650).

Ranaldo, N., & Zimeo, E. (2006). *An economy-driven mapping heuristic for hierarchical master-slave applications in grid systems.* The 20th IEEE International Conference on Parallel and Distributed Processing, IPDPS 2006.

Ranaldo, N., & Zimeo, E. (2009). Time and cost-driven scheduling of data parallel tasks in grid workflows. *Systems Journal*, *3*(1), 104–120. doi:10.1109/JSYST.2008.2011299

Rangarajan, S., Mukherjee, S., & Rodriguez, P. (2003). A technique for user specific request redirection in a content delivery network. *Proceedings 8th International Web Content Caching and Distribution Workshop (WCW'03)*.

Rangwala, S., Jindal, A., Jang, K., Psounis, K., & Govindan, R. (2008). Understanding congestion control in multi-hop wireless mesh networks. In *Proceedings of the 14th ACM International Conference on Mobile Computing and Networking* (pp. 291-302). San Francisco, CA: ACM. doi:10.1145/1409944.1409978

Ranjan, S., Karrer, R., & Knightly, E. (2004). Wide area redirection of dynamic content by internet data centers. *Proceedings IEEE INFOCOM'04*.

Ratnasamy, S., Handley, M., Karp, R., & Shenker, S. (2002). Topologically-aware overlay construction and server selection. *INFOCOM 2002. The Twenty-first Annual Joint Conference of the IEEE Computer and Communication Societies* (pp. 1190-1199).

Rayburn, D. (2009). CDN research data: Market sizing and pricing trends. *Streaming Media West: The Business and Technology of Online Video*.

Reimers, U. (2006). DVB-The Family of International Standards for Digital Video Broadcasting. *Proceedings of the IEEE*, *94*(1), 173–182. doi:10.1109/JPROC.2005.861004

Rejaie, R., & Ortega, A. (2003). PALS: Peer-to-peer adaptive layered streaming. In *Proceedings of the 13th International Workshop on Network and Operating Systems Support for Digital Audio and Video* (pp. 153-161). Monterey, CA: ACM. doi:10.1145/776322.776347

Ren, S., Guo, L., & Zhang, X. (2006). ASAP: An as-aware peer-relay protocol for high quality VOIP. In *ICDCS '06* (p. 70). Washington, DC: IEEE Computer Society.

Retnasothie, F. E., et al. (2006). Wireless IPTV over WiMAX: Challenges and applications. *Proceeding IEEE Annual Wireless and Microwave Technology Conference (WAMICON)*, (pp. 1-5). Clearwater, FL: IEEE Press.

Rodriguez, P., & Sibal, S. (2000). SPREAD: Scalable platform for reliable and efficient automated distribution. *Proceedings of the 9ᵗʰ World Wide Web Conference*, Amsterdam (The Netherlands).

Rodriguez, P., Kirpal, A., & Biersack, E. W. (2000). *Parallel-access for mirror sites in the internet*. Retrieved from http://citeseerx.ist.psu.edu/viewdoc/summary?doi=10.1.1.83.3395

Rodriguez, P., & Biersack, E. W. (2002). Dynamic parallel access to replicated content in the internet. *IEEE/ACM Transactions on Networking*, *10*(4), 455–465. doi:10.1109/TNET.2002.801413

Rodriguez, P., & Biersack, E. W. (2002). Dynamic parallel access to replicated content in the Internet. *IEEE/ACM Transactions on Networking*, *10*(4), 455–465. doi:10.1109/TNET.2002.801413

Rosenberg, F., Leitner, P., Michlmayr, A., Celikovic, P., & Dustdar, S. (2009). Towards composition as a service - a quality of service driven approach. In *Proceedings of International Conference on Data Engineering*, (pp. 1733–1740).

Rossi, D., Testa, C., Valenti, S., & Muscariello, L. (2010). LEDBAT: The new BitTorrent congestion control protocol. In *2010 Proceedings of 19th International Conference on Computer Communications and Networks (ICCCN)*, (pp. 1-6). doi:10.1109/ICCCN.2010.5560080

Rowe, L. A. (2001). Streaming media middleware is more than streaming media. *Proceedings of the 2001 International Workshop on Multimedia Middleware (M3W)*.

Roy, S., Covell, M., Ankcorn, J., Wee, S., & Yoshimura, T. (2003). A system architecture for managing mobile streaming media service. *Proceedings International Conference on Distributed Computing Systems* (ICDCS'03), (pp. 408-413). Providence, RI

Sabata, B., Chatterjee, S., Davis, M., Sydir, J., & Lawrence, T. F. (1997). Taxonomy of QoS specifications. In *Proceedings of IEEE International Workshop on Object-Oriented Real-Time Dependable Systems*, (pp. 0-100). IEEE Computer Society.

Sage. (2010). *Scalable adaptive graphics environment*. Retrieved June 17, 2011, http://www.evl.uic.edu/cavern/sage/

Sahin, O. D., Gupta, A., Agrawal, D., & Abbadi, A. E. (2004). A peer-to-peer framework for caching range queries. In *ICDE'04*, (p. 165).

Sariou, S., Gummadi, K. P., Dunn, R., Gribble, S., & Levi, H. M. (2002). An analysis on Internet content delivery systems. *Proceedings 5th Symposium on Operating Systems Design and Implementation*, (pp. 315-327). Boston, MA.

Satoh, I. (2000). A hierarchical model of mobile agents and its multimedia applications. *Proceedings of the IEEE International Workshop on Multimedia Network Systems (MMNS'2000)*, (pp. 103-108).

Sauer, S., & Engels, G. (1999). OMMMA: An object-oriented approach for modeling multimedia information systems. *Proceedings of the 5th International Workshop on Multimedia Information Systems (MIS)*, (pp. 64-71).

Schatz, R., & Egger, S. (2008). Social interaction features for mobile TV services. *Proceedings IEEE International Symposium on Broadband Multimedia Systems and Broadcasting*, (pp. 1-6). Las Vegas, NV. IEEE Press.

Schorr, A., Kassler, A., & Petrovic, G. (2004). Adaptive media streaming in heterogeneous wireless networks. *Proceedings IEEE Multimedia Signal Processing Conference*, (pp. 506-509). Siena, Italy. IEEE Press.

Schulzrinne, H., Casner, S., Frederick, R., & Jacobson, V. (1996). RTP: A transport protocol for real-time applications. *IETF RFC 1889*.

Schulzrinne, H., et al. (n.d.). *RTP tools* (v. 1.18), Retrieved from http://www.cs.columbia.edu/IRT/software/rtptools/

Schulzrinne, H., Rao, A., & Lanphier, R. (1998). Real time streaming protocol (RTSP). *IETF RFC 2326*.

Schulzrinne, H., Schooler, E., & Rosemberg, J. (1999). SIP: Session initiation protocol. *IETF RFC 2543*.

Sentinelli, A., Marfia, G., Gerla, M., Kleinrock, L., & Tewari, S. (2007). Will IPTV ride the peer-to-peer stream? *IEEE Communications Magazine*, *45*(6), 86–92. doi:10.1109/MCOM.2007.374424

Shah, P., Pâris, J. F., Morgan, J., Schettino, J., & Venkatraman, C. (2008). A P2P-based architecture for secure software delivery using volunteer assistance. *Proceedings International Conference on Peer-to-Peer Networks (P2P'08)*.

Shaikh, A., Tewari, R., Agrawal, M., Center, I., & Heights, Y. (2001). On the effectiveness of DNS-based server selection. *Proceedings - IEEE INFOCOM*, 1801–1810.

Shaikh, A., Tewari, R., Agrawal, M., Center, I., & Heights, Y. (2001). On the effectiveness of DNS-based server selection. *Proceedings - IEEE INFOCOM*, *01*, 1801–1810.

Shalunov, S. (2008). *Users want P2P, we make it work*. In IETF P2P Infrastructure Workshop.(May 2008).

Shalunov, S. (2009, March 4). *Low extra delay background transport (LEDBAT)*. Retrieved October 14, 2010, from http://tools.ietf.org/html/draft-shalunov-ledbat-congestion-00

She, J., Hou, F., Ho, P.-H., & Xie, L.-L. (2007). IPTV over WiMAX: Key success factors, challenges, and solutions. *IEEE Communications Magazine*, *45*(8), 87–93. doi:10.1109/MCOM.2007.4290319

Shimizu, T., Shirai, D., Takahashi, H., Murooka, T., Obana, K., & Tonomura, Y. (2006). International real-time streaming of 4K digital cinema. *Future Generation Computer Systems*, *22*(8), 929–939. doi:10.1016/j.future.2006.04.001

Shokrollahi, A. (2006). Raptor codes. *IEEE Transactions on Information Theory*, *52*, 2551–2567. doi:10.1109/TIT.2006.874390

Si, J., Zhuang, B., Cai, A., & Cheng, Y. (2009). Layered network coding and hierarchical network coding for peer-to-peer streaming. In *Pacific-Asia Conference on Circuits, Communications and Systems, PACCS '09* (pp. 139-142). doi:10.1109/PACCS.2009.111

SINOCDN. (2011). Retrieved May 11, 2011, from http://www.sinocdn.com

Sivasubramanian, S., Szymaniak, M., Pierre, G., & Van Steen, M. (2004). Replication for Web hosting systems. *ACM Computing Surveys*, *36*(3), 291–334. doi:10.1145/1035570.1035573

Smarr, L., Brown, M., de Fanti, T., & de Laat, C. (2006). Special Issue on iGrid2005. *Future Generation Computer Systems*, *22*(8).

Sobeih, A., Yurcik, W., & Hou, J. C. (2004). VRing: A case for building application-layer multicast rings (rather than trees). In *Proceedings of the IEEE Computer Society's 12th Annual International Symposium on Modeling, Analysis, and Simulation of Computer and Telecommunications Systems, MASCOTS'04*, (pp. 437-446).

Sobieski, J., Lehman, T., Jabbari, B., Ruszczyk, C., Summerhill, R., & Whitney, A. (2006). Dynamic provisioning of LightPath services for radio astronomy applications. *Future Generation Computer Systems*, *22*(8), 984–992. doi:10.1016/j.future.2006.03.012

Sohn, J., Robertazzi, T. G., & Luryi, S. (1998). Optimizing computing costs using divisible load analysis. *IEEE Transactions on Parallel and Distributed Systems*, *9*(3), 225–234. doi:10.1109/71.674315

Stoica, I., Morris, R., Karger, D., Kaashoek, M. F., & Balakrishnan, H. (2001). Chord: A scalable peer-to-peer lookup service for internet applications. In *SIGCOMM '01* (pp. 149–160). New York, NY: ACM. doi:10.1145/383059.383071

StrandVenice. (2010). Retrieved from http://www.strandvenice.com/

Subramanya, S. R., & Yi, B. K. (2005). Utility model for on-demand digital content. *IEEE Computer*, *38*(6), 95–98. doi:10.1109/MC.2005.206

Sun Microsystems Inc. (n.d.). *Java media framework*. Retrieved November 15, 2009, from http://java.sun.com/products/java-media/jmf/index.html

Surana, S., Godfrey, B., Lakshminarayanan, K., Karp, R., & Stoica, I. (2006). Load balancing in dynamic structured peer-to-peer systems. *Performance Evaluation*, *63*(3), 217–240. doi:10.1016/j.peva.2005.01.003

Tan, E., Guo, L., & Chen, S. (2007). *SCAP: Smart caching in wireless access points to improve P2P streaming*. In ICDCS. Retrieved from http://citeseerx.ist.psu.edu/viewdoc/summary?doi=10.1.1.116.2072

Taniuchi, K., Ohba, Y., Fajardo, V., Das, S., Tauil, M., & Cheng, Y. H. (2009). IEEE 802.21: Media independent handover: Features, applicability, and realization. *IEEE Communications Magazine*, *47*(1), 112–120. doi:10.1109/MCOM.2009.4752687

Tennenhouse, D. L., Smith, J. M., Sincoskie, W. D., Wetherall, D. J., & Minden, G. J. (1997). A survey of active networks research. *IEEE Communications Magazine*, *35*, 80–86. doi:10.1109/35.568214

Thampi, S. M. (2010). Survey of search and replication schemes in unstructured P2P networks. *Network Protocols and Algorithms*, *2*(1), 93. doi:10.5296/npa.v2i1.263

The SURFNet. (2002). *The surfnet homepage*. Retrieved June 17, 2011, http://www.surfnet.nl/

Theobald, M., Weikum, G., & Schenkel, R. (2004). Top-k query evaluation with probabilistic guarantees. In *VLDB'04*, (pp. 648–659).

Tran, M., & Tavanapong, W. (2005). Peers-assisted dynamic content distribution networks. *Proceedings 30th IEEE International Conference on Local Computer Networks (LCN'05)*, (pp. 123-131).

Travostino, F., Daspit, P., Gommans, L., Jog, C., de Laat, C., & Mambretti, J. (2006). Seamless live migration of virtual machines over the MAN/WAN. *Future Generation Computer Systems, 22*(8), 901–907. doi:10.1016/j.future.2006.03.007

Triantafillou, P., & Pitoura, T. (2004). Towards a unifying framework for complex query processing over structured peer-to-peer data networks. In *DBISP2P'04, Workshop at SIGMOD'04*, (pp. 169–183).

Turaga, D. S., van der Schaar, M., & Ratakonda, K. (2005). Enterprise multimedia streaming: Issues, background and new developments. *Proceedings of IEEE International Conference on Multimedia and Expo* (ICME'05), (pp.1-6). Amsterdam (The Netherlands).

Turrini, E. (2004). *An architecture for content distribution internetworking.* (Technical Report UBLCS-2004-2). University of Bologna, Italy.

Turrini, E., & Panzieri, F. (2002). Using P2P techniques for content distribution internetworking: A research proposal. *Proceedings International Conference on Peer-to-Peer Computing (P2P'02)*.

Vakali, A., & Pallis, G. (2003). Content delivery networks: Status and trends. *IEEE Internet Computing, 7*(6), 68–74. doi:10.1109/MIC.2003.1250586

Vanhastel, S. (2008). Enabling IPTV: What's needed in the access network. *IEEE Communications Magazine, 46*(8), 90–95. doi:10.1109/MCOM.2008.4597110

Vassiliou, V., Antoniou, P., Giannakou, I., & Pitsillides, A. (2006). Requirements for the transmission of streaming video in mobile wireless networks. *Proceedings of ICANN 2006*, Athens, Greece.

Velocix. (2011). *Advanced content distribution.* Retrieved from http://www.velocix.com/network_distribution.php

Venugopal, S., Buyya, R., & Ramamohanarao, K. (2006). A taxonomy of data grids for distributed data sharing, management and processing. *ACM Computing Surveys, 38*(1), 1-53. ISSN 0360-0300

Verma, D. C. (2002). *Content distribution networks: An engineering approach.* Indianapolis, IN: John Wiley & Sons. doi:10.1002/047122457X

Verma, D., Calo, S., & Amiri, K. (2002). Policy based management of content distribution networks. *IEEE Network, 15*(3), 34–39. doi:10.1109/65.993221

Vincenty, T. (1975). Direct and inverse solutions of geodesics on the ellipsoid with application of nested equations. *Survey Review, 22*(176), 88–93.

Voddler. (2011). Retrieved May 11, 2011, from: http://www.voddler.com

W3C. (2010). *Resource description framework.* Retrieved from http://www.w3.org/RDF/

W3C. (2010). *Timed text markup language (TTML) 1.0 – Distribution format exchange profile (DFXP).*

Wales, C., Kim, S., Leuenberger, D., Watts, W., & Weinroth, O. (2005). *IPTV - The revolution is here.* White paper. Retrieved June 11, 2011, from http://www.cs.berkeley.edu/~binetude/course/eng298a_2

Wang, J., & Yurcik, W. (2008, February 5). *A survey and comparison of multi-ring techniques for scalable battlespace group communications.* Retrieved from http://citeseerx.ist.psu.edu/viewdoc/summary?doi=10.1.1.60.7337

Wang, L., Pai, V. S., & Peterson, L. (2002). The effectiveness of request redirection on CDN robustness. *Proceedings of 5th Symposium on Operating Systems Design and Implementation*, (pp. 345-360). Boston, MA.

Wang, L., Park, K. S., Pang, R., Pai, V., & Peterson, L. (2004). Reliability and security in the CoDeeN content distribution network. *Proceedings USENIX 2004 Annual Technical Conference (USENIX'04)*.

Wang, W., & Zhang, H. (2009). Study on application layer multicast technology based on P2P streaming media system. In *2009 International Symposium on Computer Network and Multimedia Technology* (pp. 1-4). doi:10.1109/CNMT.2009.5374604

Wang, L., Pai, V., & Peterson, L. (2002). The effectiveness of request redirection on CDN robustness. *ACM SIGOPS Operating Systems Review, 36*, 345–360. doi:10.1145/844128.844160

302

Web Services Description Language. (n.d.). *Specifications*. Retrieved June 15, 2007, from http://www.w3c.org/TR/wsdl.html

Wee, S., Apostolopoulos, J., Tan, W., & Roy, S. (2003). Research and design of a mobile streaming media content delivery network. *Proceedings of IEEE International Conference on Multimedia and Expo* (ICME'03), (pp. 5-8). Baltimore, MD.

Welzl, M. (2010, May 21). *A survey of lower-than-best effort transport protocols.* Retrieved October 14, 2010, from http://tools.ietf.org/html/draft-welzl-ledbat-survey-00

Wiegand, T., Sullivan, G. J., Bjontegaard, G., & Luthra, A. (2003). Overview of the H.264/AVC video coding standard. *IEEE Transactions on Circuits and Systems for Video Technology, 13*(7), 560–576. doi:10.1109/TCSVT.2003.815165

Wischik, D., Handley, M., & Raiciu, C. (2009). Control of multipath TCP and optimization of multipath routing in the Internet. *Proceedings of the 3ʳᵈ Conference on Network Control and Optimization,* 204–218.

Wooldridge, M., & Jenings, N. (1995). Intelligent agents: Theory and practice. *The Knowledge Engineering Review, 10*(2), 115–152. doi:10.1017/S0269888900008122

Wu, J. J., Shih, S., Liu, P., & Chung, Y. (2011). Optimizing server placement in distributed systems in the presence of competition. *Journal of Parallel and Distributed Computing, 71*(1), 62–76. doi:10.1016/j.jpdc.2010.08.008

Xiao, Y. (2007). Internet protocol television (IPTV): The killer application for the next-generation internet. *IEEE Communications Magazine, 45*(11), 126–134. doi:10.1109/MCOM.2007.4378332

Xie, H., Yang, Y. R., Krishnamurthy, A., Liu, Y., & Silberschatz, A. (2008). P4P: Provider portal for (P2P) applications. *Proceedings ACM SIGCOMM'08.*

Xu, K., Zhang, M., Liu, J., Qin, Z., & Ye, M. (2010). Proxy caching for peer-to-peer live streaming. *Computer Networks, 54*(7), 1229-1241. doi:10.1016/j.comnet.2009.11.013

Yang, H., Hu, R., Chen, J., & Chen, X. (2008). A review of resilient approaches to peer-to-peer overlay multicast for media streaming. In *4th International Conference on Wireless Communications, Networking and Mobile Computing, WiCOM '08* (pp. 1-4). doi:10.1109/WiCom.2008.802

Xu, Z., Xianliang, H. M., Mengshu, H., & Chuan, Z. (2005). A speed-based adaptive dynamic parallel downloading technique. *ACM SIGOPS Operating Systems Review, 39*(1), 63–69. doi:10.1145/1044552.1044559

Yang, C.-S., & Luo, M.-Y. (1999). An effective mechanism for supporting content-based routing in scalable Web server clusters. *Proceedings International Workshop on Parallel Processing (ICPP'99),* (pp. 240-245).

Yang, M., & Yang, Y. (2008). Peer-to-peer file sharing based on network coding. In *The 28th International Conference on Distributed Computing Systems, ICDCS '08.* (pp. 168-175). doi:10.1109/ICDCS.2008.52

Yang, C.-T., Chi, Y.-C., & Fu, C.-P. (2007). Redundant parallel file transfer with anticipative adjustment mechanism in Data Grids. *Journal of Information Technology and Applications, 1*(4).

Yeun, C. Y. (2007). Mobile TV technologies. In *Proceedings 5th International Conference on Information and Communications Technology* (ICICT), (pp. 2-9). Daejeon, S. Korea.

Yoshida, N. (2008). Dynamic CDN against flash crowds. In Buyya, R., Pathan, M., & Vakali, A. (Eds.), *Content delivery networks* (pp. 275–296). Springer. doi:10.1007/978-3-540-77887-5_11

Young, J., & Faris, N. (2010, July 16). *Akamai delivers 2010 World Cup Internet coverage for two dozen broadcasters into 65 countries worldwide.* Retrieved from http://www.akamai.com/html/about/press/releases/2010/press_071610.html

YouTube. (2010). Retrieved from http://www.youtube.com

Yu, J., Kirley, M., & Buyya, R. (2007). Multi-objective planning for workflow execution on grids, In *Proceedings of IEEE/ACM International Workshop on Grid Computing,* (pp. 10–17).

Zang, Y., Stibor, L., Cheng, X., Reumerman, H.-J., Paruzel, A., & Barroso, A. (2007). Congestion control in wireless networks for vehicular safety applications. In *Proceedings of the 8th European Wireless Conference,* April, Paris, France, (p. 7).

Zhang, J., Gui, Y., Liu, C., & Li, X. (2009). To improve throughput via multi-pathing and parallel TCP on each path. In *Fourth ChinaGrid Annual Conference, ChinaGrid '09* (pp. 16-21). doi:10.1109/ChinaGrid.2009.32

Zhang, J., Lee, B.-S., Tang, X., & Yeo, C.-K. (2008). Impact of parallel download on job scheduling in data grid environment. *The 2008 Seventh International Conference on Grid and Cooperative Computing. GCC '08,* (pp. 102-109).

Zhang, T., Lv, J., & Cheng, X. (2009). Mediacoop: Hierarchical lookup for p2p-vod services. In *ICPP '09: Proceedings of the International Conference on Parallel Processing,* (pp. 486–493). Washington, DC: IEEE Computer Society.

Zhang, T., Xianghui, S., Li, Z., & Cheng, X. (2010). Multi-task downloading for p2p-vod: An empirical perspective. In *ICPADS'10: Proceedings of the 2010 International Conference on Parallel and Distributed Systems,* Shanghai, China. IEEE Computer Society.

Zhang, X., Liu, J., Li, B., & Yum, T. S. (2005). *Coolstreaming/donet: A data-driven overlay network for peer-to-peer live media streaming.* In IEEE Infocom'05.

Zhao, Z., Koning, R., Grosso, P., & de Laat, C. (2010). *Quality guaranteed media delivery on advanced network.* Demo in Supercomputing 2010.

Zhao, Z., Belloum, A., & Bubak, M. (2009). Editorial: Special section on workflow systems and applications in e-Science. *Future Generation Computer Systems, 25*(5), 525–527. doi:10.1016/j.future.2008.10.011

Zhihui, L., Yiping, Z., Shiyong, Z., & Jie, W. (2003). Study of main technology in rich media grid delivery. *International Conference on Computer Networks and Mobile Computing, IEEE ICCNMC '03* (pp. 488- 492). IEEE Computer Society Press.

Zhou, M., & Liu, J. (2005). A hybrid overlay network for video-on demand. In *IEEE International Conference on Communications,* Vol. 2, (pp. 1309 – 1313).

Zhou, J., Ou, Z., Rautiainen, M., Koskela, T., & Ylianttila, M. (2009). Digital television for mobile devices. *IEEE MultiMedia, 12*(1), 60–71. doi:10.1109/MMUL.2009.7

About the Contributors

Giancarlo Fortino is an Associate Professor of Computer Science at the Department of Electronics, Informatics and Systems (DEIS) of the University of Calabria, Rende (CS), Italy. He received his Laurea degree (Bachelor+Master) in Computer Science Engineering from University of Calabria in 1995 and a PhD in Computer Science and Systems Engineering from the same institution in 2001. He also received an MSc in Advanced Technologies of Computer Science and Communications from the IIASS (International Institute for Advanced Scientific Studies), Salerno (Italy), in 1997. In 1997 and 1999 he was visiting researcher at the International Computer Science Institute (ICSI), Berkeley (CA), USA. From 2001 to 2006, he was Assistant Professor of Computer Science at the Department of Electronics, Informatics, and Systems (DEIS) of the University of Calabria, Rende (CS), Italy. His current research interests agent-based systems, agent oriented software engineering, content distribution networks, wireless sensor networks, distributed multimedia systems, and GRID systems. He is author of more than 150 refereed papers in international journals, books and conferences. He is an editorial board member of JNCA (Elsevier) and is member of IEEE, IEEE Computer and Communications Society, and ACM. For more information, please visit http://si.deis.unical.it/fortino.

Carlos E. Palau received his M.Sc. and Ph.D. (Dr.Ing.) degrees, both in Telecommunication Engineering, from the Universidad Politecnica de Valencia (UPV) in 1993 and 1997, respectively. He is Full Professor in the ETSIT at UPV, and works in the Distributed Real-Time Systems research group of the Departamento de Comunicaciones. He is currently involved in research and development projects for the application of multimedia and real-time technologies to industry, defense and communications, wireless sensor networks, and content distribution. Dr. Palau is involved in several IPCs of national and international conferences. He has chaired IASTED Communications Systems and Networks since 2002. He is co-author of more than 150 refereed papers in international journals and conferences. Prof Palau is Senior Member of IEEE.

* * *

Jesus Martinez Barbero (Jan'59) received his formation from the Polytechnic University of Madrid (Spain). A native of Burgos (Spain), he worked for 30 years in broadcasting companies: the RTVE Corporation and Antena 3 de Televisión in Madrid as Technical Director, and then started his own consulting firm before joining Polytechnic University of Madrid as a Professor of Data Structures and Multimedia Technology in Computer Sciences. During the time he was working in broadcasting companies, he had the opportunity to be involved in live events as Olympic Games (Seoul'88 & Barcelona'92), World Cup (Korea & Japan' 04), and multiple political elections (national, regional, & local).

James Broberg is a Research Fellow at the University of Melbourne, Australia. He also holds the position of Chief Technology Officer (CTO) of MetaCDN Pty Ltd. has been working in many important areas of distributed computing since 2003. His work has appeared in some of the best international distributed computing conferences as well as top quality journals such as *Journal of Parallel Computing* and the *Journal of Parallel and Distributed Computing.* He was a Program Chair for the International Workshop on Cloud Computing, held in conjunction with the IEEE International Symposium on Cluster Computing and the Grid in Shanghai, China. He delivered an invited tutorial on an "Introduction to Cloud Computing" at CCGRID. More recently he co-edited a book on Cloud Computing entitled "Cloud Computing: Principles and Paradigms," published by John Wiley & Sons. More information on his research activities can be found at: http://www.csse.unimelb.edu.au/~brobergj

Rajkumar Buyya is a Professor of Computer Science and Software Engineering; and Director of the Cloud Computing and Distributed Systems (CLOUDS) Laboratory at the University of Melbourne, Australia. He is also serving as the founding CEO of Manjrasoft Pty Ltd., a spin-off company of the university, commercializing innovations originating from the CLOUDS Lab. He has pioneered Economic Paradigm for Service-Oriented computing, and demonstrated its utility through his contribution to conceptualization, design and development of Cloud and Grid technologies such as Aneka, Alchemi, Nimrod-G, and Gridbus that power the emerging eScience and eBusiness applications. He is a senior member of IEEE and life member of ACM. He served as the first elected chair of IEEE Technical Committee on Scalable Computing (TCSC). He has authored 350 publications. He is frequently chairing renowned international conferences and serving in the editorial boards of many international journals. For more information, please visit: http://www.buyya.com.

Carlos Calafate graduated with honors in Electrical and Computer Engineering at the University of Oporto (Portugal) in 2001. He received his Ph.D. degree in Computer Engineering from the Technical University of Valencia in 2006, where he holds the position of Associate Professor. He is a member of the Computer Networks research group (GRC) since 2005. His research interests include mobile and pervasive computing, security and QoS on wireless networks, as well as video coding and streaming. More information on his research activities can be found at: http://www.grc.upv.es/calafate/.

Xueqi Cheng is a Professor at the Institute of Computing Technology, Chinese Academy of Sciences. He is also the Director of the Key Laboratory of Network Science and Technology in the institute. His research interests include network science, web search & data mining, and P2P & distributed computing. He is a member of IEEE and ACM. He has served as an associate editor and a member of editorial boards of several international journals, a reviewer for international journals/ conference proceedings, and also as a chair and member of organizing / program committees for many international conferences.

Alfredo Cuzzocrea is currently a Senior Researcher at the Institute of High Performance Computing and Networking of the Italian National Research Council, Italy, and an Adjunct Professor at the Department of Electronics, Computer Science and Systems of the University of Calabria, Italy. His research interests include multidimensional data modeling and querying, data stream modeling and querying, data warehousing and OLAP, OLAM, XML data management, Web information systems modeling and engineering, knowledge representation and management models and techniques, Grid and P2P computing. He is author or co-author of more than 150 papers. He also serves as PC Chair in several international conferences and as Guest Editor in international journals like *JCSS, DKE, IS, KAIS, IJBIDM, IJDMMM*, and *JDIM*.

Manuel Esteve received both his M.Sc. in Computer Engineering and his Ph.D. in Telecommunication Engineering (Dr.Ing.) from the Universidad Politécnica de Valencia in 1989 and 1994, respectively. He is Professor in the ETSIT at the Universidad Politecnica de Valencia (UPV), and he leads the Distributed Real-Time Systems research group of the Departamento de Comunicaciones. He is currently involved in research and development projects for the application of multimedia and real-time technologies to command and control systems. He was responsible of the Virtual University Campus from 2000 to 2006 and currently is advisor of the Spanish Army in ICT systems. He is co-author of more than 125 refereed papers in international journals and conferences.

Georgios Exarchakos joined Eindhoven University of Technology and the department of Electrical Engineering in 2009 as post-doc researcher on Autonomic Networks. He received his PhD degree in 2009 from the University of Surrey, UK on capacity sharing peer-to-peer overlays. In 2003, he collaborated for one year with the Network Operation Center of the University of Athens before he starts his MSc in Advanced Computing at Imperial College London from 2004 to 2005. In 2010, he co-edited the Handbook of Research on P2P and Grid Systems for Service Oriented Computing published by IGI-Global. The following year, George co-authored the book Networks for Pervasive Services: Six Ways to Upgrade the Internet (Springer, 2011). He has contributed to the research community as author of more than 20 publications and chair of international workshops and conferences.

Paolo Giaccone received the Dr.Ing. and Ph.D. degrees in Telecommunications Engineering from the Politecnico di Torino, Torino, Italy, in 1998 and 2001, respectively. He is currently an Assistant Professor in the Department of Electronics, Politecnico di Torino. During the summer of 1998, he was with the High Speed Networks Research Group, Lucent Technology-Bell Labs, Holmdel, NJ. During 2000-2001 and in 2002 he was with the Information Systems Networking Lab, Electrical Engineering Dept., Stanford University, Stanford, CA. His main area of interest is the design of control policies for high-performance routers and for wireless networks.

Paola Grosso is Assistant Professor in the System and Network Engineering (SNE) group of the Universiteit van Amsterdam. She is the coordinator and lead researcher of all the group activities in the field of optical networking. Her current interests are mostly in the field of lightpath provisioning, optical network description, and modeling of e-Infrastructures. She is currently involved in several projects: NOVI, Networking innovations Over Virtualized Infrastructures; CineGrid, which makes possible to produce, send, and show high-quality digital video and sound material; GigaPort3, which researches novel network technologies to apply to the SURFnet7 infrastructure; and GreenClouds - Greening ICT clouds. She participates in meetings of several standardization bodies. She co-chaired the NML-WG (Network Markup Language Working Group) within OGF – Open Grid Forum.

Manfred Hauswirth was born in 1966 in St. Johann im Pongau, Salzburg, Austria. Since July 2006 he is Vice-Director of the Digital Enterprise Research Institute (DERI), Galway, Ireland and Professor at the National University of Ireland, Galway (NUIG). He holds an M.S. (1994) and a Ph.D. (1999) in Computer Science from the Technical University of Vienna. From January 2002 to September 2006 he was a senior researcher at the Distributed Information Systems Laboratory of the Swiss Federal Institute of Technology in Lausanne (EPFL). Prior to his work at EPFL he was an Assistant Professor at the Distributed Systems Group at the TU Vienna. His main research interests are on semantic sensor networks, sensor networks middleware, large-scale semantics-enabled distributed information systems and applications, peer-to-peer systems, Internet of things, self-organization and self-management, Semantic Web services, and distributed systems security. He has published over 100 papers in these domains, and he has co-authored a book on distributed software architectures and several book chapters on P2P data management and semantics. He has served in over 170 program committees of international scientific conferences and was program co-chair of the Seventh IEEE International Conference on Peer-to-Peer Computing in 2007, general chair of the Fifth European Semantic Web Conference in 2008, and is program co-chair of the 10th International Conference on Ontologies, DataBases, and Applications of Semantics (ODBASE) in 2011. He is a member of IEEE and ACM and is on the board of WISEN, the Irish Wireless Sensors Enterprise Led Network, the scientific board of the Corporate Semantic Web research center at FU Berlin, and the Scientific Advisory Board of the Center for Sensor Web Technologies (CLARITY) in Dublin, Ireland.

Marcel Karnstedt was born in 1977 in Halle (Saale), Germany. He received his Diploma (M.Sc.) from the Martin-Luther-Universität Halle-Wittenberg, Germany, at the end of 2003. From January 2004 to February 2009 he worked as a research associate and teaching assistant with the Databases & Information Systems Group (head: Prof. Dr.-Ing. habil. Kai-Uwe Sattler) at the Ilmenau University of Technology, Germany. That is where he also finished his PhD thesis. Since March 2009 he is employed as a Postdoctoral Researcher at the Digital Enterprise Research Institute(DERI), National University of Ireland, Galway (NUIG). He is member of the Information Mining and Retrieval Unit (UIMR) and participates in the CLIQUE project on analysing and visualising large graphs and networks, specifically social networks and biological networks. His research interests include: (i) infrastructures and techniques for large-scale graph mining and generation; (ii) universal data systems distributed at Internet scale, P2P databases: (iii) distributed query processing in P2P systems; (iv) resource-adaptive and quality-aware mining in data streams.

Cees de Laat is chair of the System and Network Engineering research group at the University of Amsterdam. Research in his group includes optical/switched networking for Internet transport of massive amounts of data in TeraScale eScience applications, Semantic web to describe networks and associated resources, distributed cross organization authorization architectures, and systems security & privacy of information in distributed environments. He serves as board member of Open Grid Forum and is acting co-chair of the Grid High Performance Networking Research Group (GHPN-RG), is chair of GridForum. nl, and board member of ISOC.nl. He is co-founder and organizer of several of the past meetings of the Global Lambda Integrated Facility (GLIF) and founding member of CineGrid.org. More information can be found at http://www.science.uva.nl/~delaat

Antonio Liotta holds a Laurea degree in Electrical Engineering from the University of Pavia, Italy and an MSc in Information Technology (cum laude) from Politecnico di Milano, Italy. He gained his PhD in Computer Science from University College London, UK with a thesis on distributed monitoring systems. He was appointed Lecturer in 2001 while he was with the University of Surrey, UK (2000-2004). At the University of Essex, UK (2005-2008) he became Senior Lecturer (2005) and Reader (2007). Since 2008, Antonio has held the Chair of Communication Network Protocols at the Eindhoven University of Technology, NL where he is leading a multifaceted team in Autonomic Networks (http://bit.ly/autonomic_networks). Antonio is a Fellow of the U.K. Higher Education Academy. He is an associate editor of the *Journal of Network and System Management* (Springer) and serves the editorial boards of four more journals. During the last decade, Antonio has investigated topical issues in the areas of network and service management and is currently studying cognitive systems in the context of optical, wireless, and sensor networks. He has three patents and over 130 publications to his credit and recently authored the book 'Networks for Pervasive Services: Six Ways to Upgrade the Internet' (Springer, 2011).

Israel Pérez Llopis received both his M.Sc. in Computer Engineering and his Ph.D. in Telecommunication Engineering (Dr.Ing.) from the Universidad Politécnica de Valencia in 1996 and 2009, respectively. He is member of the Distributed Real-Time Systems research group of the Departamento de Comunicaciones, at the UPV since 2002. Israel Perez Llopis is currently involved in research projects related to wireless communication systems using WiMAX and 3G, for emergency management, content distribution and video streaming. His main interest is focused on multimedia distribution command and control, WiMAX technologies, wireless sensor networks, and tactical communications for defense and emergency management.

Pietro Manzoni is a full Professor of Computer Science at the "Universidad Politecnica de Valencia" (SPAIN). He received the M.S. degree in Computer Science from the "Universita' degli Studi" of Milan (Italy) in 1989 and the Ph.D. in Computer Science from the Polytechnic University of Milan (Italy) in 1995. His research activity is related to wireless networks protocol design, modeling and implementation. For more information, please visit: http://www.disca.upv.es/pmanzoni/

Vlado Menkovski, MSc is a PhD researcher at Eindhoven University of Technology (The Netherlands) and he is a member of the Autonomic Networks team. He holds an MSc degree from Carnegie Mellon University (USA) in Information Networking. His research focus is in machine learning (ML), quality of experience (QoE) in multimedia applications, and autonomic networks. Recent efforts and publications are in the area of QoE management using machine learning techniques, adaptive and online learning methods for predicting QoE in streaming multimedia and design and analysis of subjective tests for QoE. Other work includes ML in security applications, AI planning, and development of GameAI algorithms for turn based games. He has published three conference papers, two in ML and QoE, and one in GameAI. In addition he has a significant work experience in the Software Development industry. Previous engagements include work as a Software Engineer, Software Architect, and a Technical Lead on numerous projects.

Benjamin Molina received his M.Sc. degree in telecommunication engineering from the Universidad Politecnica de Valencia (UPV) in 2001, and currently working to obtain the PhD on Telecommunication Engineering. He made his awarded final project about voice technologies in TISSAT. Later he became a member of the Distributed Real-Time Systems research group of the Departamento de Comunicaciones, at the UPV. Benjamin Molina is currently involved in research projects related to network simulation environments covering content distribution and scalability issues that may affect real implemented networks and semantic interoperability of services. His main interest is focused on multimedia distribution across Internet and the different related technologies, such as: multicast communications, web caching, and real-time systems.

Jewel Okyere-Benya is a Master of Science student in Telecommunication Engineering at the Politecnico di Torino, Italy. Between Sept 2008 and April 2011, he was simultaneously enrolled in the Alta Scuola Politecnica program and participated in multidisciplinary projects in underwater sensor network design. He completed his Bachelor of Science degree in Electrical/Electronic Engineering at the Regional Maritime University, Ghana. He is currently a Research Intern with the Autonomic Network Group of the Electrical Department at the Technical University of Eindhoven, the Netherlands. His main research interest is the design of Autonomic systems for next generation networks, P2P systems, and the study of quality of experience in networks.

Mukaddim Pathan is a Research Scientist at CSIRO, the national government body of scientific research in Australia. He also holds the position of an adjunct lecturer at the Australian National University. His research interests include data management, resource allocation, load balancing, and coordination policies in wide-area distributed systems such as content delivery networks, cloud computing, and sensor networks. He is the editor of Content Delivery Networks book, published by Springer. He has authored and co-authored a number of research papers in internationally recognized journals and conferences. He is involved in the organization of the UPGRADE-CN and IDCS workshops and is a PC member of several international conferences. He has edited a few research issues in reputed international journals and also serves as a reviewer and editorial board member of several renowned journals. He is a member of IEEE, IEEE Computer Society, and ACM. For further information, please visit: http://www.ict.csiro.au/staff/mukaddim.pathan.

Nadia Ranaldo received the Laurea degree in Computer Science in 2001 and the PhD degree in Computer Science in 2005 from University of Sannio, Benevento, Italy. She is currently a Research Assistant at the Department of Engineering of the University of Sannio in Benvento (Italy). She taught courses on Computer Science, Programming, and Computer Networks. She was a visiting scientist at the INRIA research institute, Nice, France, in 2008, in the context of the Research Exchange Programme of the CoreGRID Network of Excellence. Her main research interests include parallel programming, resource scheduling and brokering in distributed systems, service-oriented architectures, grid and cloud computing, content distribution networks, wireless sensor networks.

Wilma Russo received the degree in Physics from the University of Naples (Italy) in 1975,when she moved to the University of Calabria (Italy) where she is now full Professor of Computer Science at the Department of Electronics, Computer and System Sciences (DEIS). Her current research activities are focused on distributed computing and systems, agent oriented software engineering, agent-based modeling and simulation, and content delivery networks. She is author of several papers published in international journals, books, and conference proceedings.

Kai-Uwe Sattler leads the Database and Information Systems group at the Faculty of Computer Science and Automation of the Ilmenau University of Technology, Germany. He received his Diploma (M.Sc.) in Computer Science from the University of Magdeburg, Germany. In 1998, he received his Ph.D. in Computer Science (magna cum laude) from the same university, Germany. From 1998 to September 2003 he was a member of the Database research group (head: Prof. Gunter Saake) at the University of Magdeburg. From October 2001 until March 2002, he worked as a visiting Assistant Professor at the UC Davis, U.S.A. During summer term 2002 he held a replacement professorship at the TU Dresden and during winter term 2002/3 at the University of Halle. In June 2003, he received his Habilitation (venia legendi) in Computer Science from the University of Magdeburg. He joined the Department of Computer Science and Automation of the TU Ilmenau in October 2003 as Professor. Kai-Uwe Sattler is currently the Dean of the Department of Computer Science and Automation. He previously served as vice dean of the same department. His research interests include: (i) semantic interoperability: information integration & quality, peer data management; (ii) large-scale distributed data management; (iii) Autonomous database systems and self tuning.

Roman Schmidt received my M.Sc. degree in Computer Science from the Technical University of Vienna in December 2002 with distinction. Afterwards he was working in the Distributed Systems Group at the Technical University of Vienna until he joined the EPFL (Ecole Polytechnique Fédérale de Lausanne) 's Doctoral school in October 2003, where currently he is a research assistant in the LSIR (Distributed Information Systems Laboratory) lab since December 2003. His research interests relate to decentralized self-organizing information systems, in particular the structured overlay network P-Grid developed at EPFL. The goal of his thesis is to extend P-Grid towards a distributed content management system. He is also the project manager of P-Grid since the first version of the P-Grid library and the prototype application Gridella. Further details can be found on the project web page http://www.p-grid.org/ also offering the source code and libraries. He is a student member of IEEE Computer Society.

Weisong Shi is an Associate Professor of Computer Science at Wayne State University. There he directs the Mobile and Internet SysTems Laboratory (MIST) and Laboratory for Sustainable Computing (LaST), investigating the performance, trust, energy-efficiency, and reliability issues of computer systems and applications. He received his B. E. from Xidian University, and Ph.D. degree from the Chinese Academy of Sciences, both in Computer Engineering. He has served on technical program committees of numerous international conferences. He is currently serving on the editorial board of *Elsevier Sustainable Computing, Journal of Computer Science and Technology* (JCST), and *International Journal of Sensor Networks*. He served as a guest co-editor of several top journals, including *IEEE Internet Computing Magazine* and *Journal of Parallel and Distributed Computing*. He is a senior member of the IEEE and a member of the ACM.

Jeroen van der Ham received his MSc in Artificial Intelligence from Utrecht University in 2002, his MSc in System and Network Engineering in 2004 from the University of Amsterdam, and received his PhD in 2010 at the University of Amsterdam on the topic of "Semantic Descriptions of Complex Computer Networks." He is currently working as a researcher at the System and Network Engineering research group at the University of Amsterdam. His research interests are in semantic descriptions of multi-layer and multi-domain networks and (virtualized) resources, as well as associated algorithms and architectures. Jeroen is also actively involved in the OGF NML-WG as the Editor of the NML Schema document.

Tieying Zhang is an Assistant Professor at the Institute of Computing Technology, Chinese Academy of Sciences. He received his Ph.D. degree from the Chinese Academy of Sciences. His research interests include cloud computing, storage systems, computer networks, peer-to-peer systems, multimedia networking, and network security. He has chaired several conferences and workshops and served as a reviewer of numerous top journals and conferences. He received the BeWinner Ph.D Candidate Award in 2009. He is a member of IEEE.

Zhiming Zhao is a researcher in the System and Network Engineering research group at University of Amsterdam. He received his Master of Science degree on Computer Science from East China Normal University in China in 1996. He obtained his Ph.D. at University of Amsterdam (UvA) in 2004 on the subject of coordinating distributed simulation using multi agent systems. His current research mainly focuses on agent technologies and e-Science workflow management, including workflow interoperability, cooperative e-Science experiments, network QoS in workflows, and workflow provenance. He organized series of international workshops on scientific workflow and e-Science in the past years. He is also in the program committee of several e-Science related conferences and workshops.

Eugenio Zimeo graduated in Electronic Engineering at the University of Salerno, Italy, and received the PhD degree in Computer Science from the University of Naples, Italy, in 1999. Currently he is an Assistant Professor at the University of Sannio in Benevento (Italy), where teaches courses on Computer Networks, Web Technology, and Distributed Systems. His primary research interests are in the areas of software architectures and frameworks for distributed systems, high performance middleware and resource scheduling, service and Grid computing, scalable web systems, content distribution, and wireless sensor networks. He has published about 80 scientific papers in journals and conferences of the field and leads many academic and industrial research projects.

Index

CPSIA information can be obtained at www.ICGtesting.com
Printed in the USA
BVOW050746140512

290035BV00008B/21/P